Richard Hoskins is a research fellow in Criminology at Roehampton University. He has worked on many of Britain's biggest criminal investigations and is the only registered multi-cultural expert on the national police database. His expertise has been called upon in over a hundred major investigations by police and social services. He divides his time between London and Devon.

The Boy in the River

Richard Hoskins

ROTHERHAM LIBRARY SERVICE	
B53020965	
Bertrams	12/06/2012
AN	£7.99
BSU	364.1523

PAN BOOKS

First published 2012 by Pan Books
an imprint of Pan Macmillan, a division of Macmillan Publishers Limited
Pan Macmillan, 20 New Wharf Road, London N1 9RR
Basingstoke and Oxford
Associated companies throughout the world
www.panmacmillan.com

ISBN 978-1-4472-0790-0

Copyright © Richard Hoskins 2012

The right of Richard Hoskins to be identified as the author of this work has been asserted by him in accordance with the Copyright, Designs and Patents Act 1988.

All rights reserved. No part of this publication may be reproduced, stored in or introduced into a retrieval system, or transmitted, in any form, or by any means (electronic, mechanical, photocopying, recording or otherwise) without the prior written permission of the publisher. Any person who does any unauthorized act in relation to this publication may be liable to criminal prosecution and civil claims for damages.

9 8 7 6 5 4 3 2 1

A CIP catalogue record for this book is available from the British Library.

Printed and bound by CPI Group (UK) Ltd, Croydon CR0 4YY

This book is sold subject to the condition that it shall not, by way of trade or otherwise, be lent, re-sold, hired out, or otherwise circulated without the publisher's prior consent in any form of binding or cover other than that in which it is published and without a similar condition including this condition being imposed on the subsequent purchaser.

Visit **www.panmacmillan.com** to read more about all our books and to buy them. You will also find features, author interviews and news of any author events, and you can sign up for e-newsletters so that you're always first to hear about our new releases.

In memory of both Edwards.
Desperately missed.

Acknowledgements

This book would not have been written without the unswerving friendship, dedication and loyalty of Mark Lucas at LAW. I owe you a debt of gratitude beyond words.

George Morley, Dusty Miller, Jon Mitchell, Tania Adams and the team at Pan Macmillan have been wonderfully enthusiastic and committed.

Joe Fiennes and Ken McReddie have also offered me their unflinching support and much-valued friendship through an often searingly painful process.

Others that deserve particular mention include my first editor and friend Tim, who showed me the way forward in the early days; Alice at LAW; Remy and Moise in Kinshasa; Claude in London; Sue, Faith, Caroline, Silas and the remarkable Elspeth who shared so much of this journey; my mother Audrey and siblings John, Jane and Jill.

Author's Note

This is the story of an investigation with which I was involved for over ten years, and others that unfolded alongside it, during which time I found myself compelled to confront my own African tragedy. Three names, and some details, have been altered to safeguard the identity of those who might otherwise be put at risk.

The ceremony of innocence is drowned;
The best lack all conviction, while the worst
Are full of passionate intensity . . .
And what rough beast, its hour come round at last,
Slouches towards Bethlehem to be born?

'The Second Coming' W. B. Yeats

Prologue

London, a little after 4 p.m. on 21 September 2001.

As thirty-two-year-old IT consultant Aidan Minter left the office he was, like many people, thinking about the terrorist attacks on the World Trade Center ten days earlier. He climbed the steps to Tower Bridge and began crossing to the south bank. Lost in thought, he glanced idly over the parapet at the river below. In that instant he caught sight of something floating in the water. He stopped. Even from the bridge it looked strange – a dummy, perhaps, with what seemed to be a red cloth attached to it. But he couldn't be sure.

Minter walked quickly on and ran down the steps on to the south side of the river. Filled now with a need to be certain, he stepped closer to the water's edge. As he stood there his curiosity turned to horror. He was staring at a body. Or what was left of one. He pulled out his mobile and dialled 999.

Within minutes a launch crewed by officers of the Thames Marine Police Unit was searching the area around Tower Bridge. At first they found nothing. They turned up river with the incoming tide. Then, as they drew level with the Globe Theatre, they too saw a flash of colour against the bank. The boat swung across the current and a moment later a police officer hauled the mutilated torso of a little boy from the water.

The child had no name, so the police called him Adam.

I

Bath, January 2002

I was at my desk when they called.

I shared the tiny, gloriously cluttered university office with my colleague Mahinda Deegalle, a Buddhist monk from Sri Lanka. A prayer wheel and a terracotta fertility figurine from Syria fought for space among the filing cabinets, computers and shelves of books and binders. Stuck to the walls were yellow Post-it notes, family photos and postcards from colleagues in Nepal, Namibia, Nauru and everywhere in between.

Our room was in a temporary building – though the arrangement had already lasted for years – not far from the fine Georgian mansion at the centre of the main Bath Spa University campus. Our window gave out over fields, part of the estate's park which had been landscaped by Capability Brown. Dry stone walls and clumps of ash and oak trees stood in the winter light.

Mahinda would drift in from time to time in his orange robes to dispense some snippet of wisdom, or – more surprisingly – to chat about the property market. But often I had the room to myself, and would sit there for long, quiet hours, wrapped up in my research or preparing lectures. I had grown to treasure the calm of the English countryside beyond that window, and I was very much at peace there.

Until the phone rang.

'Dr Hoskins, I'm Detective Inspector Will O'Reilly from Scotland Yard's Serious Crime Group,' the caller said. I'd commented on the Adam case on BBC radio a couple of days earlier. I was often consulted by the media about African religions and related topics. 'What do you make of this mutilated body they've found in the Thames?' the journalist had asked. 'People I've spoken to in London are saying that it's a voodoo killing. Apparently a South African expert has told police that it's to do with the practice of *muti*. That's taking body parts for magic, right? What do you think?'

I knew quite a lot about *muti*, so I'd talked about that for a few minutes. The journalist must have contacted Scotland Yard after the interview and now DI O'Reilly wanted to pay me a visit. I was immediately worried that he would want me to come up with definitive answers to questions he didn't even know how to ask, on what were likely to be extremely complex issues. Perhaps I also had the first inkling that the comfortable world I had built up around me might be under threat.

I was a senior lecturer in African religions at the University of Bath Spa in the West of England and had become one of very few academics in the UK who specialized in this field.

My first marriage had ended, but it had given me two wonderful children, David and Elspeth, now twelve and ten, and my relationship with Sue, their mother, remained warm. While at Bath, I'd met Faith Warner and we'd become good friends. Faith was studying psychology, specializing in cognition among African primates, and while on a research expedition to the Congo one summer we had fallen for each other.

By the time DI O'Reilly called me, Faith and I had just moved in together. Now in my mid-thirties, I was very close to being a contented man.

I reported the imminent police visit to the university director. We booked a shiny new lecture room in one of the university's impersonal modern blocks and ordered deli sandwiches and soft drinks.

The director and I waited outside the main building as the unmarked silver car drew up.

Big, capable, serious types, painfully polite, but with a hardness in their eyes, I couldn't imagine Detective Inspector Will O'Reilly and Detective Constable Barry Costello ever going undercover. DC Costello was young, tall and wary. He spent most of his time watching me, as if he suspected I was about to make off with something. But DI Will O'Reilly was clearly the man in charge. A powerful figure in his mid-forties, he had the air of an ex-rugby player. He had dark hair and some serious stubble, which only partially camouflaged his pale complexion and the beginnings of a double chin. His voice was slightly gruff and his eyes were both keen and kind.

I opened the door to the conference room and showed them in. I was suddenly struck by how cold it was. Cold, bright and clinical. I began to wish that I was back in my own comfortably cluttered office with Mahinda calmly getting on with his work at the neighbouring desk. Will O'Reilly produced a large brown manila envelope, laid it on the table and spread eight A5 colour prints of brutally high quality in front of me. A brown torso lay on a post-mortem slab. There were several shots of the body, most showing it dressed in orange-red shorts, and close-ups of the cuts that had severed the head, arms and legs.

I had seen some pretty tough things during my time in Africa, but for a second I felt sick. O'Reilly cleared his throat. He'd seen the expression on my face. 'Obviously we all find this . . . distressing . . .' he said. 'We have next to nothing to go on, Dr Hoskins. We don't know who the child is, or where he comes from. We're guessing that he's of African or Caribbean extraction. We don't know exactly what happened to him. According to our home office pathologist, Dr Mike Heath, the cut to the neck is very precise. He thinks it was made from back to front, and that his body was drained of its blood – though you must keep that information completely confidential. We haven't released it to the press.'

As I continued to stare at the pictures, DI O'Reilly told me that the pathologist estimated the child to have been between five and ten years old. He thought the torso had been in the water for up to ten days, but not longer or the skin would have turned white. Nothing was found in the stomach except traces of what might be a cough medicine. There was no sign of sexual interference. Dr Heath also thought the shorts were placed on the corpse up to a day after death, because there were no traces of body fluids on the material.

'That's it,' he said. 'That's all we have at the moment.'

'I hear you think it's a *muti* killing,' I said. 'Linked to South Africa in some way.'

'I'll be honest with you, Dr Hoskins, I'd never even heard of this *muti* stuff. None of us had. Dr Heath thought that the injuries looked ritualistic. We took a gamble that the child might be of African origin, and flew in a South African pathologist to give us a second post-mortem. It was this gentleman,' he consulted his notebook, 'a Dr Hendrick Scholtz, who told us that in South Africa there have been cases of people being murdered and dismembered for *muti*.'

I put on my glasses and forced myself to look more carefully at each of the pictures. The first showed the whole of the torso. The next, a close-up of the neck. I looked back at the first photograph. The cut was indeed extremely precise, and unusually low. It would have been covered by a T-shirt. The arm and leg wounds, by contrast, were a strange mixture: at skin level there was a similarly stark precision, but the bone looked as if it had been hacked away from the body. I picked up my pen and made some notes.

I studied the photo of the boy's front. It didn't look as if any internal organs had been removed.

'He's still got his genitals,' I said. 'And he's circumcised.'

'Is that significant?'

'It could be.'

'How?'

I hesitated. 'Leaving his genitals intact wouldn't seem to be typical of *muti*. Also, I'd expect his internal organs to be taken. But I guess we have to start somewhere, and if your South African specialist thinks that might be the way to go . . .'

I moved to the next picture, of the boy's back, and then through the remaining photographs. I was looking for tribal markings but could find none. I sat back down in my chair and took a deep breath. 'I think I can help.'

I didn't have to say anything. The moment I got home Faith led me into the kitchen, poured a healthy quantity of gin into a couple of glasses and splashed in some tonic. It wasn't Friday – Friday was our gin and tonic night – but to hell with it.

I started to tell her about the photos as we walked through to the sitting room. When we sat down on the sofa

I started to cry. There was nothing now to hold me back and the tears streamed down my face unchecked. She put her arms around me.

After a while she said, 'It's not just this boy, is it? It's not just Adam . . .'

I shook my head.

2

Kinshasa, April 1986

I walked as nonchalantly as I could to the Swissair check-in at London Heathrow's Terminal 2. It wasn't easy; my cabin bag contained a Land Rover driveshaft and it was as much as I could do just to pick it up.

You needed this sort of thing in the Congo, or so I'd been told. The girl behind the desk wished us a pleasant flight and I hauled my burden away towards the lounge. I was wildly excited. I was breaking free. I was twenty-two years old. I was going to Africa with my new wife.

The runway at Kinshasa was rumoured to be one of the longest in the world. Some said that it was necessary for the huge transport planes that allegedly smuggled vast quantities of goods out of the Congo – everything from gold and diamonds to ivory and bush meat. Others claimed that the architects had planned two criss-cross runways, but the local contractors had misread the drawings and put them end to end.

There was little to see of N'djili Airport as we rolled to a halt, just one small building and a few lights flickering uncertainly in the kind of darkness you could reach out and touch. We stepped off the plane into a wall of lung-crushing heat.

The Congo basin sits in a bowl astride the Equator. Unlike East Africa, it has nowhere high enough to enjoy relief from the constant tropical temperatures that sap the strength of everything that moves, and quite a few things that don't. The rivers snake their way from the mountains in the east to the ocean in the west, and a vast tract of dank, steaming forest lies in between. That forest is all but impenetrable and rainstorms lash the land almost daily, sweeping away all attempts at road building in torrents of muddy floodwater. That, and the fact that the dictator Mobutu was bent on keeping the country in the Dark Ages, meant there was virtually no development outside Kinshasa. But I knew that place was going to change my life for ever.

3

Bath, February 2002

I didn't know much about police procedure, but even I could see that they were floundering.

Will O'Reilly and his team couldn't even be sure whether Adam had set foot on British soil while he was alive. They had nowhere to start; no one they could question, no potential witnesses, no alibis to check, no addresses to visit, no deposition site to search. They had the child's DNA but no one to link it with. They had no fingerprints. They didn't even have a face. That meant no dental records, no database searches, no photofit pictures.

And they had no motive. What could provoke someone to murder an innocent child, dress the mutilated torso in bright new clothes and throw it into the Thames?

I could see how the *muti* theory had caught on. Against a backdrop of bafflement and confusion, somebody had pounced on a possible answer. The police didn't know anything much about *muti* – they kept talking about voodoo – but a bizarre African cult killing could explain away a great deal. Just putting a name to the crime would be progress of a sort.

But I was uneasy about it.

In the following days I worked solidly on the Adam case, both at home and at the university. I didn't have a heavy teaching schedule and had already prepared my lectures for some weeks ahead, so I was able to give it my full attention.

African peoples are as different as their landscapes. In my travels I had encountered every sort of terrain, from barren desert to lush rainforest, from flat savannah to towering razor-backed mountains, and every variety of dwelling, from mud and palm thatch huts to gleaming city blocks of marble and glass. The sacred beliefs and practices of each ethnic group are every bit as diverse, and there are thousands and thousands of them. Now, somehow, I was supposed to try and unravel which of them might have been responsible for this atrocity, and why.

In 2000 I had attended a big conference in South Africa at which almost everyone who was anyone in the world of African religious studies was present, and I combined it with a research trip around KwaZulu-Natal Province. *Muti* had figured significantly. I had interviewed traditional *muti* workers, had visited the *muti* market in Durban and had spent some time with Robert Papini, the anthropologist curator of Durban's *muti* museum – the only one in the world.

Muti is a Zulu word, which literally means 'medicine'. The practice centres on the belief that parts of certain plants, animals, and sometimes even humans, have special curative powers. Row upon row of animal parts and plants were offered up for sale in the Durban *muti* market. Many had been smoke-dried but the smell was still intense. Among the items on display I could identify animal organs – heads, testicles, brains, hearts. And some of the animals looked to me like primates. Under a tarpaulin, more mysterious objects were being kept away from inquisitive eyes. When my camera was spotted there were mutterings around me and a small group began jostling me.

I backed away but couldn't keep my eyes off the indistinct shapes I saw under the cloth. I had heard stories that human organs were regularly used in *muti*, and this was just the kind of place a devotee might be expected to come looking for such things. But I would not be allowed to find out.

Now, sitting at my desk in Bath, I decided to go back to basics and to replay some of the interviews I'd recorded with *sangomas*, the traditional South African healers, after that market visit.

That evening I settled in front of the TV with a pile of videos. As I put the first one into the machine, I felt suddenly uneasy under the heavily lidded gaze of the Chokwe death mask, which hung on the wall behind me. I turned back to the job in hand, cross with myself. The last thing I needed right now was to start opening the door to superstition.

One interview proved particularly significant. Moses was a tall, wiry figure with prominent eyes and enormous hands, which he used to illustrate everything he told me. I rewound his tape and replayed it. His cramped and dimly lit house in downtown Durban appeared once more on the screen. I could see plant and animal parts stacked around the room and phials of traditional medicine ranged on shelves. In a dark corner was an altar covered in white cloth on which stood two large red candles, a bell and what looked like a tribal chief's fly whisk. Fading pictures of international surfing champions hung incongruously on the wall alongside a portrait of Gandhi.

'There are many different plant parts from all over South Africa that we put in our medicines,' the *sangoma* explained. His voice was surprisingly deep for so spare a man. 'We also use animals, which give power to us when we pray over them. Different parts have different powers. So when a man who is impotent comes to me I may use the genitals of a powerful animal in my remedy, because this will help cure him. If I grind down even a fragment of this and pray over it, he will be healed. Or suppose a woman comes to me who lacks the courage to do something for her good. I may give her some special medicine that will contain part of the heart or spleen of a particular animal like a leopard or a lion. These will give to her the courage she needs.'

'How do you know the right ingredient to use?' I heard myself ask.

'It takes us years and years to get this knowledge, Richard. I myself was an apprentice for eight years under a wise elder *sangoma* before I began practising. Then we also pray to our spirits for discernment of the illness and its cure.'

'What about human body parts?' I said. 'I've heard they are sometimes used. I've even heard of *muti* murders. Does that happen?'

'It's true that sometimes a *sangoma* will use human body parts,' Moses acknowledged. 'They will get these parts from mortuaries.'

'But that isn't always true, is it?' I queried.

He looked at me uncomfortably, glanced down at his lap and then back at me. 'No. No, you're right that there are also *muti* murders where a bad *sangoma* will kill someone for *muti* parts. This is very bad sorcery and I have nothing to do with it. When they kill this way, they often take the parts while the victim is still alive. They think the parts get greater power from the victim's screams. These are very bad people who do this.'

It took me two nights to get through all my video interviews. I finished the last one in the small hours of the morning. Perhaps unsurprisingly I found it hard to go to sleep that night.

The next morning I telephoned DI O'Reilly from the university and asked him if the police pathologist was sure that it was the incision to the neck that had killed Adam.

'As far as we know.' He sounded surprised at the question. 'The pathologist seemed pretty sure that the neck wound was the first, and that all the others were inflicted after death.'

'What precisely did the pathologist's report say?'

'Hang on a sec. Here we are. "The instrument came into the neck from the side or slightly from the rear and was then brought forward." That's a very unusual manner of killing, by the way. "It was then removed and another series of cuts were made."'

'Is that all the report says?'

'No, there's more.' I could hear him riffling through papers. 'OK, the pathologist thinks that the instrument was probably sharpened after each cut. He believes that the body was drained of its blood, so it's probable the child was held either horizontally or even upside down.'

'God Almighty,' I murmured.

'Something here doesn't sit right with you?'

I could hear how much he wanted me to tell him that everything fitted perfectly, but I couldn't do that. I fobbed him off with some vague response and a promise to call him back.

Taking out a blank sheet of A4 paper I wrote '*Muti* murder?' at the top. I drew a line down the middle of the page. I headed the column on the left 'Similarities', and on the right, 'Differences'.

Then on the right I wrote, 'Manner of death: cut to the neck.'

The fact that the incision had been so careful didn't fit. The perpetrators of a *muti* killing don't care how body parts are removed. If they had wanted Adam's head for some ritual purpose they could even have decapitated him with an axe. In the same column I added 'Severance of limbs'.

Moses had told me that when bad *sangomas* take body parts from humans these parts are rendered more powerful if they are harvested while the victim is still alive. This was the opposite of what had happened with Adam. His limbs were hacked off after the neck had been so precisely cut.

And then there was the question of internal organs, a third addition to my right-hand column. The body parts most keenly treasured by *muti* men were the internal organs such as the kidneys, heart, spleen, liver and above all the genitals. But none of Adam's had been removed.

4

Kinshasa, April 1986

Sue and I walked into the airport building past a line of scruffy soldiers and officials, who eyed us with a mixture of contempt and wariness. Most of them were armed with old French bolt-action rifles or pistols in webbing holsters.

'Keep in line!' a soldier shouted at us in French, gesticulating at the door. 'Go straight through there!'

I stared at him. I didn't much like being ordered around. I'd come here to help. I hadn't expected a welcoming committee, but I thought a degree of politeness might have been in order.

'What's the matter with these guys?' I asked Sue. 'Are they expecting trouble?'

'You!' the soldier shouted, getting agitated. 'Keep moving!'

'Just stay calm, Richard,' Sue said under her breath. 'We're in Africa now.'

She fixed a smile on her face, took my arm and steered me through to the terminal.

The place was bedlam. Shouting men without uniform or insignia of any kind descended on us and demanded our papers, passports, references, vaccination certificates – and when we protested they tried to grab the documents from us. There was no telling who was official and who was not. There was no sign of any system whatsoever.

We fought our way through to what was optimistically called the baggage reclaim area. The carousel hadn't worked for years, and luggage was thrown to the crowd through a hole in the wall, at which point everyone would scrum down to find their bags, or, if that proved impossible, to grab someone else's. When I finally saw one of ours I pounced on it in triumph, but so did a small fat man in a safari suit.

'*C'est à moi*!' he shouted over and over again. 'That's my bag!'

I had physically to wrest my suitcase from him and then fight off more predators when the rest of our luggage came through. I was sweating, outraged and confused. I had never seen anything like this. To be forced to fight and curse in defence of my own property upset me. I had never been aggressive. I had been, as they say, well brought up in the Home Counties. I thought that if you treated people with courtesy, they would, on the whole, return it. I saw now how far school, a brief spell in the Army and my whole background had protected me from what passed for real life. Kinshasa airport was a very rude awakening.

The concourse was stiflingly hot and full of noise, jostling and barely suppressed violence. Hugging our bags we found ourselves bundled up against a frosted glass screen, from behind which someone demanded our passports.

'I'm not letting you have my passport.' I turned for help to a soldier who lounged against the wall, smoking, but he looked at me with glassy indifference.

'Just give it to them, Richard,' Sue pleaded. 'Just do as they say.'

A hand appeared from under the screen and seized our

papers, which disappeared while another official pretended to check vaccination certificates. I felt helpless without a passport, wondering if I was supposed to bribe someone to get it back, knowing I was losing my cool, knowing I was doing everything wrong. I agonized for the best part of an hour before our papers were wordlessly returned.

Sue handled all this much better than I did. A previous trip to Africa had given her some idea of what to expect. I had none at all. I looked around for the exit but the ordeal was not over yet.

'Hey! You two – over here!'

I turned to Sue a little wildly. 'For God's sake – what now?'

'Richard, it's Customs,' she said. 'Just do as they say and everything will be all right.'

A bad-tempered officer in a sweat-stained uniform made us unpack everything. He held up our cameras accusingly. 'Have you taken photographs?'

'No,' I said.

'If you have taken photographs, I will confiscate these.'

'No, no. We haven't.'

He looked at us suspiciously, itching to confiscate the cameras, then laid them aside and rummaged on through our few things. The Land Rover driveshaft caused a good deal of mirth. Apparently this was unusual even for Kinshasa Airport, and we soon had a group of grinning brown-shirted officers examining it and passing comments – presumably unflattering ones – on anyone stupid enough to bring such a thing in their hand baggage.

It was Sue who finally extricated us: she gave the Customs officers a handful of absurd mementoes of London: fridge magnets showing Tower Bridge in a snowstorm that she had brought for just such an eventuality. The senior officer took them without comment and waved us through.

I lugged my half-packed case out into the sweltering night.

I looked back, still unable to believe it. 'This whole place is completely crazy.'

'After my last trip,' Sue muttered, 'I vowed I'd never come back. Now I remember why.'

'You never told me you felt that way.'

She gave me a significant look. 'Right now I wish I had.'

I realized she wasn't concerned for herself; she was worried about me. I was still thinking about this as we stepped outside. We were greeted by a driver called Joseph, who piled our bags into a Land Rover and took us the jolting fifteen miles over nightmare roads into the city. Soon, we were installed in a second-floor apartment in the Baptist Mission compound.

It was a plain enough place, but it was clean and there was a fan, the lights worked and there was running water. Neither of us said much until we had got inside and closed the door behind us, regaining some semblance of peace and privacy. For a few minutes we busied ourselves unpacking, then we sat at the little Formica table in the kitchen.

'We don't have to go through with this, you know,' she said.

'What?' I tried to laugh it off.

'You were never supposed to be going into the bush anyway,' she said, 'let alone for two years. If it hadn't been for us getting married, you'd have been working in Kinshasa for six months, and then you'd have been going home to university. Maybe that would have been OK for you. The way you were at the airport . . .' She paused. 'It's not a competition,

Richard. If you don't feel right about this it would be better for everybody if we pulled out now.'

'Go back to England?'

'If necessary. Or maybe apply to stay in Kinshasa, the way it was originally planned. Look, it's different for me. As a medic I was always going to be sent out into the bush. But that wasn't what you signed up for. I won't think badly of you. You know that. But we have to be a bit sensible.'

We said no more about it that night, but went to bed early and clung together in the stifling darkness, listening to the sirens and horns of this alien city. There was another sound too, the dull, insistent rumble of the Congo River.

In the daylight, some of the jaggedness had faded. It helped that the Baptist Mission compound occupied one of the most spectacular sites in Kinshasa. It was perched on the banks of the Congo, just above the start of those awesome rapids down which the river plunges for 400 miles on its way to the sea – rapids which to this day no one has conquered. Rainbow curtains of mist hung in the harsh sunlight above the falls.

We didn't have time for the sights of Kinshasa just yet, though. We had a meeting with Andrew North, the Church's head of logistics, whose office was inside the compound not far from our apartment block. I hoped, I suppose, for some encouragement after the bruising my ego had taken the night before.

His office and the lock-up next to it certainly looked the part. There was a Land Rover parked in the garage area and the floor and shelves were piled with bits of machinery, tools, drums of fuel and boxes of medical supplies. I proudly added my much-travelled driveshaft to the collection.

The office itself was dominated by Andrew's enormous kidney-shaped desk made of local wenge hardwood. On the wall hung a huge coloured map of the Upper Congo region, marked with villages, airstrips and tracks. Such maps, I was to learn, were worth several times their weight in gold, as Mobutu restricted their distribution for security reasons. There was also a CB radio, yellowing lists of call-codes pinned up above it, a fan circling lazily overhead and an impressive safe.

Andrew North was a big, dark-haired, lugubrious man with heavy glasses, rather formally dressed in slacks and a light blue bush shirt. He was in his thirties and fairly recently married.

'If you'd taken the original job you were offered, here in Kinshasa,' he told me, 'I'd have handed over to you by now and be back home.'

I knew he wasn't impressed with what he saw of me. I was obviously a complete greenhorn, and he took it as an insult that someone so utterly inexperienced should be sent to tackle problems 'up country', where life was thought to be a hundred times harder than in Kinshasa.

'Don't be afraid to say so if you can't make it work up there.' He looked hard at me through his heavy, dark-rimmed glasses.

It was clear that he didn't think I'd last two weeks. I felt myself bridle, but managed to thank him for his advice and quickly changed the subject.

'While we're here in the city,' I said, 'we'd like to pick up some stuff at the Kinshasa market. I've read you can make your own water filter with a couple of plastic buckets and—'

He stared at me through his terrifying glasses. 'You want to go to the Kinshasa market?'

'Yes, apparently it's a good place for—'

'It's not a good place for anything,' he snapped. 'You'd be mad to go there. None of us ever does.'

'But we need some rice and some lamps and some other provisions,' Sue said. 'We heard you could get all that there.'

'Yes, you can get all that,' Andrew said abruptly and looked back at me. 'You can also get your wife kidnapped.'

'Kidnapped?'

'And sold into white slavery. She'll end up in some market in Dubai. You obviously don't know what you're suggesting.'

'I want to go to the Kinshasa market,' I said in a reasonably steady voice. 'We both do.'

He glared at me for a moment.

'All right,' he said, with a sigh of resignation. 'On your own heads be it. At least I can send a Congolese driver to pick you up.'

Short of white slavery, the market was every bit as alarming as Andrew had warned.

'*M'sieur*! You like monkey?' A toothless man grinned at us over his blood-spattered table, holding up some indescribable gobbet of meat, black with flies. 'Try a bit of this one! Very tender! Or maybe you want crocodile?'

People crowded around us, shoving and shouting, thrusting fruit, vegetables, handicrafts and pots at us.

'I'm not sure this was such a good idea,' Sue said anxiously as we shouldered our way through the mêlée. 'Maybe we've seen enough.'

'I want my plastic buckets,' I said.

Everything was for sale here: every shape and colour of vegetable and fruit; the butchered remains of goats and cows and forest animals I couldn't identify; cheap tin household goods; sacks of grain; bundles of herbs; tools; bolts of brilliant cloth; bicycle components; fish and eels; carvings; sandals cut from truck tyres. Traders sold roasted maize, slices of cooked fish on skewers and globules of flour fried in palm nut oil called *minkati* – sweet, tasty and very, very unhealthy.

The din was deafening and the smells exotic, pungent and often revolting.

But I loved it.

Sue – unflappable until that moment – did not. She had an urge to be gone, especially once we had bought a couple of hurricane lamps and some rice. Although I was just as intimidated as she was by the seething throng, I glimpsed for the first time the adventure I had come for.

'Do you have plastic buckets?' I shouted across at one stallholder.

'Of course, *M'sieur*! All sizes! All colours! Very fine.'

'Good,' I said, triumphantly. 'I want two. Big red ones.'

Kinshasa at the time was something of a halfway house between the West and the heart of Africa and not yet the hellhole it has since become. If it was pretty rough around the edges, it did have electricity most of the time and running water, which was sometimes clean. It boasted some impressive buildings, stores and shops that actually had stock to sell, as well as truly chaotic traffic. The famous boulevard built by the Belgians along the south bank of the Congo was grand, sweeping and shaded by fine trees, and well-dressed people promenaded along it every evening with something approaching elegance.

We had been invited to swim at the British Embassy

pool, a favourite haunt for expatriates at the weekend. The terrace was crowded with white people lounging on sunbeds and sitting around the metal tables while their children splashed and screamed.

'First time in Kin?' a man from British American Tobacco asked me, sipping Heineken from the bottle.

'Yes, that's right.'

'Poor old you.' He gave me the kindly-wise look I soon grew to detest. 'I'm afraid you'll find there's bugger all you can do to help these people. Won't help themselves, you see? You'll find out what I mean when you've been here as long as I have.'

It struck me as intriguing that a man from a tobacco company was concerned with helping anyone.

'Going up country, are you?' a red-faced Scots engineer exclaimed, joining the group. 'Well, bloody good luck to you is all I can say. It's dreadful up there in the villages. The whole country is a complete bloody shambles. I don't know why we bother with it.'

'Why are you here if you hate it so much?'

'Dunno. Beats me most of the time. But have you been to Glasgow recently?'

I was later to discover that most people who spoke with such world-weariness of the hardships of the bush never got out of Kinshasa. Quite a few of them never moved further than the security fences of their own compounds.

Even at the time I wasn't convinced by the knowing glances they exchanged, and the endlessly repeated advice about what you couldn't do – trust anyone, eat the local food, expect to achieve anything. I hadn't come to Africa for this.

5

Bath, February 2002

A little before noon on my next free day – a Wednesday – the anonymous silver police car drew up again. The detectives had come to the house this time.

DI O'Reilly had a new companion, Detective Sergeant Nick Chalmers. Nick was taller than Will and slighter and younger. When he spoke it was as if he were measuring the weight of each word.

We decided to go straight to lunch.

'Someone has clearly handled this killing with great care,' I said. 'That may sound like a bizarre way of putting it, but it's extremely important. It's also a bit puzzling.'

'Puzzling? Why?' Will's coffee sat untouched before him.

'Because when body parts are needed as ingredients for *muti* medicine, there is usually no need for any great precision in their removal. In *muti* murders, parts are taken from dead bodies, or even while the victim is still alive. Either way, they don't need to be removed with precision. I know this sounds pretty horrible, but there are even people who believe that the medicine is empowered by the victim's screams. I know of a case in South Africa where a woman remained alive for more than two hours. They started by slicing off her breasts.'

Will was visibly shaken. I realized that whatever atrocities these men might have encountered in their day-to-day activities, we were now entering a different world.

'Adam's neck wound is precise, and it killed him. If this was *muti*, I would have expected them to start chopping pieces off him while he was still alive, and, when he finally died, to take not only his head but his internal organs and genitalia too.' I told them I wanted to do some more work on the manner of death, and on his circumcision.

Will agreed, then began toying with his coffee spoon. He shifted in his seat. 'You probably know that the police sometimes use mediums. To help locate bodies and so on. Not everyone agrees with doing it, but . . . Well, what we want to know is, what would you think of us going to an African witch doctor to see if we could get him to find out who did it? My boss Commander Baker wants to know if you think we should. And, if so, how would we go about it?'

I could see why Will was uncomfortable, imagining how a tabloid newspaper might report such a move. Until that point, I'm not sure I'd understood quite how far they were prepared to go to find justice for this unknown boy.

6

Bolobo, April 1986

'How are we going to get all our gear in?' I eyed the Cessna's under-slung luggage pod, considerably smaller than the average car boot.

'Yeah, that could be a challenge,' the pilot said. 'But don't worry, anything that doesn't fit can come up by riverboat.'

'How long's that going to take?'

'Oh, not more than a few weeks.'

In the event, there was only room for a suitcase and a bag in the hold. Everything else – our rice, most of our clothes, many of our books – would meander after us along 300 miles of the River Congo. I had one small victory: I managed to hang on to my red plastic buckets.

The tiny plane bumbled along the potholed tarmac and lifted uncertainly off the ground. Although Sue and I were crammed closely together in the back of the cabin, the din of the engine was so deafening that conversation was virtually impossible.

Within minutes we were out over the vast Malebo Pool. The Pool marks the point at which the river disgorges from a narrow gap in the Bateki Plateau to the north, before being sucked into the rapids below Kinshasa, which we had seen and heard from the Baptist Mission.

To be suspended above the vast landscape of green and silver was both magical and terrifying. As we climbed from pool to plateau, little villages emerged below us, scattered in patches of savannah carved into the endless forest. Sometime later we crossed the Kasai-Kwa River – a major tributary of the Congo that emerges from the copper belt deep in the south. Occasional orange-coloured roads snaked through the thick green vegetation then disappeared, never to emerge again.

After an hour and a half the engine noise dropped and I could make out a village tucked up against a bend in the river as it coiled away towards Mbandaka and the Equator. Some miles inland was a small yellow-brown gash: the airstrip.

Within seconds of landing children appeared from the tall grass. They all laughed and shouted their welcome, but beneath the warmth of their smiles their clothes were torn and stained and their bellies were distended with malnutrition. Lesions and discolorations covered their skin and most were barefoot.

It was my first brush with desperate poverty. The adults among them bore deep horizontal lines across their cheeks, scars which I was to discover meant they belonged to the Bateki tribe. But there was no hostility, and if their eyes were cautious they were also curious and kind.

Before we could be engulfed by the crowd a spluttering Land Rover pulled up, full of local dignitaries and staff from the medical centre. There was just one white man among them. He leapt out of the vehicle almost before it had stopped and came bounding towards us, a bustling character in his forties wearing a hectic shirt of local cotton and a pair of white shorts so incredibly decrepit they were indecent.

'Welcome to Bolobo!' He seized our hands. 'I'm David Masters. I run the medical care around here.'

'Right,' I said, slightly dazzled by his manic energy. 'So you're effectively . . . my boss?'

'What?' he looked distracted. 'Oh, yes, I suppose so. Technically. But I won't be around here much.'

I could see that he was already anxious to be gone. David, like the March Hare from *Alice in Wonderland*, was always in a rush.

'You get settled in and we'll see you at seven tomorrow. No, make it a bit before seven. That's important. You'll see why when you get there.'

And with that he was gone. I've no idea how he got back to Bolobo, which was five miles from the airstrip, because there was only one Land Rover and he wasn't in it. Perhaps he hopped.

By now our Congolese welcoming committee had lined up and was making its stately way towards us.

Papa Eboma led the group. A tall, grey-haired man in his seventies, he was the senior pastor of the church in Bolobo and held the status of village elder. Beside him was Mr Iyeti, the local headmaster and teaching administrator, as beaming and effusive as the pastor was self-effacing.

'Mr and Mrs Hoskins,' Papa Eboma began in French, in the courtly manner of African greetings, 'we thank you for coming to help us, and we hope you will both be very happy among us.'

He went on a little longer in this vein, while the children laughed and chattered and the nurses from the hospital giggled and peered round him to get a better look at us. We stood there dripping in the heat, but I was moved by the small speech. Papa Eboma had gentle, fatherly eyes and a quiet dignity about him. When he had finished, Mr Iyeti added a few words of his own.

As I climbed aboard the shabby Land Rover and the plane buzzed away like an angry hornet, I felt a sudden pang of loneliness.

From here on everything seemed to happen with extraordinary speed. We clattered along a brown rainforest track for a few miles, and all at once we were in Bolobo itself – or so they told us, because the place seemed to have no centre and no street plan. Tin-roofed and thatched houses were dotted among the trees. Groups of men sat in the shade, talking or dozing or drinking. A few exhausted women toiled along the roadside in the blistering heat, carrying on their heads sacks of yams, huge bundles of firewood or enamel dishes of fish or meal.

The Land Rover pulled up and we had our first glimpse of our new home. Set in a red earth clearing, it was a short distance from the main village and looked out over the river, a vast expanse of brown water that I could see flashing in the light between the trees. We had both expected the most primitive accommodation and it was a surprise to discover that the house, constructed as part of the medical centre complex some thirty years before, was relatively substantial. It was brick-built, had a tin roof and even boasted a single glass window in the front – possibly the only one in Bolobo.

The Land Rover could not manage the narrow track to the door, so we offloaded our few bags in the dirt. A noisy throng of helpers gathered to carry them. More villagers flanked the path, rhythmically clapping their hands as we made our way up it. As we reached the house I turned to the chattering crowd.

'My wife and I have come here to Bolobo to live with

you and to learn your customs,' I said in halting French, feeling as if I should be wearing a solar topee and sporting a big Victorian moustache. 'But first let me explain something. We have only been married a few weeks, so this is our first home. In our country, when a husband brings his wife to their first house, this is what we do . . .'

I swept Sue up in my arms with all the panache I could muster and carried her over the threshold. Everyone, adults and children alike, broke out in smiles, laughter and cries of delight. They had never seen anyone do such a thing. They were hugely amused that we Europeans had some bizarre little rituals of our own.

They followed us into the house and quickly filled every room and passageway, opening doors and poking in corners with the most guileless curiosity.

'What is the significance of this tradition?' someone asked me as I set Sue down.

I realized that I had no idea.

'It's . . . um . . . to ward off evil spirits,' I said hopefully.

This seemed to be the right answer and set off another round of admiring exclamations. Whatever the reason, carrying Sue over the threshold struck a chord. It entered local mythology, and for months afterwards the villagers talked about it, miming the gesture and laughing about it whenever we appeared.

While the hubbub continued, we took a look around. The house was dirty and both electricity and clean water were distant memories. The rooms were Spartan in the extreme: a rather imposing hardwood bedstead that might have been half a century old, a couple of rickety chairs, some cupboards providing shelter for spiders and scorpions.

But the house did come complete with Tata Martin,

an old man who greeted us with the news that he was our *domestique.* I hadn't planned on a servant – it didn't sit well with my liberal principles – but I liked Tata Martin at first sight, and grew more enthusiastic about the idea when he announced that he was preparing food for us. Wisely, I didn't argue. Tata Martin was to become a permanent feature of our household, in some ways a surrogate father to us, and we couldn't have made it without him.

Sue was beginning to find the hubbub somewhat wearing, but I was starting to enjoy it. Our visitors were so transparently friendly that I couldn't resent their presence. In any case I could see that Papa Eboma was beginning to build up to another speech, and I guessed that when this was over he would probably hand the house over to us and lead his entourage away. We only needed to be a little patient.

'Ko-ko-ko!'

In a country where there are often no doors to knock upon, this was the call from a visitor to attract attention.

'Ko-ko-ko!'

The babble faded away and the room fell strangely quiet. A fat little man in a dirty green uniform pushed through the crowd. He wore a pistol on his hip.

'Who are these people?' the man demanded, pointing at Sue and me in an aggressive and theatrical fashion.

He was sweating heavily, and had an unpleasant habit of skimming the sweat from his forehead with his index finger and flicking it over anything and anyone within range. When no one answered his question, he fixed his gaze on Papa Eboma.

'I am the immigration officer here,' he announced. 'Why was I not informed strangers were coming?'

No one met our eyes. It was obvious that though many

of these people did not know who this little Hitler was, they were all afraid of him. I was rather shocked that even Papa Eboma seemed to lack the authority to stand up to him. I could see at once that Mr Iyeti would have loved to have told this strutting bully where to go, but protocol demanded that he could not do so if Papa Eboma did not take the lead.

'I'm sorry if you weren't informed,' I said, stepping forward, 'but—'

'Passports!' He held out his hand.

I could see trouble looming. 'I'm afraid we don't have them with us. They're in Kinshasa while our residence visas are prepared.'

'No passports? This is a serious matter.' He stood up straight, flicking sweat off his forehead again. 'We have been alerted to the presence of spies from Libya.'

'Libya?' I gaped at him, not quite sure if he could be serious. Libya was some 3,000 miles to the north, on the far side of the central African rainforest and the Sahara Desert. I doubt if anyone in this village had even heard of the place. I would have been less surprised if he had accused me of being a Martian.

'I must search your bags,' he declared imperiously.

'This is preposterous.' Mr Iyeti could contain himself no longer. 'These people have been sent by the Church. They have come here to help us.'

'You must open the bags,' the officer demanded, rapping his knuckles on the table.

I didn't like the way this was developing and I could sense that Sue liked it even less. I realized that I was worried about *her* now and not the other way round. I put our case on the table and opened it. There was nothing much in it: some clothes, a few books, our mosquito net.

'What are these?' the man snapped.

He held up a box of tampons. I was stuck for a moment for an explanation that could be delivered in front of forty strangers, especially in French, and while I hesitated the officer prised open the box.

'Oh please,' Sue said, and I could hear her voice tremble. 'Please don't open those.'

He did not even trouble to glance at her, but systematically opened the box and then – one after the other – tore open every single tampon, staining the cotton with his dirty fingers, dripping sweat over our clothes and books. That, finally, was enough for Sue and she burst into tears of anger and humiliation. I put my arm around her. No one in the room said a word.

I teetered on the brink of losing my temper, which would have been a disaster. But at that moment the immigration officer, seeing me with my arm around my weeping wife, decided that he had got what he wanted.

'Very well,' he said, tossing aside the last of the ruined tampons. 'It seems you are who you say you are.' He drew himself up to his full, not very impressive height and, to my astonishment, held out his hand. 'Welcome to Bolobo.'

After that he left, pausing only to warn Papa Eboma darkly that next time the Church brought in newcomers he'd better make sure the authorities were informed in good time.

I hated watching Papa Eboma being humbled by this ignorant goon, who was obviously a Mobutu party stooge. It told me something about the real nature of power in the Congo, and it was the first time I'd seen Sue reduced to tears. We didn't talk about it after that. We cleaned the house as well as we could, and ate the meal Tata Martin prepared for us – a strong tasting fish, rice and sliced plantain dish known as *makemba*. After we had had it thirty or forty times its attraction began to fade a bit, but that first day we only knew that it was delicious.

Late that night I lay in bed under the mosquito net with Sue lost in an exhausted slumber beside me. I was too excited to sleep. It was hot, so hot my own breath felt like warm water. A constellation of tiny fireflies swam outside the ghostly folds of the net.

I got up, slipped on my sandals and padded silently through the house to the veranda. Outside, a huge golden moon hung in the trees and the African night was bursting with life: the sound of something rootling in leaf litter beside the house, the whine of mosquitoes scenting my fresh European blood and the jarring call of a night bird.

7

Bolobo, April and May 1986

It was my first morning in paradise.

The bare room was flooded with light and outside a bird I had never heard before was singing to the rising sun. I would later learn that it was the coucal. It's a dull brown bird to look at, but its haunting song would become our regular early morning call.

It was six o'clock, but already hot, and I could hear Tata Martin busying himself in the kitchen. I lifted the netting and moved to the window. Everything outside seemed lush and vividly green. I couldn't see any of the neighbouring huts: it was as if our house had suddenly materialized in a magic forest where no one else had ventured. I was strong and healthy. I was just twenty-two. The world was full of possibility.

Forty-five minutes later I set off through the trees on the short walk down to the medical centre. A score of people were milling around in the sun outside the low building. The entire Congolese staff appeared to be there – nurses in their green and white uniforms, men in overalls, cleaners, porters. David Masters came bustling through the crowd, his indecent shorts flapping.

I thought he would usher me inside, but instead he took

up position beside me, as if we were on parade. I realized that the hubbub was dying down and that the workers had formed a couple of rough ranks on the red earth forecourt. I was in the middle of the front line. I noticed for the first time that there was a flagpole in the centre of the clearing.

'Don't you dare laugh,' David said to me out of the corner of his mouth.

The singing started before I could reply, a medley of dreary and sycophantic songs in praise of President Mobutu. Too astonished to know what else to do, I mouthed a few of the words and tried to look as if I did this every morning. I couldn't quite believe what was happening. I'd come to Africa with a heart full of good intentions and here I was, miming words of praise to one of the vilest dictators the continent had produced.

Our ragged little choir was led by a prancing *animateur*, a kind of compère. I was to learn that he was a party spy who would report anyone who showed less than total enthusiasm to the authorities. We concluded with a rousing rendition of the national anthem as the flag of the Congo rose up the pole. Except that it had mysteriously gone missing some time before, so we all stood rigidly to attention in the middle of the rainforest watching the whole process in mime. I later came to suspect David of having purloined the flag himself, though I could never get him to admit it.

The ritual was absurd, grotesque, laughable, but the consequences of not taking it seriously could be dire indeed. Perhaps I sensed the dark side of this picture even then. Once it was over, David hustled me through the dispersing crowd.

'Keys to your department,' he said as he unlocked a pair of blue-painted doors and swung them wide.

The ramshackle Land Rover which had collected us the previous day stood inside, leaking oil on the stained concrete floor. Around it were stacked boxes of spares, drums of oil, paraffin and aviation fuel, a hand pump, bags of hardening cement, bits of timber, scattered tools. The space stank of diesel. David kicked the nearest crate.

'Vaccine fridge,' he said. 'Just come up on the riverboat. Need to get that installed sometime soon.'

I sensed a pet project. I had very little idea what a vaccine fridge was and no idea how to install one. 'Me?' I said. 'Install that?'

'That's what you're here for, isn't it?'

'Is it?'

He stared at me for a moment and then gave up.

'Staff,' he said, and jerked his head to where an uneven line of half-a-dozen Congolese men in green overalls had formed up behind us without me noticing. He singled out one of them, a tall, wiry, glum-faced man of about sixty. 'Tata Noah. Foreman. Speaks some French. None of the others do. Lingala or nothing for them.' He tossed me the keys. 'See you around.'

He left me and the ill-favoured Tata Noah to eye one another with mutual suspicion.

My life as logistics officer at the Bolobo Medical Centre had begun.

Sue and I learned quickly over the next few weeks. We acquired new skills and got to know new people. We both, inevitably, fell ill and got well again. We established routines. We began to find our way around.

Sue could not start work until she had completed an induction course at a hospital near Kinshasa, and that couldn't be scheduled for some weeks, so most of the domestic work fell on her shoulders. There was plenty of it.

When we had first unpacked our things the house was covered in dust and grime. Fine reddish grit coated every surface and gathered on the skin. An infestation of small scorpions – rumoured to be deadly – meant that we quickly learned never to go barefoot and shook our shoes and sandals before slipping them on. There were other tenants, too: tribes of chunky chestnut-brown cockroaches, spiders the size of a fist, and dozens of brightly coloured lizards. Mosquitoes, the scourge of Africa, were audible everywhere and all the time, not simply after dark. I often only felt or saw them after they were withdrawing from their latest feast.

Among our more engaging houseguests were two enormous rats that lived in the wood stove. Somehow they would elude us when we or Tata Martin came to light the kindling, but they would always return to bask in the heat afterwards and pick up any scraps that happened to be lying about.

Our staple diet quickly became beans, rice and eel. The eels came from the river and had an extremely strong taste and texture. Guavas, mangoes, paw paws, avocados, bananas and pineapples all flourished within a stone's throw of the house.

The people here lived much as they have always lived. They fished the great river from dugout canoes and hunted in the forest with spears and, for the last century or so, with muskets, often temperamental locally made weapons more dangerous to the hunter than their quarry. They traded where they could, carrying what few goods they had up and down the river to other villages by canoe or on their backs along rainforest tracks.

At Bolobo the Congo was some ten miles wide. In the

dusty haze of the dry season it was impossible to see the far side, so that, as I walked along the shores in those first weeks, I had the strange impression of living by the sea. Despite its girth the river flowed fast enough to drag silt up from the riverbed and to make swimming any distance from shore very dangerous. An endless flow of hyacinth islands drifted past. Introduced from Europe a century ago by a homesick missionary lady, the plant had spread the entire length of the Congo, blocking travel even by canoe and strangling the propellers of the riverboats. Only the leeches loved it.

The encircling rainforest threatened to push Bolobo into the water. Trees seeded themselves near houses and grew tall within weeks. Roots wormed under foundations and forced open gaping cracks. Creepers snaked unnoticed up the mudbrick walls, and tore them down. Giant grasses choked footpaths and engulfed anything left untended.

The rain cascaded over the village from the forest canopy, driving down so hard and flooding so fast that the water carved gorges fifty feet deep in a matter of hours.

The larger forest animals kept their distance but exotic birds felt confident enough to fly into the village clearings. The colours were vivid and dazzling. I saw kingfishers of every iridescent hue, flycatchers hovering in brilliant shimmers and sometimes spectacular bee-eaters.

Nature dictated the rhythms of life. The days and nights were of equal length here on the Equator, whatever the time of year. There was a short dry season from mid-June to mid-August, when the skies grew misty and a delicious breeze blew up the river in the morning and evening. But even in this relatively cool season the temperature remained in the eighties by day and – exhaustingly – by night too.

Outside of the dry season the sky was clear sapphire

blue. I'd watch the majestic equatorial sunrises and blood-red sunsets with a wonder that never diminished. During the day giant clouds mushroomed heavenwards as the wet land was slowly broiled by the heat of the sun. Then the air turned murky, the wind whipped into a ferocious roar, and within minutes rain lashed the ground. Then the sun pushed aside the clouds and burned down once more, repeating the endless tropical cycle.

Night was a clammy embrace. Our mattress quickly acquired a rank stench of stale sweat that we could never quite eradicate. We soon gave up trying, or even noticing.

There were no roads here, no signposts. There was nothing to tell you where you were; you knew only that you were here, now, part of the vast rhythm of forest and river. The people knew this and accepted it. They did what they have always done: build homes, have children; watch many of them die and a few of them prosper. They survived as well as they could.

And, whatever they told you, in some corner of their hearts they still believed what they have always believed. While most of the inhabitants would profess to be Christian, they'd still sacrifice a chicken or a goat to bless any new enterprise – the building of a house, for example, or the launching of a business. And everyone believed in the idea of *kindoki* – it was a catch-all for every manner of ills, anything, in fact, which disturbed the balance of body and mind.

Even though I was a Christian, I didn't find these belief systems difficult to tolerate. I thought they were rather an elegant way of viewing a capricious and often dangerous world. Perhaps I was slightly patronizing about them. Killing a chicken was no big deal, after all, and anyway it got eaten afterwards. And the normal recourse for *kindoki* was to go to a local healer, a *nganga*, who'd usually prescribe some herbal remedy and offer the Congolese equivalent of tea and sympathy. It was no great surprise, given the power of suggestion, that these treatments were often completely successful.

8

Bath and London, February 2002

I tilted back my chair and surveyed the fields outside my office window. It was a cold, misty winter's morning, still as the grave, and the dew hung in shrouds across the grass.

I now had my own library of *muti* documents in order, but getting other academics to cooperate had proved unexpectedly difficult. I knew that *muti* wasn't a popular subject among researchers, but I was shocked when a much-respected colleague and friend suggested I should quietly sweep the whole thing under the carpet. He seemed reluctant to dwell on the darker side of anyone's beliefs for fear of being labelled a cultural or moral imperialist. But the more I went through the research material, the more certain I was that Adam's killing had nothing to do with *muti*.

I sipped my third coffee of the day.

The child's blood had been drained. That wasn't typical *muti* either. The killers had made the fatal cut with precision – even sharpening the knife after each stroke. Why? Why was that part of this grim performance so important to them?

Then, after he'd been killed, his limbs had been severed, with less precision. Was this to hide his identity? If so, why dress the body in bright orange-red shorts and throw it into one of the busiest rivers in the world, where it could be seen by any one of half a million passersby? A hare dashed across the winter field, the first movement I had seen in that bleak landscape. Though it wasn't yet 8.30 a.m. I picked up the phone.

The Connex train crawled through south London's dullest suburbs. It was raining. Catford felt like that kind of place. I walked up the slip road to where DS Nick Chalmers waited in a blue, unmarked Ford.

The headquarters of the Serious Crime Squad for South London was a low office block tucked down a miserable side street behind security barriers. I was ushered into an overheated, open-plan office with a score of computer terminals, only about three of which seemed to be in use. Paper, empty coffee cups, ashtrays and tabloid newspapers littered most of the desks. There were only half a dozen people in the room, all men, all in plain clothes. Two were calling crossword clues to one another. One of them gave me a rueful look and tossed the tabloid into the bin.

An air of stagnation seemed to have settled upon the investigation. I couldn't claim to be entirely surprised. A few days earlier a TV journalist had called me for some background. He had told me that the Met were thinking about shelving the Adam investigation and moving on to cases with some prospect of solution.

Nick sat me down outside Will O'Reilly's office. A minute or two later Will ushered me into his room. Behind his desk were wall-mounted whiteboards with procedural details of a handful of operations in coloured felt-tip. Most of them were crammed with information – phone numbers, photos of suspects, details of leads. All that was stuck under

'Operation Swalcliffe' – the codename they'd given to the Adam case – was a police handout with a picture of the orange-red shorts and a large question mark. Will seemed distracted. I asked him to rate the chances of a successful outcome for the case.

'We'd have solved the toughest investigation in British criminal history,' he said simply. 'But Commander Baker is keen for us to give it a go. He wants you to join the team. And he's prepared to resource the investigation if we can progress it.'

Baker was the Met's head of homicide.

Nick Chalmers appeared and I pulled out my notes. 'The more I look into this,' I said, 'the more certain I am that it isn't a South African *muti* murder. And if I'm right, it's likely that Adam doesn't come from there either.'

The detectives exchanged glances, but neither spoke.

I went on to tell them that the people responsible probably came from the same tribe or ethnic group as their victim, and that Adam's circumcision could help identify which, and that, in turn, could point to where he came from.

Will remained silent a moment longer, then told me that he and Commander Baker were planning on going to South Africa to see if they could make some kind of appeal and possibly even enlist Nelson Mandela's support.

I read him loud and clear. They were committed to an expensive, high-profile initiative. Senior London policemen would be photographed shaking hands with the most famous man on the planet. And then I come along, suggesting that they might be barking up the wrong tree. 'It's got to be a good idea,' I said. 'Whether it's a *muti* killing or not, whether Adam's from South Africa or not, Mandela's word carries real weight.'

Will stood up. 'Let's go and get a coffee.'

The coffee room was through several double doors and down a series of neon-lit corridors. Plastic chairs were scattered around a scored table. A draining board was crowded with ill-matched mugs. Will searched for a couple of clean ones.

He seemed keen to talk. He'd never been to South Africa, and he asked me about the country, its people and the local religious practices.

They weren't heading for the *muti* heartland of KwaZulu-Natal this time around, so I recommended that they visit the *muti* market in Johannesburg. I also suggested that they visit a traditional healer, and gave Will the name of a prominent *sangoma* who sometimes received Western visitors.

'And what about your witch doctor?' I asked.

Will looked a bit sheepish. 'Commander Baker rather took to heart your point about negative publicity.' He gave a hint of a smile. 'So we've decided to put that line of inquiry on hold, pending the outcome of more routine procedures.'

'I want you to put what you've told me in writing,' he said as we were about to part. 'Give me a short report I can show to my bosses, stating why you don't think the *muti* angle is right – and what you think really happened to this kid.'

9

Bolobo, June 1986–1987

David Masters didn't give me long to settle in. I'd been in the job for about a month when he came bustling into the workshop and suggested it was about time I installed the vaccine fridge at Nko, some fifty miles away.

I felt a stab of panic. I'd just about got used to finding my way around Bolobo. I dreaded to think how the ancient Land Rover would perform on forest tracks with a heavy vaccine fridge and half my workers on board. And from my elementary studies in Lingala I already knew that the word 'Nko' meant something like 'bloody minded'. It sounded like a bad omen.

I sat on the bench after David had gone and gazed with misgiving at the crate. The fridge was a solar-powered prototype donated by an energy company. It would serve as the central vaccine repository for the whole Bandundu region, an area the size of Wales.

A little after seven a couple of mornings later, feeling like the wagon master of some pioneering trek, I kissed Sue goodbye and gave the order to roll.

There were no roads out of Bolobo, just forest tracks, and only one of these – towards Nko and then Mushie in the south – was remotely passable, even for a four-wheel drive. Nobody had tried this route for over a year; it was a nightmare of soft mud, bogs as deep as the vehicle's roof and fallen trees. It took us nine hours to cover the first fifteen miles, hacking a new path with machetes, winching or heaving the Land Rover out of holes, then shoving it forward again in a welter of exhaustion, mud and sweat. I didn't think it was possible to roll a Land Rover, but we came perilously close. I had no idea if the precious vaccine fridge could survive such treatment. By the time we got to Nko I no longer cared.

There was little to see beyond the flicker of a couple of campfires and the silhouettes of a few scattered huts. Outside the circles of firelight it was intensely dark; the sort of darkness I had not experienced even in Bolobo. A small group of children and women in shawls gathered around us. I hardly had the strength to greet them.

'I am Mr Bodio, the schoolteacher,' a voice said in French out of the gloom. 'You are welcome here.'

I suddenly knew everything would be all right. Mr Bodio was a gracious, almost saintly Congolese in his fifties, with white hair and thick spectacles. Gratefully I allowed him to lead me through the villagers to his mud-brick house.

A mattress had been laid out for me in a small room lit with a hurricane lamp. A kindly woman brought me a bar of soap, a towel and a bowl of steaming water and showed me to a small shelter of saplings and reeds. I stood there in the darkness with the night-birds calling, and washed off the filth and sweat of the journey.

When I was ready I joined the circle around the fire, all of us sitting in wooden-framed chairs of stretched antelope hide, chatting quietly in Lingala while the women prepared a meal. I tried hard to take part in the conversation and was surprised at how well I got by. At length we were summoned inside a dimly lit hut and seated around a wooden table.

I was familiar with most of the menu. *Chikwanga*, for example, was ground manioc root baked into a hard slab: it had very few nutrients and smelled like vomit, but it filled you up. *Fufu* was the same stuff, but prepared as a paste, and I always found it delicious. Tonight's last dish, however, was something else again.

'We have prepared something special for you all,' Mr Bodio said, beaming behind his spectacles. 'We hope you like it.'

A woman placed a pot on the table in front of me and whipped off its lid.

Inside was the hand of a large ape. It seemed to be beckoning me. The fingers were slightly curled so that I could see the blackened nails. It took about a nanosecond for the appropriate emotions to flit through my brain: horror, shock, revulsion. What was I to do? If I refused the dish I knew it would cause terrible offence. One of the women cut off a segment and offered it to me. I peeled back my lips in some semblance of a smile and nodded.

The dispensary was a mile or two down the track. Once a customs post between the Belgian and French Congos, it was the only brick building in the area, but it was overhung by four enormous palm trees, which I was fairly certain would play havoc with the solar panels.

'They'll have to come down,' I announced, glad that at least one task looked like being straightforward.

My irascible foreman, Tata Noah, shook his head. 'They're valuable, boss. There'll be big trouble if you cut them down without asking the local chief.'

I sighed. 'And where does this chief live?'

'Only about twenty kilometres away.'

I gritted my teeth, but sent a message to the chief in question. This was becoming as complicated as putting a skylight into a listed building in Cheltenham.

I busied myself with the cabling while we waited for the answer. A day or two later the chief turned up in person, a short, wizened old man with very deep tribal scars. He had a great air of dignity about him and leaned on a staff while a small entourage milled about him. I realized he must have walked the whole way. I knew what an honour this was, and I felt uncomfortably aware that I had been thinking less than reverential thoughts about him and his local traditions. Worse, I was in shorts when he arrived, which I instinctively knew to be bad form.

Embarrassed, I greeted him in Lingala, '*Mbote*.'

'*Mbote*,' he replied.

There was a pause. He must have been at least three times my age and esteemed for his sagacity and leadership, but I realized that he was uncertain of where he stood with me. I was the powerful white man and I had brought God knows what magical boxes of tricks with me. I was ashamed that he should feel this way when I knew myself to be so inadequate and insecure.

'*Losako*,' I said at length – Father, give me your wisdom.

There were gasps of astonishment from the entourage, and I thought for an awful moment I had committed some unspeakable gaffe. Then I saw the delight in the old man's eyes.

'*Nkoi*,' he replied – the leopard. I should go through life with the courage, guile and grace of a leopard.

As an awkward, rather immature young man from the

Home Counties, I can't say I felt much like a leopard. But I was as pleased with the chief for this blessing as he was with me for asking for it.

My new friend offered all the help and cooperation I could wish for and the palm trees duly came down. Within a few days, after a good deal of improvisation and nervous scrambling around on the roof, the solar panels were installed. A few more days and the fridge's amber 'function' light sprang on and then flicked over to green. It actually worked. I couldn't believe it. It actually *worked*.

On the last evening, I sat with Mr Bodio and the others and chatted long into the night. The fire rustled at our feet, and above us, in the gaps in the forest canopy, the southern Milky Way lay splashed across the black sky. This was the Africa I had been looking for. And perhaps, after all, I was beginning to be the man I had come to find.

I was more at peace for those first few months in Bolobo than I'd ever been in my life.

My triumph with the vaccine fridge won me a lot of kudos. It also boosted my self-esteem, something that I saw now I had always lacked. I flourished in this new atmosphere. Nobody seemed to mind what I tackled next, perhaps because virtually nothing seemed to work.

Bolobo had no running water unless it could be hand-pumped from a rain-catcher or collected from streams. The Congo itself was considered too dirty even when vigorously boiled. There was no electricity, and thus no light for the operating room at the medical centre. Within a few weeks I had repaired the centre's water pumps and installed a Lister diesel generator, which had languished in the stores for some months. When we could beg or borrow enough diesel fuel from passing riverboats we even had lights for a couple of hours in the evening.

Late one evening, when the generator was silent, I was studying my Lingala in the light of the oil lamp when I caught Sue gazing at me across the table. She was due to set off for Kinshasa the next day to complete the course she needed to start work as a midwife. We'd been apart once or twice for a few days, but this would be the first time she'd left me alone here, and somehow it felt different to both of us.

'I was about to ask if you'd be all right while I'm away,' she said. 'But then I realized how silly that was. You've done really well, you know? I'm not sure I expected it that first day in Kinshasa.'

'Thanks,' I laughed. 'Me neither.' I paused. 'I love it here,' I said. 'I just love it.'

She smiled at me. I couldn't quite fathom that smile. It struck me for the first time that by some alchemy it had been me who'd fallen under the spell of this wild and magical place, and Sue who merely lived here.

I thought about this a lot after she had gone, as I sat alone in the long evenings, listening to the scurrying of small creatures in the dark spaces of the house. The rhythms of African life had filled my spirit with peace.

This state of euphoria lasted for many months. Sue came back and started work; my own duties expanded, and I spent much of my time buying medicines and supplies for the centre, having them delivered by light aircraft or riverboat, and getting them distributed around the province.

Sometimes I took them myself, by dugout canoe or on foot, occasionally on David Masters' bucking bronco of a motorbike, bouncing down the tangled tracks like a trail rider. Filled with a growing passion for the river, the forest and the people who lived here, I used any excuse to travel. I became fluent in Lingala, so fluent that I dreamed in it.

In the middle of 1987, when we had been in Bolobo over a year, Sue told me that she was pregnant. It seemed to both of us that our world was soon to be made complete.

10

Bath, February 2002

As the First Great Western train sped through the winter countryside, carrying me back to Bath after my meeting with the police in Catford, I knew I needed to move on, to think about what sort of a murder this was, rather than what sort it wasn't.

I propped open the office door, picked up the first of five stacks of *muti* dossiers and carried them outside to my waiting Land Rover.

'Spring cleaning?' Mahinda asked, smiling up at me from his computer. 'One of your quaint Western rites, pagan in origin. Regeneration. Return of the sun. New life. It's in the same category as Easter.'

I slumped in my chair, my new sense of purpose rapidly evaporating.

The absent books had left pale rectangles on the wood where a little dust had gathered. The surface looked blank and I didn't know where to start.

Mahinda shut down the screen he was looking at and swivelled his chair to face me. 'You know, Richard, it's a credit to you that you take such an interest in the case of this poor boy.'

'It is?' The compliment surprised me.

'Yes, it is.' He gazed at me with his calm eyes. 'Although I presume that you have a more than professional interest in this awful crime?'

I thought about denying it, but there was no point. 'Yes,' I said. 'I have.'

'Then you must not allow it to take over your whole being. On the other hand,' Mahinda stood up and pointed at my bare desk, 'neither must you give up.'

He granted me one of his most beatific smiles and drifted out. With new determination I pulled out a notepad and opened the bundle of papers Will had given me.

Where did this boy come from? I decided to go back to basics. I focused on the possibility that Adam was either African or African-Caribbean. I'd already seen enough to realize that whoever did this was steeped in customs that were not exactly common in Britain, or any of the other Western countries with significant black populations. After some thought I decided that argument applied to potential Caribbean homelands too.

I pulled one of the photos out of the bundle. Adam's circumcision was well healed, so it had been carried out a considerable time before his death; most probably, therefore, when he was a baby. African circumcision practices are more often than not extremely culture-specific. Some groups circumcise their male children soon after birth, whilst others view it as the entry to manhood. Many don't circumcise at all.

I knew the Xhosa peoples of southern Africa, for example, traditionally practised circumcision at puberty. So did the Zulu, when they did it at all. Most of the East African tribes I knew about also performed circumcision at puberty. The Maasai of Kenya used the rite to initiate a boy into becoming a warrior, a *moran*. So Adam was unlikely to be Xhosa, Zulu or Maasai. Could I extend this cultural analysis across the whole African continent?

This approach wasn't without its complications. I pulled open the bottom drawer of my filing cabinet and found an article about a tribe in Uganda which was changing its cultural practices almost overnight. They'd learnt from a Western medical study that HIV spreads less readily among circumcised men, and so had begun circumcising their boy children soon after birth.

I logged onto the internet and emailed a selection of my academic contacts, asking for general information on circumcision practices among major African groups, and if the Ugandan development was becoming more widespread. I also emailed my friend Robert Papini, curator of the Durban *muti* museum, to check my Xhosa and Zulu intelligence.

I drove home and spent half an hour in the basement garage rummaging through my files and storage boxes. By the time I got back, staggering under a fresh armful of folders and books, Mahinda had materialized again. He raised his eyebrows, smiled benignly but said nothing as I dumped everything on my desk.

I worked doggedly through the heap of papers, books and articles. They dealt with cultural practices from all over the African world, and as a first step I tried to arrange them into geographical zones: East Africa, West Africa, South Africa.

By now the email replies were starting to come in. Robert Papini confirmed that Xhosa and Zulu peoples traditionally circumcised their boys only at puberty. He added that although there was some evidence of babies being circumcised in South Africa nowadays, it still wasn't at all common. I tapped my pen on the desk. Not open and shut, then, but good enough for me. I wrote on my pad, as if to reassure myself: 'Not *muti*. Not South Africa.'

I sat back in my chair and massaged the bridge of my nose. As a process of elimination, how far could I take this?

'Lunch?' Mahinda suggested hopefully.

I shook my head.

11

Bolobo, February 1988

We never knew what brought on the birth so prematurely.

Sue's pregnancy hadn't bothered her – in fact she had blossomed over the past few months. So when she slipped and fell whilst getting out of the dugout during an afternoon trip to an island on the River Congo, neither of us gave it much thought. She got up quickly and laughed it off.

If there had been any cause for concern, we would have headed straight back to Kinshasa, and probably on to England. But we had nearly three months to go before our baby was due; plenty of leeway if anything began to look out of the ordinary. We had it all planned. If the baby was a girl she was to be called Abigail, 'her father's joy'. We both loved the name, perhaps because the biblical Abigail was so winsome and feisty, if a little short on Old Testament morality when it came to seducing King David.

But a few hours later, when Sue was working in the kitchen, I heard her take a sharp breath and saw her place a hand flat on her belly.

'Something's happening,' she said.

I got up and went to her. She had been cooking fudge, of all things. It was my twenty-fourth birthday the next day, and this was to be a special treat.

I led her to a chair. She sat down and seemed to recover at once.

'I'll get David,' I said.

'No need.'

'I'll get him.'

As I hurried between the trees all the arguments we had used for staying in the village since Sue became pregnant ran through my mind. Everything would be fine. She was healthy – and a midwife herself. We worked at a medical centre, didn't we? David was back from a lengthy trip, so there was a doctor on hand. Even though he wasn't a gynaecologist, this ought to mean we were in the best place for at least 300 miles. Yes, everything would be fine.

'You're going to have twins,' David said, standing up after his examination. He kept his voice neutral. 'And pretty soon, too.'

'Twins?'

I looked down at Sue and saw something in her expression I hadn't seen there before. Fear. I knew mine told the same story.

'Twins?' I said again. 'Can that be right?'

'Look, Richard,' David said testily, 'your wife's in labour. And she's going to have twins.'

'But I'm only twenty-nine weeks,' Sue said, as if she might be able to order this thing not to be.

David kept his face averted while he washed his hands in a bowl. 'I'm afraid I can only feel one of them properly, but it's breech.'

He didn't need to say any more. Twins, and a breech birth, well over two months premature. In this place.

'I'll be back a little later,' David said. 'Call me if you need me.'

I had the impression he was leaving us alone to come to terms with this. Or perhaps because he didn't want to see us failing to do so.

I looked out of the window at the rainforest, trying to quell my rising panic. The birds were calling and somewhere nearby people laughed, as if it were any other afternoon. The house still smelled comfortingly of fudge. I tried to concentrate. I knew there would be no electric light tonight: there was no fuel for the generator and it was already getting dark.

Sue got up and paced around the room, her face lined with anxiety and – increasingly – with pain. We didn't speak. Twins. I had the most acute sense of approaching catastrophe, as if the door of an enormous iron vault was closing on us all.

It was a nightmare scene, hot and sulphurous, full of pain and blood.

I had never imagined that an event so masked in rosy myths could be as barbarous. David worked in the feeble glow of a small oil lamp. Beyond that disc of light the room and the house and the world were pitch black. The night was filled by Sue's screams, the slick glint of blood, the shadowy figures of the Congolese women helpers blocking my view.

She was born dead, our first daughter. In the confusion, I never saw her face. I don't even know exactly what happened to her. I was in shock, helpless and frantic, but unable to take my eyes off what was happening. Somehow, in the middle of all this, the child was spirited away from the room, a swaddled bundle no bigger than a paperback book. I didn't see her go. She might never have been there. Everyone's focus had already switched to the living.

David was bending over Sue, who shrieked again, and

I watched with horror the tension bunching in his shoulders as a second child was dragged into the world, mewling, gasping for breath. But alive. Somehow. Alive.

Abigail was impossibly tiny – she weighed just two pounds – and it seemed certain that she would die too. All through that suffocating night I lay listening to her pathetic struggles to breathe.

I got up every few minutes and went to the crib, just to listen for the next rasp of breath, willing it to come. I didn't know a human being could be so small and so defenceless, and I was unprepared for the strength of my need to protect her.

Sue, torn, bruised and utterly exhausted, lay beside me in the sweltering darkness. I desperately wanted to bring Abigail into our bed, but Sue forbade it; she was so fragile we might harm her. I went along with this: Sue was not only the midwife but the mother. I suspected that a more primal drama was being worked out here; that this first night was a trial Abigail must face alone.

And finally, somehow, the darkness began to thin and the song of the coucal birds floated from the forest into my half-conscious mind. It was my birthday.

Sue, I'm not sure how, had got to her feet and was standing by Abigail's cot. I couldn't hear a sound from the baby. I held my breath in the dawn.

'Well,' Sue said, with evident surprise, 'we've got a real little fighter on our hands here.'

Sometime later that day Abigail's twin was buried in a hastily dug grave in the cemetery on the hill.

Its rough wooden marker was visible from the window

in our bedroom, beneath which Sue and I lay later that afternoon. We were utterly drained, sweating in the relentless heat, stricken with the knowledge that nothing would ever be the same again, whilst the world carried on around us regardless.

'Twins,' Sue said aloud. I hadn't realized she was awake. 'I knew I felt two of them kick. I knew it.'

'A scan would have picked it up,' I said. 'Just a routine scan.' I didn't mean to sound bitter but I could hear it in my voice, and so could she. 'I never even saw her. The first baby. It all happened so fast, and there was Abigail just born and . . . she was out of the room so quickly that I never saw her.'

'I did,' Sue said in a small voice.

I rolled over to look at her. 'You did?'

'When I got up, just after Abigail arrived. I found the little bundle in the kitchen. I don't suppose they intended me to find her, but there she was, and I folded back the cloth. I saw her face.' She groped for my hand. 'You don't mind, do you?'

'No, I don't mind.' I lay back and stared at the stained ceiling. 'How could I mind? I'm glad you saw her. I just couldn't think of anything but Abigail . . .'

I knew I would always regret not seeing my first daughter's face. And now it was too late. I thought of the pathetic mound of turned earth just 100 yards from the window, baking in the Congo sun.

For Sue, our first daughter was a person who had lived, no matter how briefly, and died. For me she was insubstantial, a presence I could never give form to, nor quite lay to rest. We didn't give her an English name until well over a year later, when we decided to call her Judith. We had only expected one child, so we had only chosen one name, and naturally her younger sister had inherited that.

The lack of a name didn't seem a problem then. In this part of the Congo twins are relatively rare. The elder is always called Mbo and the younger Mpia, titles which confer some status and which imply an indissoluble bond between the siblings. There is no need for other names. So for months we referred to our lost daughter simply as Mbo, when we could bring ourselves to speak of her at all. Mbo Hoskins was the name on her grave marker.

It didn't strike me until much later that everything had been granted to the living sister and nothing, not even an identity, to the one who had died.

Sue was in a bad way after the dreadful events of that night and, though she showed great strength and courage, I did at first have rather more to do with the care of Abigail than I might otherwise have done.

I relished this responsibility, the knowledge that I could do something useful for her. I fed her through a tube and walked around with her strapped to my chest in a sling. I bonded with her in a way that I suppose would have been impossible under any other circumstances. Her eyes would gaze up into mine from her pouch. I had never loved anyone – or anything – so much.

The villagers called me a Tata Mapassa – father of twins – and as such I was eyed with much respect, but it was tinged with wariness, as if people felt it might be as well to keep their distance when dealing with me.

I was hardly aware of this at first. Or if I was, I thought the change might have been in me alone. For one thing, once Abigail had survived the first few months and was developing well, I began to travel more. I found myself driven by a relentless desire to visit the remotest villages, far away from Bolobo.

It seems strange to me now that I should have experienced this urge to journey away from the child who meant so much to me, but at the time it did not seem so. Sometimes when I was on my own in the house a sense of dread visited me like a presence. Having lost one daughter, I knew I could not bear to be near if the other was taken.

At the same time there was something much deeper at work. It seemed to me that if I now strove to do good for the people of this region, God would reward me. If I did what I thought was God's will, surely He would protect my family?

I felt useful, bringing medicines and other supplies to the villages, bringing news, making contacts, learning every day. The villagers held white people in exaggerated esteem and would talk to me for hours about their problems, their fears and their dreams. Mostly, they just needed someone to talk to, but besides that they were influenced, I think, by the fact that I was employed by the Church. For some people I almost had the status of confessor, someone to whom they could unburden with safety. I relished the role and did my best to be worthy of it, but there is no doubt that the respect and deference of the villagers was a salve for my own pain.

I found relief in the sheer physical experience of travelling. Electricity was the stuff of fairy tales for this whole area and running water meant the nearest stream. At first I took the Land Rover, but that was only possible on the track to Nko and Mushie, and even that eventually disappeared in a giant quagmire. It wasn't unusual for it to take seven or eight hours to cover a dozen miles or less, with endless stops to cut a new path through the forest.

I learned not to rely on machines. The long-suffering Land Rover, pushed beyond endurance, broke down several times. On one occasion I had struck out with Tata Mopanda for a remote cluster of villages known collectively as the Nkuboko. After passing Mushie, the track meandered through the forest for another 100 miles, little wider than people could pass in single file and yet the Land Rover was rammed through. After hours of grinding labour, the vehicle finally broke down with fuel pump failure. We spent about six hours trying to fix it and then walked a couple more to the nearest village. The monkeys screamed and gibbered in the canopy above us, ripping off fruit and letting it drop to the forest floor.

The village comprised eight shabby palm-thatch huts. Neither of us had eaten anything all day; we were filthy, exhausted and famished. There was no water to wash in and the villagers only had two eggs between them. I tried to turn them down but the villagers wouldn't hear of it and graciously made us an omelette. I stretched out that night on rushes in one of the simplest huts I had yet stayed in, staring up through the gaps in the palm thatch at patches of sky between the treetops.

I was desperately lonely that night. My resolution faltered and I remember asking myself what I was doing there when I had a wife and child back in Bolobo. Was I really doing this for God, as a trade-off for my family's protection? What kind of God would seek such self-denial from me, or impose such a price on Sue and Abigail? I couldn't find an answer.

Nevertheless, for weeks and months a great restlessness drove me on.

I usually set off into the heart of the rainforest by bicycle, stopping every few miles to hammer the wheel back into shape after the latest buckling. When I came to the frequent streams and rivers that crossed my path I would either wade out with the bicycle above my head, or try and find a villager with a canoe who could ferry me across.

Small victories over big obstacles gave me some satisfaction, but my loneliness never left me. I had a pocket radio with me and in one extremely isolated stretch of rainforest, hundreds of miles from anything resembling a town, I picked up Brian Johnston commentating on the Lord's Test. Out in the middle of nowhere, the sound of his plummy, quizzical voice filled me with almost unbearable nostalgia.

I used a dugout canoe to travel on the river. By this time I'd become passably competent at handling it the Congolese way – standing up to paddle gondolier-like from the stern. On longer trips, though, I followed the example of the wealthier local traders and used an outboard motor. I found that if I headed upriver it was possible after a few miles to turn inland through the forest along the smaller tributaries.

Once, I made a month-long trip by canoe through a series of forest streams known as the Sangassi, almost on the Equator. Villages here were built on stilts, because the forest was flooded for most of the year. I stopped to wash my clothes in a brook, beating them against the stones under an extraordinarily hot sun, and as I did so some villagers gathered round me. They seemed amazed at everything I did.

'What's so fascinating?' I asked in Lingala. 'Never seen a man washing his own clothes before?'

They exchanged bashful glances.

'It's not that,' one of them said at last. 'We've never seen a white man before.'

I stood up, tilted back my straw hat and wiped my

forearm across my sweating brow. It was my turn to be amazed. I didn't think villages still existed where a white man had never been seen.

I glanced down at my lean, tanned body, the rags I wore for clothes, my bare feet. I thought about how much had changed for me. Within the space of two years I had married and become a father, had a daughter and lost a daughter, learnt a new language with such fluency that I had trouble remembering English, and immersed myself so fully in an alien culture that I wondered if I would ever be able to find my way back to my own. I sometimes wondered if I would ever want to.

I returned down the Sangassi with a few Congolese fellow travellers. We had been paddling for hours through trees that arched over the waterway forming a solid canopy overhead. I had reached the stage of near-anaesthetic weariness I sought when, out of nowhere, a tropical storm blew up. The frail canoe was gripped by the wind and the current and in a few seconds we were swept right out into the main Congo River – a vast sweep of shining water all around and towering cloud above.

We were all awed at the sight, struck dumb by it. We stopped our ineffectual paddling and let the river whirl us on. We were impotent before its power. A man in the bow sat back on his haunches and spread his arms wide to the torrential rain. 'Behold!' he cried. 'Look upon the greatness of God!'

I found myself envying his certainty. For if I had gained some comfort during these turbulent months of wandering, I had begun to lose something too: the belief that all this toil was supposed to bolster. I had encountered suffering on a scale that had not even featured in my worst nightmares.

Children, wives, fathers, husbands, grandparents, brothers and sisters: no one was beyond death's grasp. It was a perpetual echo of my own loss, but the full import of what I had seen was not fully driven home to me until I stumbled upon a tiny village called Ntandembelo, on the very edge of the rainforest.

I got there long after dark and the villagers greeted me with their usual hospitality. They sat me by the fire, brought me a bowl of cold water so that I could wash and then gave me a meal of tough *chikwanga* and tiny fish from the local streams. We then moved under the tin roof of the church, where I was told a number of local people would like to speak to me. I sat there all evening, chatting to one villager after another in the glow of a couple of oil lamps – people asking for news, complaining of illness, looking for advice on how to deal with a troublesome mother-in-law.

Then came a woman of perhaps thirty-five, although she looked older, burdened with the weight of care and grief. I never discovered her name. She came quietly into the open mud-brick church. It was close to midnight. The others had drifted away and I found myself alone with her in the darkness.

'May I speak with you, *Moteyi*?' she asked.

She addressed me as 'teacher'. I usually tried to insist on 'Richard', but by now I was too tired to bother; so tired in fact that I had hoped to be left in peace. The church was no more than a tin shelter on poles with low walls open to the night and my ankles were being eaten alive by mosquitoes. But I knew she had probably been waiting in the shadows for her moment, and I didn't have the heart to turn her away.

I said, 'Of course.'

She sat beside me on the wooden bench.

'I have come to you for help,' she said.

'In what way can I help you?'

'You are from the Church.'

'I only work for them, you know. I'm not an actual priest.'

I had meant the response to be self-effacing, but her silence told me she had no interest in such distinctions. In the light of the lantern I saw tears rolling down her cheeks. I pulled myself upright and listened.

'I have brought nine children into the world,' she said, wiping her face with the corner of her shawl. 'Five of them are already in the ground.'

I said nothing. My own sadness illuminated her greater one with a stark clarity I had never experienced before. The endlessly repeated tragedy of Africa became, in that instant, personal to me.

'I am a good Christian.' She looked into my eyes. 'Tell me, can the Church help me to protect the babies I have left?'

She could see I had no answer.

'You know of the *ngangas*?' she asked hesitantly.

'I've heard of them,' I said.

Ngangas are diviners and healers who use traditional methods in their practices – the equivalent in these parts of the South African *sangomas*. You might go to a *nganga* for a problem involving *kindoki*, the usually low-grade witchcraft with which many Congolese felt themselves to be afflicted from time to time. He would almost certainly cure you of that with a harmless herbal draught and a few words of wisdom. Or you might go to a *nganga* for guidance on more serious questions. Questions of life and death.

'I love my children with all my heart,' she said. 'I would do anything to protect them. I could not bear to bury one more of them.'

I knew what she was about to ask and I knew what I was supposed to say in response. I knew at least what I was supposed to think, what any sane young Western man was supposed to think. I was silent.

'Would it be very wrong,' she went on, looking once more into my eyes, 'if I were to ask the *nganga* to help guard my babies from harm?'

I stared back at her, struck dumb by her intensity. She was terrified. The hardship and danger I flirted with was her birthright. She had nothing but her surviving children and she knew as well as I did that she might lose them too. Whatever my devotion to this place, I could leave any time I wanted. She was condemned to stay.

I couldn't find a single thing to say to her. Nothing I'd been taught to believe would be of the slightest use to her. No faith of mine could make sense of her and her nation's tragedy. I had travelled hoping God would protect my family, but if he wasn't protecting this woman or the millions like her, how could I dare expect special treatment?

Could I forbid her to go to a *nganga*? What did I have to offer instead? In the face of such desperation weren't all courses permissible?

She read her answer in my eyes.

'Thank you,' she said.

She stood up and moved back quietly into the night. As she vanished straight-backed between the trees, on her way to meet whatever grim future awaited her, I felt my own faith tremble.

12

Bath, March 2002

The papers and reports that Will had given to me in Catford were stacked each side of my keyboard. I'd worked through them over the past few days.

Mike Heath, the pathologist, believed that Adam's torso was put in the water up to twenty-four hours after his death. He estimated that what was left of the little boy had been floating in the river for anything up to ten days before it was found.

Tidal experts reckoned that it would have taken just one more day to wash Adam's body out to sea. They were still trying to identify the exact point where he could have been dumped, but had only narrowed it down to a twelve-mile stretch of the river. There was CCTV coverage of certain parts of the bank, but without a specific focus, examining it would have been a Herculean task.

The initial Forensic Science Service (FSS) examination had come up with very little. The upper intestine was empty, which meant that Adam had not eaten for a while, and the lower intestine contained indeterminate material which had not yet been tested. His stomach contained virtually nothing, except traces of pholcodine, an over-the-counter cough mixture, and non-indigenous pollen residues. The

Thames is full of them, but this provided an indication at least that Adam might recently have spent time outside the UK.

The body contained very little blood – none of which was fresh – owing to the child's injuries and his immersion, which also made it impossible to test effectively for antibodies that could have indicated past illnesses and might have given a clue to his origins.

The FSS had Adam's DNA, but he wasn't on any known DNA database and no candidates had presented themselves.

A number of other tests were currently underway. One was on what they called ethnic inferencing; another on the mitochondrial DNA, which, unlike DNA from the nucleus of cells, is passed only through the female line, so people sharing the same mitochondrial DNA must also share a female ancestor. Ray Fysh and the FSS team also planned to test cultural mutation against known databases, and were hoping to focus on the Y-chromosome in the male line.

Good old-fashioned police work had come up with some results on Adam's shorts. They were labelled 'Kids'n'Co' and manufactured in China. Only 800 pairs had been made, exclusively for the Woolworths chain in Germany and Austria, where they were marketed as girls' clothing rather than boys'. So it looked as if Adam might have passed through Germany before coming to Britain – but we were still a long way from pinpointing the boy's original home.

Why would someone have placed bright orange-red shorts on the torso after death? Did the colour have any significance? If randomly chosen, they weren't exactly inconspicuous. And why the river? Did Adam's killers think the body would be washed straight out to sea, not taking the tidal rip into account, or was there some other resonance behind their method of disposal?

Commander Andy Baker rang the next morning to invite me to a conference the following month at the headquarters of Europol, the Europe-wide police agency, in The Hague. 'We'd like to ask you to be keynote speaker,' he said.

He wanted me to go into some detail on the background to this killing, and outline my cultural analysis. 'I'll say a few words of introduction. Will's going to give a presentation on the police perspective of the case. Then it's over to you. After lunch we'll ask Ray Fysh to present an overview of the forensic analysis. We'll fly you out business class and put you up in a decent hotel. It'll be a chance for you to meet some other members of the team – and perhaps have a bit of a break.'

'There's just one thing,' I said. 'I'd like to bring my partner, Faith. She's been following the case closely.'

There was a slight pause, and I was suddenly anxious that I had overstepped the mark.

But then Commander Baker said easily, 'Leave that with me, would you, Richard? I'll see what I can do.'

13
Bolobo, 1988–1989

Despite the odds stacked so heavily against her, Abigail grew into a delightful impish toddler, noisy, inquisitive and affectionate. In mid-1988, when she was six months old, we took her to England.

It was our first trip out of the Congo and almost our first out of the Bandundu region, and it gave me respite from my doubts and fears, reminding me of how lucky we were to have Abigail and one another. There were new sights, the joy of homecoming, and the warmth of friends and family. If these influences did not entirely banish my uncertainties, they certainly pushed them back into the shadows.

We showed Abigail off to her relations, and then – one of the prime reasons for the trip – had her thoroughly checked out at a London clinic. It was strange to sit in a cool surgery, surrounded by gleaming equipment and crisply uniformed medical staff, while the reassuring London rain beat against the tall windows. I couldn't help thinking of the last time Abigail had received any serious attention from the medical community, when she'd been wrenched into the world by the light of an oil lamp, while the rainforest screeched and gibbered outside.

'Well, Mr and Mrs Hoskins,' the doctor stood back and

shook her head in admiration, 'you've got a remarkable child there. She's perfectly healthy as far as I can see. Perfectly.'

Abigail, at her most coquettish, gurgled up at the doctor as if she were as pleased with herself as we were.

There were those among our family and friends who urged us not to go back to the Congo, but we didn't seriously entertain the idea of staying in England. That would have seemed like a capitulation to us and would have made Judith's loss meaningless. With her death, Sue and I had given something irreplaceable of ourselves to Africa, and we both considered that we belonged there for the next phase of our lives. We had come through. Our child had come through. We had all three endured and we had all three suffered, but we were the stronger for it. We could have asked for no more potent symbol of that than Abigail herself: laughing, healthy and strong.

We returned to Bolobo in the same tiny plane that had taken us there two years earlier.

As we taxied to a halt, nothing seemed to have changed. The long grass around the fringe of the airstrip swayed in the gentle breeze. The cloying heat pressed in on us the moment the plane stopped moving. Children who had run from the neighbouring settlement were lined up near the plane, grinning and jostling one another. Our pilot Dan – sandy-haired American Dan who had co-piloted us the first time – killed the engine, and I could see adults gradually joining the throng. This time, however, the wary expressions had given way to huge smiles of welcome.

I grinned back happily as I scrambled out of the tiny cockpit. My feet touched Bolobo soil once more and I swung round so that Sue could pass Abigail down to me.

When I turned back all semblance of formality broke down. People pushed forward to shake my hand. Some of the younger ones even threw their arms around me – a remarkable breach of protocol. Out of the corner of my eye I could see some of the women and girls jostling forward to see Abigail. They smiled at Sue and two of them reached forward to stroke Abigail's cheeks.

I was suddenly aware of people reluctantly moving aside to allow someone through, and in a moment Papa Eboma appeared, smiling broadly. He came a few steps closer and cleared his throat, but if he was hoping to deliver a formal welcome his words were lost as excited chatter broke out once more. He moved closer to speak to me more privately.

'Richard, you've come back!'

'Of course, Father. Didn't I say I would?'

'Yes, yes. But people say these things, you know. It's when they come to pass that you believe them. You've come back with your wife and baby when you could have stayed in your own country. Now we know you love us.'

'Father, aren't we forgetting something?'

'What, Richard?'

'*Losako*, Papa.'

He looked at me thoughtfully before replying, '*Motema sanduku*.'

The heart is a box. He'd responded with a proverb that he thought apposite for our return. What did it mean? Was he saying that what a man stores within shows in his actions? Maybe. Or did he mean that a man's heart will be found in the place where his most precious treasure is stored? What was my treasure? My dead daughter Judith? Or was he being less literal?

I looked up quizzically at the kind old face marked with

the lines of tribal identity as well as by life's trials, and I nodded in acknowledgement and thanks.

The plane fired up and rumbled away before gradually lifting off. Sue, Abigail and I stood alongside the villagers shoulder to shoulder, watching together as the Western world receded once again into nothing.

Our return and our welcome restored the balance to our lives in Bolobo. In particular, Sue and I established a new equilibrium. We both enjoyed being back in the village and I found myself travelling away from home less often.

In those first few weeks, only one small incident troubled me.

I had come back to the house for lunch as usual. I was on my way back to the medical centre afterwards, walking between the trees and trying to keep to the shade, when I distinctly heard Sue calling me from the house in a mournful wail.

'Richard! Richard!'

I spun round. There was no sign of Sue on the track and I could not see the house from where I stood, but I had an overwhelming feeling that something was wrong with Abigail. I dropped the tools I was carrying and ran back through the trees, arriving at the door, sweating and breathless. Sue came out and looked up at me, surprised to see me back.

'What is it?' I said. 'What's wrong?'

'Nothing's wrong, Richard. I was going to ask you the same thing.'

'Why did you call me?'

'I didn't.'

I pushed past her. Abigail was sitting on the floor of the

kitchen, happily playing with Marmalade, the stray kitten we'd adopted. She looked up and cooed at me. She hadn't a care in the world and was very obviously as right as rain. I picked her up and kissed her, relieved and feeling a little foolish.

After that, life settled into its slow rhythm and soon I had all but forgotten about the incident. Weeks passed, then months, and Sue became pregnant again.

Then, one day, I had a visitor.

Abigail was running a slight fever; nothing very alarming, but I knocked off work in the middle of the afternoon and came back to the house.

As I passed the kitchen I heard Tata Martin locked in his perennial struggle with the stove.

'*Mbote*, Papa,' I called.

'*Mbote*, Richard.'

I could hear Abigail giggling as I stuck my head round the door of the back bedroom. Abigail adored Marmalade. She was playing with the poor animal's tail; the idiot creature seemed to enjoy the game as much as she did.

Abigail grinned and held up her hands – the signal for a cuddle – and as I bent down and hugged her I could feel the heat from her forehead.

At that moment I heard a voice from the front door.

'Ko-ko-ko!'

I sighed and set Abigail down. 'You be nice to Marmalade, OK?'

She giggled and instantly picked up the kitten's tail again.

'Ko-ko-ko!'

I walked back through the house. A man stood there

deferentially; he wore a stained white T-shirt and shabby brown trousers. I knew him reasonably well – Tata Mpia, a carpenter who quite often worked around the centre. He was a respected member of the Motendi tribe. I walked past his modest house almost every day and we would exchange greetings, but I wouldn't have expected him to come here.

I opened the screen. 'Tata Mpia . . .' I tried to keep the surprise out of my voice.

He stood there silently for a moment. 'Mr Richard, may I speak with you? It is an important matter.'

'Of course. Come in. Come in.'

I ushered him through to the main room and showed him to a chair. He sat on the edge of it. He had, I noticed for the first time, the most compelling face, lined with age and wisdom, and perhaps grief.

I could not begin to imagine what had brought him here, but I knew better than to rush him. I offered him something to drink. He declined. I made some inconsequential small talk. He gave minimal answers.

He cleared his throat.

'Mpia Hoskins is not well, I think,' he said.

'Abigail? Just a slight fever, that's all.'

There were very few secrets in the village; he must have heard about my early departure from the centre that day. All the same, I began to feel as uncomfortable as he looked.

'You know that I too am called Mpia?' he said. 'Because I am a younger twin.'

'Yes, I know that.'

'So . . .' He paused. 'I understand these things.'

'I'm sorry. What things?'

'She is being called.'

I felt the air in the room thicken around me. There was something almost menacing in his tone.

'My Mpia? My Abigail?' I leaned forward. 'What do you mean, *called*?'

'Mr Richard, do you understand what we mean by the living dead?'

'Well . . . only vaguely.' Trying to shut out images of B-movie zombies, I sounded more bewildered than I'd intended.

'You *must* understand this, Mr Richard. It is very important. We – you and I and everyone – we are the living living. The living dead are those whom we once knew on this earth, but who have passed on to the shadowlands beyond the grave.' His expression became still more intense. 'They guard us, Mr Richard. But they can also harm us.'

'You're talking about what we would call ghosts?'

'No, no. Your ghosts are dead. We have such ghosts too. They are the long dead – the people who died so long ago that no one can remember them. I am not talking about them. Our living dead are more alive than we are. We remember them when they were with us, and now they are beyond the grave they have much more power than we have.'

'Go on.'

'The living dead control this world and everything in it, Mr Richard. They have a hundred times more power than you or me. They are all powerful. They can build up or destroy. They bring life, and they take it away . . . And they speak to us, Mr Richard, they speak to us. They tell us what to do.'

'They *speak* to you? How?'

'They appear to us all the time,' Tata Mpia said. 'The head of my family is my living dead grandfather. Sometimes my grandfather visits me at my house. I can be sitting down and he will walk in. Sometimes I just hear him speaking to me. Other times I am dreaming and he will come and speak to me in my dream. He tells me what must be done to look after my family; he tells me what I must do to keep the living dead happy. He tells me who is trying to harm me, and how I can stop them.'

'But . . . what's this to do with my Abigail? You said she was being called? What . . . what do you mean by that?'

'Ah.' Tata Mpia nodded his head slowly. 'She is a twin. She is a Mpia – a younger twin – like me.'

I felt the heat of Abigail's fever on my own forehead.

'Twins have a special power, Mr Richard. They call to each other and you must listen to their call. Mbo is calling your Mpia to come and join her in the shadowlands. I am sure of it.'

'Her twin sister? Calling her? But she's—' I stopped myself.

'No, Mr Richard,' Tata Mpia said gently. 'Mbo is not dead. That is the thing I am trying to say to you. She is one of the living dead. And she is calling out to her twin sister, calling her to the world of the living dead.'

'Where are these shadowlands?' I heard myself ask.

'They are very close, Mr Richard. They are very close to us.'

I stared back at him, unable to speak, swamped by conflicting emotions: outrage; horror; anger; a surge of good old-fashioned righteous Western indignation. I didn't want this vile superstition in my home.

Yet I could see it had taken great courage for Tata Mpia to come and tell me this. He was well aware of the reaction he might provoke. He must have had absolutely no doubt that what he said was true.

And I realized he too was scared, scared for me, scared for my family.

'You need to see the *nganga*,' Tata Mpia went on urgently. 'The *nganga* will call upon the living dead to give your first daughter rest.' He had the look of a man coming to the end of a long and painful journey. I knew that he had one final burden he needed to remove from his shoulders. 'You must spill some blood, Mr Richard.'

'What?'

'It is the only way. If you spill blood it will satisfy the living dead and they will cut Mpia free from Mbo's call to join her beyond the grave. This is how it works with us. You *must* understand this.'

'But what does that mean?' I asked wildly. 'Spill blood? How?'

'If you do not wish to lose your daughter,' he said, 'you must perform a sacrifice.'

Sacrifice?

I stood up. In something of a daze I found the courtesy to thank him, and told him I would consider carefully what he had said. I showed him to the door and watched him walk away down the path. I went back inside and sat down heavily, but what I wanted to do was run. In the background I could hear Abigail's giggles but I didn't want to hear them now. I had to think.

I stood up and walked quickly to the outside kitchen.

'Tata Martin, can you do something for me?'

'Certainly, Richard.' Then he caught sight of my face. 'What's wrong?'

'Nothing.' I paused. 'Nothing . . . I'd just like to go out for a couple of minutes. Could you watch Abigail?' As I spoke her name a knot tightened inside my stomach.

'Of course.' He looked at me uncertainly. 'But are you sure you're all right?'

'Yes, yes.'

'You should not be outside for long. The rain is not far away.'

I left the house and headed up towards the graveyard, but stopped when I was still some distance from the railings that now seemed to mark the dividing line between me and Tata Mpia's mysterious shadowlands. I turned and walked down between the trees to the banks of the Congo. There was a storm brewing. It was very hot and the whole village was bathed in the bronze twilight that precedes a tropical downpour. The wind was starting to whip up. That gave me about ten to fifteen minutes before the rain. I was in turmoil. I desperately needed to think.

I had found out a little more about the *ngangas* and how they worked after my meeting with the despairing mother all those months before. Though sometimes called witch doctors, they were really traditional healers or shamans. I'd seen their sacrifices and had always tried to remain detached from them. I remembered the time the *nganga* had told Mama Lutondele that she needed to offer a goat to the living dead before starting to build her house. She'd asked me to come along and join the celebration. The goat had been tied upside down some time earlier. I could hear it bleating piteously as I approached the compound. The blade of the *nganga*'s knife was about eight inches long, with a white bone handle. The animal was crying like a baby, and seemed to know its impending fate.

Those cries still rang in my head. I could hear the *nganga* chanting to the living dead that the offering was theirs. I could see him lift the knife, then bring it down and draw it across the goat's throat. There was one final cry and a spurt of blood. The animal kicked weakly as he drew the knife across the wound once more, this time pressing deeper. Blood poured on to the ground and, with several further strokes, the head was severed. Mama Lutondele was hugely pleased. She knew that the living dead would give their blessing to her house.

I couldn't possibly get into this. The very idea was absurd. Sue, I knew, would be utterly outraged at the mere suggestion and I decided at once not even to tell her. I wasn't sure whether she would be more scandalized at the idea of sacrifice, or at the realization that I had not instantly dismissed it.

For I found that I had not. Not out of hand. Perhaps I had spent too long out in the villages. And besides, I loved Abigail so. Could it really do any harm to cover all the bases? No one need ever know, not Sue, not even Tata Mpia. I could go out to one of the remote villages and find a *nganga* there and get it done. What would it matter if a part of me abhorred the ceremony? For the cost of a single goat, it would be over and done with. Back in England, in time, I would laugh about it at dinner parties.

But I knew that it would not be as simple as that.

There is a bridge to be crossed when stepping into a strange culture, and once crossed there is no way back. I would be going native if I agreed to this, and would never entirely recapture the solid middle-class British persona I had inhabited all my life. If I made that sacrifice, I would cease to be entirely Western. I would open a door in my mind – and perhaps in my soul – to alien demons.

I wrestled with my conscience as the vast brown river slid past. But I knew I was not prepared to cross that bridge.

I walked back to the house, my mind made up. There would be no sacrifice.

Abigail recovered in a day or two, as she always had.

But in the weeks that followed I thought often about Tata Mpia's visit – more often than I wished to, even though his strange warning was never mentioned again. Tata Mpia continued to carry out occasional jobs for us at the centre, and I saw him almost daily, just as before, as I passed his house on the way to work and back. We spoke as we always had, and when we did I was friendly and courteous, while he was quiet and respectful. Neither of us referred to his visit.

It did worry me that his warning kept coming back to me, not just in the lonely reaches of the night, when I might have expected it, but at unpredictable times: when I was fixing a pump in the workshop, or eating, or watching Abigail at play, her blonde hair bobbing as she ran after the hens or the cat.

It weighed on me too that I had never told Sue about Tata Mpia's visit. We had always shared everything, no matter what we had been through, but I had kept Tata Mpia's words from her so that they would not trouble her. As a result, they did more than trouble me: they haunted me.

I knew that something was wrong as soon as I walked through the door. It was about a month after Tata Mpia's visit.

Abigail always filled the whole house – filled it as only a small child can – with noise and laughter and mischief. But today everything was quiet.

I closed the door behind me and dumped my gear in the corridor. I looked around for Sue, but could not immediately see her. It was a stiflingly hot African afternoon and the sun was like a battery of searchlights mounted outside every window and beating heavily on the tin roof.

I walked on through the house with growing unease. The front room was empty. In Abigail's bedroom her toys were strewn around in cheerful disorder, as if she had just been called away. The silence became oppressive. It was unthinkable that our chattering eighteen-month-old daughter, our little noise machine, our Abigail, could possibly be here and allow such silence to exist.

And suddenly there she was. My heart swooped with relief. She was all right. Of course she was all right. She was standing at the window in our bedroom, her finger in her mouth. She never came in here, but nevertheless, here she was.

'Abigail?' I stepped towards her. 'What are you up to?'

She turned her head, and the expression on her small face – normally as bright as a new flower – made me stop dead and lifted the hairs on the back of my neck. There was something in her eyes I had never seen before. Something that made her look old beyond her years.

Without a sound, she turned away from me to stare out of the window again.

I realized then what held her attention so completely. This was the only point in the house from which it was possible to see the graveyard.

Beyond the railings a haphazard collection of canted headstones and sun-bleached crosses clung to the side of the hill, shrivelled by the heat, overlooking the Congo River. They marked the final resting place of those who had lost their lives here, in a place that suddenly felt very far from home.

Abigail died in July.

That dawn – a grey, sultry morning of dry-season

summer heat – I kissed my little girl goodbye and left the house as usual. She had another very slight fever – I could feel the flush of it on her cheek as I kissed her – but she seemed fine and fevers were nothing new to us out here.

Unusually, I came back to the house at mid-morning for a wash and a rest. I found Abigail full of her usual vitality once again, running to me with her arms outstretched.

'Dadda!' she called. 'Dadda!'

I swept her up in my arms and swung her gently, thinking, as I always thought when I held her in my arms, that it could not be possible to love another being so much.

I went back to work for a while and by the time I came home for some lunch Sue had put Abigail back in her cot for a sleep. After lunch, Sue and I stretched out on our own bed for an hour.

Some time later I awoke and dressed, washed briefly and left the house without a sound, trying not to disturb the two of them. Even so, I knew Sue would be up and about at once, despite being several months pregnant and needing her rest. I was not surprised to hear her moving in the house behind me as I padded away down the earth track.

'Richard!' Sue cried suddenly from behind me. '*Richard!*'

Her tone froze my heart. I had heard her cry out in just this way once before. I had hoped then it was pure imagination, but now as I wrenched myself round I knew the impossible truth: it had been a foreshadowing of this moment, the moment I had dreaded. I ran back around the bend of the track and saw Sue standing with her hands hanging by her side in the doorway of our house, her face slack with shock. I stopped in front of her, unable to move.

'It's Abigail,' she said, quietly. 'I think she's died.'

I rushed past Sue back into the house, desperately shouting Abigail's name. I barged through to her room and found her cot empty. Sue had laid her on our bed, and as soon as I found her there – eyes and mouth open – my rational brain knew that all hope was gone. I had seen enough death to be in no doubt.

But just the same I swept her up in my arms, calling hopelessly to her, 'Abigail! Abigail! Come back to me, my darling! Come back!'

The small body was still warm from sleep, her last ever sleep, and even as I clutched her against me I saw the blood drain from her face and her sun-browned skin turn first to chalky white and then to blue.

The warmth of life ebbed from her at last and I could not replace it, no matter how close I held her or whatever prayers I screamed to my God. The child in my arms was quite cold by the time someone – I don't even remember who – was able to persuade me to lay her body down.

I'm not sure what happened over the next few hours. I was utterly helpless with grief and could maintain no sort of composure. I was long past the point of caring what anyone thought. I was aware only of certain vivid images, of certain events unreeling in front of me and around me.

Evening fell. Word had spread already and I watched, trembling and bewildered, as our friends from the village began to arrive. I sat in that darkening room, dumb with pain, by the bed where Abigail lay, vaguely aware that I had seen all this before so many times in the villages and yet had not dared to believe that it could happen to me. The scene grew into an African wake, just as I had witnessed so often over the past couple of years, the men sitting with me and the women with Sue, as tradition dictated.

Outside the light failed and cicadas began their bandsaw

chorus in the trees on the banks of the Congo, the same chorus they had sung every night for thousands of years, and would sing for thousands more, long after all of us – black and white, adult and child – were gone. Men and women wept in the darkness around me. Someone moved past me and gently dressed the child's body, murmuring to me as she did so. It was beyond my comprehension that this could happen to Abigail. She had been not so much full of life as a manifestation of life itself. It was impossible that she could die without taking all other life with her.

It was a sorry little procession that made its way up to the cemetery the next morning. I had not slept – I doubted I would ever sleep again – and I could not stop weeping. I simply could not stop. I must have looked a wild figure indeed – half-mad and stained with tears – when I laid Abigail's body in the red earth next to her twin sister. The sister who had summoned her to the shadowlands beyond the grave and who now had her for evermore.

I settled her on her last bed and looked up at the circle of anguished black faces above me. Many of them, like me, were in tears and made no attempt to hide it. Eventually someone helped me up and the gravediggers stepped forward to cover my daughter's body.

My eyes met Tata Mpia's as he sank his shovel into the soft soil. He stopped and, releasing his grip on the shovel, leaned forward to rest one hand on my shoulder. He avoided looking down into the grave.

'Mr Richard,' he said, 'now you are truly an African.'

His expression carried that unique combination of unspeakable sadness and fatalism I had seen so often in this place. But I read no trace of condemnation in his eyes, and I did not need to. I could manage that all by myself.

14

London, April 2002

The Embankment glistened that wet spring lunchtime.

I was nervous. I had looked into my own past during the preceding week or two, probing into dark corners I had never wanted to visit again. I knew the conclusion I had reached had a vital bearing on the Adam case, but I didn't like it. I was now clear that Adam's killing was indeed a sacrifice. I had gone over and over this, but when I reflected on my own experiences in the Congo, and then cross-referenced that with my academic work, I knew there was no other conclusion. The meticulous nature of the crime; the precise manner of the cut to the neck and the draining of blood; the fact that clothing of a particular colour had been placed on the body after death; and that the torso had then been disposed of in a flowing river . . .

Being confident about this didn't make the idea any easier to handle. The thought that a young boy could be the victim of a human sacrifice – here in London, one of the great capitals of the Western world – simply beggared belief. Sacrifice was quite different from *muti* killing and it was important to understand how.

Muti was all about the harvesting of plant and animal parts for later use in medicines. No one cared much how those parts were taken or whether the victim died or lived. Sacrifice was all about the blood. It was about a transferral of power via the spilling of blood, the life force. The killers cut the victim's throat very precisely. The blood was then in some cases splattered on the ground, in others over the effigies of the deities concerned, which would be standing on an altar. Occasionally those involved would even drink the blood, sometimes out of the severed head. Officially human sacrifice was banned throughout Africa. It crossed the divide into sorcery – black magic, known as *juju* in much of West Africa – and most on the continent would condemn it. But since the sacrifice of animals was rife I knew it could be a relatively short step to killing a human in the same way. The only crumb of comfort was that the victim's death was usually relatively quick.

I paused for a moment, turning to look over the wall at the swirling river below. I knew no one would want to hear this. There was bound to be some resistance.

However, I also knew that my sacrifice theory would offer the detectives crucial new lines of inquiry, and that I would be able to help with them. I had narrowed down the areas of Africa from which Adam might have come. Despite the theoretical ban on human sacrifice, there were regions where it persisted. If *muti* had its stronghold in South Africa, then human sacrifice resonated most strongly with the West.

I had spent the last fortnight poring over every document I could lay my hands on that dealt with the ethnic groups of West Africa. There were some fringe possibilities – one or two groups in Ghana, perhaps; another in Senegal – but one in particular had stood out for me, and the more I considered it the more convinced I became: the Yoruba of Nigeria and their immediate neighbours.

The Yorubans are a very powerful group, mostly from the centre and south-west of Nigeria. There are about 90 million Yorubans worldwide, with roughly a third living in Nigeria, where they are dominant in society and provide many of the country's professionals, politicians and business leaders. Many Nigerians living abroad are also Yorubans, and they wield powerful influence in some African-derived religions, particularly in the United States. In their African homeland they have about the most complex and sophisticated religious belief system of any ethnic group on the continent.

Many Yorubans believe in a high, but distant, God – Olorun (also called Olodumare). According to their traditions, Olurun commanded Orishala to create the earth, but he was delayed in this act of creation, so his younger brother Odudwe completed the work. Subsequently a further sixteen deities, known as *orishas,* descended to the earth. Many other *orishas* were added to the pantheon later on. The *orishas* are extremely important in Yoruban religion, for they act as the bridge between this world and higher realms. Some say there are 401 of them, but many Yorubans believe there are far more. Most of them are ancestors – living dead who had lived such great lives that they were elevated to the status of gods and now have huge power and influence. Each and every *orisha* has his or her own favourite colours, foods, drinks, plants, animals, precious metals, stones and feast days, and the delight of one could be the poison of another.

All the *orishas* require sacrifice. Not necessarily human sacrifice, of course, and especially not nowadays, but there was no doubt that the practice persisted in some deviant offshoots of Yoruban religion, especially, so it was rumoured, in Edo State in the south-west of Nigeria, and among their near-neighbours the Igbo.

I had other reasons to link Adam to the Yoruba area.

Yoruban males are circumcised soon after birth. I remembered the footage I had seen of a naming ceremony on the outskirts of Lagos a few years earlier. The circumcision that accompanied the service had welcomed the child into the family of Yorubans. Small offerings of salt and gin were made to the living, the dead and the relevant *orisha*. The infant whose circumcision I had seen was only a few days old. By the time he was Adam's age the scar would have healed completely – just as Adam's had.

Marshalling the facts in this way fortified me. I turned away from the river and headed with renewed determination towards the Strand.

I found Will and Nick already ensconced in armchairs in the Wellington pub with pints of lager in front of them. Nick passed me a bottle of San Miguel and an envelope. 'Two economy tickets to Holland.'

'Thanks.' I slid it into my pocket. 'It's really useful for me to have Faith alongside, but I was a bit uncomfortable about asking.'

'Don't give it a thought,' Will said. 'It works out cheaper than one business-class fare in any case. We just have to be a bit careful how these things look.'

I raised an eyebrow.

'It's the media,' he said. 'Have you seen what the papers have to say about this South Africa trip? You can't win. If you don't pursue leads they accuse you of not working hard enough, but when you do they say you're off on some overseas junket at the public's expense. It's to be expected, of course. But the fact remains that we'll have to come up with something fairly soon, or people will start making a serious fuss about police time and resources.'

'I might be able to help,' I said. 'I think I know what sort of killing this was.'

He sat very still.

'Will, I'm almost sure it was a sacrifice.'

The detectives looked at each other and then back at me.

'Sacrifice?' Will said. 'How does that make a difference? The poor kid's still dead, when all's said and done.'

'No, Will, it's critical. Look, *muti* – that's just harvesting. It's the collection of parts to be used in medicine. But sacrifice is different. It's all about the pouring out of the blood. It creates a transferral of power in the minds of those performing it.'

I explained that a sacrifice required much more preparation than a *muti* murder. It had to conform to established rituals, from the selection of the victim through to the ceremony itself and the deposition of the remains. There had to be a group involved – at least a handful of people, and maybe quite a few. 'It makes sense of everything we know,' I insisted. 'Like the shorts being placed on the torso after death, the choice of their colour and the fact that deposition was in the river. I still think the victim and the perpetrators came from the same ethnic group or same geographic area. And I've an idea that might be West Africa.'

'*West* Africa?'

I could see Will hacking through the operational tangles that would spring up if West Africa emerged as a firm front-runner days before their visit to South Africa.

'Any chance of being more specific?' he asked.

I had hoped to avoid this. I knew how easily it could be

misrepresented if I went about naming ethnic and religious groups, especially when I had no hard evidence. 'Adam was circumcised as an infant. Circumcision at that age is common among the Yoruban people, and not very common elsewhere. The Yoruban homeland is in central and western Nigeria. And there's some evidence that human sacrifice is still practised by certain Yoruban cults. They're probably not the only ones who do it, but there's a strong historical association.'

'So if I ask Ray Fysh to get the boffins to start searching for matches in West Africa, and especially Nigeria, are you confident they may find something?'

'The sacrificial victim is often forced to drink some kind of potion before the ritual act itself. That can be very specific in its make-up, depending on which deity is involved. We ought to get the contents of Adam's intestines carefully analysed with that in mind. Not his stomach. His intestine. If he was given any sort of concoction, as I'm suggesting, he probably would have been forced to drink it a day or two before the killing, so it would already have gone through his stomach and into the gut.'

'I'll see if we can push it up the list of priorities.' Will blew out his cheeks and sat back in his chair. 'Nick, while you're on your feet, why don't you get the cultural adviser another beer?'

15

Bolobo, Oxford and Bath, 1989–1999

Sue turned to her faith for the support I could not give her. She submitted to the tragedy as the will of God and found that in this way she could come to some level of acceptance.

My own response was anguished and confused. I felt betrayed by God for not keeping his side of the bargain I thought we'd made, and sometimes my mind seemed locked in one long howl of protest against his very existence. I tried to deny him on the grounds of human suffering – not just mine but the suffering I'd observed in the lives of the people of the Congo.

And yet here I was caught on the horns of a dilemma. For if I did not believe in something, if I did not allow the existence of some purposeful pattern in life, how could I make any sense of my daughter's death?

So, despite everything, I clung to faith for the time being. I could no longer even attempt to conceptualize what sort of God it was in whom I believed, but I had to believe nevertheless. I could not allow myself – not even for a moment – to entertain the thought that I had returned to the Congo with my beautiful daughter for no reason. Even worse, gnawing away underneath was the constant doubt about what might have happened if I had made the sacrifice as Tata Mpia had urged me to. Surely that way madness lay.

The Baptist Mission reacted to our loss by arranging for us to be sent back to the UK on extended compassionate leave.

On our last night before leaving Bolobo, Sue and I sat on opposite sides of the kitchen table and looked at each other through the glow of the hurricane lamp. Our hands were on the tabletop but they did not touch.

'I don't think I want to go,' I said.

'We both need to go home, Richard. We both need to move on.'

'This is home,' I said. 'And I don't want to move on.'

'What *do* you want?'

'I want to stay here with Abigail. I want to be buried here beside her.'

I was entirely serious. I did want to be buried beside my daughter, and at that moment I didn't care how soon it happened. Indeed, I would happily have helped matters along, though I had the sense not to say that to Sue.

'That's precisely why we have to go home,' she said.

The next day we lifted off in the Cessna with Dan once again at the controls. Normally so affable, he avoided looking at us directly, as if what he saw in our eyes was too painful to handle. I stared out over the canopy as the tiny plane banked. The endless forest stretched below with the silver river winding through it. Already the tiny green strip had been swallowed up. Bolobo itself had disappeared from view.

The contrast could not have been more extreme. The Baptist Church found us a pebble-dashed semi-detached in Sidcup, in London's south-eastern suburbs. And there we lived for six months or so, in a strange limbo, with no work and no particular view of the future; not quite able to believe that we were back in London, not quite sure why we were there. At first I spent the time idling, thinking of the past, wandering the grey suburban streets, staring at the television.

I cried a great deal. I had never been a particularly tearful type, but now I was overcome at unexpected moments. These bouts of emotion were like ripples spreading out from that dreadful afternoon in Bolobo. I had no control over them and made no effort to exert any. I didn't care what anyone thought. I was aware that Sue, now close to giving birth again, wanted and needed my support, but I had very little to give her. In its absence she got on with life, and managed it a good deal more stoically than I did.

She found me one day, kneeling on the living-room carpet with a pile of newspapers and a pair of scissors in front of me. Gently, she asked me what I was doing.

I couldn't meet her eyes. I was cutting out the pictures of children who had been hurt or abused in some way. 'I just thought I'd light a candle for them, that's all,' I explained.

'Abigail's gone, you know, Richard,' she said sadly. 'It's going to be best for both of us if you accept it.'

I didn't answer and after a while she quietly left the room.

Perhaps Sue called the Church in an effort to help me, or perhaps they decided to act on their own initiative, for at about this time a young man I didn't recognize appeared at our front door. It was a late summer afternoon and I had been lounging on the sofa, watching the Test match. Cricket was one of the few things that brought me relief at the time. I loved the order of it, the esoteric rules and rituals, its very Englishness. So I pulled the front door open rather grumpily when the bell rang, resenting the intrusion.

'Richard Hoskins? I'm Pete Swaffham, from the Church.' He held out his hand and I took it reluctantly. He had an open, friendly face. 'I'm here to see if I can be of any use to you.'

'Of use to me?' There was a ripple of applause from the TV and I glanced over my shoulder towards the living room, impatient to get back to the match.

'I'm here if you'd like to talk through any . . . issues. Obviously you've had a very bad time in Africa and it usually helps to talk.'

'I don't even know you.'

'It can be especially helpful to talk to a stranger, Richard. Neither of us can bring any baggage to the discussion, can we?'

I looked at him and the irritation must have been apparent in my face. I didn't need counselling, I thought, and he was interrupting my cricket. But he stood his ground and in the end I was not quite far enough gone to shut the door in his face.

'Listen,' I said at last. 'I've spent three and a half years in the middle of bloody nowhere and this is the first chance I've had to watch a Test match. So if you want to do your Samaritans bit you'll have to sit through the cricket first, OK?'

He smiled broadly. 'Sounds fair enough.'

And to his credit he came in and sat beside me in the sitting room for a good hour. We swapped occasional comments about the state of the pitch and the English batting. I don't now recall if we ever got round to talking through my 'issues', but his visit was the first useful input I'd had during this strange time.

*

Autumn gave way to winter. Then in January 1990 our son David was born in the maternity wing of Sidcup General Hospital. I thought we might have been granted an easy birth after all that we'd been through, but that was not to be. David managed to get the umbilical cord wrapped round his neck, cutting off his oxygen supply more firmly with every push Sue gave. There were some terrifying moments we could both have lived without but this was a south London hospital and not the Congolese rainforest. The problems were overcome and soon Sue and our perfect son were both doing well.

We were a family again, whatever else had changed. For the first time I began to feel a stirring of interest in the future. We returned to our limbo in Sidcup to take stock of what this meant for us. These were a strange few weeks for both Sue and me. We were aware of the fact that the gulf between us had widened. We didn't fight, or even disagree, but each of us had reacted so differently, first to Judith's death, then to Abigail's, that we could not hide from one another the distance between us in outlook and belief.

Life, however, seemed determined to go on. Here was a precious new child who needed both of us. And if life was not going to give up on us, we felt that we could not give up on life.

The seasons changed again, and across the dull suburban gardens crept the first signs of spring. One February afternoon, Sue and I were sitting in the main room of the Sidcup house. Sue was feeding David and I was alternately reading the newspaper and watching the raindrops slide down the windows.

'We can't just sit here doing nothing indefinitely,' Sue said abruptly, shifting the baby's weight in her lap.

'No,' I agreed, folding the paper. I did this carefully but it seemed to make a large sound in the quiet room. 'No, we can't.'

'It reminded me, having David,' she said. 'The help we got, the care. It reminded me how many people don't get any help at all. It makes me feel selfish. And here am I, a qualified midwife with all this experience, doing nothing. I don't think that's what God put me here to do.'

I didn't know what to say.

Sue and I went back to the Congo in March 1990 and spent another eighteen months working there, trying to rebuild our lives and to find our common purpose once more. Then, in September of 1991, events overtook us in explosive style. We were in Kinshasa when the capital was sacked by rebel soldiers. Sue – now heavily pregnant again – and David were abruptly evacuated to Britain via South Africa, whilst I stayed on, attempting to hold the fort. But after a few weeks I too had to flee, under gunfire, across the river.

Sue met me at Heathrow with David on her hip and she and I embraced awkwardly. We didn't speak for a while. Neither of us quite knew what this new life in Britain had in store for us. We had been through so much together that it was hard to imagine ourselves fitting into anything like a normal life. In many ways things should have been hopeful and positive for us. We had a young child and another baby due shortly, and we were, after all, still young. Somehow, though, it didn't feel that way. Once again we were faced with rebuilding our lives, and I think we were both beginning to ask how often two people could be expected to do that. It was as if we feared the English suburbs might prove more of a challenge to us than the Congolese rainforest.

Still, we entered into our future as positively as we could. It seemed to me that this was the ideal opportunity to return to the point at which I had left off all those years before and try to get a degree. Rather to my surprise, I was accepted by Oxford to study theology. It wasn't that I was hoping to rebuild my own battered faith – I didn't believe that I could ever lose my faith, because to do so would have made a nonsense of Abigail's death – but my relationship with Christianity had certainly come under enormous pressure. Partly because of that, the nature of belief itself – not merely Christian belief – had become intensely interesting to me, so theology as an academic discipline seemed the obvious choice.

It would be some months before I was due to start at Oxford, and meanwhile Sue and I rented a place in South Norwood, near Croydon. It wasn't much of a home but we thought we could return to some normality there after the lunacy of the Congo, and perhaps find a way of moving forward together. Those winter months brought us their share of joy. In November 1991 Sue gave birth to our beautiful daughter Elspeth. Mercifully, this time everything went well and we were overjoyed to be parents of a daughter again.

Early in 1992 I was invited back to the ravaged Congo, this time for a month to see if I could help get vital supplies up-river from Kinshasa to Bolobo. I travelled on my own, spending a gruelling time in a country that was on its knees. Whilst there the United Nations asked me if I would go to work for them on the Congo–Rwanda border. I agonized over the decision, but my place at Oxford beckoned and I knew that it would be my last chance to go to university. I turned down the UN job and came home.

*

Oxford proved to be the most liberating and therapeutic experience of my life. I loved studying and regularly worked until three or four in the morning in our tiny flat opposite Pusey House. I did well at my studies and it quickly became clear that I had found my métier in academic life. At the same time, and despite myself, my work at Oxford had a profound effect on the development of my own quest for meaning. I relished the opportunity to scrutinize the foundations of faith and, under the glare of rigorous scholarship, found them shaken once again.

Despite this, I was unable to kick the door firmly shut.

I discovered that Compline with Benediction was held in the chapel of Magdalen College at ten every Sunday evening, and I never missed it when I was in Oxford. There would seldom be more than a handful of us, and in the dim light of the candles and gently rising incense I would listen to the words in awe: '*Brethren, be sober, be vigilant: because your adversary the devil, as a roaring lion, walketh about, seeking whom he may devour. Whomso resist, steadfast in the faith.*'

When the monstrance containing the sacrament was held aloft in front of us in an act of solemn blessing it felt both sensual and surreal. Though I didn't make the connection at the time, it was in its way very African, right down to the fearsome lion, prowling beyond the circle of firelight, scenting his prey. I could never sit through this service in the ancient chapel without experiencing a sense of something supernatural, numinous, beyond the mere comfort of ritual. Intellectually, I tried very hard to argue myself out of it, but nothing quite worked.

Sue was pleased with my academic achievements, but she saw very little of me at this time and couldn't really see what my quest was about. For her faith was simply faith: it didn't need to be justified by rational arguments, nor did it find expression through clouds of incense. As a result, my studies at Oxford drove the wedge more and more deeply between us.

I left Oxford with a Double First and went on to a doctorate at King's College London. After that I considered a position as an academic theologian through the church, but finally decided I didn't have the temperament, nor really the faith, for it. In mid-1999 I was offered a lectureship in African religions at the University of Bath Spa, and I accepted. But my move there, while opening up a new direction for me, also signalled the formal end of our marriage. Sue and I had been living almost as strangers under one roof for some time, and we both knew a separation was now inevitable. We had agonized over it, trying to spare the children the worst of the pain, but in the end I moved to Bath without the family for the start of the first semester in 1999.

16

Lower Congo, April 2002

For a few weeks around Easter I was able to take a breather from the Adam case.

While Will O'Reilly and Andy Baker were in South Africa, Faith and I were planning a research trip of our own in central Africa. I wanted to take a closer look at a black Messiah movement known as Kimbanguism, which had its heartland in the south of the Congo, and Faith would accompany me as my research assistant. We scheduled an additional fortnight at the end of the trip so that she could pursue her own research into bonobos, the rare primates that survive in the Congolese rainforests.

I knew the problems of the Congo had worsened even since our visit the previous year. President Mobutu Sese Seko, whose praises I had sung under the bare flagpole that first morning sixteen years earlier, had fallen from power some years before. A brutal, half-mad despot, he survived only with the covert backing of Western powers. They – we – had turned a blind eye to human rights atrocities in return for cold war support and minerals.

With the end of the cold war came the end of Mobutu's usefulness to the West, and in 1997 Laurent Kabila's forces from Rwanda swept him from power. Mobutu fled to Morocco, leaving behind in his palace a pathetic detritus of imported Western luxuries and porn magazines, but not much else. He died of cancer a few months later.

Mobutu's disappearance had created a power vacuum, and now, five years on, the country was still embroiled in civil war that had dragged in a host of neighbouring nations. Many parts of the country that I'd freely traversed in the Eighties and early Nineties were under the control of rebel soldiers. Even places that Faith and I had visited the year before were now off limits. Dark rumours of atrocities filtered out of the country, and someone who had been into rebel territory had recently told me tales of cannibalism in the interior. For Faith it was to be very tough – the rebel area coincided with the only natural bonobo habitat in the world. If humans were eating other humans, there was little hope for our ape cousins.

Even as we cleared customs in Kinshasa it quickly became obvious that the country was in chaos. There were new bullet holes in the walls of the arrivals lounge. The airport officials wore weariness on their faces and apparently no longer struggled to repel would-be intruders from foreign lands. The noisy aggression of my first arrival here had been replaced by despair.

As we walked out of the remains of the terminal, something resembling a taxi approached. It might have been yellow once; now it was many shades of rust-brown. The rear of the car scraped along the ground, like a dog with worms. By pointing the nose at a forty-five-degree angle the driver kept to a mostly straight line. We said very little in the cab, but stared out towards the distant city, where a deadly fume-laden fog hung over the corrugated rooftops.

Kinshasa had sunk into abject squalor and lawlessness.

In the city centre, mounds of garbage towered skywards, blocking roads and pavements. There were people everywhere. Wiry and wild-eyed from hunger, they stalked the streets in search of something . . . anything. Something to eat, something to steal. Most, I knew, would find little enough before disease or violence cut short their miserable lives.

And now a new killer moved among them, more deadly than any of the diseases that had already ravaged the Congo. Roughly 20 per cent of the population of Kinshasa was estimated to be HIV-positive, of whom half had full-blown AIDS. Some 10 per cent of all Congolese people were thought to be infected, and across the whole of sub-Saharan Africa there were at least a million AIDS orphans.

The children, of course, shocked me most profoundly. As we drove into the city centre they lined the roads. Everywhere. Children on their own or in feral packs, orphaned or simply abandoned. Evening was falling and we could see them under the dim city lights, rummaging through piles of rubbish in search of food, or curled up exhausted under sparse trees or in the gutters, presumably hoping the rain would hold off. It would not.

Most distressing of all, some of them – as young as five or six years of age – offered themselves to us, seeking to barter their bodies for a day or two of survival.

At length we reached the Kimbanguist visitors' centre in the middle of Kinshasa. It was oddly reminiscent of arriving at the Baptist Mission sixteen years before. Two wrought-iron gates, the right one hanging precariously, opened onto a cracked concrete drive, which led to a large house with a green tin roof. There was a parched lawn in front and a couple of fishponds behind, with a prayer ground to the left.

We were shown to one of a row of single-storey rooms to one side of the main house. There was a small anteroom with a broken overhead fan, a bedroom and a bathroom. There was no running water but someone had kindly put a full bucket in the bath for us. Despite swarms of mosquitoes there was no net, but thankfully we'd had the sense to bring our own.

By the time we got this far, I was uncharacteristically depressed and angry – emotions I now seldom afforded myself in Africa. We unpacked in silence. After a while, Faith straightened up from her task and looked at me very directly.

'Do you want to talk about it?'

'Talk about it?' I burst out, startling both of us. 'It's an outrage!' I happened to be holding my shoes at that moment and I hurled them against the wall. 'Did you see those kids? Does anyone give a damn what happens to them?'

I stared out at the city, its lights quivering in the stifling tropical air. I wondered what atrocities were going on out there right now in those filthy streets. I thought again of the investigation back home, and determination surged inside me. If I could do something, no matter how small, to help solve this case, would it not bring some justice to the landscape?

We set off for the headquarters of the Kimbanguist movement, which was located in a tiny forest village called Nkamba, two days' drive to the southwest of Kinshasa. I had to use my most languid Lingala to avoid some potentially nasty situations at roadblocks. We also drank some decidedly dodgy water and were both sick as a result.

Worse still, the minibus I had hired broke down a couple of hundred miles out of Kinshasa, and after repair it was commandeered by our Kimbanguist hosts, who took off with it, leaving us stranded for several days. Throughout all this Faith remained her implacable, unflappable self.

The Kimbanguists fascinated me. The Movement claimed a membership of 25 million, mostly in West Africa and the Congo, and although that was surely an exaggeration, the number of believers must certainly have stretched into the millions. Officially designated a Church – at the time, at least, it was a member of the World Council of Churches – the movement blended Christianity with traditional African beliefs into an extremely seductive cocktail.

Kimbangu, the group's charismatic founder, died in 1951 in a Belgian colonial jail, where he was imprisoned for sedition. The movement was continued after his death by each of his three sons in turn. On my field trip the year before I had been granted an audience with the last of these, a strange man called Dialungana Kiangani. As a test of my faith I had had to recite parts of the Bible in French while kneeling before him, an experience for which the British public school system had only partly prepared me. From his point of view, Papa Dialungana had cause for demanding such obeisance: he had decided he was not just the herald of a new African Christ, as his more modest father had claimed, but that he was Jesus Christ himself. He had even changed the date of Christmas to coincide with his own birthday in May.

If he appeared distinctly mad, there was no doubt that under his leadership the movement had seen incredible growth. A vast temple complex seating 35,000 people had sprung up in the rainforest at Nkamba, built entirely with Kimbanguist money. The temple was regularly packed for religious festivals. Significantly too, and perhaps conveniently, Dialungana claimed to have had a vision in which he saw huge numbers of African-Americans joining the Kimbanguist Church and migrating to the Congo, presumably bringing their dollars with them. In preparation, he had Western-style apartments built on a nearby hillside at a place called Kendolo, and this was where we were lodged.

Dialungana had died since my last visit, and been succeeded as head of the Kimbanguist movement by his son, Kiangani Kimbangu Simon. I took to Papa Kiangani straight away. His beliefs were not as extravagant as his father's and I found him to be a gentle, thoughtful man of considerable insight. We were invited to breakfast at his house on our first morning at Nkamba, although Papa Kiangani himself was at prayers elsewhere.

Faith and I were greeted by an array of baguettes, margarine, peanuts, omelettes, jam and wedges of processed cheese. This was luxurious stuff for the middle of Africa, but better was to come. After the meal I was drawn to one side by Charlie, one of Papa Kiangani's aides.

'Richard,' he said quietly, 'Papa has invited you both to come and pray at the tomb of his grandfather, the founder of our Church. He would count it a great honour to share this with you.'

'Thank you. We're the ones who are honoured.'

He smiled at us and moved away, leaving me and Faith raising our eyebrows at one another. To be invited to pray at the Kimbanguists' Holy of Holies – Kimbangu's shrine – was an extraordinary privilege. I was not sure whether any other outsider to the movement, far less a white man, had ever been asked, and for Faith to be included was a particular mark of respect.

The mausoleum was a domed stone building no bigger than a modest single-storey house. It stood among the trees within a simple perimeter fence, surrounded by lesser tombs and dwarfed by the nearby Kimbanguist temple, but it possessed an aura of authority and power. Big men in white uniforms and green sashes stood impassively at the entrance with carbines held across their chests.

Papa Kiangani met us and, once we had removed our shoes, led us through the outer gate. As soon as the guards saw their leader approach they drew back and smartly presented arms.

There were several of us in a slightly awed group, led between the outer tombs to the entrance, climbing two shallow steps to green doors set in white stone. Papa Kiangani unlocked them and ushered us into a very small, dim anteroom in which someone had placed flowers from the rainforest.

We all grew very quiet as he unlocked the second door, a plain wooden one. He entered the shrine alone, closing it behind him. After a few moments, during which we could hear his voice murmuring, he emerged smiling and beckoned me to follow him in. I did, and he once again closed the door softly behind the two of us.

It was very dark inside and the only light filtered down from small openings in a cupola above. The atmosphere was stale and musty. As my eyes adjusted I saw that on a stepped dais stood a great sarcophagus of brown-flecked granite. On top of it, rather incongruously, were two vases of dusty plastic flowers. The dais was covered with a thick red carpet and Papa Kiangani gestured for me to kneel.

'Teacher,' he addressed me with gravity, his words echoing in the dark chamber, 'I invite you to pray before the remains of my grandfather. You may wish to ask him something special.'

I had not prepared anything. I hadn't known what to expect and I wanted to be driven by the mood of the occasion. In the event I had no doubt what I should ask for, and I heard myself saying, in a strong, clear voice, 'Oh, Papa Simon Kimbangu, on earth you were a force for good. You have great power. I ask you now, for the sake of Africa's children, to help. We need guidance and strength if we are to help solve the case of Adam. This continent deserves better than to have its name dragged down by this evil act against this boy. Please, Papa Simon, help bring justice.'

17

Bath and The Hague, May 2002

We got back to England in May, by which time the Scotland Yard team were home from South Africa. I wasn't surprised to learn that no solid new leads had emerged – I don't think Will himself was much surprised either.

But the visit had shown just how serious the police were, and it had dramatically raised the profile of the case. Nelson Mandela's call for information was seen on television all over the world. The two police officers were also filmed visiting the *muti* market in Johannesburg and surveying the wares on offer, and they went on to visit a famous *sangoma*, Credo Mutwa. I didn't know it at the time, but they had sounded him out about my sacrifice theory.

Attention was now focused on the Europol conference and no amount of experience as a lecturer was enough to quell my nerves.

This would be the first time my theory had been advanced in public. It flew in the face of most of the press coverage and, coming hot on the heels of the South African trip, it might appear that I was hinting that the Met's efforts were misplaced. I respected the police and was very anxious not to be seen to criticize them. In addition, the idea that a child had been ritually sacrificed in central London could all too easily cross the line into sensationalism and prejudice.

As time moved on I realized that the various forensic tests that would either back up my theories or prove them wrong wouldn't be completed before the conference, so I kept myself busy assembling a list of possible West African deities to whom a human sacrifice might be made.

On the Monday evening before the conference Faith and I flew into Schiphol Airport and took one of Holland's blue and yellow commuter trains to The Hague. After putting the finishing touches to my PowerPoint presentation in the hotel room we headed, as requested, to an Argentinian steakhouse in the main square. The guest list of sixteen or so included some of the leading lights of British policing. Besides officers from the Met there were representatives from the National Criminal Intelligence Agency, the Association of Chief Police Officers and the National Crime Faculty, as well as specialists in child pornography, people trafficking and organized crime.

A very striking figure appeared in front of us and introduced himself. Commander Baker was broad-shouldered and well over six feet tall, with an olive complexion and dark eyes. He was immaculately dressed and radiated charisma.

He took us over to the group gathered around the table, who were wary but respectful. I wasn't sure how many of these investigators, left to themselves, would have given a high priority to 'cultural analysis', but Commander Andy Baker was signalling in the clearest possible way that he took it very seriously indeed. I was immensely reassured.

Andy Baker insisted that I sat beside him with Faith immediately opposite. He flirted decorously with Faith throughout the meal and quizzed her about her work with bonobos. He was amused and intrigued by the social dynamics of these primates, and it crossed my mind that, as a top alpha male himself, he might be getting some ideas. He was attentive, drank little and was never entirely off duty. I introduced myself to Ray Fysh, the forensics expert, and asked him if the results were in yet. They weren't, largely because he had asked Professor Ken Pye from Royal Holloway College to try out a revolutionary new procedure known as geological mapping – it was the first time this had been used in a criminal investigation. The theory behind it was that everything we have eaten puts down isotopic markers in our bones. These markers can be distinctive, and specific to the region in which a person has lived. It could be possible to match the different mineral deposits in Adam's bones to the geological region where he grew up.

'We shouldn't get too excited,' Ray said, 'but if your West African steer is right, and we can get samples from that area, and if – big if – Adam did spend a sufficient length of time there, then we can get his place of origin narrowed right down – possibly even to a particular village.'

The whole idea of the Europol conference was to generate awareness – to draw together pan-European intelligence about ritual killings and to start pooling resources and ideas. The police had wanted publicity and they'd got it. It was pretty clear that the European Ritualistic Killings Conference, as it came to be known, was going to be a media circus.

Faith and I could see that as soon as we walked into the foyer of the vast new Europol building the following day. There was steel-trap security, but the main conference hall was abuzz with journalists. It was a very big room with a massive horseshoe of wooden tables facing the speaker's podium. The sound engineers and cameramen were unreeling cables, squinting through viewfinders and calling questions to one another. Kate Campbell, Scotland Yard's senior press officer, explained that Ray Fysh and I would be sitting at the top end of the horseshoe, with Commander Baker sitting to one side and acting as a moderator.

Andy would give a brief introduction, then Will would talk for maybe forty-five minutes about the investigative side of the case. After that, I would have the stage. I had an hour and then there would be a question and answer session.

'Right,' I said, with as much confidence as I could muster.

Faith squeezed my arm and moved away to find a place near the back of the hall.

I knelt down to make the final adjustments to my laptop connections and noticed my hands were shaking. The Met had never asked to see what I was going to say. They had imposed no restrictions and didn't seem to want me to clear anything in advance. But there was no time to worry about that now. The hall was already beginning to fill. Within a few minutes I was listening to Andy Baker's brief overture and after that to Will's methodical setting out of the detective work. Then I found myself at the podium.

I began by explaining some basic definitions. I pointed out that religion and ritual were by no means as clear cut as people sometimes thought. Ritual exists in many settings without religious association – the rituals of prison or Army or school life, for example. Sportsmen who wear lucky talismans, people who will only drive to work along a certain route, or daughters who ring their mothers only on Saturday mornings are all following ritualistic patterns. It is no surprise that people often say that they perform regular duties religiously, even when churches and gods are very far from their minds. When true religious belief is added to the equation there is a deeper dimension to ritual through the appeal to divine authority. This association confers power – sometimes awesome power – on the rituals concerned, and the balancing fear of dreadful penalties if they are neglected.

I then turned specifically to the Adam case and discounted the *muti* line that had been so publicly trumpeted in the media. I pointed out that, while there can be a ritualistic element to *muti*, the manner of death is quite different from sacrifice. I explained that *muti* murder is undertaken to collect body parts whereas in sacrifice the object is to spill the blood of the victim. I continued carefully through my list of differences between the two practices, illustrating my points wherever possible.

Photographs of body parts, mutilated victims, dried organs, sacrificial knives and fetish masks flashed on the screen behind me. Assuming a fair degree of resilience in my audience, I hadn't pulled any punches, and at several points there were gasps of revulsion from around the room. I could feel the tension building. I realized that, despite the fact that these were among Europe's most senior police officers and criminologists, they had little or no conceptual framework for this kind of crime. They were, quite simply, horrified.

'I don't believe Adam was butchered for his body parts,' I said. 'His genitals and internal organs were all intact. He was not killed agonizingly slowly, but quickly – at least fairly quickly – by precise cuts to the throat, his body held horizontally or upside down until it was drained of blood. And the body was dressed in orange-red shorts after death and placed in the river. For all these reasons, it is my conviction that Adam was the victim of a human sacrifice.'

I heard an intake of breath from Andy Baker and sensed

a flicker of astonishment from the body of the hall. I heard whispering, journalists scribbling furiously on notepads. No one here was going to miss the significance of this story: a child sacrificed to some jealous African god in the heart of a European capital city.

'Let me go further,' I said. 'Given that Adam was almost certainly African, he was probably sacrificed as an offering to one of the gods or deities of West Africa. Why West Africa? In my opinion, it's only there that sufficiently sophisticated religious and ritual systems exist that could account for the complexity of the awful ceremony to which he was subjected. Allied to this is the historical association of this region with the practice of sacrifice, and cultural factors such as his circumcision.

'If I'm right about that, then many aspects of this disturbing crime fall into place. The colour of the shorts will prove to be important, and similarly the deposition of the body in water. Also the precise way the killing was carried out. And the timing: the fact that the body was dressed in the shorts only after death. We do not know yet why they wanted to sacrifice a child in London, but they obviously felt they needed power for something major, which as yet is unknown to us.

'Knowing which deity is involved', I went on, 'could obviously help lead us closer to Adam's killers. But identifying the particular god or goddess is no easy task – there are literally hundreds in the West African pantheon. I will be looking further at deities associated with both the colours orange and red, and with water – especially those in the Yoruba tradition and surrounding ethnic groups. Here for now are some possible candidates on my shortlist.'

I told them about the fiery Shango, lover of the colour

red and of sacrifices. He was a distinct possibility. Then I described Shango's wife Oshun. Orange was only her secondary colour, but she was a river goddess. That might make her a credible suspect, but I described how, though capricious, she was generally seen as a benign figure. I mentioned Yemaya the Yoruban sea god, Angayu Shola who had an association with red and with rivers, and a string of other West African gods and goddesses who were, or might be, in the frame.

I drew the talk to a close. I felt a surge of relief: it was out there now.

I was still surprised that the question and answer session which followed was quite so electric. Commander Baker, Will O'Reilly and I were bombarded with questions. Predictably, some of the more ghoulish ones were bowled up to me.

'Exactly how was the boy killed, Dr Hoskins? Could you describe the precise nature of the ceremony?'

I did, as far as I was able.

'Dr Hoskins, what do you think the killers did with his head?'

I replied, 'They may have placed it on an altar, and later buried it near the place of sacrifice. It becomes a kind of remembrance of the act of sacrifice – a reminder of the power that has been invoked. Or they may have disposed of those parts separately. We just don't know yet.'

'Was he brought to Britain specifically for this sacrifice?' someone else asked, touching on something that had also begun to nag at me. 'Did he know in advance what was waiting for him in London?'

'We don't know the answers to either of those questions yet,' I hedged. 'But as far as the second one is concerned, we can only hope that the answer is no.'

'Just how many ritual murders have there been in Europe recently, Dr Hoskins?'

'That's one of the things this conference is hoping to establish. But we shouldn't get it out of proportion. This kind of thing is mercifully very rare.'

'All the same, the number is on the rise?'

'I would expect so.'

'Why would you expect that?'

'Because modern Europe is much more of a cultural melting pot today than ever before; because more people want to come here, for work or refuge, from more countries around the world, and because both legal and illegal migration is on the rise.'

'Does this mean we can expect to see African sacrificial rites become common in our cities?'

I hesitated, but Will O'Reilly stepped in quickly and gave some suitably down-to-earth answer, which defused the question.

I was glad when the session broke up soon afterwards, but I didn't have a chance to compare notes with Will or Andy Baker. In the body of the hall I was instantly besieged by reporters, but also by police officers from all over Europe wanting to ask about their own cases. I was astonished at the number – murders in Scandinavia, Germany, France, Belgium and Italy which may or may not have had a ritual connection. Cold cases on which the ritual angle might throw new light. In the middle of all this the Europol regional officer cornered me and took down my details. He told me I was to be designated an 'official expert' on ritual crime.

I fielded this sudden celebrity as well as I could, while Andy Baker stood on the fringe of the group, clearly pleased that my talk had made such a splash. When I finally managed to extricate myself from the crowd, he drew me aside and surprised me by saying that he wanted to put my contact details on the database for the National Crime Faculty, the body which selects specialists to be called in to work on major crimes when the level of expertise required goes beyond regular policing.

'You know, Richard,' he said. 'Something struck me listening to you talk, and to the questions afterwards. This isn't just about Adam. This is much wider than that. This is about something changing right across our society.' He gave me a significant look. 'You could find yourself with a good deal to do.'

He moved off silently into the press throng. I watched him go, brought up short by his words and suddenly oblivious to the clamour around me. Not just about Adam. I remembered the barrage of unsolved cases that had just been thrown at me. He was right. It wasn't just about Adam.

Kate Campbell told me that BBC's *Newsnight* wanted to film a piece about my work on the Adam case for transmission that night. She had checked with Commander Baker and he thought it was a good idea.

I hesitated: I didn't want to miss Ray Fysh's presentation. Faith stepped in, and I found myself walking up a Dutch city street as a BBC cameraman inexplicably took footage of my shoes and the interviewer, anxious to present me as some sort of ghostbuster, introduced me as 'an expert on ritual killings'.

By late afternoon Faith and I had escaped to our hotel room. We sat on the bed, side by side, completely drained. I wanted to ask her how Ray's briefing had gone, but we were both too tired even to talk about it. Instead, we went downstairs and wandered for a while as the cool spring evening settled over the waterfront. We ended up in an Italian restaurant, sharing a bottle of indifferent Chianti.

I looked out over the quay. It was well lit, very orderly, very clean, very Dutch. But just beyond the neat railings lay the sea, dark and mysterious.

'Do you think it's just chance', I asked Faith, 'that I, of all people, get called in on this case? The sacrifice of a child? With my history?'

'It's your history that qualifies you. That's the point.'

'But they don't know that. The police don't know anything about what happened to me in the Congo. They don't know about Abigail and Judith. A few months ago I was an obscure West Country academic. Now, apparently, I'm Witchfinder General. Doesn't that strike you as weird?'

She looked uneasily out of the window. 'I don't believe in things that go bump in the night, Richard.'

'Neither do I,' I said. 'That's why it's weird.'

18

London and Bath, May 2002

Over the next few days newspapers in Britain continued to carry stories connected with the Adam investigation. They exhausted the most clear-cut approaches to the case on day one, and almost immediately after that it was obvious that they were scratching around for something new to say.

They began publishing stories about apparently similar killings in the UK and elsewhere. Some of these had been mentioned in The Hague; others looked as if they had been trawled up out of the archives and subjected to a little journalistic licence.

I was sitting at my desk in Bath, having just read one of the more fantastic offerings.

'You know, Mahinda,' I said, 'I'm beginning to wonder whether this high-publicity strategy isn't something of a double-edged sword.'

'Indeed?' he said. 'This is, I'm afraid, the nature of journalistic inquiry.'

He was standing at the window, gazing with obvious delight at the springtime fields. He looked rather like a gigantic spring blossom himself. The foot-and-mouth crisis of the previous year was behind us now and the fields had been restocked with dairy cows for the first time in many months. Mahinda liked cows.

'They're beginning to publish some pretty iffy stuff,' I said unhappily, folding the paper. 'A lot of it's really speculative and sensational.'

'The authorities have stimulated the media with the promise of great news,' he said. 'But for the moment they have nothing more to tell. Naturally, the gentlemen of the press have no choice but to try to make much of little.'

An enormous Guernsey lumbered right up to the window – so close that her big soft nose rested on the glass – and gazed at Mahinda with adoration. He gazed back.

The phone rang.

It was a journalist. I didn't think his timing was great, given my growing disenchantment, but on the other hand I knew that what Mahinda had said was true. Trying to hold back from the media now would merely encourage more speculative stories. We couldn't blame reporters for flying kites if we didn't talk to them when they asked. So I spoke to him about the case and answered his questions as fully as I could.

'They didn't send me to The Hague, I'm afraid, Dr Hoskins,' he told me. 'I wish they had. Could you tell me something about what you said to the conference?'

I gave him a precis. I explained to him that Adam's killing was a sacrifice. I told him that I thought the crime was related to a Yoruban religion, and I told him my reasons, mentioning my shortlist of a dozen possible deities to whom the sacrifice may have been dedicated.

Pretty soon I began to feel wary, as he came back repeatedly to the river goddess Oshun. I sensed that he had already worked out his own agenda, and that he was probing not for information but confirmation.

'Oshun's just a possibility,' I stressed. 'There are several others. She's not even top of my list. And I'm not just saying Yoruba itself, but neighbouring groups like Igbo.'

'Oh, I understand that. But she is a contender.'

'Yes, but—'

'And she does have a very strong following. Am I right?'

Alarm bells went off.

'Listen,' I said, 'if you're going to use me as a source I need to see this piece before you run it.'

'That's absolutely no problem, Dr Hoskins,' he assured me.

I put the phone down. Mahinda was tickling the glass and making baby noises to the Guernsey, which was luxuriously licking the window from the other side.

'She can tell I'm a Buddhist,' Mahinda told me, 'and thus a vegetarian.'

'Great,' I said, thinking of the time I could have sworn I'd seen him eat a beefburger. 'You two were meant for each other.'

The journalist never contacted me again, and that weekend his paper published a story linking Adam's sacrifice directly to the Yoruban people. It specifically cited the river goddess Oshun as the most likely deity to whom Adam had been sacrificed and quoted me as the authority for this. I shuddered.

My anger was not just a matter of professional pique. There were some serious issues here. Oshun has a large number of devotees worldwide, and they would be offended to be singled out in this way and to have their faith linked with such an abomination.

Two days later I came in to work, turned on my computer and went off to make a cup of coffee while the machine booted up. Things had quietened down a bit and I was glad about that. I had gone forty-eight hours without a media inquiry, and that was OK with me. I was at my desk, sipping my coffee, when the phone rang.

'Dr Hoskins?'

The caller was a woman with a West African accent. I didn't recognize the voice but I instinctively didn't like it. There was an edge to it, as if it were being released under pressure.

'That's right,' I said. 'Who's this?'

'I am Princess Tania Olesungo. Dr Hoskins, you have done the Yoruban people a very great wrong.'

I held my tongue for a second or two. I didn't like the sound of this. I wasn't overawed by the 'princess' part of it – Yoruban royalty is tolerably numerous and in Lagos I have been in taxis driven by princes of the blood – but I could hear the hostility in this woman's voice and I didn't like her phoning straight through to me on my direct line. I asked her what she wanted.

'Oshun has nothing to do with this murder case,' she said. 'I am myself a worshipper and I know this. It is an outrage that you say so.'

'I did not say so,' I told her. 'The article in the paper last week put too much weight on that side of the issue, if that's what you've been reading. For the record I never said Oshun devotees were behind this. But I'm afraid I am convinced that a Yoruban group of some kind was involved.'

She was silent for a moment and I could hear her breathing. 'You have no evidence for that,' she said. 'You must tell me now why you are making such a grotesque assertion.'

I told her that the evidence was confidential and I really could not divulge it. But I assured her I wouldn't have stood up in front of Europe's leading police officers – and the press – unless I believed I was right.

'You must retract this at once,' she hissed. 'Or we are going to ruin you.'

I said, 'Are you threatening me?'

'Dr Hoskins, there is no basis to these charges. They are a slur against Yorubans and against all Nigerians. You will be in very serious trouble if you persist in these slanders.'

'Don't be ridiculous.'

'We will ruin you,' she whispered again, her voice tight with malice. 'I am warning you of this. There are more of us. We will ask Oshun for help to bring you down.'

She hung up. I sat for a long time staring at the telephone.

'I think we should call the police,' I said to Faith that evening.

'You don't think she's just some silly woman going over the top because she thinks her people have been insulted?'

'Probably. But there is a murder at the centre of this case.' The next day I called Nick Chalmers. I half expected him to laugh at my concerns but his reaction surprised me. The police had received calls from the same person and others who claimed to be her associates. Nick sounded guarded, even a little cagey, and that didn't reassure me. I sensed that he was not altogether comfortable with this turn of events himself, and I asked him if he thought I should be concerned.

'Well, you know more about these people than I do, Richard,' he said carefully. 'We tend not to worry too much about this kind of thing, unless there's a direct physical threat, of course.'

'Do you think that's likely?'

'No. Not likely. But anything's possible in this big bad

world, as we all know only too well. In all probability these are just angry people letting off steam. But, well, you know . . .'

'No, I don't know.'

'Well . . . just keep your eyes open, that's all. That's common sense. And stay in touch.'

He hung up, rather too quickly I thought.

A day or two later I let myself into the office, made coffee and settled with it in front of my computer. I opened my email inbox. I saw a message headed '*Observer* article', and my stomach knotted.

It had been sent from London and came from two people claiming to be Oshun devotees. Both of them, apparently, were postgraduate students studying in London.

They denied absolutely that Adam's death had anything to do with either Nigeria or the Yoruban people, or indeed with Oshun. I was, they said, steeped in ignorance and prejudice and had publicly discredited myself. They went on to attack everything I had said about the Adam case. They didn't stop there. They threatened to make sure everyone knew of my gross misinterpretations and they planned to smear my academic reputation around the world.

As the day wore on, I began to receive similar emails from people overseas. When the language of the messages started to strike me as familiar I became suspicious and decided to scour some of the internet forums I regularly used, to see where all this was coming from. Sure enough, I found that the first two correspondents had posted a statement vehemently attacking the *Observer* article and me, and this statement gave my contact details.

Some of the incoming emails continued to sound threatening. I was told that for daring to suggest a Nigerian link

I would be ruined as an academic and that my name would be dragged through the mud. It was unpleasant enough to have abuse heaped on me in this way, but all the more so that it should come from complete strangers. In more than one case writers told me that they would not be responsible for the consequences if I failed to retract my allegations or – worse still – dared to repeat them.

I told myself that a physical threat wasn't high on my list of concerns. People say all sorts of unpleasant things when they are angry, especially via phone and email, when abuse can be hurled from a safe distance.

All the same, I took to locking my office door.

This precaution caused a good deal of distress to Mahinda. He had his own key, but was forever losing it in the folds of his robes, or leaving it inside the office, so that he had to beat on the door and piteously plead for me to open up. When I did he'd drift in, full of karmic energy. There were times when I thought Mahinda was driving me crazy, and other times when I thought he was just about keeping me sane.

Over the next few weeks I continued to receive abusive correspondence from around the world, and there wasn't much I could do except sit and take it. Some of it was merely unpleasant, some of it downright lunatic.

By no means all of these messages came from Yorubans or from Princess Tania's acolytes. I had one phone call from a seriously disturbed man in Wales who claimed he could help crack the crime and wanted to send me a video of a child being raped. I got straight on to Will O'Reilly about that one.

'Oh, yes. We know about this character,' he said, and added darkly, 'leave him to us.'

The silence from Wales was deafening after that.

An outraged teacher from Yorkshire accused me of deliberately undermining racial harmony. Nigerians who had barely heard of Oshun were scandalized that I had implicated their nation in such an obscenity. Some academic colleagues and friends fell unaccountably silent when I mentioned the Adam case to them.

And then I got one message I could not ignore.

It began with the words, 'I think I know who killed Adam.'

The message was from a British woman called Jean, who was working with her husband at a hospital in Lahore. I had got used to people writing to me with crackpot ideas, but Jean's email had a convincing ring to it. No mention here of spirit guides or conspiracy theories. She had seen me interviewed on Arabic television. She worked with a Nigerian colleague whom she called Vincent, and whom she suspected of smuggling African children into Europe. She believed that one of his victims had been Adam and claimed she had good evidence to back it up.

If I wanted to know who this man was, I could find his full name and even his photograph in an issue of a certain medical journal, for which she gave details. She would tell me more over the phone in seven days at a strictly specified time.

I called Will O'Reilly at once.

I could almost hear him yawn. 'Forward it to me and we'll see what we should do. If anything.'

I reminded myself that the police must have hundreds of calls like these every day. But a few minutes after I had sent him Jean's email, Will called me back. This time he sounded a good deal more interested.

'I think we'll have to follow this up,' he said. 'Can you ask her to be a bit more specific? Get her to put something more in writing so we can see if she's wasting our time.'

Jean's next message only strengthened the feeling that we might be onto something. Her husband was also a colleague of this man Vincent, and she was afraid that if her husband knew what she was doing he would somehow let it slip and alert him. She was terrified of that, which was why she had to talk to me directly, when she was alone in the house, and she would be able to convince me she had hard evidence. I was to ring her as and when she had requested and at no other time. She could not even risk emailing again before then.

'I'll tell you what we'll do,' Will said. 'We'll come over and listen in to the conversation.'

I told Faith what had happened at home that evening while I was preparing a curry. She dipped a spoon into the black Colombian pot.

'Not bad: you're clearly picking up my culinary methods.' She looked at me. 'So you really think this could be it?'

'Someone somewhere must know something. Maybe Jean does.'

'Wouldn't it be fantastic to put an end to this?'

I didn't need to answer that after the weeks of malevolent phone calls and emails.

'Are the police checking on this medical journal?' she asked.

'I got the impression they wanted to do the phone tap first. I suppose they don't have unlimited resources.'

'On the other hand, if the medical journal doesn't check out, then the phone tap is probably a waste of time.'

I gave her a sideways look. 'What are you building up to?'

'Well, it wouldn't do any harm to see if that part of her story stacks up, would it? We're going up to London anyway this week. We should be able to track that journal down easily enough.' She glanced at my beloved curry, seething on the stove. 'You really ought to stir that, you know.'

Faith and I spent that Friday morning in the reference library of the Royal College of Obstetricians and Gynaecologists at Sussex Place near Regent's Park. I had dressed for the occasion in a sombre suit and tie, and allowed the receptionist to believe my doctorate was a medical one, so that she personally ushered me into the hallowed precincts.

There on the shelves was the relevant issue of the medical journal Jean had named, and inside it was a photograph of our Nigerian suspect, Vincent, giving his full name and contact details. He was one of the authors of a medical research paper and his smiling face looked out from the page. The photograph showed a confident, professional-looking middle-aged man. I wondered what he would think if he knew that two total strangers half a world away were linking him to the murder of a boy called Adam.

19

Bath and London, June 2002

I knew the police disapproved of amateur sleuthing, so I didn't report our discovery to them.

A few days later Nick Chalmers and Will O'Reilly were sitting opposite me in our living room in Bath. We were waiting to telephone Jean, who had given us a time slot during which we could reach her. There were just the three of us as Faith was away on a research trip.

As the minutes counted down Nick passed me a list of questions.

'You want me to ask her all this?'

'If you get the chance.'

I dialled Jean's home in Lahore. There was a long pause and then I could hear the phone ringing at the other end. The receiver was lifted.

The voice was fairly young, educated; tense but controlled. I pictured an intelligent woman of about thirty-five. It would not be easy to dismiss this person as a crackpot and that made me, if anything, even more nervous.

She told me she didn't have much time, then took a couple of breaths to compose herself. 'All right. I've told you that Vincent is a colleague. Naturally, I've had a good deal of contact with him. I became aware that he was acting very strangely during the year 2000—'

'2000?'

'I mean 2001, of course. I get so jumpy I make mistakes.' Jean told me Vincent had visited Britain and Nigeria several times during 2001. She thought he was in London that September, but couldn't be entirely sure. After one of his trips to Nigeria he came back through Lahore on his way to London with a young Nigerian boy, perhaps five or six years old. Jean didn't know where the boy came from or who he was. She didn't think he was a relation. Vincent made no secret of the boy's presence but then he took him to London and neither she nor any of her friends or colleagues in Lahore had seen him since.

I suggested that Vincent might just be chaperoning the child for a friend.

'No, no, there's more. He's involved in voodoo. *Juju*, or whatever they call it.'

'How do you know that?'

'He was quite open about it. He said he believed his career was being held back by a jealous rival at the hospital – another Nigerian – and that this man had put a *juju* curse on him. He told me he was going to do something that would cancel out the curse and clear his path to a successful future. Apparently a *juju* man back in Nigeria had told him what he needed to do.'

'I don't suppose he said what that was?'

'No. But pretty soon after he told me this, Vincent made one of his visits to the UK. When he came back later that month he seemed much more confident and relaxed. He told me everything was going to be all right now . . .'

In the silence I could hear her breathing. 'What are you frightened of, Jean?'

'I can't talk about this to my husband. I'm terrified that if he gets wind of what I think, he'll somehow let Vincent know – they might even have a good laugh about it. I'm really frightened of what Vincent might do if he knows I suspect him, but I can't just sit quietly and forget about it, can I? As soon as I saw you in that TV interview I knew you were the person I had to tell.'

'I'm sure you did the right thing,' I said.

I heard a muffled sound in the background.

Jean whispered, 'Oh, my God! My husband's coming back. You must phone next week, same time. I've got to go . . .'

The phone went dead.

I put down the receiver. Will and Nick glanced at one another, and then looked at me. I tried to read their faces, without success.

'You did fine, Richard,' Will said. 'But I wanted her to say more, to tell us something that would be actual evidence.'

Nick nodded. 'Why don't you try and get some more details out of her by email, Richard? We can talk before you call her again next week.'

I tried not to show my disappointment.

Nick went on to say that they'd heard from the disgruntled Yorubans again – more than once. This was news I didn't want to hear. Jean's messages had helped me put that episode to the back of my mind.

'They gave me quite an ear-bashing,' Nick said. 'I told them you were confident of your theory, Richard, and that's the line I'll stick to.' He paused. 'So long as you *are* confident . . .'

I took a deep breath. 'I'm confident,' I said.

'Good. Because there's more at stake here than the feelings of a few brassed-off Nigerians.'

I looked from him to Will.

Will said, 'Ever since you gave us the possible West African link, we've kept an eye out for anything that matches it.'

'And?'

'There's a woman in Scotland who's rather caught our attention. I'd prefer not to say any more about it just yet.'

'It would be great if you could come up to London,' Nick said. 'I'll be able to fill you in. And ask Faith along.' A smile played around his mouth. 'We always enjoy her company.'

Several emails arrived from Jean over the next forty-eight hours. She explained that her husband had come home unexpectedly and she'd had to get off the phone fast, but that she already felt better now that she'd made contact. It was an immense relief to unburden herself to someone who understood.

It struck me that her messages were getting rather prolix; natural enough, perhaps, for a woman who had at last found an ally after months of suspicion and secrecy, but I was aware too that her information still lacked the kernel of hard evidence the police needed. All the same, I dutifully collected all her messages and sent them off to Nick.

Faith and I were running late on the morning of our visit to Catford. I logged into the email account I was using for Jean, rather hoping the inbox would be empty – we would be pushed to make the London train as it was – but Jean had sent me five emails and they all seemed pretty lengthy. Casting a quick eye down the pages, they appeared to give further information about the mysterious Vincent, but I didn't have time to read them properly, so I hit the print button.

We arrived flustered at Bath Spa Station just as the train drew in and found a pair of seats with a table. I pulled out the emails and began to read.

I knew almost at once that something was wrong, but said nothing as I passed them to Faith. I didn't need to ask her. '"My songbird"?' she quoted, with some scorn. 'That's a bit of a bloody odd thing to call you, isn't it?'

'Yes, it is, rather.' I cleared my throat.

'"Such a lovely man",' Faith read on, breathlessly. '"Such a caring, kind, intelligent individual."' She flattened the sheet on the table. 'Are you sure this woman's got all her marbles?'

'Because she calls me kind, intelligent and caring?'

'If I was feeling generous I could cope with that. But *songbird*?'

'It's worse than that, though, isn't it?' Tell me she's not in a total muddle over timing.'

'She's not just in a muddle; she's gone completely haywire. She's a whole year out, surely?'

'I'm afraid so.'

'And you told me she got the year wrong on the phone too . . .'

I nodded. 'Vincent was in Lahore all through September 2001. He was nowhere near London. He couldn't possibly have killed Adam. The whole thing's been a waste of time.' I stared out of the window. 'My playing at Sherlock Holmes in London, the phone tapping. Everything. All because of some lonely woman with a taste for the dramatic.'

'I don't know,' Faith said. 'I think she's sincere. She really does suspect this character of Adam's murder.' She shrugged. 'She's just wrong.'

'Great,' I said. 'Hear that clattering sound? That's the whole house of cards collapsing in a heap.'

As the First Great Western train sped towards London I wondered how often the police must have to put up with this sort of thing. I understood now how Will and Nick had managed to stay so cool about Jean's 'information' even while they were diligently checking it out.

Well, at least I'd learned something. I'd learned how easy it is in an investigation to allow yourself to believe what you most want to believe.

20

Catford and Bath, June 2002

We didn't say much as we caught the tube at Paddington. When we finally reached Catford Station, Nick Chalmers was waiting for us.

'You two look a bit down in the mouth,' he said.

Before we reached his car I had given him a brief summary of Jean's latest messages.

'It happens,' he shrugged.

'I feel a bit sorry for her,' Faith said. 'I think she meant well.'

'Maybe.' He opened the driver's door. 'But I can't say I'm completely surprised.'

We headed for a nearby Japanese restaurant. The place had blue walls and black wooden tables and benches – colours that pretty well matched my mood.

Nick had seen it all before.

'A high-profile case prompts a never-ending stream of calls like that. Some are obviously loopy. Some are loopy but don't look it. Some are malicious. A lot are well-intentioned but rubbish. But we have to make some sort of attempt to follow them all up. So anything that helps us sort the wheat from the chaff is useful. Like your tip about West Africa.'

Nick told us he'd received a telephone call back in February from a PC McGlyn in Glasgow. He'd been the duty officer at a care hearing for Jacqueline and Precious Osagiede. Social workers were worried about their welfare. Their mother, Joyce, had been found guilty of minor breaches of the peace and she'd come out with a bizarre argument for getting her children back: that she was a member of a cult, that she needed the children for a ritual ceremony that night or there would be terrible consequences.

Kevin Williams, the social worker, confirmed that Joyce had indeed told him that she was a member of a cult. And when he'd been in her flat he'd seen all sorts of strange looking artefacts and what he assumed were medicines.

Joyce Osagiede had originally presented herself at the Croydon Immigration office in south London in November 2001, claiming asylum. It seems she had already been in the country for some time. She had two young girls with her, aged six and four. She said they were her daughters and that she was from Sierra Leone in West Africa.

'But the Immigration people weren't so sure,' Nick said. 'Nigerians quite often claim they come from Sierra Leone – they think it helps their chances of asylum. I guess all this may be nothing more than another interesting diversion, but the cult is Yoruban. I've found her file. She admitted under questioning that she had travelled from Sierra Leone to Benin City in Nigeria in the mid-1990s to marry one Tony Onus, a prominent member of a cult calling itself "the Black Coat Eyes of the Devil Guru Maharaj", if you can believe that. She says he has messianic status.'

Guru Maharaj sounded distinctly Eastern. I had a hazy recollection of a similar sounding mystic guru in the Seventies. But then again, new religious movements sprang up by the hundreds every year in Africa. It was hard to keep up.

Nick leaned towards us. 'Joyce says that this group has participated in a number of human sacrifices during initiation ceremonies, that her husband took a prominent role in these sacrifices and that her own newborn son was sacrificed in 1995.'

The lunchtime hum faded into the background.

'He was sacrificed by his father?'

Nick nodded. 'According to Joyce, anyway. It was supposed to bring power to someone who was a devotee of the cult.'

According to Joyce, her husband sacrificed ten people in Nigeria in that one year. She went on to say that – not surprisingly – she grew more and more scared of him, and finally ran away because he wanted to sacrifice one of the two girls next. She fled to England to save them.

Immigration sent Joyce to Glasgow, as part of their policy of spreading asylum seekers around the country. There the social services became very concerned about the state of the children and put them into care. It was at the care hearing that Jim McGlyn heard her beg for them back so they could take part in this ritual.

The social workers' case files mentioned 'strange items' in her flat and what looked like packets of some unidentifiable substance. Kevin Williams confirmed these sightings in court. Interviewing Joyce had become a priority.

My next task was to look more closely at the Guru Maharaj cult.

Before we left, I asked Nick if there had been any progress with the analysis of the contents of Adam's intestine. Nick said he would check and get back to me.

*

The investigation seemed to have shifted into a different gear. Within a week I'd changed our home phone number and made the new one ex-directory. I had the locks changed at the house and started making sure the car was in the garage and not left in the street overnight. I became wary about picking up the phone, and at the university I often waited until someone else answered it. I became conscious of who got off the train when I did and who walked behind me at night down Bath's leafy suburban streets.

Worst of all, I became conscious of colour for the first time in my life. For all the years I had spent in Africa, for all the friends I had made there, for all my love for the continent and its people, I started to see black people, and particularly West Africans, as a potential source of threat. I was furious with myself about this. I found it profoundly shaming. But whenever a man of West African origin got into the lift beside me or passed me in the street I felt my heart beat a little faster.

21

Devon, July 2002

The university granted me sabbatical leave ostensibly to allow me to continue my research on the Kimbanguists, but actually to allow me to concentrate on the Adam case.

Faith's parents owned a fifty-acre farm in rural Devon, and offered us use of a cottage, so on a hot summer Friday we crammed ourselves and as much of our gear as we could into the Land Rover and headed down the A39.

Within a couple of days I had established my Adam site office – an old caravan in an orchard – and filled it with my books and dossiers on the case. Faith's dad, a computer buff, amused himself by installing a phenomenal communications system so that I actually had faster and more reliable contact with the outside world from this tatty little cabin than when I had been part of the university's high-tech network.

Faith settled herself in the farmhouse a few hundred yards away. Every now and then we would convene in the garden or at the caravan and compare notes.

Andy Baker's prediction at The Hague conference began to come true. The occasional request for advice from the Met and elsewhere began to escalate to a point where I was more and more deeply engaged with the machinery of police work. I was becoming fixated on the role of religion in crime.

These developments were not altogether healthy. Nothing in my life had prepared me for continual exposure to such violence and depravity, and I was wrong to assume that Faith and I could involve ourselves in these investigations without cost. At the time, though, I was intrigued by the intellectual challenges that were being presented to us, and encouraged by our success in dealing with them. Every academic must wonder from time to time about the usefulness and relevance of their work in the 'real' world. At least we had no doubts on that score.

The stream of new cases began with an approach from the Norfolk Police. The violated body of a young woman, Domingas Olivais, an asylum seeker from Guinea-Bissau in West Africa, had been found in the River Bure. It was quickly established that the injury had been inflicted after death, and they thought there might be a ritualistic angle.

I could see very little sign of it, and told them so. I thought the killer's behaviour had more to do with his own state of mind. It turned out that the woman's partner, Filomeno Lopes, had strangled Domingas because he suspected she was having an affair. He'd dumped her body in the river, probably hoping it would float out to sea and never be found. A jury at Norwich Crown Court found him guilty and he was sentenced to life imprisonment.

My involvement with the case was relatively confined, but it indicated that the idea of ritual murder had taken root. A couple of years earlier no one would have considered it. I made a mental note to discourage the people I was dealing with from seeing it as exotic and bizarre, and reminded anyone who would listen that there was no need to invoke ritual crime just because the victim was African – or to discount it if they were not.

Despite the stream of cases, work on the Adam investigation remained my priority. Since Nick's request a couple of weeks earlier I had been trying to find out about the cult to which Joyce Osagiede's husband apparently belonged.

I'd brushed up my knowledge of the original Guru Maharaj. He was an Indian mystic who founded the Divine Light Mission in 1960. His son took over as head of the movement on his death in 1966, even though he was only nine. In due course the son took the title of Maharaj Ji. He was recognized by his followers as the latest *satguru* in a line that included Krishna, Buddha, Christ and Mohammed.

The 1970s was a vintage decade for mystical Indian movements. For the gurus themselves those years were good karma and big business. A few of the sects – such as the movement led by the Bagwan Shree Rajneesh – gained a high profile by attracting celebrity adherents, most notably members of The Beatles. So in 1971, hoping to carry forward the Divine Light Mission (DLM) on the crest of this wave, the very young Maharaj Ji undertook a world tour. He briefly became a controversial figure in the United States where, like some other spiritual leaders, he found self-indulgence more attractive than the self-denial he recommended to his followers. His tour was a financial disaster following a doomed attempt to launch the New Age at Houston Astrodome in 1973.

In the mid-1970s, faced with financial ruin, Maharaj Ji moved away from the DLM. In response, his mother back in India deposed him as leader. Maharaj Ji changed the name of his movement in the USA to Elan Vital, and associated himself with the realization of human potential rather than with the preaching of any recognized form of religion. Maharaj Ji long ago renounced his status as divine guru and now lives quietly in the States. Elan Vital has about 75,000 followers worldwide. The Divine Light Mission, which continued to have its spiritual base in India, claims about 250,000 adherents.

Elan Vital and DLM have some notable followers in the world of religious studies. I'd known for a while that quite a few academics in my field had more than just a research interest in their subject matter. Even so, it was a surprise to find quite so many devotees of Eastern movements behind the study doors of Western universities.

Was the Nigerian Guru the man who had founded the DLM back in the 1960s, or someone else altogether? There was indeed a Nigerian movement known as the Divine Light Mission, but the present Maharaj Ji had no connection with it, and neither had the founders of the worldwide DLM. The Nigerian group had merely hijacked the name, and the name of the original DLM's founder. By so doing they had given themselves an instant – though entirely spurious – pedigree.

I needed a contact on the ground in Nigeria. My academic contacts there had proved less than helpful. They either ignored my requests for information or advised me to back off. There was still a lot of resentment about the Yoruba link I'd made, and some fear. I was given some strong hints that this line of inquiry wasn't likely to bring results and was very unlikely to do anyone any good.

Then I remembered Afe Adogame, a Ghanaian specialist on West African beliefs. I had met him a year earlier at a conference at the Institute for African Studies in Bayreuth, Germany, where he worked as a senior lecturer.

I told Afe as much as I thought I could about the Adam investigation, about my sacrifice theory and the cult that Joyce was supposed to belong to. I left room for him to protest, or perhaps even to hang up. He did neither.

'I'm not getting much help on this, Afe,' I said. 'You can see the problem. This is a dreadful crime and there are people who will use it to smear the good name of Africans generally, and Nigerians and Yorubans in particular.'

He recommended contacting Blessing Adekunle, a young PhD student of religion at the University of Lagos.

I was concerned about putting her at risk, though, and left it a few days before I set about calling her in Nigeria. This took the best part of an hour. Despite the worldwide advances in technology, things didn't seem to have improved much in Nigeria over the last decade. I grew increasingly anxious as I listened to the symphony of clicks and buzzes, the repeated disconnections and engaged tones and call diverts. I looked out at my English orchard as the rain started to slap down on the roof of the caravan. The phone cheeped and squawked in my ear and I wondered if I should forget the whole thing.

Then, miraculously, I got through.

'Dr Adogame told me that you might call, Dr Hoskins,' Blessing Adekunle said. She had a quiet, unhurried voice. 'He has outlined the problem. Of course I will help, if I can.'

She sounded both competent and resolute. The people I was interested in, she said, were evil men who brought shame on her country, and she would be happy to help with any investigation of their activities. I stressed that some of these people were potentially dangerous, that what I wanted was strictly academic research, and I could pay her only a pittance.

Just then Faith pushed the door ajar and peeped in. She looked uneasy. 'You're going to think I'm nuts. It's that damned mask. There's something weird about it.'

I'd never liked the Chokwe death mask. I'd been uncomfortable when Faith had seen it on a trader's table in the Brazzaville market. It would have been shaped around a dead girl's face so that whoever wore it thereafter might draw up the spirit of the deceased. It was strangely beautiful, but the first night we'd had it in the room with us we'd both had chilling nightmares. We'd hung it on the wall of our home in Bath, and occasionally, when I'd been working late, the thing had given me the creeps.

'I put it up on my study wall when I unpacked,' she said. 'And I've been getting blinding headaches ever since.'

She hadn't told me before because she couldn't see how her headaches could possibly have anything to do with the mask. But as soon as she took it out of the room, the headaches stopped. As an experiment, she'd passed the thing on to her mother, for whom it had no connotations. But her mother had started to have awful nightmares in which the mask featured, and now she wouldn't have it in the house.

'And she smells,' Faith went on, 'of wood smoke. She always did a bit. But sometimes it's really strong. Almost choking.'

I didn't like the way Faith had called the mask 'she', as if it had a personality of its own. That wasn't something I wanted to consider.

'Burn it,' I said.

'We can't do that, can we?'

'It's just a lump of wood,' I said with as much conviction as I could manage.

She chewed her lip. 'This shouldn't be happening, should it? Two rational people . . .'

We'd both been upset by the phone calls, the emails and all the weird material we'd been digging around in. That was natural enough. But if we started thinking like this . . . It felt as if we were giving in to the very thing we were trying to expose.

I said, 'If it really worries you, and you don't think we should destroy it, then give it to me. I'll keep it in here.'

'Is that a really great idea?'

'We have to draw the line somewhere, don't we?' I said, rather grandly. 'It's one thing to get the creeps, but it's another to start believing.'

Within an hour I had set up the mask next to my computer screen. I'd forgotten how lovely it was, with its full lips, slanting almond eyes and hempen hair. When Faith had gone I spent quite a long time admiring it. It had stopped raining and the weather had cleared, and the mask was framed in the sunlit window with English trees shifting in the summer breeze.

The phone rang, making me jump. It was Will O'Reilly. Professor Ken Pye had finished his geological mapping. A meeting of key members of the Adam investigation team had been called at Royal Holloway College to hear the results.

22

Royal Holloway College, July 2002

It was a swelteringly hot July day, one of the few England produces that reminded me fleetingly of the tropics. The train ground to a halt at Sunningdale. Sunshine on the tracks, perhaps. I hailed a cab outside the station.

The college is a vast Victorian red-brick pile set in extensive grounds at the end of a sweeping drive. I hadn't been there before but despite my wanderings I still found myself standing outside Professor Pye's room half an hour early. I opened the door on to a tiny office stacked with files and folders. A computer and two or three microscopes jostled for space on the narrow bench. Ken and his colleague Nick Branch greeted me warmly and we filed into a conference room where we were joined by Ray Fysh, looking as if he'd just got out of a sauna.

The police contingent was the last to arrive. Will O'Reilly introduced me to another member of his team, DC Mark Ham, who I hadn't met before. Ray Fysh began by describing the killing: 'Adam was held horizontal or upside down, and his throat was sliced in such a way as to cause maximum blood spillage . . .' He put Adam's murder in its forensic context and then indicated that I should take up the baton.

'As I said at The Hague,' I began, 'I'm sure that this crime is strongly linked to West African religious beliefs, and that it was in fact a sacrifice—'

'I don't like that word,' Commander Baker cut in. 'I'm not comfortable with it.'

I'd known at the time that I had dropped something of a bombshell at the Europol conference, but this was the first time I'd been confronted openly.

Andy nodded at Ken Pye.

Ken set out the principle behind his geological mapping, starting with the basics Ray had sketched out to me in Holland. Every individual on the planet carries levels of mineral and other deposits in their bones which are determined by the environment in which they live, picked up from the plant and animal foods in their diet. Isotopic data testing made it possible to determine the levels of strontium, carbon, nitrogen, oxygen and neodymium.

Since every environment leaves its own unique geophysical signature, it is theoretically possible to match the mineral content of bones to an exact location anywhere on the planet. Ken explained that isotope levels take years to change. He'd developed a number of specific tests which gave an accurate record of where someone had lived over a period of up to ten years. The problem was that whilst isotopic databases existed for most Western countries, only patchy information was available elsewhere.

He'd analysed the samples taken from three sections of Adam's bones.

'One thing we can say straight away', Ken said, 'is that Adam wasn't brought up here. The strontium levels in his bones, and traces of copper and lead, are about two and a half times higher than for a child of the same age brought up in south-east England. The Caribbean and the rest of Europe are completely ruled out for similar reasons: his strontium levels don't match. So we looked elsewhere. If Adam didn't come from London or the Caribbean, there was a good chance he came from Africa. But Africa is a big place and the isotopic information available is extremely sketchy. The question was where to look. Initial indicators suggested South Africa, but that began to look less likely as the investigation progressed. Then Will told us to look in West Africa, where we do have some isotopic information.

'Some places leave a more characteristic signature in the bones than others. It's not always possible to be sure where an individual has come from. However, I am confident of our results. The West African information precisely matches the geological composition of Adam's bones. Moreover, there are three relatively small areas of Nigeria that match the results very closely indeed: between Kano and Jos; the highlands towards Cameroon; and the Yoruba Plateau. The evidence points most vigorously to the last of these. With further soil samples from that area I should be able to determine within a very small radius where Adam spent most of his life.'

I caught Will O'Reilly's smile.

'We also tested the carbon levels in Adam's bones,' Ken said.

Carbon will show up after a much briefer exposure; even a short stay in the UK would have left its mark.

'From these results, Adam could not have spent any length of time here in the UK. He might have been in the country for six months at the very most, but probably for a considerably shorter time than that.'

Nick Branch got to his feet, looking slightly overawed.

He explained that as an archaeopalynologist – a pollen archaeologist – he was more used to working on old cases. Very old cases, in fact, including bodies found preserved in peat bogs. Most of his ritual killings dated from the Iron Age, but the same principles of detection and analysis could be applied to modern bodies. He had found pollen spores in Adam's lower intestine which could only have come from British or other north-western European sources – most notably from the alder tree. The fact that these spores were found in the lower intestine meant that they couldn't have made their way in from the Thames after the body was dumped. Adam must have ingested them, and some time must have subsequently elapsed for them to have got that far down his intestinal tract.

'This doesn't help us determine the upper limit of his time in this part of the world,' Nick said, 'but it does give us a lower limit. It means that Adam was in the UK or north-western Europe for at least three days prior to being killed.'

A picture began to emerge of a child who had been brought all the way to London from Nigeria, and had been kept here for between three days and a few weeks before his murder. I think the same thought occurred to all of us at that point: given the meticulous nature of the crime, it was likely that Adam had been brought to London for only one reason. I was overcome by a sense of the loneliness of his final days, and I wondered at what point he had begun to realize the true purpose of his great adventure.

I wondered what else Adam might have ingested. If they could test for pollen grains, why couldn't they analyse the other material in his gut?

'I'll avoid the S-word,' I said, glancing across at Commander Baker, 'but I think it's more than possible that

Adam was deliberately fed something. Victims are often given a potion or preparation of some kind before they're killed, to make them a more acceptable offering to the deity in question. Have we had a chance to look more closely at whatever else was in Adam's lower intestine?'

'There is something there,' Ken said. 'But we haven't completed our analysis yet.'

I told them that if Adam had been given such a potion, and we could analyse it, it might help us understand what happened, and why. If the ingredients were sourced from Nigeria, they could corroborate the derivation of the victim and killers. The potion could in fact provide us with the signature of the person who prepared it.

I explained that in Yorubaland such potions were prepared by traditional healers, usually after cooking them for hours in a small pot over a fire. These healers were the equivalent of South African *sangomas* and Central African *ngangas*. In Nigeria they were known as *babalawos*. It sometimes took up to twelve years to train as a *babalawo*. Apprentices were assigned a mentor, a senior *babalawo*, with whom they spent considerable time, often in the depths of the rainforest learning the ways of nature and the properties of animals and plants, perhaps studying just one tree variety, learning how to harvest its sap, bark, leaves or roots for use in medicine.

If a healer had prepared a potion for Adam to swallow, it would have had his own signature. The particular ingredients, the quantities and the manner of preparation would be distinctive. I told Ken I could give them some pointers; certain plants, animals and minerals which stood a fair chance of finding their way into the mix.

We concluded the meeting by agreeing that Ray and a

police officer would head for the Yoruba plateau to gather samples of local soils, local foods, animal bone and tissue, and so on.

Andy Baker took me to one side before I left. 'Maybe I came on a bit strong. It's just that "sacrifice" is such a powerful word. And we had scientists present . . . I don't want them to go bandying that word about to anyone who asks . . .'

23

Glasgow and London, July 2002

The police raided Joyce Osagiede's Glasgow flat one afternoon later in the month.

It was on the first floor, up a couple of flights of steps. Will O'Reilly, Nick Chalmers and DC Mark Ham arrived with two Glasgow policemen. Nick thumped on the door. There was confused and aggressive shouting from inside, and then silence.

The police knew more about Joyce Osagiede than Nick had let on at the Japanese restaurant. Glasgow officers had gone to see her twice before the raid. Joyce had allowed them into her flat. They didn't have enough evidence to arrest her, but while they were trying to persuade her to give a DNA swab, Jo Veale, a sharp-eyed female detective constable, noticed a letter bearing a London address. She memorized it. A few days later Nick and DC Mark Ham sought it out: a run-down terrace, the home of another Nigerian woman and her family.

She denied knowing Joyce Osagiede, but admitted to recognizing the woman in the picture from Joyce's social security dossier. She said that Joyce had appeared at her door one day looking for a priest. When the officers pressed her for more details she remembered that Joyce had mentioned that she'd recently been in Germany.

Outside Joyce Osagiede's Glasgow flat a decision was taken. The door was smashed open.

Joyce stood against the far wall. A big woman in her mid-thirties, wearing a baggy brown blouse and blue trousers, she was alone and seemed frightened.

Mark Ham walked into the back room. Clothing was tossed over the unmade bed and across the floor. There was a cupboard against the wall; Mark tugged it open. Tucked away at the bottom, out of sight, were some more odds and ends. He held them up to the light.

Their washing instructions were in German. Their labels said 'Kids'n'Co'. Mark and Nick had seen this label before, on a pair of orange-red shorts.

Nick asked, 'Can you explain where you got these clothes, Joyce?'

'I bought them,' she said. 'I was living in Germany. I bought them there.'

'Where would that be in Germany, then? What store?'

She looked from one to the other in confusion, perhaps trying to gauge the advantages of answering honestly.

'Woolworths,' she said at last.

Mark unearthed more hidden items of clothing, all with the same German markings.

'Mrs Joyce Osagiede,' Nick said, 'I am arresting you in connection with the murder of a young boy known as Adam in London during September 2001. You do not have to say anything, but it may harm your defence if you do not mention when questioned something which you later rely on in court. Anything you do say may be given in evidence.'

It was a long way from a conviction or even from a

charge, but it was the first arrest and, after nearly a year of painstaking work, it was the first moment when everyone involved thought they might at last be on the trail of Adam's murderers.

The police brought Joyce back to London for questioning. She clammed up at first and then began to talk in a confused and illogical way. The duty solicitor encouraged her to respond 'no comment', as was her right, and the police got very little out of her.

Now that she was under arrest, however, they did get an all-important DNA sample. Forensics got to work on it at once.

Joyce was taken back into the interview room with her solicitor the next morning. The detectives faced her over the plain wooden table. Nick Chalmers took the lead. This time, Joyce spoke more freely.

She said she was from Sierra Leone, but that she had moved to Nigeria to get married and lived in Benin City. From there she went to Germany, where her two children were born. She'd lived near Hamburg, where she had bought the clothes. No, she had never claimed benefits in Germany. She hadn't needed to. She had lived with her husband.

Joyce began to grow visibly nervous at this point.

'So his name was on your passport,' Nick Chalmers said. 'What was that name, Joyce? The name you originally had on your passport?'

'Onojhighovie,' she said, and looked around wildly.

'I didn't quite catch that, Joyce. Would you please write it down for us?'

Nick slid across a ruled pad and a pencil. She picked

them up, toyed with the pencil for a moment and wrote, 'Tony Onus'.

After that she denied everything. She denied that she had mentioned the name Onojhighovie, and claimed that she had never been to Germany. She said she had come to Britain directly from Lagos by ship. She knew nothing about clothes, nothing about rituals. Her version of events grew more contradictory at every turn.

Nick believed she was either very confused or very scared. Will thought it more probable that she was being deliberately evasive. Meanwhile, time was running out.

Forensics worked miracles with the DNA tests, and within a few hours of being given Joyce's sample they phoned the results through to the team. They were negative. She was not related to Adam.

Joyce Osagiede was driven to Heathrow Airport in an unmarked police car and put on a plane back to Glasgow. For the moment at least, she was a free woman.

24

Devon, August to September 2002

The frightened voice coming down the line from Lagos didn't sound anything like Blessing's cool, measured tones from a fortnight earlier.

She'd been researching the Nigerian Guru Maharaj cult to which Joyce Osagiede's husband apparently belonged and had already sent me three packages of literature and notes. But her fourth package had failed to reach me. Now Blessing feared some sort of conspiracy. The cult was extremely powerful. I tried to reassure her, pointing out that mail went missing all the time. She didn't sound convinced, perhaps because I couldn't entirely convince myself. Blessing's fourth package never did turn up.

'And other things have been happening,' she said darkly.

A friend of hers had been badly hurt a few days ago, knocked from his motorcycle by a hit-and-run driver. She had often ridden that motorcycle herself, and now no witnesses could be found to the crash. There had been strange phone calls to her department at the university, from people she didn't know. She thought she was being followed, and had seen men hanging around outside her apartment at night. She paused. 'They are using *juju* against me, Dr Hoskins. I am sure of it. And I think it is beginning to work.'

Now thoroughly rattled, I told her to stop everything, to ask no more questions and to undertake no more research.

I said, 'Blessing, I can't thank you enough for what you've done. But maybe I shouldn't have asked you to get involved.'

'Someone asked you,' she said, some dignity returning to her voice, 'and you agreed to help. So I did the same.'

After the phone call I spent some time looking out of the caravan window. The sun blazed on the paddock. I glanced down at the death mask, which was still sitting next to my computer. It was black as obsidian. The light streamed through the eye sockets in long spokes. I stretched out my hand towards it, pushed it away and reached instead for Blessing's research material.

I had pieced together a picture of the 'Black Coat Eyes of the Devil Guru Maharaj' and could see why Blessing had been so spooked by them.

The real Divine Light Mission had suspended all its own operations in Nigeria for fear of being tarnished by the cult's reputation, and with good reason.

The man who ended up leading the Nigerian sect was a Yoruban by the name of Muhammed Saib. His family had lived in Ghana, where he was born in the 1950s, but had moved back to Yorubaland when Saib was in his mid-twenties.

He'd been a security guard, worked for a transport firm in Lagos and in a factory. He once played Father Christmas at the YMCA. Then Saib had come to London illegally in 1975 after enrolling on a course at the Institute of Marketing, and encountered the teachings of the Maharaj Ji. Blessing had done sterling work: she'd even sent me copies of Saib's letters from there to his faithful devotees. In one he described attending a Halloween party, where the rituals reminded him of his homeland river gods. He went on to emphasize the importance of sacrifices to these deities.

Saib had gone back to Nigeria in 1980 and declared himself to be the new and rightful Maharaj Ji, the new *satguru* for the world. Most Nigerians were not fooled, but a small and significant number of mainly Yoruban followers signed up to the cause. Ostracized by DLM International, Saib set up his own breakaway group, interchanging the names Divine Light Mission, Elan Vital and others, including variations on the theme of the Guru Maharaj. The most common name the cult used was the singularly inappropriate 'One Love Family'.

As I told Will O'Reilly, Muhammed Saib was then variously known as the Guru, Black Jesus, or Perfect Living Master. I'm not sure I had his full attention until I told him their sacred colour was a warm orange-red.

'The Guru always dresses in orange-red robes. He drives a big, flashy Mercedes, and even that's been re-sprayed orange-red.'

Will wanted to know whether I thought they had any real power.

'The group's got twenty-nine cult compounds – ashrams, really – all around Nigeria, in all the major cities. And there have been a lot of complaints about them. The Guru was accused of killing a Ghanaian in 1999. The man went into the Iju ashram to try to find his sister. Apparently she'd been virtually held captive there for years. He never came out. The Guru was arrested and even jailed for a while, but in the end he was acquitted. There had been accusations of torture and of people disappearing, none of which had been conclusively proved.

I knew Will was growing weary of these increasingly

bizarre complexities. He was going to Nigeria with Ray Fysh in a few weeks to focus on the kind of policing he preferred – collecting forensic evidence, gathering facts, interviewing potential informants.

Maybe they could all forget about cults and pagan sacrifices and red-clad gurus who played Father Christmas before allegedly butchering people for a pastime. I looked at the mask. The afternoon light had shifted and shadows fell across it at a new angle so that it leered at me. I could almost believe that it was watching me.

'Right, that's it,' I said.

I scribbled a note to the Pitt Rivers Museum in Oxford.

'I'm a professional academic,' I wrote. 'I'm not supposed to believe in curses and spells. But I can't have this artefact anywhere near me or those I love for a day longer. It's a genuine death mask, and I'd be grateful if you'd take it off my hands. If it's not suitable for your collection, please destroy it.'

I bundled the mask into a plastic bag and taped it up into a rough package, ostensibly to protect it but in fact so that I would not have to look at it again. I left the caravan at once, got in the Land Rover and drove through the dusty lanes to Okehampton. I bought a cardboard carton at the post office and shoved in the mask. 'Goodbye,' I said under my breath, as the silver-haired lady behind the counter dropped the package into the post sack. 'Rest in peace.'

She smiled nervously at me. I hadn't spoken quite as softly as I'd meant to.

25

London, September 2002

A full year after Adam's body had been found in the Thames, the Met organized a memorial service at the splendid new offices of the Greater London Authority near Southwark Bridge.

I'd learned over the last few months that they were not the hard-nosed cynics they were often thought to be, and many had developed a truly personal commitment to giving this child back his identity and finding his murderers. At the same time, they hoped the service would refocus the public's attention on the crime, and provide the opportunity to broadcast a fresh appeal for information.

Faith and I met John Azah of the Kingston Racial Equality Council at London Bridge station. John was an engaging Ghanaian with a huge moustache and a ready smile. We walked along the river, chatting about the case.

'You know, Richard,' John said, 'some of the police didn't like your sacrifice theory much.'

This wasn't news to me. I told him about the meeting at Royal Holloway.

'They don't necessarily think you're wrong. Andy Baker just wants to avoid the press running away with it.'

After the hammering the Met had taken over the

Stephen Lawrence killing, they seemed to be trying to treat Adam's death as a more conventional murder than it really was in order to minimize further controversy. I had some sympathy with that, but believed strongly that if they didn't face the truth, the result would be much more damaging.

I'd sent the list of likely ingredients through weeks ago but had heard nothing more. Not for the first time I wondered if they now secretly wished Adam's body had been flushed out to sea on the Thames tide.

The service was moving and simple. The room was just below ground level and seated around a hundred people. TV crews crammed the back of the auditorium.

There was a reading from the Bible and an address from Commander Baker and Will O'Reilly, followed by some words of reflection from a police chaplain. Afterwards the TV crews moved forward like vultures, circling the desk beneath the Metropolitan Police crest. Will O'Reilly made his appeal for new information, reminding everyone that there was a £50,000 reward.

A short while later, as traffic on the river fell silent and bemused tourists looked on, Will and John leaned over the side of a police launch and cast a wreath on the water.

We moved on to a bar, a light and airy place with a view over the Thames. Mark Ham, Nick Chalmers, Will O'Reilly and Barry Costello, the wary DC who had accompanied Will to our very first meeting in Bath, were there with Ray Fysh. With a conjuror's flourish, Mark produced a brown envelope and tipped a number of glossy photographs onto the table.

We all stared at the sequence of geometrical shapes and irregular patches of colour which bore testimony to the painstaking analysis of Ken Pye's team.

'Well, what it boils down to is that this stuff hasn't got any nutritional value at all. Nick Branch says it's bits of bone, and clay, and flecks of gold and things. It's not food. It's some sort of preparation.'

The clay apparently came from a river in West Africa. So the concoction, or its ingredients, had been brought into Britain and given to Adam right here, in London.

Will was not slow to grasp the implications. He called an urgent meeting.

26

Royal Holloway College and London, October 2002

This time there weren't so many of us. Ray Fysh, Will O'Reilly, Mark Ham and I sat around a big table, while Ken Pye stood at the front of the room, flashing images up on the screen and tracing the outlines of the shapes with a laser pointer.

'These are the clay pellets found in Adam's intestines,' Ken said. 'In my opinion the clay came from a riverbank, or a flood plain or lake margin, and its composition is consistent with a West African origin. The pellets are very high in minerals and metallic particles, especially quartz and gold, and that might eventually give us a more precise location, even a specific deposit.

'Among the other ingredients in this concoction are bits of ground-up bone. I can't tell you yet whether they are animal or human, but we've contacted the Office of the Chief Medical Examiner in New York. After the 9/11 attacks they gained a lot of expertise in analysing DNA from small pieces of bone. There's also some plant material, but it's too degraded for us to tell immediately what it is.'

'Just for the record, then,' Will said, 'this is a preparation of some sort? It's definitely not food?'

'Hardly. It would have been a pretty revolting mixture.

We have traces of carbon and they don't match the normal sources such as coal, charcoal or charcoal filters. They're almost certainly the result of the mixture being burned down in a pot, and that's backed up by traces of tin we've also found.'

All the reports I'd gathered suggested these potions were ground up together and then burned down in a pot over an open fire. They were then fed to the victim, typically between twenty-four and forty-eight hours before he or she was killed.

'A black, claggy, gritty mess,' Ken said. 'It would have tasted vile.'

'Poor kid,' Will muttered.

It had occurred to me that the cough medicine found in Adam's stomach might have been used as a linctus, to help him swallow the potion. I'd originally thought that he must simply have had a cough, and his killers wanted to cure that before the ceremony, in order to make a perfect offering to the god. I wasn't sure whether this made things better or worse.

Will asked if Ken could analyse the mixture any more precisely.

'It's not easy with the non-mineral content,' Ken said, 'despite Richard's pointers. This material is very degraded. It's possible we might be able to cross-reference with the samples you and Ray pick up in Nigeria next week.'

Will turned to me. 'What kind of stuff was on your list?'

I explained that different deities had different offerings, and that a tasty morsel for one might be anathema to another. With hundreds of deities on offer, we might have to sort through thousands of unique ingredients. To start the ball rolling I'd picked out the likeliest deities, and suggested

Ken should look for kola nuts, yams, palm fronds and various beans.

'What about animal material?' Ken asked. 'You didn't mention that.'

'I don't know how much of that could still be identifiable, but there could be bits of roosters – feathers or bones – or bulls' or horses' testicles. Then there might be bones from rams or dogs. Leopards, crocodiles, monkeys and various birds are also possibilities.'

Will made some notes. 'Ken's already identified bits of bone. Do you know anybody who could make a stab at identifying which animals they might have belonged to?'

I said that the Natural History Museum would be an obvious place to start, and that Faith probably had some contacts there.

Ray and Will asked me to stay behind for a few minutes after the meeting. They wanted some tips for their trip to Nigeria. I ran through a list of recommendations, which seemed second nature to me: they should take their own mosquito nets, drink only bottled water wherever possible, never neglect their anti-malarials. I threw in the occasional cautionary tale: the Englishwoman I had met on a riverboat on the Congo who told me that she did not need anti-malarial pills because she had natural immunity. The other passengers had buried her on the riverbank three days later. I didn't mean to be alarmist, or to play the old Africa hand. But I did want to get across to them just how different it was out there.

Mark Ham seemed to be hugely amused by Ray Fysh's lack of enthusiasm for the idea of bucketing around Nigeria in a four-wheel drive for nearly three weeks. 'If you go the same way,' he called, 'can I have your stereo?'

*

In the meantime, Nick Chalmers was continuing his own painstaking police work. Joyce Osagiede might be innocent, but he was still interested in her movements and her associates.

After searching the Scottish social services files, he came up with two addresses for Joyce before she moved to Glasgow. One was in south London, the other in the East End. Though she had supplied these details herself, Joyce later maintained that she had only ever lived at one of them. She had heard of the other, but never lived there.

Armed with a search warrant, Nick Chalmers and Mark Ham arrived at the south London house on a wet day in mid-October. It was a dingy brick Victorian place in a nondescript street. The occupant, a West African woman, struck them both as shifty and scared. They could get little sense out of her, so went inside and began to turn the place over.

They made some interesting finds.

Among them were a number of forged travel documents and tickets, and Nigerian and British passports. One was in the name of Omovbiye Joyce Airhiabere, giving her date of birth as 14 June 1971. The picture inside was of Joyce Osagiede. The others were in the names of various men and women, apparently West Africans, none of whom rang any immediate bells with the police, but whose activities and legal status would obviously need checking out.

Nick and Mark also found a video labelled 'Wedding of Joyce Airhiabere to Samuel Onojhighovie' and dated February 1997. When they played it at the station they weren't too surprised to see that Joyce and Sam had celebrated their wedding with the sacrifice of a live goat, whose blood was spattered over an altar in an offering to the gods.

Now that Samuel Onojhighovie's name was confirmed,

the detectives ran it through the Europol database, and came up trumps almost at once. Onojhighovie was a wanted man in Germany, where he lived under yet another alias, Ibrahim Kadade. The Bundespolizei had been after him for some time for a variety of serious offences, including forging travel and immigration documents, and for trafficking illegal migrants. He had jumped bail and been sentenced in his absence to seven years in jail. The Germans had information on Joyce, too. She was known to them as Bintu Kadade, had lived in Hamburg with her two daughters and drawn benefits there.

At the same time as the South London raid was under way, police visited Joyce's other previous address in the East End. They were able to establish that the occupant was a Kingsley Ojo, but the premises were empty when they arrived and Ojo never returned to it. There was nothing of interest to be found inside.

A few days later, just before ten o'clock on a grey London morning, I climbed up the steps of the Natural History Museum. I glanced impatiently at my watch. Mark was late and I was growing edgy. I particularly wanted this meeting to go well as it was the first day I'd be charging the police for my time.

I pulled out my mobile.

'I'm at the front entrance to the museum,' I said, 'and you aren't.'

'You're right about that,' he agreed. 'I'm a bit lost in here.'

'Describe where you are and I'll come and find you.'

'I'm standing next to a bloody great lizard. Does that help?'

I tracked Mark down in the dinosaur hall. Our bone specialist, a severe woman with brown hair and large glasses, eventually appeared in the foyer to collect us. She didn't look happy that we were late.

We followed her through an unremarkable door into a hidden world of corridors and tiny offices. Hers was a cupboard-like space on the second floor, piled with journals and tagged plastic bags of bone samples.

I explained the situation briefly. Mark, after his adventure with *Tyrannosaurus Rex*, was finding the whole situation more amusing than she did.

'The concoction we've been able to extract from Adam's intestine seems to be made up of bone residues and plant matter, plus some minerals,' I said. 'We wondered if you could help us work out from which animals the bones came.'

Mark was carrying a folder with hugely enlarged photographs of the various materials Ken Pye had found. He spread them on the desk in front of her.

She frowned. 'Is this all?'

'All?' I said. 'I'm not sure I understand.'

'We couldn't do anything with this,' she said. 'There are thousands of different animals! We wouldn't have a hope of working out which bones are present in a sample as degraded as this.'

Mark stopped grinning and put on his policeman voice. 'Doctor, we have forensics experts in the USA who've been working on the aftermath of the World Trade Center terrorist strike. They advise us that they might be able at least to differentiate between human and animal bones.'

She frowned again. 'Well, I suppose we could manage that much. But as to differentiating between one animal and another, that's going to be nigh on impossible.'

'Even if I suggested what sorts of animals you were most likely to find?' I said.

She shook her head. That could take months, and even then it wouldn't be conclusive. Mark and I exchanged glances. He picked up his photographs, we thanked her and shook hands all round, and within five minutes of entering her office we were standing in the corridor outside it.

'And just how much were you planning to charge Will for that?' Mark said out of the corner of his mouth.

He was joking, as usual, but my heart sank all the same. It hadn't been a smart idea to let DC Ham know that my meter was finally ticking. He would get hours of fun from my embarrassment.

The office door behind us opened again and our bone specialist reappeared.

'Dr Hoskins? I wouldn't want you to have had a wasted visit. I've just had a thought. You could go and see our mineralogy people while you're here. They might be able to help. No guarantees, of course, but if you like I'll call through and ask who would be free to see you.'

A few moments later we were following her down the narrow corridors and my faith in human nature was beginning to revive. I didn't hold out much hope that the museum's minerals specialists would be able to add a lot to what Ken Pye and his team had already discovered, but I was willing to try anything.

Our guide took us to a room below ground level in a dim corridor smelling of polish and chemical reagents. Benches were cluttered with computer terminals and microscopes and equipment I didn't recognize. In among all this stood two men in spectacles. Both clutched coffee mugs and beamed at us.

We handed them the photographs and, without further ado, the larger scientist slid the prints out of the envelope and pushed his glasses up onto his forehead so that he could focus on them from a range of three inches. The smaller man moved his own glasses onto the end of his nose and crowded in beside him.

'Good Lord . . .' They launched into an enthusiastic exchange while Mark and I sat back and listened.

'Well, that's mineral, all right. So's that. See the structure?'

'Not much of a shot, but it could be gold. Wouldn't you say?'

'And there's some quartz. We know someone who could track this down, maybe even to the actual mine it came from.'

'But that's not mineral. That dark mass: see? I'd bet any money that's not mineral. Plant material, I'd say.'

'It's pretty degraded. Must have been burned.'

I said, 'Yes, it was. We think it was burned in a—'

'If anyone would know, Hazel would.'

'You're right. It might be burned to a crisp, but Hazel would have it flowering in a window box by next spring.'

And so it went on for about forty minutes. Mark and I eventually emerged into the drizzle outside the museum, filled with new hope.

27

London, December 2002

In December the Home Office dropped a bombshell.

The immigration authorities had been alerted to Joyce Osagiede's case. They ruled that she had not followed correct asylum procedures and had lied about her country of origin. She would not be allowed to keep her children and she would be deported.

The police protested that they still had questions for Joyce, and that several lines of inquiry might still show that she or her associates had been involved in some way with Adam, but this fell on deaf ears. The Home Office decreed that unless she was charged immediately, she must be returned to Nigeria. There was no question of arresting her a second time. Apart from her immigration violations, there was no evidence that she had done anything wrong. Accordingly, she was picked up by immigration officers and placed in Northolt Detention Centre pending deportation.

Later that month, with as little publicity as possible and at taxpayers' expense, the Home Office hired a private executive jet to fly her back to Nigeria. The jet had last been used by a world famous footballer. Now Will, Nick and Joyce Osagiede, violator of immigration rules and possible associate of murder suspects, were the only passengers. The plane landed at Lagos and Joyce Osagiede was taken through Nigerian immigration.

And then she was set free.

I heard about this on the phone from Will O'Reilly. I was as incredulous as he was. After the discovery of the clothes in her flat, her link with Germany and what she had said about her involvement with a Yoruban cult, I couldn't believe anyone would have sent her back to Africa.

'There may be method in somebody's madness,' Will said loyally. 'If we'd kept sniffing around her it might have scared off some bigger game.'

I wasn't convinced. I suspected some stickler for the rules in the corridors of power had failed to see how important she might have been to the inquiry.

'You can't hold people without charge,' Will said. 'Not in the UK. And, besides, the order to send her back came right from the top, and I mean the top. It's unfortunate, but these things happen.'

Ironically, within days of her deportation, police inquiries into Joyce's life in Germany began to yield dramatic results.

German social services revealed that she had arrived in Germany via Italy in 1992 under her alias of Bintu Kadade, a year after her partner, Ibrahim Kadade. He was undoubtedly the man known to UK police as her husband Sam, who was still on the run. Joyce's two children, whom the Germans knew as Esther and Eseoghen, had been born in Germany in 1997 and 1999. Her first child, a son, was reported dead at birth in 1995. That matched the year Joyce had given the British team for Sam Onojhighovie's sacrifice of the boy. The two daughters had briefly attended a nursery near Hamburg in September 2001.

Will and Nick went to Germany to interview staff at the nursery. The girls had only been there for two weeks, but a local woman, Frau Dibbern, had fostered them for a short while. Frau Dibbern, her daughter and her husband all remembered something striking about the oldest girl when they had last seen her in August and September 2001.

The child had been wearing bright orange shorts.

A couple of weeks later there was another breakthrough in London. Police tracked down Kingsley Ojo, the mysterious figure whose name had been on the lease of one of the two addresses Joyce Osagiede had given Immigration. Ojo had evidently fled as soon as Joyce was apprehended, leaving the flat bare.

A resourceful and unscrupulous man, Ojo had adopted a new identity as Mousa Kamara and taken lodgings at Quested Court, Brett Road, in the East End of London. It was a respectable flat in a modestly prosperous street. He'd been lying low there since Joyce's arrest and eventual deportation.

On a wintry morning, Nick Chalmers, Mark Ham and some heavyweight uniformed officers arrived at Quested Court with a search warrant. Nick immediately suspected that the flat was empty. He signalled to the uniformed officers, who broke down the door and burst in. The stove was warm, unwashed plates were stacked in the sink, and the window in the back bedroom was open. It was clear that this time they hadn't missed their quarry by much.

Mark Ham noticed a pile of video cassettes beside a television. He held one up. Helpfully, the scrawled label read, 'Rituals'.

The rest of Kingsley Ojo's apartment was thoroughly

searched and various items carted back to headquarters at Catford. The haul included dozens of immigration and travel documents, including passports, some forged, some genuine; tickets; money and reference letters.

The 'Rituals' video, which I was invited to see within a few days of the raid, purported to show the beheading of a man as a sacrificial offering, apparently to propitiate a Yoruban deity. His severed head was offered up to speed the recovery of an elder from a serious illness. The video looked as if it had been made for sale as a cheap movie, using third-rate actors. On the other hand the acting may have been so bad because it wasn't acting at all. None of us was ever quite sure whether or not we were watching an actual beheading.

Two small packets of an unidentified sandy substance were also found. Nick sent them off to Ken Pye for analysis.

Kingsley Ojo was soon found and arrested. An imposing man of about forty, he was softly spoken, articulate and expensively dressed. He faced the police with brazen denial. He knew nothing about the documents found in his flat, or any murdered child, or any cults and rituals. He claimed that another person rented the bedroom out, and neither the videos nor the packets found there had anything to do with him. He had never heard of Joyce Osagiede, and could not explain why she had given his flat as her address. When Nick pointed out to him that he had Joyce's name and number stored in his phone, he was unfazed. He simply denied everything, and when faced with an incontrovertible fact, fell into a stony silence.

There were certain things Kingsley Ojo could not deny, among them that he was a Yoruban, originally from Benin City.

The police weighed their options. They could charge

Ojo straight away with relatively minor immigration offences and deport him. But, perhaps still smarting from Joyce's premature departure, both Commander Baker and Will O'Reilly had other ideas. So they released him with a caution and Kingsley Ojo walked free on to London's streets, presumably hardly able to believe his luck.

It took some time for Ken Pye and his team to analyse the great mass of material Will and the others had brought back from Nigeria.

When they had finished, they were able to check Adam's bone samples against the new data. Their work showed definitively that Adam had spent most of his short life in the suburbs of Benin City in the heart of Yorubaland.

So Joyce, Kingsley and Joyce's vanished husband Sam all came from Benin City. And so did Adam.

28

London, December 2002

I accepted an invitation to become visiting lecturer in African Religions at King's College London, though I knew I'd miss Devon and Bath. Meanwhile, since my name had been added to the National Crime Faculty database, new cases were coming in from all over the United Kingdom.

I developed my own set of yardsticks to filter out the ones I knew did not require my input, but would usually go and visit the officers concerned and collect as much information as possible. Sometimes this involved going to the crime scene itself. Needless to say, I always found this a distressing experience. I discovered that I could be most useful if I simply took the information necessary for my analysis, and no more. I knew that what I produced had to be independent, academic and objective, though for all the distance I tried to maintain, I found it excruciatingly hard to deal with anything involving children.

Our move to London coincided with further progress on the Adam case. Faith and I met up with the team at a bar in Fleet Street.

Andy Baker, smiling and expansive, called me over at once. 'You know we released Kingsley Ojo?'

I told him that I did, and that I'd been surprised by it,

especially now that Joyce was out of reach. He dismissed it, maintaining that they could find her again whenever they wanted to.

'Funny thing,' he said. 'Even though he obviously knows we're on to him, as soon as he was released he went straight back to his old haunts and habits. What do you make of that?'

I said that Ojo probably believed that he was protected from the police by *juju*. His release would have reinforced that.

They were putting Ojo under surveillance, and though it would take some time, Commander Baker was confident they were going to come up with something a good deal bigger than passport fraud.

I felt my spirits rise. Across the room I could see Faith sharing a drink with officers from the Marine Police Unit – the men who had retrieved Adam's body from the Thames. I made my way over to Ken Pye.

Ken doesn't often betray excitement, but that day he looked like a man on a mission. 'You know those packets of sandy stuff from Kingsley Ojo's bedroom? It's remarkably similar to the contents of Adam's intestine.' He touched my arm. 'I mean *remarkably* similar.'

He couldn't yet say for sure that it was all from the same batch, but the quartz grains might have come from the same river, and the only rivers that fitted the profile were in West Africa.

29

London and Nigeria, January–April 2003

Operation Maxim went into action early in the New Year.

Maxim was the codename for Scotland Yard's people-trafficking surveillance unit and they were giving Mr Ojo their full attention. They bugged his phones, his flat and his car. Teams of officers trailed him whenever he moved. When he travelled overseas he was watched or followed by British officers and their colleagues from other forces.

Maxim began to produce results almost at once, helped significantly by the fact that Kingsley Ojo continued to behave with remarkable indiscretion. It was as if he felt himself to be beyond the reach of the law. He spoke freely on the phone. He implicated associates and himself and visited their addresses in London and overseas. The surveillance was gradually widened to draw these new subjects into the net.

Meanwhile, Nick Chalmers had a breakthrough. He always carried photographs of Joyce's husband Sam Onojhighovie, and he showed one to a Nigerian who had been detained on unrelated charges. The man immediately recognized Sam and claimed that he lived in Dublin. Nick Chalmers contacted the Irish Garda, and within days they found a direct match in the immigration files with a man who had entered the Irish Republic in 2001.

Sam Onojhighovie had taken a new name and a new wife. She had arrived in Ireland illegally from Nigeria in 2001. She was pregnant on arrival and gave birth to a son in the autumn of that year in Cork. A loophole in Irish immigration law allowed Onojhighovie to join her there under his new false identity. The German authorities were going to be very interested to learn of his whereabouts: he would face seven years in a German jail if they could get their hands on him.

The British police were tempted to make arrests at this point, but decided to hold off and maintain the surveillance a while longer.

By the first months of 2003 we knew that Joyce Osagiede was connected with both Ojo and Onojhighovie, and that she should never have been repatriated. British police made a request to the Nigerian authorities to find her and re-arrest her, but despite Andy Baker's confidence, it didn't happen. In February a small British contingent went out to Benin City in an attempt to narrow down the search for Adam's relations. They also looked for Joyce, and they too failed to find her.

But then the police had a bit of luck. Commander Baker heard from the British High Commission in Lagos that a woman named Osagiede had made an appointment. She wanted news of her children, who were still in care in Scotland.

When Joyce turned up for her interview, Nigerian police officers acting on behalf of the Met arrested her and took her away for questioning. The two key Nigerian officers present were Dr Wilson Akiwu and Detective Superintendent David Kolo, who had accompanied Will and Ray on their Nigerian travels the previous October. Dr Akiwu was himself from Benin City, spoke the local language and understood local customs.

Joyce could not be charged. She had committed no known offence in Nigeria or in the UK, apart from breaking immigration regulations for which she had already been deported. But she made a statement to Akiwu and Kolo under caution.

Joyce admitted membership of the Guru Maharaj cult from 1994 to 2002, when she left because of 'too much evil'. She said the sect was widely involved in *juju* practices and black sorcery, and claimed to be too frightened to give more details. The movement had devotees in Germany and London, she asserted, and said she had played a role as an organizer for them. She confirmed that her husband, Sam, was a messiah in the cult and she repeated that he had been involved in the murder of children.

When asked specifically about Adam for the first time, Joyce said, 'I do not know anything about the murder of the child in London.' But she later asserted, 'I know the child was killed in Lewisham. I don't know where the head and limbs are. I think the boy was sacrificed because his parents had been brainwashed by Maharaj Ji's teachings.'

She confirmed that she had bought the orange-red shorts, which witnesses in Germany had seen her eldest daughter wearing. She couldn't explain where these shorts were now. First she said she had given them to a friend, then she said she had left them in her flat in Germany.

By chance her former landlord in Hamburg had been unable to rent the flat after Joyce's departure, and it was still exactly as it had been left when she had walked out. However, no orange-red shorts were found there when police searched it. When this was put to Joyce, she said that they must be in her place in Glasgow. But that flat had already been thoroughly searched by Mark Ham, Will and the team, and no orange-red shorts had been found there either. Joyce could not explain this. Nor did she know, she said, how identical shorts had turned up on Adam's mutilated body.

After the interview, and with the reluctant agreement of the Metropolitan Police, Joyce was released by the Nigerian authorities.

30
Dublin and London, June 2003

On a hot midsummer morning, just after dawn, armed officers of the Metropolitan Police and their Garda colleagues broke down the door of a flat in Dublin and arrested Sam Onojhighovie and the woman claiming to be his wife. Both were taken to Dublin's central police headquarters for questioning and their home was exhaustively searched.

Onojhighovie seemed astounded to have been hauled in, almost as if he too felt he was shielded by some higher power. He denied having anything to do with Kingsley Ojo, although the latter's contact details were found in his diary. He denied ever visiting London. He denied any knowledge of Adam's murder, or of cults or rituals, and even denied knowing Joyce herself, even though he was or had been married to her.

The German authorities, with the cooperation of the British police, began extradition proceedings.

Two weeks later, police launched a series of dawn raids on nine addresses across London, a considerable feat of co-ordination involving more than 200 officers. Twenty-one people were arrested on suspicion of people trafficking, immigration and passport offences; ten men and eleven women. Two more were pulled in the following day. Nineteen of them proved to have direct links with Benin City. The raided premises were all searched and hundreds of suspicious items and artefacts were bagged and removed.

Simultaneously, Kingsley Ojo was picked up by a joint force of Italian and British officers. Under constant surveillance, he had been followed to an under-age brothel in Brescia, which acted as a transit depot for juveniles he helped to smuggle into Europe. Some young people got no further than the brothel and worked there as sex slaves.

Ojo was flown back to London and taken to Shooters Hill police station, the new headquarters of the Met's southern area murder squad. He, like Onojhighovie, was thunderstruck to be re-arrested. He seemed to find it unthinkable that the police should be able to trace him and pull him in, even though he had made no attempt to hide his whereabouts.

Faith and I sat in front of the midday television news.

Will O'Reilly came out onto the steps of police HQ to face the cameras and field a barrage of questions.

'This is the trafficking side of the Adam investigation,' he said. 'We have uncovered what we believe is a criminal network involved in people trafficking, particularly from mainland Africa, through Europe to the UK.'

Shortly afterwards, Andy Baker also emerged. 'Children brought into the UK on false documents are often used to carry out elaborate benefit fraud,' he said. 'Many arrive at British airports travelling alone, and once here they are used as slave labour, or forced into the sex industry.'

Most of those arrested were small players and eventually deported after questioning. Several were charged and ultimately jailed for periods of between a few months and a few years for trafficking and passport offences. There was no doubt that the real prizes were Sam Onojhighovie, wanted for his previous offences in Germany, and Kingsley Ojo, whom police had already identified as the ringleader.

Two Nigerian girls freed by the police raids told horrific stories of how they had been initiated into a cult in Benin City in a chamber draped with bright red cloth, forced to drink a potion and bound to the cult by secret spells and rites. They were told that they would die if they ever broke the vow of secrecy to which they had been sworn. They had to obey whatever they were told which, it soon became clear, involved enforced under-age prostitution.

I got up and turned off the television. Moments later Will O'Reilly rang to ask if I could come over to Shooters Hill and take a look at the proceeds from the raids.

'We've got a shed load of weird and wonderful stuff we took from these addresses.' He paused before answering my unasked question. 'No missing body parts, I'm afraid.'

Shooters Hill police station was an altogether more impressive building than the old Catford HQ.

'Welcome to Aladdin's cave,' Will said. 'Have a look at all the voodoo gear we've got for you.'

He grinned. He knew I hated him calling it that.

We were in a large conference room with a long table at its centre, heaped with exhibits in plastic bags – dozens of them; perhaps even hundreds. Large bags, small bags, boxes and bottles. Will told me that no one had touched anything since the raids. They had been waiting for Ray and me.

'We know you get off on this kind of thing.'

It took us all morning to work through the mass of material. It was an unpleasant and disturbing collection:

powder and herbs, horseshoe nails wrapped in twine, bundles of plants, indeterminate pieces of dried organic matter, feathers, bones and a bottle of oil with a miniature cross floating in it. Probably the most striking object was the skull of a large rodent, probably an African cane rat, with a nail driven through it.

Most of it was obviously *juju* related, and I classified it as well as I could, setting aside samples to go to Ken Pye for analysis. By the time we had completed the task our hands were filthy and the room foetid. As we were finishing up, a call came through for Ray Fysh from the Horticultural Society at Kew.

Dr Hazel Wilkinson, the plant specialist who had been looking at Adam's intestinal contents, had found traces of *Physostigma*, the Calabar bean. I knew it by another name: the ordeal bean. In anything but very small quantities, it was deadly poisonous. The bean was found in Adam's intestine and not his stomach, which meant that he had digested it without it killing him. So he must have been given a very small amount, and some time before his death.

'How long would it take to digest?' I asked.

'Well, we reckoned the potion was swallowed between twenty-four and forty-eight hours before he was killed,' Ray said. 'But if this bean somehow speeded up digestion, it could have gone through in a matter of a few hours.'

I could see that we were beginning to think the same thing. We agreed that before we spoke to anyone about this – especially to the press – we ought to do some further research. I called Faith. By the time I got home that evening, she had already found out a good deal.

The bean was named after the Calabar region in West Africa where it grew, and had been used traditionally in cases of suspected witchcraft to distinguish the innocent from the guilty. It worked along the same lines as the old ducking stool. The victim was fed a concoction containing the bean, and if he or she vomited it up and lived, they were guilty. That was rare, however. Usually they died, which belatedly proved their innocence. Half a ripe bean would kill an adult, so whoever administered it could pretty well determine who was 'guilty' and who wasn't.

In small doses, though, the Calabar bean was known to paralyse the victim. It didn't just knock them out: they would know what was happening to them, but they wouldn't be able to scream or struggle. I didn't like to think about that.

One direct outcome of the Calabar bean discovery was that Andy Baker described Adam's death as a sacrifice for the first time on the television news that evening. It was, I suppose, a victory of sorts, but I didn't feel like celebrating. I got up and walked out onto our balcony. It was a warm summer night. A small child had breathed the same London air not so very long ago. He would probably have found it chilly, coming from where he did.

No one had yet proved exactly what had happened to Adam. But in my imagination, as I stood on that balcony, I reconstructed his journey from what I knew and what I could reasonably assume.

In my mind I found myself sitting with him in a stiflingly hot room in Benin City. What had they told him? That he was going to have a better life in Europe? Or had he been traded for the twenty-five dollars it costs to 'buy' a child in parts of Africa today? Perhaps they told him nothing at all, but drove him straight to the airport, leaving him to guess for himself how his life was about to change.

Almost certainly Adam would never have been on a

plane before. The flight would have seemed interminable, but I liked to think the stewardesses were kind to him, and that he dozed off before the night gave way to a creeping grey dawn. The plane landed in Germany, a country he had never heard of, on a chill morning.

Sometime later he was probably taken on a ferry in Hamburg. He would never have seen a boat of such size, like a floating city. It was exciting. And his carers really did seem to care, though he had begun to notice something odd about them. They whispered a lot when he was with them.

When the ferry arrived at its destination, two more strangers drove him away from the docks. Who were they, and why were they paying him so much attention? In a couple of hours they came to a huge city, and drove through endless streets to a house where he was told he would live for a while. After that they said he would have earned a special treat.

He was kept in a room in that house for two weeks. It troubled him that they did not want to let him go outside. They always kept the curtains closed and the doors locked. He wasn't sure about the food, either. Perhaps as a result of all the travel, but more likely because he was exposed to germs that were new to him, he'd developed a cough. It was keeping him awake at night, but his carers had brought him some good medicine.

Then one night they drove him to another house. They seemed less gentle than before. He was jammed between two people in the back of a car with blacked-out windows. This time they made the journey in complete silence. His carers kept looking nervously around them.

The next day he was given only water to drink. He grew very hungry, but nobody would listen to his pleas for food.

In the early evening there seemed to be a lot of noise outside the door of his room. The door opened, and for the first time he felt real terror. For there in front of him was a *babalawo*, a gaunt man, half-naked and smeared with white chalk. He came into the room carrying a pot with a small spoon sticking out of it, flanked by two men Adam had never seen before.

As the *babalawo* drew near, he muttered some incantations, took the spoon and gave Adam a black, paste-like mixture which made him retch. The two men stepped forward and grabbed his arms. One of them pushed his head back and forced a bottle of water to his mouth, to wash the black substance down his throat. The *babalawo* repeated the process twice more.

I leaned against the balcony rail in the darkness. What had that poor child been thinking when he arrived in this city? Could he sleep that night? And on his last night how quickly did the drug begin to work, making his limbs leaden, numbing his hands and feet? I couldn't dismiss his imagined face from my mind. I had no doubt that he had known something terrible was about to happen. The thought made me shudder.

I turned away from the view, went back into the flat and slid the door closed behind me. I poured a couple of drinks. I could feel Faith's eyes on me as I did so.

At least I'd been able to do something, I told myself fiercely. Soon, I hoped, there would be more arrests, extraditions, convictions. Adam would get justice and I would have played some part in getting it for him.

'Are you all right?' Faith asked.

I looked at her. Was I all right? Well, yes. Yes, perhaps I was all right. Because if Adam could be laid to rest, then so could my own ghosts. Couldn't they?

31

London and Dalkeith, July–September 2003

For a while it seemed that they could. Faith and I were married that summer.

After the ceremony we spent two blissful weeks in Europe, travelling to Perugia, Florence, Venice and Verona. In contrast to the time I had spent in the murky netherworld of the Adam case, the days now seemed full of sunshine and hope. On our return to Britain we sealed our good fortune by buying our first proper home, a flat with a view over the Thames near Putney Bridge.

I felt I had reinvented myself and turned my back on a grim past. For her part, Faith had finished the research for her Masters, and it seemed a good moment to cement the idea that we could work together in a formal capacity as a husband and wife team. Our skills seemed complementary, and Faith had overcome her earlier reservations. The work we'd done on the Adam case was becoming well-known in police circles. Just married, and full of confidence that we could make anything work if we tackled it together, we decided to give it a try.

I was unpacking, still very much in holiday mood, wearing shorts and a luridly coloured shirt. People had not yet discovered I was back in London and right now the only thing on my mind was finding my favourite CDs in the pile of boxes that blocked the hallway.

And then the phone rang.

The caller spoke with a Scottish accent, quiet and formal. He almost made me feel inappropriately dressed. The Scottish National Crime Faculty wanted to know if I would be willing to help on a high-profile case involving the murder of a child, which possibly had a religious aspect. If so, I would receive a call shortly from the senior investigating officer.

Detective Superintendent Craig Dobbie came on the line soon after. He wanted to talk about the brutal murder of a schoolgirl called Jodi Jones. It had taken place while we were away on honeymoon, and I had missed the headlines. Within a few days Faith and I were taking the Flying Scotsman to Edinburgh. It was glorious weather, holiday weather. We spent some of the time re-reading the case notes that Superintendent Dobbie had faxed us, which outlined the events with harsh brevity.

Jodi, a fourteen-year-old schoolgirl, had been murdered at around 5 p.m. on 30 June – just a couple of weeks earlier. Her body was found off a well-used woodland path known as Roan's Dyke, outside the Lowland Scottish town of Dalkeith. She had been mutilated. Some seventy cuts and slashes had been inflicted on her body. Murders involving frenzied attacks were not unknown to the police, but according to the forensic officer some of the cuts to Jodi's body had been made, with apparent precision, after she had died. Rumours of the extreme brutality of the crime had leaked to the press, but no precise details had been released.

I closed the file, sat back in my seat and tried to concentrate on the sunlit countryside slipping past the window.

We stayed at the Balmoral, a rather grand old hotel in the centre of Edinburgh, and that evening we dined in the hotel's dark, old-fashioned restaurant. We were to see the police at Dalkeith the next day. I wasn't sure what that meeting would bring, but we were both calm and resolute. We were going to play our part.

When the cab arrived the next morning we were ushered out by a uniformed doorman as if we were A-list celebrities rather than on our way to a murder inquiry.

'Have a good day, sir, madam,' the commissionaire smiled.

I felt a frisson of discomfort. Everything about us – our clothes, our Italian tan, and even our attitude, seemed out of kilter with reality. We drove out of the city and into the wooded countryside to the southeast. Faith hadn't spoken since we had got into the car and I felt sure she was having the same doubts as I was.

Dalkeith proved to be an unlovely town built of grey stone. The police station was a squat modern block set back from the main road. The sergeant at the desk was a hard-faced man in his forties who told us gruffly to wait and made us a truly vile cup of coffee. He kept looking from me to Faith. She was wearing a red jacket and bright red lipstick and seemed to set the room on fire.

I heard footsteps on the stairs and a moment later we were shaking hands with Detective Superintendent Craig Dobbie.

He was just as I had pictured him: capable, quiet, softly spoken and as solid as granite. One of the most senior police officers in Scotland, he had been assigned to the West Lothian force to take on the highest profile murder investigation in the country.

He sat us down at a large table in the incident room. A drowsy bluebottle buzzed against a window that looked out on lowland fields and farms. Rather to my surprise, Superintendent Dobbie suddenly stood up, asking if we would excuse him for a few minutes.

I glanced around at the walls – maps and charts, large arrows and photographs, and several whiteboards with names and numbers written on them in coloured felt-tip – as he conferred with a group of officers in the corridor. The knot of men kept looking over in our direction, while Dobbie spoke earnestly to them. I had the distinct impression he was trying to reassure them about the bearded academic and his attractive young wife.

Superintendent Dobbie returned to the table with several of his colleagues in tow. Within minutes the room was a hive of activity. Faith and I had taken seats at opposite ends of the table, and watched a large pile of material appear between us. Nearly everything was in clear plastic bags, and I glimpsed clothing, books and one or two items that looked stained, perhaps bloody.

Finally, Craig Dobbie set a large folder down in front of me and told us that he was going to leave us alone for a while. He delegated a Detective Sergeant Campbell to help if we needed anything, and pointed out a small collection of books and papers, which weren't sealed in evidence bags.

'They're Jodi's diaries and some personal papers. I'd like you to look at them as well. If you want to examine any of the items in the bags, Sergeant Campbell will call me over and we'll go through things for you.'

The photographs were extremely detailed large-format prints; shots of the area around Dalkeith, aerial views of the housing estate where Jodi had lived, and of Roan's Dyke, the footpath where she'd been found, and some neighbouring estates at the other end of the path. As I turned the pages we returned to ground level and moved down the track.

The body was sickeningly mutilated. Picture after picture showed wounds across the girl's face, her neck and breasts, her stomach, even her eyes. The case notes had not prepared me for the gross nature of the injuries and the depravity of the killer. I didn't trust myself to catch Faith's eye.

Superintendent Dobbie returned and placed his large, strong hands together on the table. 'Do you have children, Dr Hoskins?'

I told him I had a son and a daughter just a bit younger than Jodi had been.

'Then I'm afraid you'll find the diaries as distressing as the photographs.'

He explained that the prime suspect was Luke Mitchell, Jodi's boyfriend. He was fifteen years old. Forensic evidence linked him to the crime scene, but Luke had claimed to have found Jodi's body. He was not under arrest. The police didn't have sufficient evidence. But Luke did have some unusual interests.

For one thing, he had an obsession with Marilyn Manson, the American singer. Superintendent Dobbie felt this might be significant. An alert pathologist had noticed that Jodi's wounds were mainly inflicted post-mortem, in a pattern resembling the ritualized injuries inflicted on the victim of the Black Dahlia murder in 1940s Los Angeles and which Faith immediately recognized. She had come across the case during her psychology studies. Elizabeth Short, a Hollywood B-movie actress, had been found dead, her body mutilated. The killer was never found. Marilyn Manson was apparently fascinated by it.

I made a few meaningless notes and tried to clear my head. I knew Superintendent Dobbie was observing me. He could see how affected I was, and he probably thought I was thinking of my children. That was true, in a way. If Abigail had lived, she would have been within a few months of Jodi's age. I felt confused and inadequate. I couldn't see why this quiet Scottish policeman needed me: he appeared to have already made the obvious connections. He soon supplied the answer.

'I don't just want to solve this crime, Dr Hoskins,' he said. 'I want to know what gets inside the minds of people and makes them do this. I want to know what tips them over the edge. I'd like you to help me understand that. Because if we don't understand it, I don't see how we can ever work to prevent it.'

Later that day we visited Roan's Dyke. There was little now under the birch trees to mark the atrocity that had been perpetrated here – striped police tape, some trampled undergrowth, coloured marker pegs stuck in the leaf mould.

Faith and I returned to our hotel in silence. I lugged my briefcase across the lobby, laden with photos, notes and reports, some of them copies, others originals that I had to guard with my life.

I dumped the bag on the bed and slumped into an armchair. Faith sat opposite me. I flicked on the television. Sky News was on and the screen filled with the face of Luke Mitchell.

Faith and I were transfixed. The boy was cool, articulate, intelligent. He accused the police of harassment and calmly protested his innocence to the interviewer over and over again. He insisted he knew nothing about Jodi's murder. He spoke with what sounded like complete candour, directly into the camera. He was fair-haired, good-looking, clear-eyed. He looked like an angel.

Faith got up abruptly, walked into the bathroom and shut the door. After a moment I heard the shower. I looked at the closed door for a second then turned off the television. I opened my case, removed several of the photos from the folder and laid them out on the bed.

I stared at them for some time, totally absorbed and utterly repelled. At length I became aware of Faith standing beside me.

'What were we thinking of?' she said. 'That we could build a glittering career together based on obscenities like this?'

'I'm sorry.' I shuffled the photographs together and locked them in my case. 'This was all a mistake.'

'Did you see the way those policemen looked at me? You could hear them asking, What's *she* doing here, that wee blonde girl with her shiny lipstick? What could *she* know about all this? And they were right. This is way out of my league, out of any league I want to be in. How could anyone stand it, dealing with this kind of material, day after day? How could anybody mix in this world and not be contaminated by it? Do you think you can?'

We didn't talk much more after that. We checked out, took a cab to the station and got on the first train back to London. The train was packed. The trip back was a nightmare. The weather had held and it somehow made it worse to see the fields and hills slipping brightly past. We couldn't look at one another. We seemed unable even to offer each other comfort.

*

Back in London, I locked myself away for a couple of days with Superintendent Dobbie's material. I spent a lot of time with my books and on the internet. I wanted to give us some time to recover. And I wanted to get this case off our hands.

It didn't take long to confirm the Black Dahlia hypothesis. The cuts to Jodi's body, especially the ones made post-mortem, echoed those inflicted on Elizabeth Short sixty years ago. And there was also a clear link with cult singer Marilyn Manson, who, as Dobbie had pointed out, was fascinated by the Elizabeth Short killing. The promotional video for his song 'mOBSCENE' featured dancers dressed in 1940s gear with their faces made up so that they appeared to have wounds similar to Elizabeth Short's. In the summer of 2003, the time of Jodie's death, the song was in the charts. It was hard to avoid the notion that Jodi's killer had been influenced by it.

But even if Mitchell was obsessed by the Black Dahlia, there were no indications that this was a religious crime. I had hoped there would be: it might have helped explain Jodi Jones's dreadful death and the equally dreadful things that had happened to her afterwards. As it was, I was left wondering what Superintendent Dobbie expected from me.

But then, sitting in my study one dull afternoon, thinking bleakly over the case for the hundredth time, I remembered his words to me as we sat around that table in Dalkeith police station. He didn't just want to solve this crime: he wanted to understand it.

He was not alone. How could anyone in our society do such things? What had happened to Adam had been horrible enough, but at least we could tell ourselves it was performed by people of an alien culture and beliefs, people who were profoundly *not like us*. Jodi Jones and

Luke Mitchell, though, were disturbingly like the kids next door. They were rebellious and confused, perhaps, but no more than many other adolescents struggling to come to terms with a bewildering world and their own sexuality.

I realized that this admirable Scottish policeman, who must have seen most of life's horrors in his time, had been deeply shocked by this case. Superintendent Dobbie gave me the impression of a man fighting a doomed rearguard action against a new and incoherent world that threatened to engulf him and all he stood for.

I talked to him on the phone several times over the next few days and weeks. I was painfully aware that I wasn't giving him the answers he sought, but he was too courteous to say so, and instead he listened to all my observations with calm dignity.

Not long afterwards, Luke Mitchell was arrested and once again questioned by the police. New searches revealed that the boy's alibi was false. His mother had lied for him. Neighbours reported that he had been seen burning various items in his backyard early on the evening of the killing. One by one, doors were slamming on Luke.

32
London, October 2003–January 2004

The Jodi Jones case affected me profoundly and I began to think about turning away from this wrenching line of work altogether. I could have stepped back into the sheltered life of an academic – Faith would probably have preferred it if I had – but the abuse of children had become a high-profile media issue by this stage, especially when religion or ritual was involved. There were frequent television reports and articles in the newspapers and I was often asked to contribute, making backing away more and more difficult. Besides, I didn't feel that I could be free of all this until the Adam case had been resolved. And that seemed to be taking longer than anyone had anticipated.

After the arrests of the previous summer everyone had expected more action to track down Adam's killers, but there was little sign of it. Every time I called Nick Chalmers for news he was as confident as ever, but had little new information to share with me. Sam Onojhighovie's lawyers were fighting his extradition to Germany tooth and nail, and there was every chance they'd be able to delay it indefinitely. In London there was talk of further surveillance operations with the promise of new arrests. But nothing seemed to happen. The only big fish to be reeled in so far –

Kingsley Ojo the arch people-trafficker – remained in custody awaiting trial.

As the closing months of 2003 dragged by I grew steadily more frustrated, and Faith told me that she had been offered the chance to do a PhD at the University of Exeter. I knew this set the seal on her retreat from the work we had once approached together with such confidence.

The story of the eight-year-old later known as Child B started on a bleak day in late November.

A community warden, Kwame Agbo, who was patrolling with a colleague, spotted a child huddled alone on the steps of an apartment block in Hackney, east London. She was shivering in the cold, bruised and sobbing. She was softly spoken and clearly intelligent, but seemed to be unable to say why she was sitting alone out in the winter drizzle. Kwame Agbo did not press her for answers. Instead, he wrapped his coat around her and sent his colleague to a local café.

As he chatted to her, he noticed that her eyes were inflamed, blood-red and oozing. Mr Agbo's colleague came back with a cup of hot chocolate and the child drank it gratefully, almost greedily. It was, Kwame Agbo was to recall later, as if nobody had shown her any kindness for a very long time.

When the girl had finished her drink, the two wardens led her to the nearby school, where she should have been in classes for the day. Over the next few hours the head teacher called in social workers and doctors to examine her. Finally the police were called. Child B had been subjected to horrific injuries. Forty-three separate wounds were found on her emaciated body.

*

I was at my desk in King's College on the Friday afternoon when my mobile rang. Detective Constable Jason Morgan introduced himself as the Child Protection Officer on the North London Child Abuse Committee. He wanted to meet.

'I'm afraid I'm rather tied up at the moment,' I said. 'I've a lecture to give in a few minutes, and after that I'm going away for the weekend.'

'Anywhere nice?'

'The West Country.'

'Driving?'

'No. Getting the four thirty-three from Paddington. That's why I'm in a hurry.'

'No problem. I can meet you for ten minutes in the British Transport Police office there.' He waited, and when I continued to hesitate he said, 'Dr Hoskins, I've heard about your work. This case has got your name all over it.'

The British Transport Police's office at Paddington was just this side of squalid, with a lot of frosted glass, scarred pine tables and a permanent fog of cigarette smoke.

DC Morgan told me about Child B, a girl of eight who lived with her aunt and mother, apparently, and one other child. The family were Congolese. There was no father on the scene, but the aunt's half-brother was a pretty constant presence. He slid a photograph of a pretty child with huge eyes across the table. She had been cut with a knife, beaten, starved, tied up in a garbage sack, threatened with drowning in the local river and with being thrown out of the window of the family's high-rise apartment. Someone had also rubbed chilli peppers in her eyes.

Now I was sure where this was going.

'Is this something to do with *kindoki*?' I asked.

'I'd never heard the word before,' DC Morgan said, 'and I thought I'd heard of most things. The girl says it's her aunt and her mother, mostly, who did this to her. They're born again, or something. Christians, anyway. They were trying to drive out this *kindoki*, the girl says. That's like witchcraft, isn't it? Like casting out devils? Is that the sort of thing they believe, these people?'

I didn't answer at once. I was familiar enough with *kindoki* from my days in the Congo and I knew it was just as widespread a concept in other African countries. But to my knowledge there had never been anything sinister about it. It was seen as an affliction, often a passing one. It was a catch-all phrase that covered a multitude of minor ills, rather like saying one had the blues. A bout of depression or simple low spirits might qualify as *kindoki*, or some low-grade physical illness. It was usually quickly dealt with by a traditional healer who would offer a sympathetic ear and then prescribe herbal medicines. To describe it as witchcraft, as many Westerners did, was technically correct, but conjured up images of voodoo dolls and curses. In my experience *kindoki* was nothing like as dramatic.

Recently, though, through my contacts in the London Congolese community I had begun to hear whispers of exorcisms organized by revivalist churches for children affected by *kindoki*. It was more usually called 'deliverance' in African circles, but they were talking about exorcism all right. I hadn't really credited these stories with much weight. Exorcism is not that outlandish a prospect in itself: most Western churches believe in the casting out of demons in exceptional circumstances. But I couldn't work out how the church had come to see *kindoki* as the work of the Devil.

In the African world view, virtually everyone suffered from *kindoki* from time to time. To talk about having it exorcized was a bit like having radiotherapy to treat a cold – it wasn't necessary, it wouldn't work and the treatment would be far worse than the disease.

All the same, I wasn't about to scoff at such a notion. I didn't like the reference to witchcraft, however mistaken it might be. Like everyone else I knew about Victoria Climbié. Victoria, an eight-year-old from the Ivory Coast, had died in London in February 2000 after the most appalling mistreatment by her family and carers. She had been beaten, burned with cigarettes and forced to sleep in a bin liner in an empty bath. When she had finally been taken to hospital it was too late to save her life; 128 separate scars were found on her body, all of them believed to be deliberately inflicted. In 2001 her great-aunt, Marie Therese Kouao, and Kouao's boyfriend Carl Manning, were convicted of murder and sentenced to life imprisonment.

I had not been involved in that case, but I knew that her torturers had claimed to be trying to drive out demons from the little girl. They believed – or said they believed – that she was possessed, and that she was a witch. And it may have been pure coincidence, but they were also members of a new revivalist church. So it could happen, and it could happen to children in London.

Was it happening again? Was Victoria Climbié's awful death part of some unspeakable new trend?

DC Morgan hefted a bulky document case onto the table. I didn't want to touch it, but a few minutes later, as Paddington station slipped away behind us, the case lay on the seat beside me.

*

After our weekend away I took the case to my study and shoved it under the desk. It caught my eye accusingly every time I walked in and after a while I put it away in a cupboard. I even locked the door on it. I was afraid to look inside. I put off opening that document case for weeks.

I didn't call Jason Morgan, so he finally called me. I bluffed. He asked me to ring him back. I didn't. He rang again: I recognized the number and ignored the call.

Faith saw the effect this was having on me. She was on her way out of the apartment one morning in January of 2004 when she turned back to face me.

'I don't want you holding back on my account,' she said. 'You know you won't rest until you've tackled this.'

Without waiting for an answer, she walked away down the corridor.

I went straight into the study, hauled the case onto the desk and opened it. Four hours later I was still reading.

Child B had lived in Hackney with her mother, who could not be named for legal reasons, and with the woman whom she had known as her aunt, Sita Kisanga. Kisanga's half-brother, Sebastian Pinto, also stayed in the tiny apartment, as well as Kisanga's young son. All of the adults were asylum seekers, the two women were Congolese nationals and Pinto was apparently Angolan.

When found, the girl had bruises all over her and the scars of several knife cuts; she was also severely malnourished. As DC Morgan had told me at our first meeting, someone had rubbed chilli peppers in her eyes, causing the most acute agony. She told a story, echoing that of Victoria Climbié, of being left to sleep in the bath, cold, terrified and alone. She had then been bundled into a sack, which was zipped up, and her mother and aunt had discussed throwing her off the third-floor balcony, after which she was to be drowned in the nearby canal.

The adults, while all quick to blame one another for abusing the girl, were quite clear about why Child B had been so cruelly treated. She was infected with *kindoki*. They knew this because one night Kisanga's son had been visited by Child B in a dream and she had threatened to fly back to the Congo with him.

Sita Kisanga was a member of a fundamentalist Christian church known as Combat Spirituel. Founded in Kinshasa, it now had a branch in Hackney and was enthusiastically patronized by members of the Congolese community. Notes made in Kisanga's Bible confirmed that she was a worshipper there. In her early statements she suggested that she had gone to her church for guidance about Child B's *kindoki*.

The police interviewed Pastor Raph, who headed up Combat Spirituel's operations in London. He didn't know Sita Kisanga, he said, or any of the others. Perhaps they had attended his services: he had a large congregation and could not be expected to know everyone, but Sita Kisanga was not personally known to him. Pastor Raph told police that she was certainly not a prominent member of the church community, as she had at first claimed. In any case, he said, Combat Spirituel would never have condoned frightening a child in the name of deliverance, far less hurting her.

It seemed clear that the two women and Pinto were clutching at any straw to defend themselves against the charges.

Two days later I took the tube to Seven Sisters, an area I knew well as I'd been a Spurs fan for years.

Jason Morgan led me up to a small meeting room at Tottenham police station and introduced me to Detective Inspector Brian Mather. The two made an intriguing contrast – DC Morgan portly and casual, DCI Mather tall, lean and immaculately turned out. I was to learn that Jason Morgan was a master at interviewing children, able to put them at their ease with his gentle, affable style, while Brian Mather was the hard-edged investigator of the partnership.

'The fact is, Richard,' Jason began, 'we don't know anything about this sort of stuff. To us, abuse is just abuse.'

'To me too,' I said.

'I'm relieved to hear you say that,' Brian Mather said. He'd evidently expected a different answer, perhaps something more culturally correct. 'But just the same, we need to understand what drove them to do this sort of thing to a young girl.'

I had been here before. I remembered Will O'Reilly grappling with the concept of sacrifice, and Craig Dobbie asking me to help him understand how anyone could do what Luke Mitchell had done to Jodi Jones.

'Would they do this sort of thing where they come from?' Brian went on. 'Would they consider it . . . normal? In Africa?'

I tried to explain that there was nothing African about this crime, that Africans love their children and generally take a great deal better care of them than we do of ours. Nor was there anything particularly weird about *kindoki*. It was a great mistake, I said, to believe that because people held unfamiliar beliefs they were somehow predisposed towards child abuse, or any other crime. What we were seeing was the perversion of a belief system that was otherwise benign: it was the perversion we should be looking at, not the belief.

Furnished with a handful of addresses, I left the police station and began walking the streets of north-east London. I wanted to get the atmosphere of the place, to catch a flavour of what life must have been like in this alien and often hostile city for these Congolese migrants. I wondered if it might give me a sense of what had gone so badly wrong here.

I visited the Woodberry Down estate in Hackney where Child B had been found. It was a dismal place, bleak tower blocks with washing on balconies and litter blowing in the courtyards. After that I took the train to Dalton Kingsland station, crossed the A10 and walked through Hackney's Ridley Road market.

In contrast to the rain-swept streets and concrete overpasses, the market was a mass of vibrant colour, thronged with shouting people. The place reminded me strongly of markets in Kinshasa, except that every possible ethnic group seemed to be represented here: Indian and Pakistani traders selling clothes, Thai and Chinese food stalls, a Caribbean steel band, tables of West African produce. I wondered if Sita Kisanga and the others had come here for their shopping, searching out the okra and pawpaw that reminded them of home.

Certainly they'd have passed through on the way to their church, for according to the police, Combat Spirituel's Hackney branch had been situated just across the road, though it had since moved. I went looking for the building.

I found the address quite easily, but there was nothing to indicate that it had been a church. It was a shabby three-storey block in a run-down commercial street just off the main road, and it looked like a cross between a warehouse and a multi-storey car park. A 'To Let' sign with an estate agent's number was fixed to the wall above the double doors.

I took out my mobile and called the estate agent's number. I was interested in commercial property in the area, I told the woman who answered. I was outside the address right now, if she could get someone down here quickly and let me have a look at the place.

With the speed of an emergency call-out an Asian youth screamed up in a silver BMW, parked on double yellow lines and hurried across the pavement. The place appeared not to have attracted many prospective tenants.

'I just want half an hour in the place on my own to get a feel for it,' I told him brusquely. Feeling bad about the subterfuge I slipped him a ten pound note. 'That way we won't waste one another's time. All right?'

He backed off at once, unlocked the doors and was gone. I was faintly surprised that he was prepared to let me have the run of the place, but perhaps he knew there was nothing worth stealing there.

A strong smell of urine and mould hung on the chill air inside. Tattered posters sagged from the wall. Plastic cups and plates lay scattered on the floor. I climbed the concrete stairs.

The whole of the second floor was an open area the size of a bus garage. The blue carpet was faded and stained. A wooden dais faced the door, with more squares of carpet scattered on and around it. On the walls were religious posters, many in Lingala and some in French. One read *Je Suis Conquerant!* Sheets of A4 paper with the Combat Spirituel letterhead were taped to the walls. It looked to me as if the church had decamped in a hurry.

I spent some time there, growing steadily more depressed. I wandered through to a kitchen area at the rear.

A dripping tap, a split sack of rubbish, the smell of damp. More A4 Combat Spirituel letterhead on the walls. I stopped in front of a roster of some kind, perhaps for kitchen duties. Towards the bottom of the typed list a name caught my eye: Mama Sita.

33
London, February 2004

One of my first tasks after I got back home was to translate the Lingala notes made by Sita Kisanga in her Bible. Most of them referred to sermons she claimed to have heard preached by Pastor Raph. The two detectives wanted to know if the notes would help them build an unassailable case against Child B's torturers.

At first I seemed to make little progress. I'd renewed my contacts in the Congolese community, but this had yet to bear much fruit. My enquiries focused on the revivalist churches. I knew from my experience of the Kimbanguists and other neo-Christian movements in the Congo that their influence could be profound. Combat Spirituel was no doubt a thoroughly responsible church, but I needed to make sense of the fact that Sita Kisanga had a connection with the revivalist movement, and yet had been evasive about just what that connection was. I wondered if she had been given advice on exorcism by someone purporting to speak in the name of Christianity. But material on revivalist churches in London was proving remarkably hard to find.

Before I could make much progress, events overtook me once more. Sarah Beskine, a partner in a legal firm with close links to local government, wondered if I could help her with an 'odd request' she had received a day or two earlier from the social services department of a London council.

Among the children in their care was Andrew, a twelve-year-old boy from a Congolese family. Apparently he had been causing problems at home. He was bright, but aggressive and disruptive at school, and he'd been involved in a lot of truancy and some petty crime. There were signs that he'd been assaulted, and his family said he was possessed by demons.

She explained that Andrew's family were devout Christians and wanted to send him back to Kinshasa to be exorcized – at the council's expense. Apparently such an exorcism was beyond the power of their local church in London, and they believed that only in Kinshasa would the boy get the proper treatment for his *kindoki*. Indeed, they had already been in touch with a pastor there.

The council was asking Sarah if this was appropriate from a legal point of view. She found this as staggering as I did. 'Send a child to Kinshasa, against his will, for some religious ritual? I don't think *legal* comes into it. It can't be right, can it?'

We met in Hopkin Murray Beskine's elegant offices not far from King's College. Sarah was a smart woman in her thirties with cropped blonde hair. We talked for a while, and she repeated her concern that a child might be sent to a place as lawless as Kinshasa for an exorcism, and at British taxpayers' expense.

I could see she was afraid that Andrew might be removed from care and sent to Kinshasa simply because no one in authority had the courage to stand up and dismiss the decision as ludicrous. Local government would be extremely wary about offending the family's cultural sensitivities.

Our worry was that they might put these concerns above the welfare of a child.

Sarah Beskine arranged for me to visit Andrew in the secure psychiatric unit. He clearly had psychological problems, but I found him articulate, intelligent and open. He had lived in London for some years; he thought of himself as a London child. The idea of being flown to Kinshasa terrified him.

'I don't even know what *kindoki* is,' he protested. 'I've never even heard of it. I don't know what they're all talking about.'

Andrew was scared and confused, and with good reason. Where his relatives saw a boy witch, I saw a child with no one to turn to. And a London council with responsibility for his care was considering sending him into the unknown out of a twisted adherence to the principle of political correctness.

Two weeks later, Sarah and I met members of the council in their shabby Fifties office block. Several of the social services team were black, and more than one of them was openly suspicious of a white academic and a white lawyer presuming to give advice on 'black' issues. These people worked at the rough end of life on the streets of London, and they'd had enough of white middle-class liberals who knew what was best for black communities.

But beneath the prickliness they too were concerned for the boy, and they were all painfully aware that they had very little idea of what awaited him in Kinshasa. I said that I'd been thinking about going to Kinshasa for some academic research on the Kimbanguists, and would be prepared to look into the exorcism issue for them while I was there, if the council would contribute something to the cost of the trip. Maybe I could visit members of Andrew's extended family who still lived in Kinshasa, and the pastor who they had in mind to perform the exorcism, and report back on what I found.

They agreed at once.

34

Kinshasa, February 2004

Within a few hours of leaving King's College I was flying over the Sahara, and the following morning, somewhat bleary-eyed, I was walking through the glass doors of the Grand Hotel in Kinshasa, which had long since ceased to live up to its name.

It was violently hot. There was an air conditioning unit on the wall, but it didn't work. Neither did the electric sockets, and nor did the toilet.

Outside, Kinshasa sweltered, cars and trucks bucking over the potholed streets, horns blaring, market traders shouting. I had bought cigarettes at Heathrow, even though I'd given up smoking years ago. I lit one now. I lay back on the sagging mattress, watching the smoke curl up towards the ceiling. I was probably imagining it, but as I drifted between sleep and wakefulness I thought I could hear the thunder of the rapids on the River Congo as I'd heard them on my first day in Kinshasa, so many years before. Now, as then, I wondered what I was doing here.

Things looked a little better in the afternoon. Fortified by a few hours' sleep, I went out into the blast furnace of the forecourt and was immediately surrounded by clamouring drivers, beggars and street women, all tugging at my sleeve and clutching for my backpack. All this felt reassuringly familiar. It was the Kinshasa I remembered.

I selected a driver with a Peugeot 404 that seemed slightly less dilapidated than the rest. His name was Jean-Pierre – he called himself JP – and after a token negotiation I hired him for the next few days.

Delighted, JP made a great show of ushering me into his cab, displaying me like a trophy to his less fortunate fellow drivers. I went along with it. I've always loved the African sense of theatre, and it was good to hear Lingala and French spoken again, and to speak them myself. I gave JP directions to the pastor's compound in the Kasa-Vubu district.

As soon as we pulled away from the hotel I realized that this was not the city I had known fifteen years earlier. It was not even the city I had visited with Faith two years ago. I'd been outraged then by the lost children on the streets, begging and offering themselves for a pittance. Now the situation seemed ten times worse. The city itself had slid into crushing poverty – broken pavements, derelict buildings colonized by squatters, shuttered shops, stalls with only a few pathetic items of merchandise, and over it all a stifling pall of pollution. It was like the set of an apocalyptic movie, with desperate people forced to live like scavenging animals amid the ruins.

The occasional knots of desperate youngsters I had seen when I was here last, had given way to scores, hundreds even, some as young as four or five, begging in ragged gangs, or sorting through the hillocks of garbage piled in side alleys and on vacant lots. Others hung around on street corners, eyeing the cars and their occupants with hard and knowing eyes.

I needed some bottled water and pointed JP to a nearby stall.

'Don't get out, M'sieur Richard,' he said, stopping the car. 'Give me the money; I'll fetch the water. You stay here.'

Except during the riots in the 1990s I'd never been worried about walking the streets of Kinshasa, at least not in broad daylight, but I did as he advised. He locked the car and went over to the stall. The taxi grew oven-hot and sweat ran down my neck. Curious faces peered in at mine. Pleading beggar children tapped on the window. I turned away to avoid their eyes.

On the far side of the street, in the gutter, lay the body of a child. The afternoon crowds stepped over and around it as if it were a bundle of old clothing. No one registered the remotest surprise.

JP reappeared with the water. He saw me staring at the tiny corpse.

'*Chegué*,' he said with distaste.

The Lingala word meant urchin, but without the hint of charm. Rabble. Scum.

I had some trouble taking this in. The Africa I knew didn't abandon its children wholesale, not even in its sprawling cities. That Africa did not look down on the dispossessed and homeless with contempt. It did not let children die on the pavement, and leave their bodies in the gutter to rot. It maintained its poor and defenceless, somehow, through networks of extended family and friends. What had happened to change that?

I found my contacts book and thumbed through it, then read out another address to JP.

'Take me to this place.'

'We don't go to Kasa-Vubu, M'sieur Richard?'

'Later. Take me to this place, please.'

*

I'd heard of Remy Mafu from a friend in the United Nations High Commission for Refugees. He was something of a legend, a Congolese married to a French woman. He could have emigrated to France, but instead stayed on in Kinshasa to toil tirelessly for the street children, giving shelter where he could, lobbying such government as existed in Kinshasa, begging funds from foreign agencies.

We found ourselves opposite the stadium where, in 1974, Muhammad Ali had fought George Foreman in the Rumble in the Jungle. The grandiose new stadium nearby had been built in the 1990s, as a monument to Mobutu's ego, and, if the rumours were to be believed, upon foundations that provided the last resting place of many of his opponents. The new stadium was used on Sundays by revivalist churches for noisy prayer meetings. Around it, the whole area was semi-derelict – a sinister inner-city wasteland of cement blocks and wrecked cars, with a scattering of huts and hovels.

Remy Mafu's compound stood beside a huge stack of rusting pipes. Gaping holes served as doors, window frames hung loose, half the roof was missing and the walls had never been painted. But the floors were swept, and men and women clattered busily at old manual typewriters in what passed for offices. Boxes of dried milk, food parcels and clothing were stacked in odd spaces. There were children everywhere – perhaps fifty of them – sitting listlessly in the shade, taking lessons in a roofless courtyard, playing football in the dust.

Remy Mafu was working at an old desk in a back room. A solidly built man of about forty-five with a deeply furrowed face and thick-rimmed glasses, he looked as though he'd been carved from ebony. He listened while I told him why I was in Kinshasa, then led me to a conference room of sorts, furnished with a table and half-a-dozen mismatching chairs.

'You have seen the situation in Kinshasa with your own eyes,' he said gravely, speaking in French. 'You can make your own judgment about whether this boy Andrew should be sent back here.'

I looked out through the rough window at the ragged children playing in the dust. 'How many of these kids are out there on the streets?'

'Fifty thousand, by the Social Affairs Ministry's estimate, so the true figure is probably much higher.'

I goggled at him. 'Fifty *thousand*?'

'At the very least. A lot of them are AIDs orphans. Then, of course, four million people have died in the civil war since the late 1990s. That means a lot of children without parents.'

I knew this figure, but it never ceased to shock me. Four million dead in a war most people in the West had never heard of.

'All the same,' I said, 'it never used to be like this. The war's been going on for years, and AIDS has been here for years, too, but it was never this bad.'

He took off his thick glasses and polished them. Without them he looked older and wearier. I wondered how long he could go on with this sort of work before the awful weight of what he saw every day finally crushed him.

'You know the Congo, Richard. You speak the language. You have lived here for many years. You know that the family holds society together against all trials and hardships. Only family. It is the cement which binds us.'

'And that's breaking down? Why now?'

He eyed me steadily. 'You said you were going to visit

a church pastor. Perhaps you should put your question to him.'

'I don't follow, Remy. Do you mean the church is involved?'

'Not every church. The new revivalist churches. If there are fifty thousand children running wild on the streets, at least another fifty thousand are held in church compounds throughout the city.'

I frowned. 'They're prisoners?'

'Effectively. Parents in Kinshasa cannot afford to keep their own children, not with so many orphans. Many go onto the streets. But many more are taken into the church compounds. Some pastors try to help them. Others are dishonest. They hold the children to ransom, forcing their parents to pay for their keep, and pay more to get them out. Most cannot afford to, so the children stay there and the parents go on paying. Some pastors spread this idea of *kindoki*.'

'But *kindoki* isn't that serious, is it?'

'That is not what the new churches preach. The pastors claim it is witchcraft, the work of the devil. They say that only they can help children infected with *kindoki*, and refuse to set them free until they have been exorcized. All the while the parents must pay and pay.' Remy sighed. 'Richard, many of these pastors may really believe this witchcraft nonsense. But whether they believe it or not, the effect is the same. Thousands and thousands of children are held awaiting exorcism.'

I thought of Andrew, waiting fearfully in London. 'What form does this exorcism take?'

'That, I think, you must see for yourself.'

*

I met Pastor Henri at his compound in the Kasa-Vubu district the next morning. He was a jolly, rotund figure, warm and welcoming, and seemed happy to discuss the work of his church. Despite what Remy had told me I found it hard at first to dislike him.

His compound was far more substantial than Remy's, with evidence of a new roof and fresh building work. About the only thing it had in common with Remy's place was the presence of children, though the ones here were far more subdued.

The problems only began when Pastor Henri sat me down on a bench by a wall and produced a shoebox full of trinkets.

'You see the kind of trouble we have,' he said, showing me the contents. 'We have confiscated these things from children infected with *kindoki*.'

I stared into the box and saw a few pieces of broken mirror, a toy car, a comb.

'They use this', he said, holding up a piece of mirror, 'to see into other worlds. And the car – they travel to Europe in it at night.'

I forced myself not to say anything.

'Oh, yes, many, many children are infected with *kindoki*,' he went on, his voice taking on a steely edge. 'They have eaten *kindoki* bread or drunk water tainted with it. Now they must be exorcized. The boy in England, too, this Andrew. He must come here to be exorcized.'

'And how will he be exorcized, Pastor Henri?'

'He must fast for up to four weeks. Water only. He must be kept alone. And then there is the ceremony, the casting out of demons. That is deliverance.'

'And this is in the name of Jesus Christ?'

'Certainly.' He looked puzzled. 'Who else?'

Over the next few days Pastor Henri allowed me to witness several exorcisms and gave me introductions to see others in other churches. He was completely open about the practice, which he considered commonplace. But these Kinshasa exorcisms were brutal and terrifying affairs. Children were starved, shut up alone in the dark, shouted at, beaten and traumatized. Some had chilli peppers rubbed in their eyes – the same torture that Child B had endured. Others were cut with razors. In Britain, the practitioners would have been jailed for child abuse, and somebody – I hoped – would have thrown away the key.

I managed to speak to some of the children in private. They showed me their scars and told me their harrowing stories. Several had been denounced by priests as infected with *kindoki*, so that their own families disowned them and they became virtually the property of the church that had stigmatized them.

'They've destroyed my life,' one girl told me simply.

It moved me to tears.

Afterwards I went back to my room and tried to process what I'd seen and heard. I ate very little during the next few days and chain-smoked constantly. At night I sprawled sweating on my bed and wondered what the good and politically correct council social workers would think if only they could see this. And I asked myself how much of it was going on. Were other British children being sent to Kinshasa to be tortured in this way?

What bewildered me most was that this was so utterly un-African. In all my years in the Congo, moving in and out of Kinshasa and living in the city for lengthy periods, I had never come across it. The idea of *kindoki* has existed in

Africa for centuries, probably millennia, but this taste for exorcism was something new. It seemed to have sprung up in recent years as a result of a fatal cocktail of desperate poverty and the new revivalist brand of Christianity that was sweeping Africa.

JP drove me south out of Kinshasa to a rural area called Mbetenge, which was well known as a centre for traditional healing. It was a gruelling twelve-hour trip over roads almost as ruinous as the ones I used to travel when I first lived up-country in Bolobo. The roadside was dotted with huts with palm leaf roofs, market stalls and beaming children selling roasted cane rat on skewers. Wrecked vehicles lay rusting in the lush undergrowth. Several times we had to dig the car out of soft sand. This was the Congo I knew and loved. I felt at home here, and almost as soon as we arrived I felt some of the tension slip away from me.

We were made welcome by the head man in a village at the centre of the Mbetenge region, and very soon word of my arrival and news of my interests had spread. The next morning half-a-dozen traditional healers – *ngangas* – had gathered. They were keen to speak to me and I didn't need to prompt them. They were as outraged as I was.

'In the old days,' said a wizened old man with a nap of white hair, 'we would never have said *kindoki* could affect a child. To us, that's ridiculous. And even for a person who did have *kindoki*, we would never go in for all this beating and shouting. We would just make up a potion of plant extracts and the sufferer would drink it for a few days and be cured.'

He and the other *ngangas* were anxious to make the point that *kindoki* was nothing to do with demons. There was no question of sufferers being possessed, so there was no need for anything to be driven out. And they all condemned the idea of beating, hurting or frightening children. Such behaviour was totally alien to them. I knew this was true: when I had lived here I had never once seen an African mistreat a child.

'It's these new churches,' the village headman said. 'They spread these stories so that simple people will pay them to drive the demons out of their children. Then they can hold the kids to ransom for as long as they like. It's a racket! A corrupt racket!'

I returned to Kinshasa with my resolution firmer than ever. Andrew must not be subjected to this nightmare.

I had to tread carefully, though. If his family in Kinshasa insisted on his return, and the London relatives remained firmly committed to the idea, there would be huge pressure on the British authorities not to hold the boy. He was not, after all, a British citizen.

I met Andrew's family in the pastor's church, with its sand floor, red-brick half-height wall, rotting wooden pillars and heat-inducing corrugated iron roof. It was stiflingly hot.

A grandmother, an elder brother, at least three aunts, an uncle and a cousin or two clustered on a couple of benches. Pastor Henri sat to one side, smiling like a Buddha. They had all greeted me courteously, and warmed to me further when I sent out for Coke and peanuts. As soon as everyone had a bottle in their hand I described the situation from my perspective. Andrew was probably unhappy, I said, because life in London was stressful and it was hard to settle there. Perhaps that accounted for his behaviour. There were nods from the relatives. It looked as if they could buy that. I seemed to be making progress.

'If he really does have *kindoki*,' I said, 'well, that's a

traditional affliction, and maybe it could be cured by traditional medicine. I could give him this.'

With something of a flourish I produced an amulet of herbs I had obtained from one of the *ngangas* in Mbetenge. 'Oh, no,' Pastor Henri broke in severely. 'That is *juju* medicine, the work of the devil. The Bible tells us we must turn our back on such superstitions.'

I backed off. 'Have you heard the story of Jesus and the centurion?'

Pastor Henri said nothing. The others looked at me warily.

'It's in the Bible,' I said. 'I'll show you.'

Someone produced a Bible and I found the passage.

'A centurion comes to Jesus and tells him that his son is sick,' I began. 'Jesus says he will go with him to his house. But the centurion replies, "There is no need, Lord. You have only to speak the word and the child will be cured." And Jesus is overjoyed, and says that he has never yet encountered such faith in the whole of Israel, and the child is healed.'

I had their attention now.

I said, 'Surely the lesson here is that if we all pray together and ask Jesus to help young Andrew, then Jesus will be pleased with our faith and will cure him. Then there will be no need to bring him all this way to go through an exorcism. Do you believe God is powerful enough to heal this boy from a distance? If you do, the only question is whether you have as much faith as that centurion.'

The family members were divided about this. A stricter faction thought it was all very irregular and that there could be no substitute for the ministrations of Pastor Henri, who sat in disapproving silence. Others felt the gauntlet had been thrown down: to see if they really had faith. In a few moments we had all joined hands and, kneeling on the crumbling concrete floor, we prayed aloud for the boy's deliverance.

I called Sarah Beskine as soon as I arrived back in London.

'There's no way this boy should be sent back. I don't think the family over there will insist.'

'I don't quite know how you swung that,' she said.

'Don't ask.'

She told me she'd already informally advised the council they'd be on very shaky ground. And better still, the boy had suddenly shown a remarkable improvement in behaviour over the last couple of days.

35
London, April–July 2004

I was pleased with this small victory, but sensed a wider battle looming over the whole question of *kindoki*, of witchcraft and exorcism. I began to express my concerns more and more frequently in articles and interviews.

'This might be the tip of the iceberg,' I said, and I must have repeated the phrase once too often, because one reporter dubbed me 'Mr Tip-of-the-Iceberg'. I tried to back off a bit then, for fear of weakening my case by overstating it, but the epithet stuck.

I passed my fears on to the police working on the Child B case. They wanted hard evidence of what was happening here in London, and as luck would have it, a young Congolese man called Claude phoned me soon afterwards.

'I've seen your stuff in the press, Dr Hoskins,' he said. 'You're on the right track with what you're saying. About the kids, I mean. And *kindoki*, and deliverance rituals. All that.'

I was cautious at first, but his outrage was plain. We met at a café in Islington.

Claude was an engineering student at London University, having hauled himself out of the hopeless morass of his native Kinshasa with brains, guts and relentless persistence. What I liked most about him was his compassion. He was

Catholic, although not particularly religious, and his indignation sprang mainly from a profound sense of outrage at what he saw as the abuse of children in some revivalist churches, and of the damage this would do to the reputation of Africans and African beliefs.

'This should never be happening, Dr Hoskins,' he said. His voice was gentle but urgent. 'Children should not be put through this. Most African people in London who know about it are horrified. Ashamed, even. And you know what it will do to the way the wider community looks at us. There are a lot of us who would do something about it, if anyone would listen.'

He said that he wanted to expose these practices, that he knew of my research and thought that maybe he could help me.

'It would be easier for me as a Congolese to approach the right people and ask the right questions,' he said.

I told him I wanted to find out more about revivalist churches in London, and that I'd like someone to go along to some of their services and tell me what was really going on.

He took out a small spiral-bound notebook and wrote in it, then looked up at me. 'OK,' he said, as if I'd asked him to drop by the corner shop and pick up a pint of milk. 'Anything else?'

I hesitated. 'One other thing keeps nagging at me. I just came back from Kinshasa. I was looking into the case of a London boy whose parents wanted to send him back to the Congo for . . . deliverance. Maybe that was a one-off. But then again, maybe it wasn't. I'd like to know if other children in London are in the same danger.'

Claude closed his notebook. 'I'll look into it.'

*

Claude was as good as his word, and gradually built up his contacts within the community. I met him several times during the course of that spring and summer. Quite soon he was uncovering evidence that *kindoki*, and so-called deliverance from it, were major issues for many African people in London. Once the idea of *kindoki* as a form of demonic possession took root, the worried parents of apparently afflicted children would frequently seek help from their local pastor. As a result, these new revivalist churches, which had sprung up in their hundreds across London, wielded extraordinary influence.

Many of the pastors, perhaps most of them, were as worried as I was about this state of affairs. I contacted several during my research and found myself in the company of responsible churchmen, deeply worried about the dangers of the *kindoki* phenomenon.

'It says in the Bible that there are witches,' one told me, 'but it is possible to accuse a child of being a witch who is not a witch at all. And that is very wrong.'

'We are absolutely against hurting or frightening a child under any circumstances,' said another.

But none of them denied that such things happened, or that pastors were sometimes responsible.

Claude secretly filmed an interview with a young pastor who claimed he could tell merely by looking into a child's eyes if he or she 'had' *kindoki*. He matter-of-factly described a witch-child who had levitated in front of him, and explained how demons could be driven out by exorcism.

Claude joined more than one congregation and attended services almost weekly. It was clear that exorcism rituals in Britain were, as we had suspected, the product of the fundamentalist Christian movements. Occasionally exorcisms took place in church, or what passed for church, by professional exorcists – itinerants who wandered from Christian splinter group to charismatic church, casting out demons from helpless and terrified children. But it appeared that demand had grown so rapidly that more and more parents were attempting exorcism in their own homes.

DI Brian Mather remained determined to achieve a conviction for Child B, but pointed out that without evidence of abuse they had no case to prove. The problem remained that the police were hamstrung by their lack of knowledge of the wider picture. British detectives, in my experience, were decent and hardworking, but usually mono-lingual and white. Interviews with church officials, for instance, had to be conducted through an interpreter, and against a background of cultural and religious references that were utterly alien to them. As a result, I suspected that some questions that needed to be asked were not being asked.

As the summer of 2004 drew on I became increasingly committed to the Child B investigation. Like Claude, I also wanted people to understand that this was not the African way. If and when the case finally got to court, I wanted the prosecution to show beyond any doubt that the abuse of Child B owed nothing to traditional African beliefs, just as it owed nothing to any reasonable person's interpretation of Christianity.

In the meantime Kingsley Ojo, alias Mousa Kamara, was to go on trial on 10 July.

It had taken nearly a year to get him to court, but a number of his minions had already got their comeuppance. Some had received prison sentences of up to three years. Of those arrested, many hailed from Benin City in the

Yoruba region of Nigeria, and several had been immediately deported for breaching immigration regulations.

It left a bitter taste that these people should be free to walk around their home city. They were no better than modern-day slave traders, and I would happily have seen them suffer a harsher fate. But I very much hoped that Kingsley Ojo, the mastermind of the whole nefarious racket, would receive a sterner punishment.

I arrived at Southwark Crown Court, a huge modern building with a cavernous foyer. After going through security I made my way along a softly lit corridor. At the far end, silhouetted against the window, was a huddle of figures, heads bent in earnest conversation. As I drew near, Will O'Reilly broke away. I could see at once that something was wrong.

'There's been an almighty cock-up,' he said. 'And I mean *almighty*.'

Despite the fact that Ojo had been arrested more than a year earlier, some of the court papers hadn't been served until the end of the previous week which meant they were too late to be taken into consideration as evidence. Operation Maxim had been set in motion to keep tabs on the traffickers, but the existence of two parallel sets of dossiers had created the potential for confusion.

'The prosecution counsel put a rocket under various people last week . . .'

Nick Chalmers emerged from the lift. He grinned at me, but looked more worried than I'd seen him at any time in the investigation. The prosecution counsel came over too and we were introduced. As the barrister drew on his cigarette I noticed his hand was shaking.

Half an hour later, an usher summoned all parties on

the case of Mousa Kamara into Court Seven. Ojo was to be tried under his favourite alias.

I looked around the starkly lit courtroom. The barristers' benches were immediately in front of us. The prosecution and defence counsels were already in place, piles of paperwork stacked in front of them. To our right was the dais where the judge would preside. To the left, behind a glass screen, was an enclosed space with a door in the far corner.

The investigation had taken nearly three years to reach this point. Was it really about to collapse in failure? The door behind the glass screen swung open, and in walked Kingsley Ojo. He was flanked by security guards, one of whom locked the door after him.

Ojo was a big, heavyset man with an incongruously thin moustache. He looked straight at me and we held each other's gaze. Was he wondering who I was? Or did he know? With all the press coverage since The Hague, my involvement on the case had hardly been a secret.

'All rise!'

As everyone stood, Judge Hardy appeared. Ojo was asked to confirm his name and everyone sat down.

Over the next couple of hours, the prosecution barrister meticulously guided the judge through the dossiers in front of him. His tone was modest and understated. Though much of what he described was dramatic enough, he avoided grand statements and instead heaped fact upon fact, allegation upon allegation, listing them in a quiet, precise, level voice. The impression conveyed by the end was of a mountain of incontrovertible evidence.

Judge Hardy sat hunched slightly forward, watching impassively. Finally, when the barrister was finished, the judge simply stated that the court would be adjourned while he checked that all his paperwork was in order. As we filed out the defence counsel motioned to the prosecution team.

We all reconvened in the corridor, avoiding one another's eyes, shuffling nervously. Thirty minutes later our barrister emerged from the courtroom and motioned for Will and Nick to join the conference that was already taking place inside. When Will came out again a few minutes later, his shoulders seemed a little less hunched.

'The defence have taken a pragmatic view,' he told me quietly. 'The evidence that was submitted within the time limit is still overwhelming, and they know they won't succeed in getting him off, so they've offered us a deal. Basically, he'll plead guilty to some of the charges in exchange for us not pushing the ones we have the greatest problems with. He'll try and get a reduced sentence, and in the process avoid a three-week trial.'

I wasn't sure whether this was good or not, but it sounded better than I had feared.

'I've insisted that we'll only go along with this if the conviction states that he's the mastermind of the trafficking ring,' Will said. 'I'm not just accepting a few petty charges. He's the ringleader and I want him banged up for it.'

Within hours, Kingsley Ojo faced Judge Hardy again. A list of trafficking and immigration charges was read out. One by one Ojo softly muttered the word 'guilty'.

At the end of the trial, Ojo, who had been identified as the ringleader of a major people-trafficking operation that had come to light during the Adam investigation, was sentenced to four and a half years' imprisonment. The judge recommended that he be deported back to Nigeria at the end of his term.

Later we all gathered on the embankment. Tower Bridge

stood to our right – and beneath it the spot where Adam's torso had been found three years earlier. The police were in jubilant mood. They had broken up a massive trafficking operation. Who knows how many young people had been saved from crime, prostitution and death? Even from sacrifice?

A clearer picture had emerged during the investigation of just how extensive the trafficking operation had been. Young people had been recruited in Benin City with false promises of a better life in Europe. Others – many of them children, and some as young as Adam – had been bought outright. They were flown usually to Germany or Italy and transported from there to other parts of Europe.

Some were virtually enslaved into domestic service and others put to work in brothels. They were trapped, unable to approach the police for help because they feared deportation, and in terror of the traffickers themselves. Many, whose families had mortgaged themselves to pay for their journey, were too ashamed to contact their relatives back home. In some cases girls as young as twelve or thirteen had been forced into prostitution through pseudo-religious ceremonies in Benin City, and made to swear that they would never tell who was involved. Two such girls had been picked up by the police in leafy Surrey. They were traumatized, perhaps scarred for life.

As I gazed downstream, sunlight glanced off the river. The police had a right to be pleased, I thought. They had a result.

Nick Chalmers gave me a thumbs-up and Will O'Reilly smiled at me. But as soon as our eyes met, I knew we were thinking the same thing. No matter how pleased the team was about smashing the trafficking operation, the fact remained that they had not been able to charge those responsible for the ritual slaughter of a small boy.

It wasn't over, and it never would be until we knew who had been responsible for sacrificing the child we knew as Adam. For the first time, I began to fear that we never would.

There might, however, be a chance to get justice for another damaged child. Now that Ojo had been convicted I could give my full attention to the Child B case.

36

London, September 2004–June 2005

I decided to take another look at Combat Spirituel. I headed for the church that Sita Kisanga, Child B's great-aunt, had said she attended, and whose former premises I had inspected after my first visit to the police at Tottenham. The warehouse in which they now met was grey and down-at-heel, but the atmosphere was anything but. I was met with smiles and happy greetings whichever way I turned, and I was led to a seat right up at the front.

I had told the elders on the phone that I was lecturing on African religions at King's College, which was true, and that I had a purely academic interest in the revivalist movement, which wasn't. They were delighted by my fluency in Lingala, and fascinated to hear something of my six-year history in the Congo. Yes, of course I was welcome to come. Why not? Their services were open to everyone.

It was easy to be swept up by the exuberance of the congregation, men in their best suits and women in traditional African dress, vibrant with colour. I was glad I had come. It reminded me of why the church was so important to these people. Many of them, I knew, had grindingly hard lives, often eking out an existence on the margins of London society. They crowded into squalid accommodation and took on jobs nobody else would do, often for illegally low wages. A fair proportion of them lived in fear of immigration officials, whose power over them they only half understood, dreading repatriation to countries engulfed by violence and poverty.

But here, for one day a week, they blossomed. Here they came together and were accepted, could dress with dignity, celebrate their faith, pray together and sing. And sing they did, joyfully swaying to the music and throwing up their arms in exultation. It was very moving and I saw just how powerful a figure their pastor must be for them, a guiding hand and a mentor, a leader of the only community to which they could fully belong. The pastor, as Claude had once told me, was 'a little god'. To be cast out by him was to be thrown into exile.

Pastor Raph, head of Combat Spirituel in London, arrived in some state, his chauffeur-driven black vehicle sweeping to a halt in the street outside. Out leapt a brace of bulky sidekicks who looked very like bodyguards. They held the door for him, peering into the middle distance the way CIA agents do in movies, and ushered the dark-suited pastor up the stairs and into the room where we had gathered.

There was a certain *froideur* between Pastor Raph and me from the moment we met. He shook my hand briefly and loftily bestowed a greeting. I could see that he regarded me as a nuisance, and I guessed that he was annoyed with the elders for inviting me. Within moments he strode away to begin his preaching.

He marched around the packed room to cheers and acclamation, microphone in hand, whipping up excitement. In his dark glasses he looked like Ray Charles working a crowd.

'Today you will witness something amazing!' he promised, and jubilant voices rose around him. 'Your lives will be changed! There will be a new beginning, in the name of Jesus Christ! Yes, many new lives will begin here today, and they will be dedicated to the glory of *Jesus*!'

'Alleluia!'

'You will be powerful and free, in the name of *Jesus*!'

'Alleluia!'

And much more of the same.

I watched, fascinated, for about an hour, swept up by his masterly technique and the ecstatic responses of the crowd behind me. Then, right at the end, he crossed the floor to stand directly over me.

'It is possible for a man to have evil spirits, even though he comes here,' he asked, quite softly. 'Isn't that so?'

Murmurs of agreement rose from the congregation. I sat very still, wondering what was coming next.

'In that case, you must have the devil cast out of you!' he cried.

'Yes!' the congregation shouted.

'You must be rid of these spirits!'

'Alleluia!'

'You must turn aside from your life!' Pastor Raph swung his arm up and then down, pointing directly at me, jabbing his finger and then punching his fist in the air again and again, within inches of my face, hurling his whole body into the gesture. 'You must have the devil cast out! Cast out! CAST OUT!'

The effect was extraordinary. I felt like a rabbit caught in the headlights. I just about kept my composure while his energy burst over me.

*

After my visit to Combat Spirituel, I had to keep reminding myself that my discomfort was at least partly cultural. In common with most people brought up in a secular state I tend to regard religion as a private matter. That's how the British normally conduct matters of faith, and it's one of the reasons they are suspicious of exuberant expressions of belief, and perhaps blind to the fact that some 87 per cent of the world's population remains fervently religious. But looking beyond our comfortable and sometimes hypocritical secularism is one of the challenges we all face in a rapidly changing world, if we are to understand the forces working on our society.

On 21 January 2005 Luke Mitchell was found guilty of the murder of Jodi Jones and sentenced to a minimum of twenty years in prison. I had known the trial was under way, but had avoided following it. I still had memories of the utter despair Faith and I had experienced during our brief involvement with the case.

But I could not avoid hearing the outcome of the trial, which was splashed over every newspaper and TV channel. The murder was tagged the most gruesome in recent Scottish legal history, and Judge Lord Nimmo Smith described the photos of Jodi's body as the most shocking he had ever seen in his long career.

I remained keenly aware that I had failed to answer Superintendent Craig Dobbie's fundamental question: how could people do such things? The further I went into this landscape, the more distressing I found my inability to answer, for others or for myself. However, with the Child B case coming to court it was a question I needed to face.

Patricia May QC was to lead the prosecution team in the Child B trial. I could have mistaken her for a kindly headmistress. I later came to understand that the air of gentle eccentricity she projected, if not exactly an act, was a weapon she used to extraordinary effect in the courtroom.

We met at her chambers near the Royal Courts of Justice in the Strand. Ms May sat at the head of the large boardroom table with two or three members of her team and a prim secretary to one side, taking notes. Brian Mather, Jason Morgan and I faced her. With us was Michelle Elkins, press officer for the Metropolitan Police in North London. An attractive and compassionate woman in her late twenties, she did a great deal to soften the harder edges of the largely male police contingent on this case.

In a quiet, unhurried voice, Patricia May summed up what was known about the crime, the defendants and the evidence against them. She asked for confirmation of a number of points, jotting down the answers on her pad. A brief discussion followed, and when it was over, she turned to me.

'This is much more than a matter of building the evidence against Sita Kisanga and her co-accused for what they've done to this girl, isn't it?'

At last someone was interested in the wider picture.

'As I see it, Richard, it's crucial that Child B's abusers are not only convicted and punished, but that they are not allowed to hide behind the smokescreen of religion. Everyone at this trial needs to understand that nothing can excuse this.'

That was the message she wanted us to get across. Most people saw Victoria Climbié's death as the result of sheer sadism, or grotesque neglect. An isolated atrocity. But the Child B case must not be seen as isolated. We had to link it with this new pseudo-religious movement, and at the same time show that no religion, or set of beliefs, could possibly excuse it.

She needed me to establish in my evidence that what had happened to Child B had no foundation in African tradition either; that it was down to the perverted behaviour of cruelly misguided people. We mustn't allow them to call on either Christianity or African beliefs to justify their actions. If we succeeded in making that point, the crime was clearly indefensible.

The meeting launched a period of intensive work: writing reports, briefing the prosecution team and preparing myself to testify as an expert witness. Not all Ms May's colleagues, middle-class professionals that they were, understood the central issues as readily as she had. I felt that I constantly needed to steer lawyers and policemen away from the suspicion that the defendants had done these awful things *because* they were African and held African beliefs.

My argument was that the crimes had been committed *despite* their African heritage. I was even more determined than Ms May that the defence must not be able to use their African origins as an excuse. That would not help British society tackle such crimes, and would be a betrayal of all that I knew and loved about Africa and its people.

The Child B case came to court on 9 May 2005. After emerging from the City Thameslink station, I arrived at the Old Bailey. The narrow street was jammed with camera crews, witnesses, lawyers, police officers and members of the public queuing for entry – some of them with folding stools and picnic baskets. Technicians tested their equipment, glamorous young women presented early pieces to camera.

I pushed through the crowd and up the steps, and as I

did so I caught sight of Sita Kisanga and her co-defendants emerging from a taxi. In that instant I saw Kisanga the way millions would see her on television and in the newspapers, an iconic image of her walking towards the crowd, her head and face swathed in a red scarf. She was trying to disguise herself, but the effect could not have looked more sinister if she'd tried.

I shoved my way into the gloom of the lobby. Behind the scanners and the uniformed guards was a great sweeping staircase beneath a vaulted ceiling. I looked around me in something like awe, overwhelmed by a sense of occasion. So many infamous criminals had been tried in this building – Dr Crippen, the Kray twins, Myra Hindley, Ruth Ellis, Peter Sutcliffe, Ian Huntley and Maxine Carr. The Old Bailey could rightly claim to be the heart of British justice, but no trial like this had ever been heard within its walls.

Jason Morgan met me on the far side of security. The prosecution's witness room was a bleak chamber with cream walls, high windows and plastic chairs. There were half a dozen people in there already, one or two talking in animated whispers, others silent, avoiding one another's eyes. I didn't recognize any of them.

I had only been there a few minutes when Jason returned and called me out again.

'The prosecution team's asked if you'd like to sit with them,' he said, leading me away down the crowded corridor. 'I'm assuming you'd prefer that?'

'What happens when I'm called to testify?'

'You probably won't be. Word is, the defence won't put you on the stand. The judge has ruled that your written evidence is to be accepted as it stands.'

'They won't even challenge it?'

'Patricia May reckons that the defence think that if they tried giving you a grilling they'd only shoot themselves in the foot.'

Throughout the days that followed, my research was constantly cited by both sides without my ever having to stand up and defend it.

I had a ringside seat at a groundbreaking trial. The benches all around me were jammed with lawyers, every inch of table space stacked with files and papers. The defendants were all blaming one another, and each had to be separately represented.

The jury sat to my right. I noticed a large lady with bottle-blonde hair, an elderly man in a suit and tie, a younger man in a T-shirt. Immediately facing me was the clerk of the court, a young woman who was forever holding hushed conversations on a phone that stood on the desk before her – ordering documents, I assumed, or lining up witnesses. Judge Christopher Moss, resplendent in ermine and very much in control, sat high up above the body of the court.

The four defendants entered the glass-shielded dock no more than five metres behind me. I twisted in my seat to study them. Sebastian Pinto was young, tall and slender. The three women – Pinto's girlfriend, Child B's aunt Sita Kisanga, and the girl's mother – were all full-figured after the African fashion and brightly but formally dressed. They avoided eye contact with one another and gazed around the court with some of the awe I felt myself. I had the impression that none of them understood quite what was going on, or why they were there.

On the first day, Child B gave evidence by video link.

Though the trial would go on for another three weeks, this was its defining moment. I doubt anyone who was present will ever forget that girl's face. She was pretty, with large eyes and her hair in cornrows, but she had a calm and resolute air that was extraordinary in a child of eight. The room was utterly silent when she spoke, her voice clear and unhurried. Once or twice she wept, and I saw several people around the court moved to tears in sympathy.

Child B was evidently highly intelligent and mature beyond her years. I wondered if perhaps that precocity was part of the reason her family had decided she must have *kindoki*. She was certainly in no doubt about what had happened to her and who was responsible. She immediately cleared Pinto's girlfriend – who was then released – of any involvement, but roundly condemned the other three.

There wasn't much they could say in their own defence. It was suggested to them that Child B's exorcism had been carried out at the behest of someone in the revivalist movement, but Sita Kisanga denied this. She insisted that she had rarely even visited her local church, Combat Spirituel, though her earlier statements, her diaries and the marginal notes in her Bible all indicated that she was a regular worshipper there, and I had seen her name on the list of helpers pinned to the kitchen wall. Perhaps simple desperation was making her deny everything that was put to her.

On the last day of May, Judge Christopher Moss concluded his summing up and sent out the jury.

The jurors had to consider a number of different charges against each of the three defendants, including conspiracy to murder and child cruelty. They deliberated for three days, but finally we were all summoned back.

The atmosphere was electric. The courtroom was packed

with journalists waiting for the verdict, and when the foreman read out that first 'guilty', several of them rushed for the exit.

The defendants were cleared on the conspiracy to murder charges, but all were found guilty of child cruelty. The two women in the dock shrieked aloud as they realized what had happened and Pinto shouted in disbelief.

Judge Moss restored order with his gavel.

'I'm remanding you in custody,' he told the defendants when the hubbub had died down. 'When I am ready to pass sentence you will be brought back to this court. But I will tell you now that each one of you can expect to spend a long time in prison. Take them down.'

The three were ushered away to the cells, the women still wailing and Pinto looking stunned.

The courtroom emptied with all the noise and excitement of the last school assembly before the holidays. I slipped away from the jubilant prosecution team, and managed to avoid Jason Morgan and Brian Mather too. I pushed through the packed corridors outside the courtroom and found a bench in a relatively quiet corner.

I wanted to keep out of the way. There had been intense press coverage of the trial and I knew that Brian and Jason would be swamped by reporters the moment they stepped outside. I had attended a news conference with them a week or two earlier and the media interest had been overwhelming. *Witchcraft? In London? And you're an expert on this?* I didn't think I could face any more of that at that moment. I felt drained, wrung out.

I hadn't realized quite how much this case had taken out of me, and now that it was over I felt a crushing sense of anticlimax. I stayed on that grubby bench watching the life of the Old Bailey bustle around me for at least an hour and a half. The Old Bailey. Now that it was over I couldn't work out quite how I had got here. A few years ago I had been pursuing a quiet career as a West Country academic.

Finally I made my way to the door and slipped out with a group of people into the summer afternoon.

'It's Mr Tip-of-the-Iceberg!' a voice called and I was instantly engulfed, microphones and lenses thrust into my face and questions shouted from all sides.

I didn't have the will or the tactical nous to escape. Child B was the news of the day and there was no way the press were going to let me go without an interview. I answered such questions as I could, hardly knowing who I was talking to. The Child B case was the lead story on the BBC six o'clock news and on ITV's six-thirty bulletin, and clips from interviews with me featured in both.

Eventually I allowed myself to be bundled away by a Channel 4 team, more or less to get away from the noise and confusion. Apparently, I was to be interviewed live by Jon Snow.

I calmed down a bit on the way there. I'd wanted publicity for Child B, I'd wanted people to realize what was going on and to be outraged by it. That was the whole point.

Snow talked briefly to me before the programme, suggesting the line he was going to take, checking facts, asking what I particularly wanted to say.

'I can tell you that in a nutshell,' I said, suddenly sparking up. 'It's that we in this country have to stop sitting on the fence. The Child B case shows that we can't close our eyes for fear of being labelled cultural imperialists: it's time to stand up and be counted on this. Child abuse is wrong, and it has to stop.'

Snow raised his eyebrows, surprised by the passion in my voice. I was surprised by it myself.

'Fifteen seconds, Jon,' somebody called, and the studio fell silent around us.

Faith had managed to make it to the Channel 4 studios in time for my interview, and watched from the observation box. When it was over, we took a cab to a pub near the Old Bailey, where the police team were still celebrating their win. They had been there some time, and despite their beery camaraderie, we both felt rather out of it, so after an hour or so we decamped to a quiet Italian restaurant.

My mobile didn't stop ringing with calls from national newspapers and TV and radio stations, and then later from the regional media. I was a little wired and couldn't settle. I wanted to catch my breath, but the process had a momentum of its own. I was wary of the media's determination to feed so greedily on the torture of a young girl, and I rather despised myself for being part of it, but I still wanted to get my message out there. I knew that I had to strike while the iron was hot.

'Where to now?' Faith said, as I folded away my mobile for perhaps the tenth time.

'I'm not sure,' I said. 'There's so much still to be done.'

'There is.' She reached across and took my hand. 'But don't fall into the trap of thinking that it's your responsibility to do it all, will you?'

The mobile buzzed again.

'No, no,' I said distractedly, releasing her hand to pick up the phone. 'Of course not.'

37
London, July–October 2005

On Friday, 8 July 2005 Mr Justice Moss identified Sita Kisanga as the instigator of the worst of Child B's abuse and sentenced her to ten years, the longest jail term allowed by law for her crime. The girl's mother got the same sentence, and Pinto got four years.

It should have brought closure of a sort, but I found that it did not.

As further cases continued to come my way over the next few months, I grew increasingly unhappy. I was depressed by the sheer nastiness of the crimes I examined, and frustrated by my inability to do anything significant about them. I never became hardened to what I saw and heard.

Faith watched this change in me, and gently pointed out that I was always working, and that even when I did take time off I was increasingly introverted and strained. I knew she was right, but I seemed unable to do anything about it. I began to feel I was marooned in the flat – still living high above London, but no longer part of it. Not really part of anything, in fact, except the distressing landscape of my work.

I was working late as usual one evening, having appeared for long enough to eat dinner in silence before going back to my desk. Faith brought me a cup of cocoa and put it beside me on the blotter. I discovered it there, cold and congealed, when I looked up hours later. Faith told me that she had spoken to me when she'd brought it in, had even put her arms around me and kissed the top of my head. I had no recollection that she had ever been there.

My life was getting more surreal by the day. A bright young woman from a production company called me with a proposal. They wanted to make a reality TV show in which I would set up a bogus religious cult.

'Pardon?'

'We want you to act as the guru. The idea would be to show how easy it is to get people roped in, and to believe everything you say. And to see how far they would obey you, too. You might tell them, for instance, to sign over all their worldly goods.'

'Are you quite mad?' I asked.

'Oh,' she protested. 'It would just be a bit of fun. We'd give everything back afterwards, obviously.'

Quite apart from such foolishness, the lack of progress on the Adam investigation was a continuing source of tension. But I called Nick Chalmers every month or so, and he remained upbeat. There was talk of renewed surveillance, of fresh suspects, of Joyce Osagiede's imminent return to the UK, of breakthroughs in identifying Adam's family. Everything was always on the point of happening within the next fortnight, and each new proposed initiative was garnished with a mass of procedural detail. But nothing actually happened, and I could feel the investigation losing what was left of its momentum.

I continued my research into child exorcism, and even began to wonder whether it was becoming a personal obsession, but exchanges with people in the communities echoed my convictions. I still saw Claude regularly. One Wednesday in September, as he sat opposite me in the steamy café, wearing his trademark white baseball cap, I decided to be straight with him.

'Maybe I'm getting carried away with this exorcism thing, Claude,' I said. 'Maybe I'm not seeing things clearly any more.'

'No,' he said in his calm but formal way, sipping his Coke. 'Matters stand just the way you think they do. In fact, I believe the situation may be getting worse.'

He reminded me that when we had first met I had asked him to listen out for London children being sent to Kinshasa for exorcism, as had so nearly happened to Andrew. He told me that he now had strong evidence that this was indeed happening. My heart sank. I remembered the lost children in the church compounds, waiting to be bullied, starved and cut until they achieved deliverance.

'You know of an actual case?' I asked.

'I've heard of thirty or so.'

'*Thirty*?'

'Yes: kids who've either been sent, or whose families are preparing to send them. I think there are probably a lot more.' He took out his spiral-bound notebook. 'Here. I made a list.'

The names were in a column down the left hand margin. I stared at them. Most stood alone, but beside one, a boy called Londres, was an address.

'That's his uncle's place in Kinshasa,' Claude said. 'Where he's been sent. One of his relatives let it slip.'

For days after meeting Claude the thought of this boy gnawed at me. For an ordinary London child to be trapped in an alien city and forced to undergo what I had seen those Kinshasa children go through seemed like a kind of hell to me. I racked my brains for some way I could help him or draw attention to his fate.

Since the blaze of publicity surrounding the Child B case I had received regular calls from journalists and TV documentary producers. One of the more persistent had asked if I'd be interested in fronting a film about Britain's 'child witches' for the BBC. The project would involve a trip to Kinshasa.

I had been cool about this up until now. I knew Faith wouldn't want me to go back to Kinshasa merely to make a TV programme. I wasn't anxious to go myself, but my meeting with Claude put a different complexion on things.

Three days later I found myself sitting in the production company's North London offices. I told them that I wanted to shine a spotlight on the abuse of children in the name of Christian deliverance, and especially to draw attention to the fact that London kids were being shipped back to Kinshasa for exorcism. There was one child in particular I had heard about who had been sent on that journey and I wanted to follow him there. Sacha, a slender and thoughtful director in his early thirties, was enthusiastic.

Faith, however, was distraught – more upset than I'd seen her at any time in our relationship.

'The boy's name is Londres,' I said. 'London. Funny name.'

'I know what it means. Why do you have to go to Kinshasa?'

We had been over this several times.

'To talk his relatives out of putting him through exorcism.'

'And you think you can do that?'

'I managed it once before.'

'That was different. The boy wasn't already there. And besides, what makes you think this is your responsibility?'

'He's fourteen years old. He's spent most of his life here in London. He *is* a Londoner. I've seen what they do in Kinshasa. Can you imagine being put through that as a child of fourteen?'

'Richard,' she sighed, 'you can't just make this all right.'

But I was in full flight by then. I told her I knew his uncle's address in Kinshasa. I could go straight there and talk to the relatives. Perhaps they'd even let me bring the boy back. We'd do a little filming and maybe we'd be back in a couple of days. The rest of the documentary could be done in London.

Faith walked over to the window. She stood with her arms crossed, silhouetted against the night-time city.

'I'm worried about you, Richard,' she said at last. 'Truly I am. What kind of sense does it make to go charging out to the Congo to try to find one child? A child you've never even met?'

'I'll be there with a film crew. And the documentary's for the BBC. That gives it some weight, even in Kinshasa. It's not as if I've launched into this all on my own.'

'You're not some sort of superhero in red tights, you know, swooping around the world righting wrongs.'

'But I know the place. I speak the language. I understand the problem. And I know where this boy is. Who else can say all that?'

'I think you're pushing your luck going there again,' she said. 'I know how important this is to you, but I don't want you to go. I'm serious. I have a very bad feeling about it.'

She stood there in silence for a long time. I thought perhaps there were tears in her eyes.

Then she said, 'Richard, I'm not sure I can take a lot more of this. Seeing you getting chewed up by every new case. You have no life outside your work, and so neither do we. Can't you see that I'm really, really unhappy? I hate London. I hate the way we live here.'

I stared at her. While I was still groping for a response she said, 'I want to stay down in the West Country during the week. Just during the week, that's all. But I need some space, away from here.'

'But . . . we'll hardly see one another . . .'

'We hardly do now.' Her voice was heavy with sadness. 'I could go and stay with my parents in Devon. They'd enjoy having me around.'

38

Kinshasa, August 2005

Sacha met me at Heathrow and introduced me to the crew. Soundman Andy was tall, lanky and relaxed, with designer stubble and wearing T-shirt and jeans. Camerawoman Petra was his virtual opposite, a tough, direct and highly experienced professional who specialized in filming in war zones. I took to both of them at once.

The trip began to go wrong from the start. There were endless hassles getting our gear checked in. An over-eager sniffer dog took an entirely misplaced interest in one of Andy's bags, so that we were interviewed at some length by customs officers and barely made the flight.

When we were finally on the plane and strapping ourselves in, Sacha joked a little nervously that someone must have put *juju* on our journey. I wished he hadn't said that.

In Kinshasa, the crew had been booked into the Memling, one of a tiny handful of places in the capital that still functioned roughly like a real hotel. It had lifts that worked most of the time, the food on the menu was quite often available in the restaurant and prostitutes were only permitted in the lobby by invitation.

It was evening by the time we got there. I saw the others into their rooms, grabbed a quick meal with them, then took a taxi to a much less salubrious hostel downtown. I had an urge to be close to the real Kinshasa, and the Happy Day Hotel was just that, a run-down rest house patronized entirely by Africans – traders, travellers and people visiting relatives.

The large woman at reception was startled to see a white man check in, but when I greeted her in Lingala my arrival was met with huge good humour and I was shown off to guests and staff like the curiosity I was.

The Happy Day was a ramshackle three-storey structure roofed in corrugated iron, built around a courtyard with ill-matching tables at which men lounged in the hot darkness drinking beer. Fitful electric bulbs hung from a neem tree in the centre. Guests could get French fries in the dining hall, if they were lucky, or maybe rice or cassava and beans.

My room was a cubicle on the first floor with a small balcony that looked directly down onto a chaotic road junction packed with people, traffic and vendors' stalls lit by oil lamps. I leaned on the rail, perched just above the heads of the passers-by, listening to the cries of traders and the blaring horns of the traffic, returning the amused shouts of greeting from people who spotted me there, a lone white man in the heart of a black city. The smoke from my cigarette mixed with exhaust fumes, rotting garbage and the reek of burning tyres from a dump on the far side of the junction.

Immediately below my window was an informal drop-off point for taxis and taxi-buses. Kinshasa cabs were supposed to be yellow, though the interpretation of this rule is subjective. Every few seconds battered vehicles in all shades from ochre to canary to acid lemon would pull up and disgorge their passengers while drivers bellowed for new fares, bawling their destinations into the hot night – *N'djili! Kimbanseki! Ndolo!*

At about midnight I tossed away my last cigarette, turned away from the window, and crawled under the tatty mosquito net. I lay there sweating in the darkness for a long time. I had left the balcony door open, partly to help with the heat, but really because I enjoyed the anarchic din of the street just below, especially the cab drivers' cries, with their promise of action, movement and adventure: *N'djili! Kimbanseki! Ndolo!*

It went on all night, and every now and then I would surface into full wakefulness and listen to it. Tomorrow we would go to find a boy called Londres. Maybe this would all work out well after all. *N'djili! Kimbanseki! Ndolo!*

By the time I got back to the Memling Hotel the next morning, Sacha, Petra and Andy were busy loading their gear into the back of a glossy white Land Cruiser with tinted windows. I eyed the car and the pile of gear that lay around it uneasily.

Sacha handed me a new Nokia mobile phone he had bought on the street for twenty dollars, with unlimited calls for another twenty. He'd got one for each of us. Sacha was pleased with this bargain, and wondered how the locals managed to provide such a service.

I wasn't so sure. The sheer mass of expensive equipment worried me – cameras, lenses, tape recorders, microphones and palmtops. I saw too that the vehicle itself was a mistake. I could hardly blame the team: I had given them the contacts to hire the car, and they had picked something that seemed to make sense. It was large, air-conditioned and powerful, and its dark windows hid the equipment from prying eyes and would even allow Petra to film undetected.

I liked the look of the driver who had come with the vehicle, a quiet, capable man called Apolossa. But the Land Cruiser itself was impossibly opulent for the slums we were due to visit. A single tyre would have cost more than a poor Kinshasa family would earn in a year. It was a platinum panzer, money on wheels, and would mark us out at a glance as rich foreigners. Voyeurs. Exploiters. Targets.

I tried to put these thoughts behind me, though, and within a few minutes we were heading off through the loud and glaring morning with Apolossa at the wheel. Away from the main streets the city was just as I remembered: a riot of low concrete buildings, broken storm drains, tin roofs and daubed graffiti. Crudely painted shop signs of startling explicitness advertised butchers, dentists, haemorrhoid specialists. Most vividly of all from my time living here I remembered the people, crowding everywhere on the broken footpaths, dressed in hectic colours, loafing on crumbling concrete walls, cramming the empty shops, weaving between the potholes on elderly bicycles.

The address Claude had obtained for me wasn't far from the Boulevard Kasa-Vubu, in the same area as Pastor Henri's church compound, which I had visited on my last trip. The neighbourhood didn't have a lot to recommend it, but at least I was familiar with the area. In the cool cavern of the car, with the competent and laconic crew surrounding me, I began to relax.

It didn't last long. We hadn't gone far through the choked streets before a stone was thrown, clunking against the bodywork. A few people jeered. As we crawled through a crowd, horn blaring, someone smacked hard on the shiny window and pressed his face grotesquely against the glass, nose flattened. I could hear angry shouts in Lingala.

'Bloody Westerners! What d'you want here?'

'Give us dollars!'

'Bugger off back to America!'

Inside the car, suddenly there were no more jokes.

'What's going on?' Sacha asked.

I caught Apolossa's eye in the rear-view mirror. He and I were the only two people who understood the language, and thus the depth of hostility directed against us.

'We'd better back off,' I said.

Nobody argued, and Apolossa gratefully swung the car round in a vacant lot. We headed back towards the centre of town more quickly than we had come.

The incident troubled me. I had travelled these streets scores of times, often alone and on foot. But none of that counted for anything when I was insulated inside this arrogant and overbearing vehicle. All the street people saw was our power and insufferable wealth, thrown in their faces. No wonder they wanted to hit back.

I cursed myself. I should have thought of this and briefed the crew more thoroughly.

'Well, that's terrific,' Sacha was saying. 'How are we going to find this boy if they won't even let us drive the streets?'

'I'll walk,' I said.

He looked at me. '*Walk*?'

'I'll be safer out of this damned great tank. I'll go this afternoon.'

Boulevard Kasa-Vubu is a long, broad avenue that was once grand. The shady trees had long since been cut down for fuel by this time, and most of the tarmac had gone. A strip of blacktop down the centre had survived, just broad enough for a two-way traffic jam of belching trucks, taxi-buses and motorbikes. The sides of the road and the laneways were covered in grey sand, deep enough in the dry season to bog a regular car. Flanking the boulevard were hideous one- and two-storey commercial buildings, offices and dim shops and garages, and between them private houses and shacks, their multi-coloured doors glaring in the sun.

Londres' uncle's place proved to be one of these, a miserable hovel with a red door set back between two lock-ups. I knocked. People jostled past along the crowded margin of the road. Almost in front of the door two women in violently coloured head ties sat at a rough table, chatting and laughing. They were selling – or failing to sell – the ubiquitous trade goods of African stallholders: tiny tins of pilchards in tomato sauce, milk powder, bottles of Fanta. No one took any notice of me. I knocked again.

The sweat was running down my body inside my shirt. I wondered if it would affect the radio transmitter I had taped round my midriff, and which ought to be relaying my every sound and movement to Sacha and the crew in the car, which was parked out of harm's way half a mile distant.

I knocked for a third time and shouted through the flimsy door.

'Ko-ko-ko!'

'Not home,' one of the trader women called. 'As you see.'

'Do you know these people?' I asked her in Lingala.

She tossed up her chin. No. Maybe. What's it to you?

'I'm looking for a boy. From London. A boy called Londres.'

Again the chin came up. 'There are many boys.'

That was self-evidently true. A gaggle of children had gathered around me, most of them boys in faded T-shirts and torn shorts, barefoot, wide-eyed, laughing and nudging one another, cracking jokes at my expense.

'Does anyone know a boy called Londres?' I asked them.

They jostled one another and giggled, all bright teeth and eyes.

'Londres,' I tried again, 'a kid of about fourteen? Speaks like an English boy, maybe?'

They exchanged glances of elaborate puzzlement and several shook their heads. I had no way of telling whether their ignorance was genuine, and I began to feel ridiculous. I was a big rich white man asking questions about one of their own. Whether they knew anything or not, these youngsters weren't about to help me.

I gave them a few coins and walked away through the hot sandy streets, trailing for a while a comet-tail of children begging for more money until the last of them grew bored and peeled off.

'Well, you tried,' Sacha said consolingly, as I climbed into the chill cavern of the Toyota. 'But what do we do now?'

'I've got an idea,' I said, and pulled out my mobile.

At his run-down compound near the stadium Remy greeted us like long lost friends.

The courtyard still swarmed with threadbare children, a few more roofs had fallen in, more walls had crumbled, but otherwise little had changed since my last visit. Remy's courage and his devotion to Kinshasa's street kids were as extraordinary as ever. Sacha, Petra and Andy had experienced many of the world's incredible people, but they were uncharacteristically quiet as we sat in Remy's office, sipping Coke we'd bought from a hawker. I could tell they were awed by the scale of the problem and by this man's determination, against all the odds, to tackle it.

'You think you can get this boy – this Londres – back to London?' Remy's glasses flashed eagerly at me.

'I don't know, Remy. This film's for the BBC, so at least we can publicize the story and make the British public realize this is going on. Maybe help stop it. But we won't know any of that until we find him.'

'It's the street kids themselves who'll know where he is,' Remy said. 'I'll put a team onto it.'

'A team?'

'Sure.' He waved airily. 'We're used to tracking down missing kids. We'll have someone set up nearby as a street trader ask some questions. Have someone else cycle past every couple of hours. That sort of thing. If he's there, they'll spot him sooner or later. Meanwhile, we should ask some questions ourselves.'

'I tried that. I think I scared them off.'

'No, we won't ask at the uncle's house.' Remy leaned forward. 'Richard, did you know a street child was killed by some soldiers yesterday?'

'No. That's terrible.'

'Of course, and it's one of the reasons the kids are wary about sharing information with people who look official. I hear there's going to be a big funeral for this child tomorrow. There'll be a lot of street children around. We should go. Keep our ears open.'

'You'd come with us?'

'Sure. I know these kids. They won't talk to four whites.'

Sacha picked up on this at once. 'Will we be able to film? That's what we're supposed to be doing.'

Remy thought about it for a moment. 'You're here

for the BBC,' he said. 'That should help, so long as they understand we're on their side. You have to be careful, though. People don't like cameras being pushed in their faces.'

'The vehicle's not very discreet,' I said. 'We've already discovered that.'

'We'll leave the car in a side street and go in on foot.' Remy said. 'You should be all right with me. I've never had any trouble.'

The funeral was to take place in a slum east of Kinshasa centre, a place of shanty buildings and dirt streets.

It was very hot when we got there. An open space between the buildings was seething with people, their backs to us. A dull roar rose from this mass, a threatening sound that I could feel in the pit of my stomach, not unlike the hum of a disturbed hive on the point of swarming.

We started through the crowd, with me and Remy in the lead. Just behind us Petra, half hidden by our bodies, was already filming. Andy was manoeuvring his cumbersome sound gear behind her. Remy, who knew more about the street kids of Kinshasa than anyone alive, was speaking gently and respectfully to the people around him in Lingala, parting the mob, looking for anyone who had authority.

All at once, through the shimmering heat, I caught a glimpse of the murdered child's body. He lay on a makeshift bier, a boy of five or six, killed the day before by a Congolese soldier. I didn't know why he had been killed – I didn't even know the poor child's name – but I could see the livid machete wound on his head.

We pushed on. Remy and I had come up with a plan of sorts. If we could find a relative, or a pastor who held some sway here, we'd give them money to see the child got a church burial. That at least would show our good faith. But I was already having my doubts. In the gathering glare of the Kinshasa morning, tempers were beginning to fray. There were outbursts of angry shouting up ahead and some hysterical weeping. We were well into the crowd by now, and the mass had begun to close behind us. I didn't like it. I had been around danger in Kinshasa before and I could smell it in the air, like high-octane fuel, waiting for a spark. People started to notice us. One or two pointed and others called questions.

I began talking in Lingala to the people in front of me, trying to explain that we only wanted to help. Beside me I could hear Remy doing the same. But I knew we weren't getting through to them. I could see that these people were in no mood to trust our motives, no matter what we said.

We edged on just a little further. Out of the corner of my eye the red light glowed on Petra's camera as she filmed from the shoulder. Sacha shouted from behind us, a warning of some sort. I could hear the tension in his voice. All at once a wild-eyed Congolese man in a faded AC Milan T-shirt materialized in front of me.

'Thief!' he shouted in my face. Then he screamed at all of us, 'Thieves!'

Was that what we were? Thieves? Was this entire exercise for our benefit rather than theirs? I caught a glimpse of a twenty dollar bill being incautiously offered by one of the crew, presumably to demonstrate our good intentions. Then someone stole Petra's cigarettes out of her jacket and I knew it was all going to go badly wrong. I heard, or sensed, the small commotion behind me as Andy cursed at the pickpocket, I half turned and the hot Kinshasa sky fell in.

The twenty-dollar bill was snatched from the upraised

hand. Someone jumped on me and I staggered and almost fell, catching a glimpse of Remy going down and the crowd surging around him, suddenly frenzied, kicking and screaming. I tried to straighten up. Another man got hold of my jacket, and another and another. I felt myself being smothered by their weight and their fury, their hands ripping at my clothes, the rank smell of their bodies stifling me. Someone was wrenching at my finger, trying to get my wedding ring off and prepared to take the finger with it.

A couple of yards away Petra and Andy were in retreat, dragging what they could of their gear with them, Sacha struggling to help, everyone shouting. My wallet went, then my new mobile phone, followed by anything else I had in my pockets. My shirt was literally torn off my back, and after that I only cared about getting my head down and somehow barging and shouldering my way through the screaming throng, with bodies hanging off me, pummelling and gouging at me. My only advantages were my size and the strength of my desperation. I had a fleeting vision of a bison dragged down by wolves, and I knew I was fighting a losing battle.

Without our driver, Apolossa, we would all have been torn apart. He had stayed with the car, parked in an alley a few metres away. Suddenly he reversed hard into the crowd, the Land Cruiser's doors flying open, and somehow we all scrambled into or onto the vehicle. He then floored the accelerator and we took off, bouncing down the rutted alleyways of Kinshasa's slums with men from the mob still insanely hanging on to the swinging doors, clutching at us. As we pulled out of the slums and on to the main road they eventually dropped off.

*

In another universe, though in reality perhaps only ten minutes later, we stood around the Land Cruiser at the side of a busy main road in the heart of Kinshasa, trying to come to terms with the fact that we were still alive.

Apolossa had gone to a roadside stall and brought back cigarettes and drinks. The drinks were the usual African selection – Coke, Fanta orange, Primus beer. I took a beer and leaned against the hot bonnet of the car. I hadn't tasted anything as good as that beer in a very long time, and I lingered over it, drinking in sips.

For a long while we were very quiet. We all had scratches, cuts and bruises. We'd lost most of what we'd been carrying – money, watches, bits of clothing and quite a lot of the gear, including Petra's $20,000 wide-angle camera lens.

Petra, who had filmed under fire in Iraq, Afghanistan and Bosnia, told me through the smoke of her third cigarette that this was the nearest she had ever come to death while on an assignment. Andy was visibly shaking as he busied himself with his equipment to keep his hands occupied. Sacha, who had managed to hang on to his mobile, was speaking into it, his voice quivering a little. He was talking to London, filing an incident report. After a moment he took the phone away from his ear and asked if any of us had any messages to pass on. I said I'd be grateful if someone from his office could put in a call to Faith and tell her I was OK. This was a mistake, since Faith had no reason to think otherwise, but I wasn't exactly thinking straight.

Sacha said, 'Sure. Anything else?'

'How's England doing in the Ashes?'

Sacha smiled wanly and went back to the phone to file his incident report.

I stole a glance at Remy. He was deeply shocked. He

had worked with Kinshasa's poor for thirty years and nothing like this had ever happened to him. I could see he felt responsible. At that moment none of us had enough spare courage or generosity to contradict him.

He looked up and met my eye. He had got it badly wrong and we both knew what that meant: Kinshasha was no longer a place that even a man with Remy's matchless experience could fully understand. It was a frightening thought. When I'd last been here, no one would have thought the city could get much worse. But it had.

Petra leaned against the bonnet beside me and tapped the ash from her cigarette.

'Tell me something, Richard,' she said with the glimmer of a smile. 'I know why I'm here. It's my job. But what's a nice guy like you doing in a place like this?'

At that moment Remy's mobile rang, startling us all. He fumbled it out of his pocket, perhaps surprised to find that he still had it after the mêlée. He spoke briefly into it, then looked at me.

'It's one of my team,' Remy said. 'Londres' uncle is at the house now.'

Sacha and I agreed that I would grab a taxi. He would take the crew to Boulevard Kasa-Vubu in the Land-Cruiser via the main roads. They would get close enough to film unless it was actually dangerous, but would stay as inconspicuous as possible.

When I arrived at the boulevard, I told the driver to wait and crossed to the red door between the garages. This time when I thumped on it the door was opened by a shifty man in a blue T-shirt and flip-flops. He looked startled to see me. I took advantage of the fact that I towered over him, and before he could marshal his thoughts I barked, 'Are you the uncle of a boy called Londres?'

'Who gave you this address?' he blustered, but under the bravado he looked guilty, as if I had caught him out, and I felt sure he had been inside the house and deliberately avoiding me on my earlier visit.

'It doesn't matter who gave it to me. Are you the boy's uncle or not?'

'Well, yes, but—'

'Is he here?' I looked past him into a shabby room with a plastic chair and a dirt floor.

'No.'

'Where is he, then? When are you expecting him?' I glimpsed the white Land Cruiser pulling up on the far side of the boulevard.

'I'm not expecting him,' he stammered. 'He's at my sister's.'

'Which is where?'

He gave me an address and I turned on my heel and marched to the taxi. I gave a cautious thumbs-up to the Land Cruiser across the road, and as we pulled away I had the reassurance of seeing the shiny vehicle nose into the traffic behind us.

To bitter complaints from the taxi-driver the route took us down a maze of sand-choked and potholed alleyways, into which the beaten-up cab bounced and bottomed. After about half an hour we stopped in a surprisingly well-to-do district, at least by Kinshasa standards. A lane shaded by palms led away from the street where we had parked, dwindling to a footpath a few metres down.

'There,' the driver said, jerking a surly thumb. 'The place you're looking for is down there.'

I paid him and he drove off at once. It was quiet after the mayhem of Kasa-Vubu. I started to walk down the narrow street. I felt very alone and a little afraid, and I was relieved when the white Land Cruiser appeared behind me and pulled up near the entrance. From there, I guessed, Petra would be able to film the house. I reached the address I had been given, a respectable dwelling with a security gate and – as I could glimpse over the wall – a couple of acacias growing in an inner court. I knocked on the door.

It was opened by a sullen woman of about thirty in a scarlet and white cotton wrap.

'I'm looking for a boy called Londres,' I said. 'Are you his aunt?'

She squared up to me. 'Why? Who are you?'

Evidently my bully-boy tactics were not going to work on this one.

'I've come from London,' I said, more agreeably. 'I'm a university researcher, and I'm writing a book about African churches. I'm very interested in Londres' story.'

'What story?' she demanded.

'I understood that he had come back to Kinshasa to undergo deliverance?'

'So? What of that?'

I hesitated, and in that moment a withered old woman appeared beside the aunt. She was toothless and keen-eyed and she peered narrowly at me.

'It's about that boy, is it?' she demanded. 'That Londres?'

'Yes, madam,' I said quickly, my heart beginning to thump. 'Is he here?'

'Nothing but trouble, that boy,' the old woman muttered. 'I should know. He's my grandson. They put him through deliverance at the church, but it didn't do much good. We sent him back for another lot. But the *kindoki*'s too strong in that one.'

'He has *kindoki*?'

'Of course he has. There's a lot of it about, but he's got it bad.'

'He's not here,' the younger woman put in before I could go on.

'But he lives here?'

'Sometimes.'

'Will he be back soon?'

'Who knows?' she said. 'He may be on the other side of the city. How should I know when he'll be back?'

'Could I wait for him? He's not in any kind of trouble, not with me. I just want to talk to him.'

She paused, but then gave in, perhaps realizing she was not going to get rid of me easily, or maybe convinced by my reassurances. Perhaps she even saw me as a potential source of profit.

'You'd better come in, then,' she said grudgingly. 'But like I say, I don't know how long he'll be. Maybe he won't come back at all tonight.'

I thought of the camera crew in the car just a few yards away. I didn't want them to lose sight of me.

'If it's not too much trouble,' I said, 'perhaps we could have a couple of chairs out here? It's so much cooler in the breeze.'

She shrugged, contemptuous of the eccentricities of foreigners, but brought out a couple of chairs and went back for another. In a few minutes, Londres' aunt, his grandmother and I were sitting in the gathering dusk waiting for the boy's return and chatting with stilted formality.

By this time we had an audience. A considerable crowd

of children had gathered around us, steadily filling the lane. Most looked better cared-for than the kids along Kasa-Vubu, but they behaved in much the same way, some standing and staring, mostly at me, and a few scuffling and shoving one another. When they grew boisterous the aunt would snap at them and they would fall silent for a minute or two before starting up again. They knew who I was looking for: I could hear Londres' name whispered among them.

I sat there in the mosquito-humming gloom for perhaps an hour. I dreaded the moment when the aunt would declare that we had waited long enough and tell me to clear off and not come back. I strongly suspected she thought I was trouble and I feared she'd got a message from someone to keep the boy away.

Just then one of the kids near my chair sidled up and jostled my arm. When I glanced at him he nodded down the alley to where a thin boy had just turned the corner and had stopped at the sight of the crowd.

'Londres,' the lad whispered in my ear.

I jumped up before anyone could speak to the new boy. I walked over to him, and as I drew closer I recognized him from his photographs. The gauntness of his face made his eyes look very large, and his whole aspect was wary and fearful, but he was the boy I was looking for. I felt a rush of relief.

'Hello, Londres,' I said slowly in English, not really sure if this child in the middle of the Congolese capital would really follow.

'Who are you?'

He wasn't tall for his age, but he had a certain breadth to his shoulders, and I guessed in England he would have been called stocky. Now the flesh had fallen away and left him looking pinched and underweight.

'My name's Richard,' I said. 'I've been looking for you.'

'For me? Why are you looking for me?' He looked cowed and unhappy, but his accent was pure street London, all flat vowels and glottal stops.

'He wants to hear your story,' the aunt called scornfully. 'I don't know why.'

The boy's eyes were full of suspicion.

I told him I'd heard he had been through deliverance, and that he'd been brought back to Kinshasa for that. He watched me in silence.

'They tell me you miss London,' I said.

'Yes.' I could see hope jump in his eyes. 'I miss London. I hate it here.'

'Nothing but trouble, that boy,' the toothless grandmother spat. 'Trouble and ingratitude.'

'Let's not talk about it now,' I said, leading him over to the two women and addressing myself to them. 'Why don't I come back in the morning and I'll take Londres out somewhere for the day?'

'Take him where?' the aunt demanded.

I said I'd take him somewhere respectable, and suggested the Portuguese Club, which wasn't far away and had a pool and a restaurant. I told the women I would buy the boy lunch and bring him back before dark. Before they could object I turned to Londres and asked him if he'd like a chance to chat about England, and especially football. He tried to look nonchalant, but in his eyes I could see a gleam of collusion, as if a secret message had been exchanged between us.

39

Kinshasa, August 2005

I was back outside the door by 9 a.m. the next morning.

I worried that Londres' family might have had a change of heart; when I arrived and the aunt opened the door to me I could see no sign of him.

'He'll be around,' the aunt told me, offhandedly. 'You can wait inside.'

She walked off into the house, her flip-flops slapping on the cement. This time I followed her, and she led me into a neat room off an internal courtyard. A tall, elderly man I had not seen before was already sitting there. He was grey-haired and had a certain bearing, and as I entered the room he rose and greeted me coolly.

He explained, with some dignity, that he was Londres' grandfather, and asked me to tell him what I wanted with the boy. I went through my patter: I was an academic, writing a book on the phenomenal rise of African revivalist churches, and I was interested in the experiences of someone who had gone through deliverance.

'Not that it did him any good,' the grandmother put in, shuffling past the doorway. 'Trouble, that boy.'

'I am concerned about this,' the grandfather said. 'I hear you want to take him to some club?'

It was a fair point. A foreigner appears out of the blue and wants to whisk your fourteen-year-old grandson off for the day? He had a right to be suspicious.

I said that I would take Londres for lunch, and maybe a swim, and that he would be back by the afternoon. I made a big thing of saying that naturally I wouldn't want to do any of this without the grandfather's agreement, and with that I produced a consent form. I had thought this piece of bureaucracy might be an obstacle, but now it worked to my advantage. Impressed by the formality of my important document, and with his authority acknowledged, the grandfather barely hesitated before signing.

As he did so, Londres walked into the room.

His face lit up when he saw me. Perhaps he hadn't truly believed I would come back.

'Hello, Londres,' I said. 'Shall we go?'

'Yes,' he replied, nodding rapidly. 'Yes.'

When we arrived at the Portuguese Club at ten that morning we were its sole guests. The only sign of life at all in the gathering heat of the day was an old man listlessly sweeping up between the poolside tables.

The club is one of those fading expatriate social clubs that can be found in every former colonial city. I had chosen it because it wasn't far from Londres' house and because I slightly knew one of the Congolese chefs. The crew set up under one of the thatched shelters that surrounded the pool.

Londres was surprised to find that he was to be filmed, and a bit overwhelmed by all these unexpected professionals bustling about, but the crew – Andy in particular – were wonderful with him and he soon relaxed. Within a few minutes, with a Coke on the table in front of him, he was telling me his story.

'I've been in London since I was four,' he said. 'I didn't know anything about this *kindoki*, or whatever it is.'

'And you didn't want to come back to Kinshasa?'

'Why would I? I don't even speak their language. All my mates are in London. Besides, I was always afraid of coming here.'

'Afraid? Why do you say that?'

'It's a place people try to get out of. Refugees and that. They only come back if they get caught or they've messed up.'

I could hear the faint whirr of the camera over my shoulder and could almost feel the crew engaging with his story. I was desperately sorry for Londres. I couldn't miss the sadness in his large, pleading eyes. I had been told he'd been in trouble at school, and I didn't have much difficulty imagining that, but to me he seemed like a typical fourteen-year-old London boy. He liked rap music and McDonald's and was passionate about football. He supported Manchester United and idolized Cristiano Ronaldo.

'Londres, do you have a British passport?'

'I would've had in another month. I was sent here just before I was going to get it.'

Just one more month.

'Tell me how you got here,' I said.

'My mum told me we were going on holiday. Switzerland, she said. I'd always wanted to go to the mountains, the snow and that. I was really excited. I thought she meant it. I really did.' He was quiet for a moment, thinking back to this betrayal, still wounded by it. 'I only caught on we were going to Kinshasa when we changed planes in Paris. Too late by then.'

'What happened?' I asked.

'When we landed, my mum handed me over to this bloke from the church. That's where he said he was from, anyway. I'd never seen any church like it. He took me away to some compound and locked me in a shed. Just like that, like I was a prisoner or something.'

'And your mum?'

'I saw her once more, a bit later. Then she went back to London and left me there.'

'And what happened to you in that place?'

'They call it deliverance. They're mad, this lot. I mean, seriously mental.' A flicker of fear entered his eyes and his voice. 'I was kept in this church place for four weeks. I was alone most of the time. I got bread and water, and not much of that.'

'For four weeks?'

'Every now and then these people would come in and shout and rave at me and sometimes slap me about. I didn't know what they wanted me to do. I couldn't even understand what they were saying. They just screamed and shouted and then went away and locked me up again on my own.'

'And then?'

'They said it hadn't worked. They moved me to some other compound and it all started again.' His voice became urgent and he leaned across the table. 'They're bad people, Richard.'

'The church, you mean?'

'Yes. They're bad news.' He looked around as if he might be being watched. 'They run all sorts of shit in this town. They can get anything done. You wouldn't believe.'

Londres was clearly very frightened, and I could see why. I was filled with an intense pity for this lonely, scared boy, marooned in what looked to him like a madhouse. It seemed very like that to me too.

'Can you take me back to London?' he asked suddenly. His tough-kid attitude had deserted him. 'Please, Richard. Take me home with you. I'd do anything to get out of here.'

'Londres, your family would never let me do that.'

'Please. I'll be stuck in this place for the rest of my life. I'll never get out.'

I couldn't answer him, and I sat staring stupidly at the boy for several seconds. It was Andy, the lanky soundman, who saved the moment. He took off his headphones and punched Londres lightly on the shoulder.

'Bollocks to this,' he said. 'Time to cool off.' And with that he stepped to the edge of the pool and threw himself in, fully clothed. In a couple of moments Londres and the rest of us were all in the water, in various states of undress, splashing around like kids. Someone found a ball and a half-hour game of improvised water polo followed, which continued as soccer once we had dragged ourselves out of the pool. I could see why Londres was so passionate about football: he was extraordinarily good, and ran rings around even Andy, who was no slouch when it came to ball skills.

Perhaps for the first time in months Londres became a teenage boy again, laughing and shouting, squelching around after the ball in his sodden clothes. It felt to me as if this was all I could give him, this hour or two of normal, boisterous life. I suppose it was something.

After that we treated him to lunch. He sat wrapped in a towel while his clothes dried in the sun. I told him to order anything he wanted – he had two main courses and a vast confection of a dessert – and at about three in the afternoon I called a cab and prepared to take him back.

He was laughing until the last moment, high-fiving the crew and cracking jokes, but once inside the cab his mood grew instantly tense again and his expression hangdog. We drove away from the club in silence, and he barely acknowledged the waves and shouted farewells of Andy and the others.

As we approached his aunt's house, his distress became even more evident and I felt desolate. I took him to the door, hugged him quickly and walked away, leaving him a forlorn and tearful figure, with his aunt and toothless crone of a grandmother flanking him like jailers. An ordinary London child, delivered into a ghoulish nightmare from which he could not escape.

Later that afternoon I contacted the British Embassy in Kinshasa.

'We're sympathetic, of course, Dr Hoskins,' an official told me. 'But if I understand you correctly, the boy isn't even a British citizen.'

'No, but he's been a resident of London for most of his life.'

'Hmm. Not good enough, I'm afraid. He's Congolese. He's a minor. He's here with the consent and approval of his parents. From what you're telling me, his mother actually brought him out here.'

'He doesn't want to be here. Doesn't he have any rights?'

'Of course he does, Dr Hoskins, but none that we can enforce.'

'So what do you suggest I do?'

'You could contact the Kinshasa social services department.'

'Are you serious?'

'I'm sorry. Truly.'

*

The next morning I took a cab straight round to the social services department of Kinshasa, a huddle of cinder-block offices in a littered backstreet. The visit proved to be every bit as much of a fiasco as I'd feared it would be.

I was greeted by a bad-tempered man in a white shirt who claimed he was the director. Speaking to me across a dusty desk entirely devoid of any signs of ongoing work he made it clear that he was profoundly uninterested in Londres' case. I didn't like him, but he had a point. The streets outside his barred windows were full of destitute kids – tens of thousands of them – stealing, starving, selling their bodies. Every one of them had a tragic story, many of them more tragic than Londres'. What was special about Londres, the director seemed to imply, except that I chose to think of him as British?

'I will make inquiries,' he said, and stared stonily at me to show that the interview was over.

I suspected that he had forgotten me and Londres by the time I had left the building.

Back at Sacha's room in the Memling hotel I called DC Jason Morgan in London.

'We have no jurisdiction, Richard,' he told me bluntly. 'We're the London Metropolitan Police, and you're in bloody Kinshasa.'

'You'd have jurisdiction if he was in England, wouldn't you?'

'Yes. But he's not.'

'He's a boy from London. In everything except citizenship he's as British as you or me. He deserves our help.'

'They all do. Get real, Richard. What do you want us to do? Send in a squad car?' When I said nothing his voice softened. 'Half the world deserves our help, mate. Almost no one gets it. It's not right, but it's the way it is. You know that.'

I put the phone down and went to the bar, where the crew were drinking. They knew what I'd been trying to achieve, and they'd known I would fail. They lowered their voices when I appeared, the way people do around the bereaved.

'Cheer up, Richard,' Sacha said at last. 'I've got us on a flight tomorrow. We can get back home and watch some cricket.'

Andy put a Primus on the bar in front of me. 'We could always kidnap the little blighter.'

Of course he was joking. But as I stared into the frosted glass, I wondered if I might do just that – take a cab round to the house in the morning, bundle the boy in and escape with him. I knew the system well enough. I could bribe our way through the airport and onto the plane. I might just get away with it. And in London? Presumably I would be arrested for abduction. But Londres would be back home – and what headlines we would make with the case! Could it be worth it?

'I want to get a sunset shot,' Petra announced, putting down her glass and breaking the thread of my insane reverie. 'Palm trees and rapids. Richard standing by the Congo River as the sun goes down. You know the sort of thing.'

We all followed her outside into the hot dusk and, helped by security guards from the hotel, we lugged the gear across the road to the riverfront promenade. I went along with it, allowing Sacha to tell me what sort of a piece to camera he wanted. I no longer cared much one way or the other, but there didn't seem to be anything else I could do, and I stood on the broken pavement while Petra framed her shot.

Mosquitoes whined off the riverside vegetation and

the soft boom of the falls filled the air. The sky above the vast river was a brilliant scarlet, as gaudy as a parrot's wing, and the mist from the rapids floated blood red, blurring the lights of Brazzaville on the far bank.

The usual little crowd had gathered to watch, laughing Congolese kids and passers-by, keen for any kind of entertainment. Traffic slowed while passengers got a look at us.

I paid no attention until an elderly Datsun pulled up almost at the kerb in front of me. The driver wound down his window and looked me in the eye, his face a mask of contempt. He spoke a short sentence of Lingala, then wound up his window and sped away with a screech of tyres.

Andy glanced at the receding tail lights. 'What was that all about?'

'You want a translation?' I asked him.

'Sure.'

'He said, "You fucking Westerners. You've stolen everything else, now you want our sunset too."'

At noon the next day I sat in the ruined departure lounge of Kinshasa airport and stared out at the acreage of tarmac as it wobbled in the heat.

I had found a place for myself some distance from the others, and I was grateful that they – sensing I wanted to be alone – had respected my privacy. I was depressed. I seemed unable to get my mind in order. I was in part suffering a delayed reaction to the riot in which we had all so nearly died. But the image which kept coming to mind was not the screaming aggression of that day, but the picture of Londres standing forlornly between his aunt and his grandmother, a tearful and abandoned child.

I was desolate at the thought that I had opened a

window onto his old life, without being able to offer him any way of escaping through it. We'd got our documentary, but what good would it do Londres? For that matter, what good would it do anyone in Africa? We had raised the *kindoki* issue and tried to show it for what it was. But would it make any real difference?

I gazed bleakly around the terminal. It was battered and bullet riddled, the seats broken and the glass cracked. I had been through here a few times now. During the riots of the early 1990s, when these bullet holes had been made, South African troops with machine guns had guarded the place against rebel assault while I saw off my wife and child from this spot. I remembered too the very first time I had come through this building, close to twenty years ago, a callow young man from the Home Counties. Then, I had been aghast at the confusion, the aggression, the shouting and chaos, but also seduced by the colour, heat and din. I had fallen in love with it all.

Had it all been worth it, my relationship with this place? What had it cost me and those around me? What had I really achieved? Had the sacrifice been worthwhile?

I thought of my two girls, buried 300 miles north of where I was sitting. And then I thought of Faith, sadly packing her bags to go and stay at her parents' in Devon, not quite leaving me. Not quite. Just during the week, I should understand, because I wasn't with her anyway. I was off trying to solve the problems of the world, problems which no one could solve, not alone. I missed her desperately. I missed her comfort, her love, her companionship, her warmth and affection.

I swore I wouldn't come back to the Congo again.

I'd had enough.

40

Devon and Sheffield, August 2005–2007

Faith was waiting for me when I walked through the barrier at Tiverton Parkway station. We held on to one another for a long time, oblivious to the people we forced to edge and shuffle past us. Eventually she broke away and handed me the keys. She asked me if I wanted to drive. Her voice was unnaturally high and she kept her face away from me.

It was full, glorious, Devon summer, the trees still and heavy in the afternoon and the air as warm as a scented bath. We got into the car and I drove a couple of miles out of town before either of us spoke again.

'I gather you had some trouble in Kinshasa,' Faith said, studiously looking out of the window at the hedgerows and golden fields.

'Yes. A bit.'

'That's what that mysterious call was about, was it? Saying you were all OK?'

I confessed that it was.

'You know the most frightening thing in the world, Richard? It's getting a phone call telling you not to worry.'

I told her I hadn't been thinking clearly at the time. Apparently she knew what had happened, at least in outline: she had shouted at the girl from the production company until she'd told her. Now Faith wanted the full story from me, but I couldn't face talking about it at that moment and I said so.

'We have to talk about it sooner or later,' she retorted, but something about my attitude was confusing her. She decided to change the subject. 'Dad's in hospital,' she said. 'Nothing too serious, at least I hope not. It's to do with his diabetes. But the timing's not great, with the hay all cut and just ready to be brought in, and this is the first spell of really good weather we've had. David Wood – the farmer up the road? – he's going to bale it up for us, but he can't do it all on his own. Mum's running the farm at the moment, and we're trying to hire someone for a day or two to help get the hay in.'

'No need. I'll give him a hand.'

She stared at me. 'You?'

'Yes, I realize I'm a bookworm of advancing years, but I might have a few days' honest work left in me yet.'

'But I thought you'd have to get straight back to London after the weekend. What about your casework? You won't have time.'

I had deliberately chosen the back road home from Tiverton. We were deep in the Devon countryside now, narrow lanes bordered by high hedges of beech and hawthorn, white cow parsley dense on the verges. I wound down the window so the soft air flowed over my face. When I saw the lay-by ahead I pulled over.

'What are you doing?' Faith asked slightly nervously.

I felt in my pocket for the police mobile, the one the new cases came through on. I weighed it in my hand for a moment and tossed it into the hedge. Then I slammed my foot firmly to the floor, the soft gravel spinning behind me as we pulled away.

Faith twisted in her seat and looked out of the rear window, as if she might be able to pick out where the mobile had fallen. After a moment she turned back to face me.

'Are you going to tell me what's going on?' she said.

'I put the London flat on the market.'

'You did *what*?'

'Just before I got the train down here. I went back to the flat and I looked around and I knew I couldn't live there – *we* couldn't live there – any more. I called the agents and put it on the market.' I looked at her. 'I know I should have discussed it with you first, but somehow I felt I didn't need to.'

'No,' she said, her voice tight. 'You didn't.'

We began work at noon the next day, when the heat of the morning sun had dried the cut hay. For hours I followed the tractor as it bumbled and clanked across the dusty field. The tractor was supposed to be fitted with an appliance for loading the bales, but naturally it didn't work, so it was left to me and Faith's mother to load the trailer by hand.

All through that afternoon I heaved bale after bale off the ground and into the trailer, then unloaded them again in the barn and stacked them eight high. Mice and voles scrambled away to safety and crickets bounced from under my feet. Faith kept up a steady stream of lemon squash and tea throughout the day, laughing at me as I wrestled with the heavy bales.

Finally, David silenced the tractor's engine and walked over to me, his boots crunching on the stubble. He was a lean, thoughtful man of about my own age, not much given to talking, which was just as well, because his West Country accent was so strong I could barely understand him. We stood in companionable silence. The sun was low above the western horizon, and the first bats began to flicker from the wood.

'You can't beat it, can you?' David said. 'Working the land.'

The path home took me past the lake excavated by Faith's parents, which was now well stocked with trout, close to the caravan where I had sat for weeks on end studying the Adam case. I stopped in the long grass, looking out over the lake and listening to the soft trickle of the stream that fed it. It was here that I'd been spooked by the Chokwe death mask. I had phoned Blessing in Lagos from that caravan, and briefed Will O'Reilly, and tried to help build the case that had come to determine the course of my life over the last five years.

'Hello,' Faith said. 'You look as if you could use a drink.'

I hadn't seen her, sitting on the bench by the water's edge. There was a tray and a couple of bottles of beer on the seat beside her. She handed one to me as I sat down beside her.

'There's something I've been meaning to tell you.' I looked out over the water. 'When I was back at the flat the other day I took a call from Nick. He'd been trying to get hold of me while I was out in Africa. They buried Adam.'

Faith was startled. 'I didn't see anything about that on the news.'

'No, well you wouldn't have. Apparently there were only a couple of police officers present. They wanted it done without fuss. They just buried him quietly in an unmarked spot in Southwark cemetery.'

I pictured a tiny grave, a couple of thoughtful policemen standing to one side. Adam had been buried not a mile from where his body had been found, in the heart of the grey city that must have seemed so alien to him. I wished he could have known how much effort the people of that city had made to find justice for him.

After a while I broke the silence. 'David Wood just told me that you can't beat it. He's right, isn't he? This. The land. The countryside. It's magical down here.'

'Then let's find somewhere not far from my parents. They could use our help around the farm.'

At that moment I wanted nothing more.

Over the next year I combined work on the farm with heading up the religious studies department at the local school. And, of course, coaching the under-13 cricket team.

One afternoon as the clouds lifted and the sun eventually broke through, I stationed myself at the bowler's end. The distant horizon was dominated by the dark mass of Dartmoor, the foreground by green fields dotted with English oaks.

Callum marked his run-up for the first delivery. Jack, the new batsman, stood back to survey the fielders. I followed his gaze. Anna, Jack's sister, was at fine leg. Picking her had been controversial. The boys had muttered darkly about girls playing cricket. One or two of the more sophisticated ones thought it was political correctness. I enjoyed their mild cheekiness but I knew I was right. Her first over of the new season she'd bowled out three of the top batsmen.

This game meant so much to me. Here was a chance for these children to do something as a team. This was a place where they could find the space to grow and, in some cases, to heal. I had heard their stories. Many were, of course, from loving and stable environments, but few were born with a silver spoon in their mouth, and some had suffered trauma, tragedy, abuse or neglect. A fair number were from broken homes.

As Callum thundered forward I leaned in slightly, keeping an eye on the popping crease. Jack planted his back foot firmly outside his off stump and cracked the ball square to the boundary.

Elated, I signalled to the scorers.

In February 2007 I was summoned to Sheffield Crown Court to give evidence in a case I'd worked on a few years earlier.

I stood to the right of the defendant, Martin Paul Brown, not more than a few feet away from him. The jury returned their verdict of guilty for the 1988 murder of Keith Slater. Brown was jailed for a minimum of thirteen years.

Had I really been any help to all the people who had asked me to explain these horrors to them over the last few years? I certainly hadn't found all the answers. All I could hope for was that they would never stop asking for one, never stop being shocked. God help us all if we ever reached the stage when this kind of behaviour seemed normal.

After I left court I was collared by BBC *Crimewatch*, who wanted to make a special feature on how the case was solved. As I concluded the final interview for the programme I vowed it would be my last, and then slipped back to Devon.

For six years I had been exposed to the darkest underbelly of human nature. The cases involving children had left me close to despair. I needed some distance. Devon was giving me that. Faith was now heavily pregnant; I had a new life on which to focus. I did my best to ensure that the police and social services could no longer track me down. Enterprising media types occasionally broke through, but I politely declined all comers.

In the late summer of 2007 Faith gave birth to our son Silas and I felt more settled than at any time since Bolobo. Tucked away in our West Country idyll, I had successfully shut out the 'madding crowd's ignoble strife' and it seemed as if my life was complete once more.

41

Devon, 2007–January 2011

The police hadn't entirely abandoned their attempts to find Adam's killer. With some audacity they had secured an early release for Kingsley Ojo, hoping that they could persuade him to work undercover for them. Although Nick and Will believed Ojo's denials about his involvement in the actual sacrifice of Adam, despite his involvement in trafficking, they hoped he would take them to the killers. But for the next year, Ojo led them on a series of wild goose chases, then disappeared back to Africa.

With what seemed like the last throw of the dice, Nigerian police traced Joyce Osagiede in the spring of 2008. They interviewed her under caution, hoping that she might help them trace Adam's movements during his final weeks. She gave them a lead about the boy's true identity, and aimed the British police towards a potential new witness in Germany. It proved to be another blind alley.

With that, Will O'Reilly and Andy Baker retired from the force, Nick Chalmers was given new responsibilities, and it seemed as if the last vestiges of the investigation had melted away. Desperately disappointed, I withdrew still further from the world of murder enquiries. Teaching consumed much of my time, and the rest I was able to devote to family.

At the start of the new school year a notice appeared in the staff common room asking for runners to join the 2009 London Marathon in aid of the Joint Educational Trust, a National Children's Foundation charity that places kids who are at risk of abuse, trauma or tragedy in healing environments.

I'd never run a marathon before. In fact, I had done little running of any kind since my schooldays. I was overweight, unfit and in my forties. But the aims of JET so perfectly matched the goals that had been central to my life for so long that I couldn't turn my back on the challenge.

A few weeks later I was in training. I began to run to school in all weathers, along the winding Devon lanes, and lost four stones in the process. I'd discovered the ultimate stress reliever. I never ran to music; the rhythms of running and breathing generate their own entirely natural and refreshingly meditative cadences. As April arrived I was fitter than at any time since my first few months in Bolobo. I raised a couple of thousand pounds for the cause and managed to run the marathon well inside three hours and fifteen minutes, which guaranteed me a place for the following year. Running was becoming addictive.

The whole student boarding body was waiting up to greet my return to north Devon. I stood there feeling sheepish, sore and ridiculously proud as the pupils cheered and applauded. It was one of the great moments in my life.

We moved into a house on the farm itself and added two Kunekune piglets and a cat to the family circle. I kept up the running and, of course, the cricket, even dusting off my boots to play for the local side.

Then, early in 2011, I received an email from an ITN address. A freelance called Rienkje Attoh had tracked me down through my former head of department at Bath Spa University. I emailed back politely, putting her off.

Or so I thought.

Her response arrived two minutes later. As the leading expert on the case, it claimed that if they didn't interview me about 'the sensational story' their reporter Ronke Phillips had uncovered, the piece would be the poorer for it. They had intelligence from a key source, which supported all my theories.

I couldn't resist responding: 'Which case are we talking about?'

'Adam.'

I sat at my desk and stared out of the window. It had been bitterly cold. Like much of the country, north Devon had taken a battering from blizzards and severe frost. Now it was as if a switch had been flicked and spring had suddenly appeared. I stared out at the mulberry tree that seemed to have sprung straight out of a nursery rhyme and taken root in our front lawn.

I'd already hesitated a fraction too long.

I knew Ronke Phillips, a highly educated Nigerian with dual citizenship, from the Child B case. As ITV's crime correspondent she'd covered the darker side of London's rich and varied multicultural criminal tapestry. A few days later, we settled into a café near Waterloo Station.

Will O'Reilly had called her. He'd retired at around the time I'd gone into hiding, but he still had sleepless nights about the Adam case. 'It's the one that got away,' Ronke said. 'It's the only unsolved child murder in the capital. He knows they should have solved it. He knows they let one of the chief suspects slip through their fingers.' She paused. 'But I've found her.'

We'd leapt through these hoops in 2008. The Nigerian police had elicited some sort of statement from Joyce under oath, but it had petered out through lack of corroborating evidence. I was beginning to regret having come.

'She's confessed to the whole thing: bringing him in from Germany; handing him over to someone here.'

She told me how at the end of the previous year she and Will had flown out to Lagos at ITV's expense. With a bit of robust journalism Ronke had tracked down Joyce's brother and then Joyce herself. The interview had contained some prompting and Joyce had appeared a little short of marbles, but Ronke was in no doubt about the weight of her confession to the trafficking. She corroborated my theories about the preparation for and act of sacrifice, as well as the ritual deposition in the river. And she repeated her claim that she knew the boy's identity.

'She has given me an actual name.' Ronke looked at me expectantly.

I leaned forward.

'Ikpomwosa.'

I repeated the name slowly, separating each syllable: 'Ik-pom-wo-sa.' If Joyce was to be believed, the boy in the river now had a name.

She then passed me a photograph.

It was the one the police had seized from Joyce, taken in Germany at the time she was trafficking him to London. The image will always be etched on my mind: a young boy in a blue buttoned-up jacket, with innocent eyes and a smile that carried all the cheekiness, delight and zest for life a boy of six should have. Joyce had kept it because her own two children, now in care in the UK, were standing alongside him.

42

Devon, February 2011

'Phone call for you.'

Faith leaned out of the window.

'Very bad moment. I'm teaching Silas how to play a Pietersen chip through mid-wicket. Tell them I'll call back.'

I placed the plastic ball on the grass in front of us and together we pinged it into a nearby rose bush.

'He says it's really important . . .'

The voice at the other end of the line sounded strangely euphoric.

'Dr Hoskins? I'm Simon Metcalfe and I've spent the past three years looking for you. You did an excellent job. Kicking over the traces, I mean.'

I racked my mind. Metcalfe?

'Are you familiar with the National Policing Improvement Agency?'

I confessed that I wasn't.

He explained that the NPIA pulled together all the major cases in the UK, and sometimes beyond, then sought specialist assistance for the senior investigating officers.

'There's been another African child murdered in London. Witchcraft case. The *kindoki* thing you used to talk about. Terrible torture; days and days of it. We need you back. Please. For this poor little bugger's sake.'

I stared at the picture on the desk in front of me. Those sparkling eyes gazed back.

I sat down and nudged the mouse. My computer screen flickered into life. I nestled the receiver under my chin and clicked the Word icon. Without quite realizing it, I was about to start taking notes.

Sometime later I wandered back into the kitchen. Faith was setting a plate of tea down in front of Silas, who was busy trying to describe what the Pietersen shot should look like. His glass of milk seemed as if it might be about to get the treatment. It was the perfect family scene. The one these children should have had. Faith saw the expression on my face.

'You . . . are . . . joking . . .'

I shook my head weakly.

'I knew he was a police officer. I just knew it.'

I nodded.

She looked down at Silas. 'Flipping heck. After all these years.'

'It's another African boy, in London. A *kindoki* exorcism.' I lowered my voice so Silas might not hear. 'It's very, very nasty. They say they need me . . .'

'All I ask is that you don't bring it into our lives like you did last time. I don't mind, honestly. If they really need you, they need you, and you must help. But keep it separate this time, OK? Keep this as . . . well, *this*.' She nodded from me to Silas.

'That seems reasonable,' I said quietly.

'No, I mean it. Keep it away from here. From him. From

us. Find a place to work on it, and then have your fix here. Just don't bring the darkness back into our family life. Or our marriage.'

As a coping strategy, it suddenly seemed blindingly obvious.

43

London, March 2011

It was a warm day in early spring as the DLR train approached Royal Albert Dockside station. The Olympic stadium rose like a toadstool from the flat wasteland of the East End. Brash developments were interspersed with sections of marshland and rows of houses unimpressed by the sudden presence of flash new money. New-builds looked as if they had been parachuted in, untouched by their surroundings. The ExCel Centre glistened in the sunshine.

Newham Dockside, as it was nicknamed, had apparently cost the local borough – working amongst some of London's most deprived inhabitants – at least £130 million. Melanie Adegbite had sounded quite sheepish when she'd given me directions. Now I could see why. The central atrium looked more like the Eden Project than a council office block. Giant palms soared upwards, surrounded by a glass fortress. A reception desk was tucked furtively to one side, doing its best not to detract from the spectacle. I'd witnessed such misplaced opulence in parts of Africa; I hadn't expected to find it here.

Melanie was in her late thirties. She greeted me with a warm smile and explained that she was a safeguarding intervention officer. We would be joined by representatives of the different parties in the case.

For the next two hours I sat in a conference room answering questions on Congolese culture, witchcraft, exorcism and attitudes to children. The assembled company needed guidance on motivation as well as assistance with the family network involved in the case. The tentacles of this crime seemed to spread far and wide and I was their link to a dark and unfamiliar world. I outlined the basic tenets of *kindoki* and deliverance. As the meeting closed Melanie reminded us of the Section 39 court order imposed on the case – effectively gagging the media until the trial.

I emerged into the late afternoon sunshine. As I climbed up to the DLR platform I looked out across the rooftops. I paused there for some minutes, oblivious to the arriving and departing trains. Somewhere to the right of the Olympic stadium lay Hathaway Crescent, Manor Park. One of the most brutal cases of child torture and murder in this country's history had taken place there, with possible paedophile links in the UK and in Europe. I pulled my jacket more tightly around me and headed back into the city.

That evening I laid out the case documentation on my desk and began to go over it once more. I'd taken a flat in London. It wasn't anything grand – it didn't need to be: I had all the space and beauty I could wish for in the West Country – but it gave me a way of keeping my work on the case physically separate from our home life. I spent the week in London when required, and went back to Devon for long weekends.

Kristy Bamu arrived in London on 16 December 2010. His parents had sent him and his four siblings to stay with their older sister Magalie, her boyfriend Eric Bikubi and their young son.

The mother and father were from the DR Congo but now lived in Paris. They travelled regularly to Britain and worshipped in a revivalist church in North London. During the autumn they had become concerned that at least one of their children was possessed by *kindoki*. Magalie and Eric, who both held British citizenship, were members of the same church; the London trip would enable them to properly investigate the matter. What triggered the parents' conviction was not clear, but it seemed they had begun suffering from bad luck and bad dreams – 'voodoo dreams' as their father described it. They seemed particularly concerned that the sorcery would affect the other children.

Between 19 and 24 December all the children underwent sustained and systematic torture. They were made to stand in a line for all four days without food or drink and were beaten with a horrifying variety of instruments until one of them cracked. Police later found over thirty weapons, including light bulbs, a six-inch knife, four-inch pliers, large floor tiles, a wooden stick, a table leg, a large black metal dumb-bell, a small metal pole and a hammer.

When the eldest son, Kristy, wet himself in terror, it appears that Eric and Magalie focused on him as the most likely conduit for the *kindoki*. Kristy had tried in vain to cover up his incontinence. The poor boy must have been absolutely terrified. During a graphic phone call to his parents on Christmas Eve, a traumatized Kristy told them he thought he'd be killed by Eric unless they came to rescue him. The phone call ended. Nothing happened.

*

A ferocious onslaught was now unleashed on the boy. The two adults took it in turns to torture him. When Eric grew tired, Magalie took over until he felt sufficiently recharged. They forced other siblings to join the torture on pain of death if they didn't conform. Teeth and nails were pulled out, fingers smashed with a hammer. Pliers were used to cut off parts of Kristy's body. He was forced to drink the urine of one of the other siblings and he was beaten and stabbed with a variety of instruments, suffering over a hundred serious injuries.

Later that day Kristy was dragged into the bathroom and submerged in water. The other children were forced to sit on top of him and watch the final moments of his life. Once his struggle was at an end, Eric and Magalie sprinkled the water from the bath over the children in some sort of purification rite. Both Victoria Climbié and Child B had also been put in the bath.

Magalie Bamu then telephoned for an ambulance.

When the crew arrived there was blood splattered all over the floor of the flat, and all over the walls, curtains and ceiling. They found blood-stained instruments strewn everywhere. CPR on Kristy proved almost impossible as dislodged teeth were stuck down his throat.

I got up from my desk, tears welling and feeling physically sick. I needed some air. I stepped out into the cool evening. People bustled back and forth, jostling for position on the pavements. I'd chosen this place, not far from Clapham Junction, as it offered me a quick escape route on Southwest Trains. It also had a vibe I liked. Right now the busyness was a good antidote to the horror of what I'd just been reading.

I wandered down to The Falcon, the pub on the intersection of St John's Hill, Falcon Road and Lavender Hill. There was a reassuring hum from within, and the familiar smell of beer wafted out. I pushed the door open and within minutes was being served by a smart barman in black trousers, matching apron and white shirt.

I was too shaken by the case to want to dwell on which of the dozen real ales I should choose, so I let him decide for me. A moment later I was settled at my own table looking across the street to the old Arding and Hobbs department store building.

Boisterous young people spilled onto the street from the Slug and Lettuce next door, but in here the hum was comfortingly restrained. The horseshoe-shaped bar helped induce a sense of cosiness and tradition. It was perfect. I cradled the glass in my hands and reflected on what I had been reading. The attack on Kristy was brutal. I wondered if such sustained savagery against a child had been seen before in this country.

I sipped my beer and watched the buses turning through the intersection. A kaleidoscope of light. Cars whisked their passengers to all quarters of the city and beyond. Immediately outside the window strangers of every gender, colour, age and belief moved along the pavements. Laughter erupted from next door and someone struck up a song. It might not have been pretty, but it was blissfully normal. Psychopathic killers were still rare, and I had to keep remembering that. I downed the last of the ale, thanked the barman and made my way back to the flat.

I picked up the pathology report.

There were three concurrent causes of death: haemorrhage at the base of the brain below the cerebellum; drowning and internal bleeding. A second post-mortem revealed a screw in Kristy's intestine, showing it had been ingested some hours before death.

I didn't sleep well that night. I was out of tune with London's ambient noise, and the combination of radiator heat and case notes sent me into a state between wakefulness and fitful dreams that included screams, witchcraft and soapy warm ale being served by a leering barman carrying a hammer.

At first light I pulled on my running gear and headed out onto Clapham Common. I'd never needed much sleep and I knew a few miles at dawn would prepare me for the day ahead. Besides, I had another marathon coming up soon.

44

London and Devon, April–May 2011

Over the next few weeks my new police mobile began to ring with ever greater frequency. A queue of new cases formed, from gangland attacks to child abuse; Africa to Malaysia; it seemed as if the dam had burst. I was suddenly extremely busy.

The coping strategy seemed to be working.

On Friday afternoons, as the train pulled out of Crewkerne station, bound for the Devon border, a simple flick of the thumb switched off my email until I headed back up to the metropolis the following week. The NPIA knew how to get hold of me in an emergency, but this way I could keep the regular casework at bay. Faith was right, but it was for *my* sanity as much as hers.

April saw me run the London marathon again for the National Children's Foundation. I'd shed so much weight in training that I was looking gaunt, but I was becoming a fairly serious runner for my age. Some sponsors were prepared to shell out extra donations for the children if I could break the three-hour barrier. As I set out from Blackheath in the great throng of 32,000 participants I felt positive and confident, despite the effects of a nasty migraine a few days before.

By the time we reached the halfway point at Tower

Bridge I was worried. The sun was beating down fiercely, my right hip was starting to ache, and the brand-new white shirt I had donned for the charity was stained red by my bleeding nipples.

I was hurting, and for the first time in a race I seriously felt like giving up. There was another marathon in Edinburgh in a few weeks' time, and I could regroup for that. Dropping out might be sensible.

As I pushed up the incline of the bridge I found myself glancing to the right over the parapet towards the distant water. The river was the colour of steel. Another man had glanced over this parapet at this very point as the world was still reeling from the events of 9/11. He had glimpsed a flash of orange in the water and hurried down the steps to discover the mutilated body of a small boy. A boy who became known as Adam.

There was nothing sinister in the water now, just some scummy foam and a cluster of plastic bottles.

I pictured Ikpomwosa's beautiful face, as I had done many times in recent months. The boy in the river, who now had a name and an identity, but whose life had been taken so cruelly.

I pulled the cricket cap down over my eyes and dug deep, very deep. I don't remember much of the remaining miles except pain, but I crossed the finish line in two hours and fifty minutes.

Ronke Phillips also ran the marathon for a children's charity that day. We'd continued to swap training notes up until race day, and we swapped congratulations as we finished.

Eric Bikubi and Magalie Bamu appeared before Mr Justice Ryder at the Old Bailey a few days later, to be remanded in custody pending trial. The media were starting to circle, and Ronke had a proposal from the ITV news team.

Shortly after, I was sitting in front of a bank of computers assigned to the *London Tonight* team.

'We obviously wouldn't broadcast until the day of the convictions,' Ronke said. 'The usual rules apply. We prepare the piece as much in advance as we can, then hit the transmit button on the day of the verdict.'

'Sounds good,' I replied. 'So where do I fit in?'

'We want to take you to Kinshasa for a week's filming.'

'Oh fuck.'

The expletive had come out before I could stop it. Faces peered over screens, eyebrows raised. One lady looked at me particularly sternly. Ronke was clearly expecting some explanation.

'The last time I went out there with a TV crew I was nearly killed. I swore I'd never go back.'

Ronke looked at me firmly. 'I do understand,' she said, not altogether unkindly. 'I know what it can be like out there. We will film it very low key, with just a cameraman, you and me.'

The BBC crew had been bigger – and white: we must have stuck out like a sore thumb. This would be very different.

I was still wavering when I caught sight of the photo she had pinned to her monitor. The photo of Ikpomwosa.

It didn't take more than a moment to agree.

But on the train home, as Devon approached I found it increasingly hard to explain to myself why I'd agreed to do this film, let alone to Faith and Silas. Until I thought once more of a little boy's smiling face. The boy in the river.

45

Kinshasa, August 2011

N'djili Airport, Kinshasa, on a tropically misty evening in the middle of August: my fellow passengers erupted in applause as we landed – a delightfully African response to the wonder of air travel. I wasn't in the mood to join in. The last time I'd been here, broken and exhausted by the heartrending cases I'd witnessed, I'd vowed never to return.

Six years later, I was back with another film crew. Persuading Faith of the wisdom of the trip had taken some doing, but I think she'd always known why I needed to make it. She was holding the fort in Devon, her energies focused on our family home, and she looked forward to seeing me return. That was all I needed to know as I set off once more for Central Africa.

It seemed incredible to me that a quarter of a century had passed since I'd first landed here, complete with Land Rover driveshaft. As I walked into the terminal building with Ronke and Bill, the cameraman, little seemed to have changed. Except for the conveyor belt: tonight it was working. The bags were still hurled through the hole in the wall, but they now made their way relatively smoothly to their awaiting owners.

No one batted an eyelid at our camera equipment. I

didn't believe in omens, or so I told myself, but if my last visit here with a camera crew had seemed doomed from the outset, this one appeared to be off to a good start.

Our host for the first two days was Isabel del Arbol from Save the Children. She had previously worked in-country with the United Nations, and was now overseeing their project for children accused of witchcraft. She and her colleagues took children off the streets and worked, where possible, towards rehabilitating them with their families. Under Isabel's careful eye we visited the children in their housing centres and talked with some of them who'd been accused of having *kindoki*, and suffered beatings and torture as a consequence.

On the third day I met Remy Mafu again. The pipes were no longer in evidence outside his offices but everything else was much as I'd last seen it. Remy greeted me like a long lost friend, and as we embraced I felt acutely conscious that in withdrawing from these cases I had also withdrawn from people who'd been very good to me. His best news was that Londres, the boy we'd tracked down on my last visit, had been returned to London by his family. Perhaps, after all, we had done some good. I promised myself to try and get in touch with him on my return.

The rest of our day was rather more depressing. There were still thousands of children on the streets, many because they'd been accused of *kindoki*. New churches were continuing to spring up, peddling the same twisted message of witchcraft and childhood possession. A little girl sleeping rough in Limete district talked of a church nearby where she'd been subjected to a ceremony of deliverance. Someone left the metal compound door open and she'd escaped.

It wasn't difficult to find the Church of Deliverance – its

name was emblazoned across a pair of large blue gates. I walked through the entrance with some trepidation as Bill and Ronke followed with the camera. A number of children sat forlornly on benches in the foyer. One girl – she couldn't have been older than five – stared out at us like one of those glazed Somali famine pictures. I wondered for a moment if she was still breathing. I crossed the dirt floor to where she sat, but as I did so a middle-aged man moved swiftly to intercept me.

'*Que voulez-vous ici?*'

'Is this girl OK?' I said.

'I ask you what you want here?'

I tore my eyes away from the girl. The man was around forty, with a pronounced beer belly straining against the buttons of his white shirt and the waistband of his blue trousers.

'I need to speak with this girl.' I stepped forward and crouched alongside her. In the gentlest Lingala I could muster, I asked her how she was feeling.

Her reply was not much more than a whisper. 'I feel . . . bad . . . hunger . . . no water . . .' She pointed at her mouth. Her tongue was cracked and dry. I felt my compassion give way to rising anger. I turned on the man now standing over me. 'What the hell is going on here?'

He took a step back. 'You must await the pastor.'

So he wasn't the top man. I wasn't surprised.

'I am not awaiting anyone. I asked you a simple question, which you can answer yourself. What is going on?'

He looked at me, then at Ronke and Bill, who were filming the exchange. He licked his lips slowly. 'She is . . . fasting.'

'What kind of fasting?'

'She has not had food or drink for three days. She has

kindoki. We are preparing her so that she will be delivered of this evil witchcraft.'

This was too much for Ronke. She exploded. The tirade that followed, mostly in English, was one that only an African could deliver. As Ronke harangued him for child abuse, I noticed another gentleman approaching. He was wearing a shiny light blue suit that looked as if it had been carefully tailored. His gold-framed glasses, cufflinks and watch seemed like the real deal. I glanced down at his shoes and guessed that only the choicest slivers of crocodile skin had gone into their manufacture.

The pastor had arrived.

His unabashed nonchalance was immediately infuriating. Right next to us, staring vacantly into the distance, was a young girl who had neither eaten nor drunk for three days, whilst the man towering over her, claiming to be a representative of Christ on earth, explained how her evil *kindoki* meant she needed to fast in preparation for deliverance.

I shuddered to think what this might entail. We had to do something.

'I'm seeing the Children's Minister tomorrow,' I lied. 'You are, presumably, happy for me to bring the minister here so she can see your ministry at work?'

For the first time there was hesitation.

'We have all the government documents to say we can operate—'

'Excellent. So there's no problem then. What time shall we make the appointment?'

There was silence. The pastor looked from me to Ronke, then to the girl, then nervously at the camera.

We waited.

'What do you want us to do with her?'

'Give her something to drink!' Ronke and I shouted in unison.

'I would rather not,' the pastor eventually responded.

'What does that mean? *Rather* not?'

'Jesus said that this type of demon can only come out through prayer and fasting. She needs to be deprived of food and water. It's nearly over for her. Tomorrow we will deliver her. I would rather she didn't eat or drink.'

'Look, she desperately needs water,' I said. 'She's in a bad way. This is tropical Africa. She has got to have something to drink.'

We seemed to be at an impasse.

Ronke was seething. In English, we quickly discussed removing the girl, but knew that could be construed as kidnap. We were powerless to do anything except carry out my original threat.

We left the compound and clambered wearily into our ageing Land Rover. As the driver turned over the engine, I realized there was one other tack I could try. 'Hold it. I'm going back in.'

Ronke made to follow.

I shook my head. 'Just me. I want a quick word with the pastor. There's something I want to talk to him about. Off camera, please.' Before I slammed the door behind me, I added, 'And if I'm not back in ten minutes you'd better follow.' I meant it half-humorously; I didn't really think the church team would be violent towards an adult, but one could never be sure.

On the other side of the gate a sizeable group had gathered round the pastor. He was talking animatedly whilst the little girl still sat motionless. He stepped towards me, a face like thunder. I held up my hands. 'Pastor, there's no camera this time. I just want to talk with you about one thing that's troubling me.' I motioned to some seats. 'May we . . .?'

The pastor hesitated, then finally nodded.

I waited until his companions had settled around us.

'What is it?' he asked. 'You came in here and insulted Christ's ministry. You'd better have a very good reason for daring to come back.'

I ignored the undercurrent of threat. 'Pastor, I honestly want to ask you just one question.' I paused, trying to remember my Bible verses. 'It's very simple really. I just want to know what you are doing here.'

The pastor's faint look of astonishment gave way to laughter, which rippled through the gathering. His smile faded again as he turned to face me again. 'That's what you came back in here to ask me? I'm a busy man. Isn't it obvious? I'm here to do the work of Jesus Christ on earth.'

'No, sorry, that isn't quite what I meant. Let me rephrase it.' I paused. 'Why aren't you in Troas?'

'Troas? Who, what or where is Troas? I don't know it.'

There was a further ripple of laughter. One or two of his entourage began whispering behind me. The white man had lost it. Perhaps the sun had addled his mind.

'Actually, it's not even in Africa. It's in Asia Minor. Quite a long way from here. I just wondered why you aren't there?'

He was clearly beginning to get exasperated with me, but I pressed on.

'Look, it says in the Bible, "Go to Troas and search for my cloak."' I just wondered why you're not following that biblical command.'

I looked around the crowd. 'Can one of you bring me a Bible, please?'

It took only a few moments for a young man in a blue T-shirt to fish one out of a small rucksack.

'Now read it, please. Paul's Second Letter to Timothy, chapter four, verse thirteen.'

There was some fumbling, and murmured debate about where in the New Testament this verse could be found. After a while, he appeared to have found the relevant passage. He cleared his throat: '"The cloak that I left at Troas with Carpus, bring it with you when you come . . ."'

I waited for a few seconds, then turned again to the pastor. 'So . . . why aren't you in Troas, getting Paul's cloak?'

There was some muffled laughter behind me. They were getting the drift. I thought I caught the faintest smile on the pastor's face.

'That was written for someone a long time ago: an instruction for a specific time and place.'

'Exactly. So how do you decide that? How do you decide which instructions are for a specific time and place, which you can just ignore, and which you must obey now? How do you know that instruction about fasting wasn't also written for a specific time and place, just like the command to find and bring Paul's cloak?'

'It's what we believe.' The pastor sounded suddenly weary.

I took my chance. 'Look, as a favour to me, given that we're not one hundred per cent certain about the meaning of that instruction today, could you just give her one glass of water?'

The pastor looked at me, then at those gathered around me. Finally, he spoke. 'OK, just this once, you understand – I will do this. If, and only if, you now leave us alone.'

I agreed and he nodded to one of the ladies behind him.

'Give her a cup of water.'

'Thank you.' I stood and watched as the girl's tentative, bird-like sips turned to gulps and I knew it would see her through until the morning.

Ronke looked at me quizzically as I got back into the Land Rover.

'It's OK,' I said. 'I just needed to clear up a small matter of biblical interpretation.'

I knew it was a pyrrhic victory, but it might at least have helped this one casualty.

A few days later we flew out of N'djili Airport.

On a purely journalistic level, the trip had been a success. My Lingala had proved useful and I'd worked my socks off. But it was a sober team that landed back at Heathrow the following day. The *kindoki* poison had spread throughout the Congo, but nothing we had seen there matched the ferocity of what had taken place in one London flat.

I didn't believe that Europe was just seeing a momentary overspill of misguided religious fundamentalism. Something much worse was beginning to flourish beneath the farcical ignorance and superficiality of the pan-European multicultural agenda. Children were being trafficked and used for benefit fraud, sold into sex slavery and subjected to physical and mental abuse. Porous national borders, splintered churches, broken family ties and a fundamental lack of understanding and communication amongst the relevant authorities had fostered a litany of depravity. Victoria Climbié, Child B and now Kristy Bamu were unlikely to be the only victims.

46

London, October–December 2011

A few weeks after we got back from Kinshasa I received another phone call from the police working on the Kristy Bamu case. Detective Inspector Paul Maddocks introduced himself as the senior investigating officer.

Fresh from the successful conviction of Levi Bellfield in the Milly Dowler murder trial, Brian Altman QC was to be lead counsel for the prosecution. The interview transcripts and witness statements had shown him how fundamental belief in *kindoki* was to the proceedings, and he was concerned that the jury would not know how to handle the complexities. He was also prepared for the possibility that either of the two accused might try and defend themselves under the guise of religious and cultural self-justification. As a result, he wanted to instruct me to investigate the case in depth and produce a report for the court.

I met up with Paul Maddocks in a bar near the Old Bailey early one Monday evening. The DI had described himself as 'very tall, wiry and with a moustache: think John Cleese and you won't fail to spot me.' He wasn't wrong. We shook hands and he introduced his colleague Detective Sergeant Dave Boxall, a burlier individual who seemed to be studying me in much the same way as DC Barry Costello had when I'd first encountered him and DI O'Reilly on the Adam investigation.

'The coroner described it as the worst case she has dealt with.' Paul pushed his half-finished sandwich to one side. 'This lad was singled out because he couldn't get into the bathroom to do a wee. He effectively signed his own death warrant.'

'It's the ambulance officer's statement that really got me.' Dave shook his head dolefully. 'He couldn't do CPR because Kristy's teeth were stuck in his windpipe.'

'He went from asking to be saved to begging that they finish him off . . .' Paul's voice tailed off as he looked out onto Ludgate Hill.

The sadness of these habitually robust men was tangible. None of us spoke for a while, and when he did, Paul sounded choked. 'One of the issues we'd like you to look at, Richard, is Eric Bikubi's previous form in this area. It seems he attacked a girl, Naomi Ilonga, three years ago. Naomi is Kristy's mother Jacqueline Bamu's niece; Naomi's mother is Jacqueline Bamu's sister – although the family relationships are complex to say the least. Naomi says Eric accused her of having *kindoki*. Have a look. At the very least the allegations suggested false imprisonment. It wasn't followed through, though.'

I looked at them both, oblivious to the chicken burger that was being placed in front of me.

'The implications of that are massive,' I said.

Paul nodded and proceeded to set out the terms of reference. The circumstances of the crime were so outlandish that most people would struggle to understand them. I was to examine the whole case and pick out any areas where my cultural knowledge might help the jury navigate the case. I had four weeks. Any later and I'd be serving up my report too late for the court to accept it.

I was involved in another murder trial in the northeast, in which the defendant claimed that the victim's drunkenness so offended his faith that he stabbed him to death, but it wasn't due to start until February. I told them I'd get to work immediately.

I began poring over the documentation at once. For the next two weeks I worked night and day, juggling part-time teaching, family life and very little sleep. Faith agreed that I should stay in London as much as possible; I needed the time, and it was easier for her emotionally if I kept the horrifying details of the case well away from home.

The evidence against Magalie Bamu and Eric Bikubi appeared very strong. The testimony of the other children and the conclusive DNA evidence at the scene of crime seemed incontrovertible. The motive also seemed clear cut – the central dynamic ran through all the witness statements: they thought Kristy was possessed by *kindoki*.

The families involved or connected with the case were known previously to social services in other boroughs. Magalie Bamu and Eric Bikubi had been living in the UK since 1996. Paul Maddocks had mentioned that Eric had been on Westminster Council's radar in 2008. There were also incidents in Barking and Dagenham. Naomi Ilonga had indeed made allegations against Eric Bikubi, and Westminster had begun a core assessment of the family. Somehow – and it was difficult not to put this down to incompetence – these enquiries were not followed through. According to Newham social services, their counterparts at Westminster appeared to be gripped by inertia.

The French authorities were no better. I could now see why both the Met and the Newham social services department were incensed. The French police had refused to pursue allegations that included child rape, enforced imprisonment, trafficking and sex slavery. In immigrant communities throughout France, it seemed it was increasingly common for young girls of twelve or thirteen to be assigned domestic duties, usually when the mother of the family was pregnant. Known as *menagière,* this included various forms of sexual servitude. Astonishingly, French social services claimed that they had never heard of witchcraft and had 'no clue' what it was. Neither the police nor Newham could get them even to entertain the idea of looking into it. The Congolese community was, apparently, of no interest.

After two weeks I produced my forty-four-page report, shining as bright a light as possible on the issues. I cross-referenced the witness statements and constructed a vigorous challenge to any notion of a 'cultural' defence. Despite the widespread prevalence of belief in *kindoki* I made it clear that in Congolese culture the torture and murder of a child would never be condoned, and that the majority of Congolese would be appalled by what had happened. Indeed, the Congolese Government had now made it officially illegal even to accuse a child of being infected by witchcraft, let alone perpetrate any physical damage to the 'sufferer'.

I tried to keep my statement as objective as possible, but my sadness for Kristy threatened to overwhelm me. For five days he had experienced a living hell. Within a stone's throw of the new Olympic Stadium, a teenage boy had been slowly and savagely tortured to death without anyone noticing.

*

I escaped back to Devon for a respite.

Or so I thought.

On a family walk along Widemouth Bay during the Christmas holidays my police mobile rang. The distant voice of Susannah Beasley-Murray from Newham Children's Services did battle with the pulsating wind and the roaring Atlantic breakers. She was calling on behalf of the head of Safeguarding in Newham Borough, Gareth Flemyng. They were concerned about the way the case was going to be reported, and were attempting to get a wider court injunction gagging the media from using any of the names, including those of the two accused. Could I produce a report for the following morning, and then attend a hearing at the Royal Courts of Justice at the end of Christmas week?

I looked at my watch. 'It's nearly 4 p.m.! Are you serious?'

She was. A bundle of emailed documents would be awaiting my return to the house.

At eight fifty the following morning I pressed the Send button on my report and crawled upstairs for a few hours' sleep.

Just before New Year's Day, I climbed the steps of the Royal Courts of Justice and walked along the deserted marble hallway. I was the sole witness in Court 39 of the Family Division and I didn't have to wait long. I took the card with the oath in my hand and promised to tell the truth. Religious beliefs were what seemed to have pushed Bikubi and Bamu over the edge; I wasn't in the mood to rekindle mine, so had chosen to affirm rather than swear on the Bible.

I was cross-examined by barristers for the next half hour, during which I stated my case. Despite the Council's concerns there was also a public interest issue at stake. I suggested that the court shouldn't lose sight of the fact that there was more than one child involved in this case, and that we owed Kristy a trial that was conducted in the full light of day rather than one that was clandestine and quickly forgotten. Thinking back to the Child B case in 2005, I added a heartfelt plea. I told the court that I did not want us to be back again in five years' time with another child abuse or murder trial, knowing that we had missed an opportunity to place this issue under public scrutiny because the media had been stifled.

We awaited the verdict with some trepidation. The Judge found in favour of the public interest and the injunction was overturned. The media could report the case, name the accused and show photos. I knew this might open the floodgates to some lurid coverage, but the matters that needed to be aired drove to the heart of 'multicultural' Britain. It was also vital for Kristy's memory that we knew what he looked like and what he had endured, rather than allow him to be shunted aside as London's pristine Olympic image was presented to the outside world.

47

London, January–February 2012

There are eighteen courtrooms in the Old Bailey, and Court 5 is located up two flights of stone stairs. The room was hushed as Brian Altman QC rose to open the prosecution case. He made a point of not sparing us any of the details; we needed to understand the terrible savagery that had been meted out to the deceased. Two porter's trolleys were stacked high with bags containing weapons recovered from the flat. The boy had suffered 131 separate injuries. The final week of his life had been one of almost unparalleled suffering.

Altman drove home the fact that *kindoki* was central to the case, and told the court they would hear from me on the subject in due course. The two defendants were, he said, obsessed with the notion that the siblings were possessed, eventually fixing on Kristy as the source and conduit for the witchcraft.

The days following were dominated by the testimonies of the surviving children, except for the eldest, Yves, who was very autistic, and another who was too young to give evidence.

Kelly Bamu was twenty at the time of her brother's death. Over two days she described in graphic detail, through racking sobs, how again and again they had begged for mercy; how Eric and Magalie began to focus on Kristy, taking it in turns to rain blows upon him. She looked at the jury: 'Magalie deserves to die for what they have done. I have no pity for her. She had no pity for us.' Later, after she was given time to compose herself, Kelly said she thought the two accused still believed the siblings were witches to this day. 'She didn't give a damn and said we deserved it.'

The court watched the evidence from the other brother and sister by video link because they were not yet eighteen and their names could not be reported. They backed up everything Kelly had said.

Kristy's parents Jacqueline and Pierre were the final members of the family to take the stand. They claimed they had been unable to intervene from Paris, even after Kristy had telephoned on Christmas Eve to tell them he was going to be killed. Jacqueline broke down as she described the loss of her son.

After the family's evidence came the reports from the paramedics, police, pathologist and coroner. Those attending the scene of the crime described it in graphic detail. Forensics showed Kristy's blood spattered all over Eric and Magalie's clothing.

I met Brian Altman the day before I was due to take the stand. He talked me through the report I had written and told me which elements of it he would refer to. The jury needed to understand the belief systems that lay behind the killing. Eric was attempting to plead insanity, whilst Magalie believed that people can be possessed by *kindoki*. For her, it was the norm. Clearly they couldn't both be right. Altman wanted to draw a distinction between what was 'normal' to the Congolese, and the terrible actions of the accused. He wanted me to take those present deep into the world I had inhabited for the past quarter of a century, but which would be alien to most of them.

The following morning was overcast and drizzly. I walked eastwards along the viaduct, approaching the Old Bailey from the north side to avoid the media scrum. I looked up at the dome and saw the gilded figure of Justice, the sword in her right hand pointing heavenwards, the scales balancing in her left. The inscription carved into the stone beneath her reads: *Defend the children of the poor and punish the wrongdoer.*

Barristers, jury members, witnesses and journalists mingled in the corridor outside Court 5. DS Dave Boxall ushered me away from the advancing reporters. Cedar panels lined the walls, and a large flat screen monitor for video evidence was mounted opposite me. A perspex box led to a closed, padded door, through which the defendants were brought from their cells.

Ushers and recorders scurried around tables at the centre of the room, preparing files, making calls and checking on those present. Journalists clutching notepads and mobile phones began to settle like locusts in the green leather seats around me. The case was being tweeted live. The public gallery above my head sounded as if it was filling fast. Barristers in wigs and gowns strutted into position. Dave whispered in my ear, 'Eight of them.' He grinned. 'Imagine that lot cross-examining you.'

I couldn't smile back. I was beginning to feel nauseous at the prospect. Dawn, the court usher, came over to see if I was all right.

The jury took their seats and the recorder called, 'All rise.'

Mr Justice David Paget was presiding over his final case before retirement. In his gown, wig and spectacles he looked as formidable as the occasion demanded. After some brief discussion, Brian Altman announced the next prosecution witness: 'Dr Hoskins.'

The witness stand faced the jury. The judge sat slightly to my left, the court officials below me, as if in an orchestra pit. Further to the right the defendants were ensconced behind the perspex screen. It was the first time I'd seen them. Eric's hair was ruffled and he looked unkempt. He was flanked by three staff, who I guessed were from Broadmoor, the secure hospital where he was awaiting further psychiatric assessment. Magalie, looking altogether more demure, had just one guard by her side.

The preliminaries over, I began to outline the significance of *kindoki* to the case, and how the fact that the accused thought Kristy was possessed ran through every witness statement. I was hitting my stride when Magalie's lead defence barrister leaned across and whispered to Brian Altman. He nodded and rose to his feet.

'I don't normally agree with the defence, Dr Hoskins, but your evidence is very important, so I'm going to stop you right there. You're going too fast. I want you to slow right down. The court needs to go back. Back to when *you* started, twenty-five years ago. I want you to tell us about the traditions and beliefs that *you* know about. I want this court to understand where this all comes from, and how normal it is for people who believe in it. So please don't rush. Why don't we start with the African spirits that you mention in your report? Tell us about the living dead, would you? Take us back.'

Take them back?

The air was heavy with anticipation.

In another life, the breeze stirred the palm fronds and I saw Tata Mpia's face.

'The living dead are those whom we once knew on this earth, but who have passed on to the shadowlands beyond the grave.'

Tata Mpia's words echoed down the years, filling the courtroom.

'The living dead control this world and everything in it. They have a hundred times more power than you or me. They are all powerful. They can build up or destroy. They bring life, and they take it away . . .'

'And so, traditionally, where did *kindoki* fit into that, Dr Hoskins?'

'Any of the living dead can be evil, but it's the long dead, the distant ghosts who are no longer remembered, who were associated with *kindoki* – witchcraft, as we call it.'

'And that's different from how it is today?'

'Totally different. Back then, back when I first went to Africa, *kindoki* was just an external force. It was bad, for sure, but it was nebulous, diffuse, out there. It was just like an evil eye, something to ward off.'

'And how did they deal with it then? How did the traditional healers – the *ngangas,* as I think you call them in your report – control it?'

'The *ngangas* have three methods for dealing with these things,' I said. 'First are protective amulets—'

'A bit like a St Christopher medallion?' the judge queried.

'Yes, my lord, that's exactly right. The traditional belief in *kindoki* isn't so very different from what people the world over think: that there are good and bad forces. And a great many people in all cultures take steps to keep good luck, whether it's wearing a cross, reading their horoscopes, or making sure they don't walk under a ladder.'

Mr Justice Paget nodded and signalled for me to continue.

'Next there is scapegoating, where the *nganga* will lay his hands on an animal and banish it, along with the evil, to the wilderness – usually the desert or savannah.'

'And the third?' Altman asked.

'The third', I said, 'is sacrifice. It's the most powerful of all. It's the spilling of blood, the transference of power. And they believe it works.'

'You need to see the *nganga*,' Tata Mpia said. 'It's the only way. You must perform a sacrifice.'

For the sake of one small sacrifice – a chicken, perhaps, or a goat . . . Abigail was the apple of my eye. So why hadn't I?

I glanced at Eric and Magalie.

I knew why I hadn't. I think I'd always known.

'And so tell us about *kindoki* today, in the hands of the churches. What happens now?'

I cleared my throat, regaining some equilibrium. I took the court through the way fundamentalist Christianity had blended with those traditional beliefs to create a monstrous new mix. In the minds of these pastors and their believers, *kindoki* was no longer an outside force that could be controlled by the *ngangas*, as they had, untroubled, for thousands of years. Now *kindoki* was a power that possessed people, particularly children, and they could only be delivered through exorcism.

I described services of exorcism in the Congo, and the abusive methods often employed there. But I then told the court that the violence meted out to Kristy by Eric Bikubi and Magalie Bamu was on another level altogether. Cut loose from normal social restraints, this pair had been able to commit acts of atrocity without anyone apparently noticing or stepping in to help.

It took all afternoon to complete my evidence, with the judge putting questions as well as counsel. Mr Justice Paget suggested that exorcism was not an alien concept in this country. I agreed, though I added that in northern Europe it is more usual for a place to be exorcized than a person. I also pointed out that it was a literal interpretation of the Bible that prompted some pastors to starve the apparently afflicted children; fasting for deliverance had its roots in the New Testament.

Only Eric Bikubi's barrister cross-examined me. He wanted to demonstrate that Eric was deranged both in action and belief. I told the court that whilst the Congolese Government had made it illegal even to call a child a witch, the beliefs that lay behind the notion, however repugnant they might seem, were well founded in their culture. I told the court that the actions of the two accused should not be confused with the belief system in which they sought shelter.

Brian Altman approached me as I left the court.

'The trial's back on track,' he said. 'Back to where we should be. It's not the *What?* now, but the *Why?* You did that. The jury were taking reams of notes. I think we've lanced the Bikubi defence.'

'What about Magalie?' I asked.

'I reckon she's going to try and blame Bikubi for the whole thing. I reckon that's why her team didn't cross-examine you. Doesn't stack up, though, with the evidence.'

I felt completely wrung out. I'd kept my emotions in check – even when I heard Tata Mpia's voice in my ear – but only just. Dodging the cameras, I returned to Clapham.

At four in the morning I woke and sat bolt upright in bed, tears streaming down my cheeks. I wasn't only thinking of Kristy; I was remembering Abigail.

48

London, March 2012

After I'd given my evidence, four eminent psychiatrists spent a week trying to persuade the jury that Eric Bikubi was insane and that I was wrong to attempt to place his beliefs within the context of an established cultural paradigm. Eric didn't take the stand.

Magalie Bamu's defence focused on her inability to say no to Eric. She described a lifetime of servitude – under the thumb of another relative and his wife – since arriving in Britain at the age of thirteen.

Brian Altman's opening question set the tone of his response: 'Now you're not telling the court the truth, are you?'

He began to systematically undermine her testimony. He argued that she had only recently hatched the 'blame Eric' defence. I scrutinized her face as she stood in the dock, looking for hints of the darkness within. How could she have turned so violently against her own brother?

Suddenly aware that I was watching her, she stared back at me. I felt myself recoil. The challenge in her eye seemed more appropriate to a nightclub than the dock of an Old Bailey courtroom. Her defiance bubbled to the surface with increasing frequency over the next two days as she gave her testimony. She became steelier and more impatient under questioning. Perhaps most remarkably of all, she showed no sign of remorse.

'Do you admit striking your brother Kristy Bamu with a curtain pole?' Mr Altman asked.

'Yes.'

'Around the head?'

'Yes.'

He nodded towards one of the trolleys. Detective Sergeant Dave Boxall handed him a package. The barrister held it horizontal, for the benefit of the jury.

'This it?'

'Yes,'

'There's a dent in it, do you see?'

'Yes.'

'It's a dent in the shape of his skull, isn't it? It's bent completely out of shape like that because you struck him so hard on the head.'

He flourished photographs of the front door, showing that it had not been locked with a key, as she had claimed. She could have run for help – even removed her brother Kristy from further harm – at any point. Any lingering sympathy for her evaporated.

'And then, when Kristy staggered across the room, blood pouring' – Altman paused, betraying his own distress for the first time – 'all you could say to your *own* fifteen-year-old brother, who was *dying* in front of you, was, "Don't sit on the sofa, or you might *spoil* it . . .".'

'All parties in Bikubi and Bamu to Court 5.'

Reporters swarmed through the entrance, clutching their mobile phones. The verdicts would be tweeted around the world before anyone had left the courtroom. Mr Altman ushered me across to the prosecution benches.

The twelve members of the jury had chosen a woman to speak for them.

'To the first count of murder against the defendant Eric Bikubi, how do you find?'

'Guilty.'

'To the first count of murder against the defendant Magalie Bamu, how do you find?'

'Guilty.'

Some journalists dashed for the door, others began typing furiously into mobile devices. But in the central well of the court we all sat quietly, pausing to reflect on the enormity of what we had witnessed.

Judge Paget thanked the jury. Owing to the harrowing nature of the evidence, he exempted them from further service for the rest of their lives. Then Brian Altman read a searingly dignified statement from Pierre Bamu on behalf of the family.

'The pain is unimaginable,' Pierre said. 'This was done by people we loved and trusted. To know that Kristy's own sister, Magalie, did nothing to save Kristy, makes the pain that much worse. We are still unaware of the full extent of the brutality. We cannot bring ourselves to hear it.'

A few days later Judge Paget sentenced the two to life imprisonment. The severity of the torture meted out to Kristy in the name of *kindoki* exorcism was reflected in the minimum tariffs before which they could even be considered for parole: thirty years for Eric Bikubi and twenty-five for Magalie Bamu.

Epilogue

Scotland Yard, London

I am waiting in the foyer of New Scotland Yard, near St James's Park. The iconic triangular box revolves outside the glass frontage of the Metropolitan Police HQ. A tall, wiry figure appears and ushers me upstairs.

I have received a rather unusual invitation from Chief Superintendent Chris Bourlet.

The Yard's Crime Museum is located on the first floor, in Room 101. Unless you're seeking it out, you might not know of its existence. Chris tells me he has served here for years without being invited inside.

We walk along a shadowy corridor until a white door emerges out of the gloom. Chris knocks twice. We pass through and it clicks shut behind us. I hear a key turn.

A sandy-haired man in his fifties with a slightly nasal twang introduces himself as the curator. He explains that the museum dates back to 1874; it is the oldest establishment of its kind in the world. He then demonstrates, with some relish, how nooses are tied. He points to the wall where I see a row of them, all of which were used to hang some of Britain's most notorious criminals.

As he talks I glance around. I can now see that there are two rooms, forming an L. Their spines and outside walls are lined with glass display cases, with larger objects on show between them. I can make out a badly stained apron, a bath and a large pot perched on an old cooker.

The curator reaches into a wooden box near the door and hands me a state-of-the-art audio handset. He points out the numbers displayed on each cabinet, and tells me that I can follow the exhibition in any sequence I like so long as I tap in the relevant digits on the keyboard.

Reggie and Ronnie, the infamous Kray twins, would have been pleased; they command twice the space of their fellow criminals. Newspaper cuttings and photos give mute testimony to the terror in which they held the East End of London during the Fifties and Sixties, alongside the gun Ronnie used to shoot fellow gangster George Cornell in the Blind Beggar. I feel slightly queasy, but move on.

A display devoted to the 7/7 London Bombers includes the items recovered from the car they left outside Luton railway station when they set off on their last journey, containers of bomb-making equipment found in their flat, a laptop used by one of the suspects and a rucksack similar to the ones they so devastatingly deployed.

I'm momentarily captivated by the bullet with which Mark David Chapman killed John Lennon, but when I ask the curator how or why it's there he cannot – or will not – say. The ricin pellet recovered from the body of the Bulgarian dissident Georgi Markov is close by. Markov was waiting at a bus stop on Waterloo Bridge in 1978, en route to the BBC, when he felt a stinging pain in the back of his thigh. The deadly projectile had been fired from an umbrella designed by the Soviet KGB. There is a replica of the weapon alongside the actual pellet. The poison had been coated in a sugary substance designed to melt at 37°C, the temperature of the human body.

The bath I had spotted earlier is made of steel, and stands alongside a number of drums. It belonged to John George Haigh, the infamous acid bath murderer of the late 1940s. Close by is the cooker upon which sits the pot in which Dennis Nilsen boiled the heads of his fifteen male victims in Muswell Hill between 1978 and 1983. A voice in my ear describes how Nilsen lured and dispensed with his victims.

There are medical instruments used by Harold Shipman, the biggest serial killer in British – if not Western – history, with over 200 alleged victims of his depraved 'mercy killing' spree. Dr Crippen's display includes macabre remains recovered from his cellar. The blood-soaked apron belongs to John Reginald Halliday Christie, who murdered at least eight women, including his wife Ethel, in 10 Rillington Place between 1943 and 1953.

When I finally come across the Child B exhibit, I realize why I'm here. Chris appears at my elbow as I take in the sack that confined the little girl, a series of photos and the diary kept by her aunt, Sita Kisanga. The commentary describes my contribution to the unravelling of the case, and the twisted belief system that Child B's torture had forced us all to confront.

Child B seems awfully lonely in this company. But the depravity of her treatment does not stand out here. I'm forcibly reminded that the world in which I work is not defined by race, culture, age or gender. Whether or not its darkest actions can be shielded from the full force of the law by claims of custom, diminished responsibility or insanity, the cocktail of ritual and manic fundamentalism, however horrifying, does not set it to one side. We cannot comfort ourselves with the thought that the heart of darkness lies beyond our horizon. It lies squarely within the world we inhabit, and within us.

I hand back my audio set and thank my guides. As I walk away from Scotland Yard through the gentle rain, my mind is not filled with images of acid baths and gangland killing – or even Child B – but once more with the case that isn't there: the cold-blooded murder of the little boy we knew first as Adam, and more recently as Ikpomwosa. The boy in the river.

No expense was spared in the decade-long investigation. The people who were responsible for trafficking him and countless other children into this country have been sent down, but no one has been convicted of his killing. His death still haunts me. And I know I'm not alone.

The rain is falling heavily now. I pull my jacket more tightly around me as I picture again that innocent, smiling face: the victim of an unimaginable sacrifice, here in the heart of our capital city.

extracts reading groups
competitions books new
discounts extracts
competitions
books new
events books
extracts
new reading groups
interviews
events extracts
discounts
new books events
events new
discounts extracts discounts
www.panmacmillan.com
extracts events reading groups
competitions books extracts new

D0860725

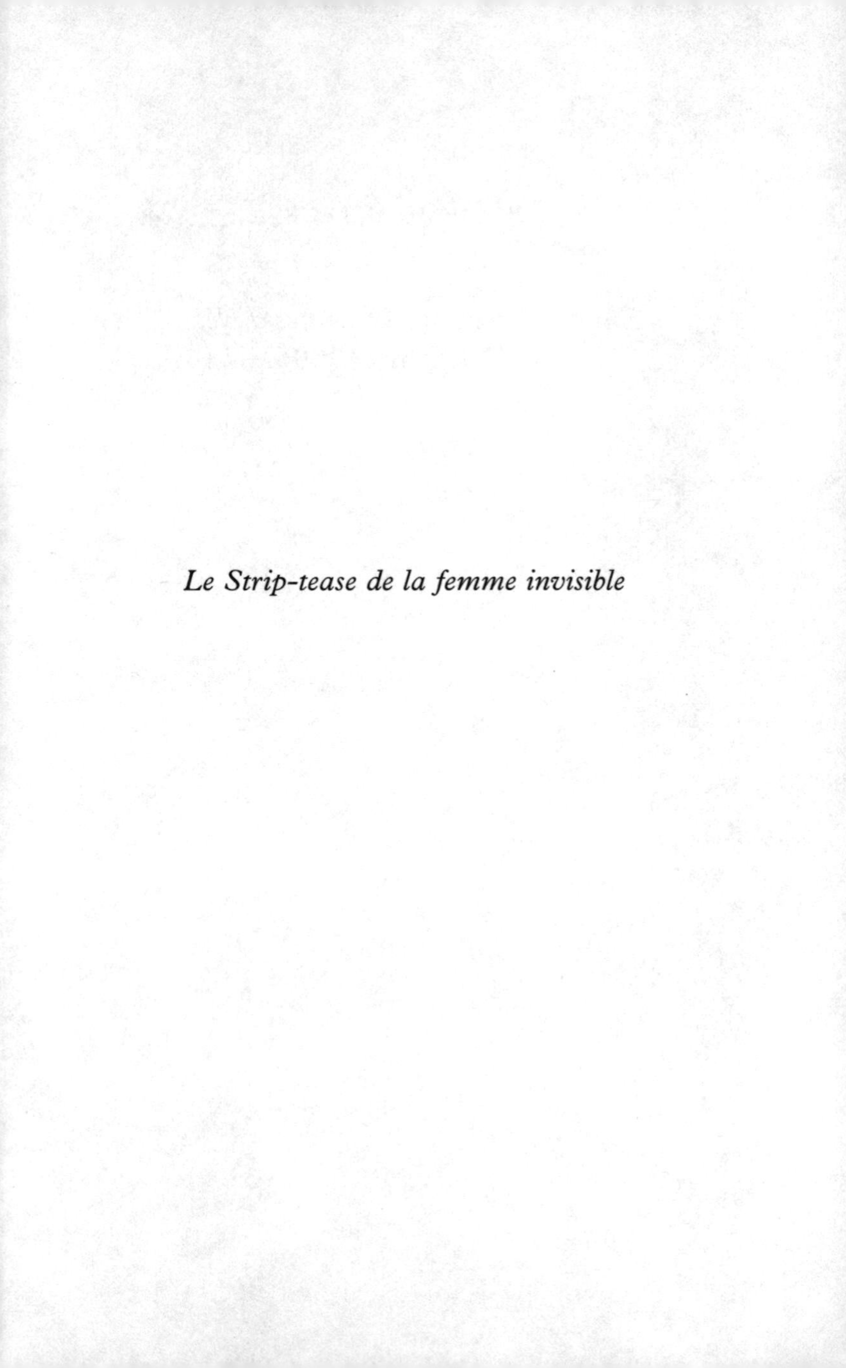

Le Strip-tease de la femme invisible

DU MÊME AUTEUR

Enfin la vérité sur les contes de fées,
Le Dilettante, 2006.

Murielle Renault

Le Strip-tease de la femme invisible

le dilettante
19, rue Racine
Paris 6^{e}

© le dilettante, 2008
ISBN 978-2-84263-148-2

Quinze ans

Je n'ai jamais compris en quoi une rentrée des classes pouvait être excitante. À part les fringues neuves et le nouvel agenda, j'avais beau chercher, je ne voyais pas.

« Tu n'es pas excitée à l'idée de connaître tes nouveaux profs, ton nouvel emploi du temps ? Cette année, c'est le lycée, tu vas rencontrer plein de nouvelles têtes ! », m'a dit ma mère hier.

J'avais l'impression qu'elle aurait adoré y aller à ma place.

« Mouais super, les nases de l'autre cité, là, trop génial… »

Je n'avais aucune envie d'y aller dans ce lycée pourri. Je voulais aller dans le même établissement privé que ma copine Lucie, mais ma mère m'avait rabâché trente-six mille fois le couplet sur l'école publique, l'égalité des chances et d'autres conneries dans le genre. Il était hors-de-ques-tion (je détestais cette manière qu'elle avait de détacher les syllabes quand elle montait sur ses grands chevaux !) qu'elle déroge à ses principes et blablabla.

J'avais beau lui répéter les histoires sordides de racket, de drogue et même de viol qui circulaient à propos de ce lycée, c'était peine perdue, elle ne voulait rien entendre. J'étais vouée à finir étranglée au fond d'une salle de classe au nom de ses idéaux.

Ce matin, elle m'a emmenée en voiture.

« Allez, pour ton premier jour, tu ne vas pas prendre le bus ! », m'a-t-elle dit tout sourire.

Ben voyons ! Au collège, tout le monde connaissait ma mère. Elle venait souvent me chercher à la sortie des classes. Trop souvent. Et au lieu de rester dans la voiture comme les autres parents, elle paradait sur le trottoir avec ses jupes trop courtes, ses décolletés trop profonds et ses talons aiguilles trop hauts. Je pressentais qu'il n'y avait aucun changement à espérer avec mon entrée au lycée.

Je suis sortie de la voiture en marmonnant un vague « Salut, à ce soir ! » auquel elle a répondu avec un excessif enthousiasme dans la voix. Ça m'a donné envie de lui balancer une vanne, mais ça n'en valait pas la peine. Autant garder mes forces pour la suite des événements.

Je me suis dirigée vers l'entrée du lycée. À gauche, un parking plein de scooters. Devant, l'allée qui menait à l'entrée. À droite, la sculpture moche qui orne chaque entrée d'école. Partout, des groupes de gens qui discutaient et qui rigolaient. Au milieu de tout ça, moi, les yeux cachés derrière ma frange. J'observais. Personne de ma connaissance. J'ai ouvert la porte du hall. Je me suis sentie agressée par les cris, les rires et l'agitation ambiante. Une adulte compatissante s'est adressée à moi. Est-ce que j'avais l'air si paumée ? Peu importe.

« Seconde ? Première ? Terminale ?

– Seconde…

– Panneau d'affichage à gauche. Seconde ? Première ? Terminale ? »

Elle bouclait grave.

Je me suis dirigée vers le panneau d'affichage. Seconde 1. J'ai parcouru la liste. Je n'y étais pas. Seconde 2. Non plus. Seconde 3. Pas mieux. Je commençais à stresser. Ah ! j'étais là, seconde 8. Rendez-vous salle F120. J'ai sorti de ma poche le plan des salles. Je devais monter au premier étage, prendre le couloir E qui débouchait sur le couloir F et c'était tout au fond.

J'ai rangé mon plan avant de rentrer dans la salle. Peu d'élèves étaient arrivés. J'ai murmuré un timide bonjour que personne à part moi n'a pu entendre, et je me suis dirigée vers une table, au fond, où il n'y avait encore personne.

« Bonjour, vous êtes ? »

Tous les yeux se sont tournés vers moi.

« Mélanie Lagrange. »

Il a cherché mon nom dans sa liste.

« Bienvenue Mélanie.

– Merci. »

J'ai posé mon sac à terre avec l'air le plus cool possible. Je m'étais donné cette peine pour rien, plus personne ne me regardait. J'ai observé les autres élèves. Certains étaient comme moi, dans leur coin, en train de scruter la salle. Deux filles discutaient et riaient. Elles avaient l'air de bien se connaître. Elles avaient de la chance.

La salle commençait à se remplir. Personne ne s'était assis à côté de moi. Tant mieux. Jusqu'à ce qu'arrive cette fille toute maigre avec ses piercings et ses fringues délire. Elle est venue droit sur moi.

« Bonjour, vous êtes ?

– Fanny Simon.

– Bienvenue Fanny. »

Elle lui a adressé un signe de main, genre « trop cool mec », puis s'est tournée vers moi.

« Et toi, comment tu t'appelles ?

– Mélanie.

– Mélanie, c'est cool comme prénom. Tu viens de quel collège ?

– François Ier.

– Eh ben, ça va te changer. Tu vas voir, c'est moins bourge ici mais on se marre bien. C'est ma troisième seconde. J'arrête pas de dire à ma mère que ça sert à rien de me faire passer le bac mais elle y tient. Moi, je veux être esthéticienne alors le bac, j'en ai pas grand-chose à foutre... et toi, qu'est-ce que tu veux faire ?

– J'en sais rien. »

Je n'ai pas osé lui dire que j'étais plutôt bonne élève et que j'aimais bien l'école. Je ne voulais pas passer pour une fayote. Les rentrées, je détestais. Mais après, c'était le train-train.

Le prof s'est raclé la gorge avant de prendre la parole. J'ai sorti mon agenda.

« Ouah ! Trop cool ton agenda, montre ! Moi, ma mère, elle veut jamais m'acheter de marques, elle fait chier ! »

Je le lui ai passé, sourire aux lèvres.

M. Colin s'est présenté. C'était notre prof de maths. Il nous a distribué des feuilles avec notre emploi du temps. Un brouhaha s'est aussitôt installé, chacun y allant de son commentaire. Il nous a ensuite remis la liste des profs.

« Putain, c'est pas vrai ! Cette conne de Forestier en français ! Tu vas voir, c'est pas une marrante !

– Ah…

– Oh nan ! Stillman en anglais, il peut pas me saquer !

– Ah bon, pourquoi ?

– Il aime pas mes piercings.

– Ah… »

Fanny les connaissait presque tous et pas un seul d'entre eux ne lui plaisait. J'avais dans l'idée qu'il ne fallait pas que je m'affole, que son avis sur la question ne voulait pas dire grand-chose.

Après quelques infos d'ordre général sur le fonctionnement de l'établissement, le prof nous a distribué un QCM pour évaluer notre niveau. Je l'ai terminé en un quart d'heure. Fanny, à côté de moi, ne semblait pas très inspirée. D'un signe, je lui ai fait comprendre qu'elle pouvait copier sur moi. Elle m'a remerciée d'un sourire et a noté quelques résultats de-ci de-là.

À la pause, elle m'a présenté ses potes. Ils étaient tous en première ou en terminale. Ça me plaisait. Fanny parlait beaucoup et très fort, elle interpellait les uns, les autres, elle s'agitait, grimaçait, lançait des blagues en rafales, de temps en temps elle me faisait un clin d'œil, puis elle repartait dans une nouvelle histoire. Elle a tenu comme ça jusqu'à ce que la sonnerie nous oblige à retourner en cours.

« Ils sont cool hein ?

– Ouais, ils ont l'air...

– Comment tu l'trouves Karim ?

– C'est lequel Karim ?

– Celui qui était à côté de moi avec le tee-shirt rouge.

– Ouais, pas mal.

– Pas mal ? Il est beau de chez beau tu veux dire. J'aimerais trop sortir avec lui ! T'as un mec toi ?

– Nan.

– On va t'en trouver un. J'ai un pote, Samuel, je suis sûre qu'il te plaira. »

Je lui ai répondu d'un sourire. C'était gentil de sa part de faire comme si de rien n'était, comme si j'avais toutes mes chances, mais la vérité, c'était que les petites grosses comme moi n'intéressaient pas les garçons.

Je n'étais pas ce qu'on pouvait appeler un top-modèle. Je pesais soixante-deux kilos pour un mètre cinquante-huit, soit une dizaine de kilos de trop d'après moi, trois ou quatre d'après ma mère et une bonne quinzaine d'après les nanas qu'on voyait dans les magazines.

Je ne suivais aucune mode. Je m'habillais avec des jeans larges, des tee-shirts informes et des sweats assez longs pour masquer mes fesses. Ma mère était désespérée par ma garde-robe. Elle disait à qui voulait l'entendre qu'elle ne comprenait pas que sa fille puisse à ce point renier sa féminité. J'aurais voulu la voir, elle, être féminine avec mon gabarit.

Ma mère était pleine de contradictions. Elle piquait une crise dès que j'approchais du frigo en dehors des repas, mais elle refusait ca-té-go-ri-que-ment qu'une jeune fille de quinze ans (moi en l'occurrence) suive un régime parce que blablabla j'étais encore en pleine croissance (je n'avais pas pris un centimètre depuis au moins deux ans) et blablabla c'était comme ça que l'on finissait boulimique ou anorexique (ou les deux) et blablabla il était hors-de-ques-tion qu'elle me laisse m'engouffrer dans cette spirale infernale.

Eh oui, elle était comme ça, avec des opinions tranchées sur tous les sujets. Il n'y avait pas moyen de discuter. Pas d'école privée. Pas de régimes pour les ados. Et c'était tout.

Je tiens à préciser que ma mère, elle, prenait grand soin de son apparence. C'était une championne des régimes. Elle n'avait jamais dépassé les cinquante-cinq kilos (une de ses grandes fiertés !), sauf pendant sa grossesse, et mesurait dix bons centimètres de plus que moi. Elle avait une jolie silhouette qu'elle entretenait en allant à la gym plusieurs fois par semaine et de magnifiques jambes fines et galbées. Elle se maquillait beaucoup et s'habillait de manière sexy. C'était une belle femme. Séduisante. Elle plaisait aux hommes, je le voyais aux regards qu'ils lui lançaient. Elle le savait et elle en profitait. Mon père en était la première victime, une victime parfaitement consentante. Il disait oui à tous ses caprices et prenait parti pour elle en toute situation. Lui aussi était beau. J'avais du mal à comprendre comment ils pouvaient avoir donné naissance à quelqu'un comme moi. J'avais effleuré l'hypothèse de l'enfant adoptée, mais sans vraiment y croire, juste pour le plaisir de m'imaginer avoir d'autres parents.

À midi, nous sommes allées manger avec quelques personnes de notre classe. À la cantine, j'ai observé Fanny. Elle picorait plus qu'elle ne mangeait. Elle attrapait une frite du bout de sa fourchette et, prise par la conversation, faisait tournoyer le malheureux bout de patate pendant de longues minutes dans les airs jusqu'à ce qu'elle en ait fini avec la discussion. Alors que tout le monde avait terminé son plateau, celui de Fanny était encore presque intact. Nous n'avons cependant pas eu à l'attendre. Elle a reposé sa cuillère après avoir tout juste goûté sa compote de pommes.

« On y va ? Toujours aussi dégueu la bouffe ici. »

Moi, je n'avais pas trouvé ça mauvais. Plutôt bon même. C'était ça mon problème. Je trouvais toujours appétissant ce qui se trouvait dans mon assiette, dans le plat, voire dans les assiettes des autres.

Fanny a proposé que nous allions prendre un café au bar, à côté du lycée. Personne n'était tenté. Je n'étais pas non plus emballée. J'ai quand même suivi Fanny avec l'air détaché de celle qui fréquente les bars depuis toujours. J'ai bu le premier café de ma vie mais j'ai refusé la clope qu'elle me tendait. Si je disais oui à tout ce qu'elle me proposait, je craignais de me retrouver à sniffer de la cocaïne avant la fin de la journée.

« Tu sais quoi Mélanie ?

– …

– Tu me plais ! Je trouve ça cool de passer l'année avec toi. »

Nous allions passer l'année ensemble ? D'accord. Ça me convenait. J'étais flattée. Même si je trouvais ça un peu bizarre qu'elle me dise ça alors que nous ne nous connaissions que depuis quelques heures.

« Ouais… moi aussi, je trouve ça cool… d'habitude, je trouve ça nul les rentrées… là, je trouve ça… ouais… cool… c'est cool. »

Elle m'a regardée avec un grand sourire.

« T'es marrante. Tu parles pas beaucoup mais on voit que ça cogite là-haut. Ça va me changer de passer mes journées avec une nana comme toi ! Merde ! T'as vu l'heure ? Faut qu'on y aille ! »

Nous sommes arrivées au cours d'anglais avec cinq bonnes minutes de retard.

« Miss Simon, toujours aussi ponctuelle à ce que je vois. Et vous, vous êtes ?

– Mélanie Lagrange.

– Welcome Mélanie. Sachez que je n'apprécie guère que les gens arrivent en retard à mes cours. Je ne saurais donc que vous conseiller de ne pas prendre exemple sur miss Simon. »

J'avais les joues cramoisies.

« Je t'avais dit qu'il pouvait pas me saquer », m'a murmuré Fanny à l'oreille pendant que nous sortions nos affaires.

Je ne lui ai rien répondu. Je lui en voulais de m'avoir mise dans cette situation. Je me suis donc concentrée en ignorant ses essais répétés pour me distraire.

« What's your name ?

– My name is Stéphane.

– And how old are you ?

– I'm fifteen.

– Where did you spend your holidays ?

– In Spain.
– And what about you ? »

Le prof déambulait dans la classe en posant des questions aux uns et aux autres. J'étais obnubilée par l'éventualité qu'il puisse m'interroger. Je me cachais plus que jamais derrière ma frange, persuadée que la mauvaise impression donnée en arrivant en retard n'allait pas tarder à m'être facturée, et cher. C'est sur Fanny que c'est tombé. Elle a répondu avec une mauvaise grâce évidente mais s'en est bien sortie.

Je n'ai retrouvé un semblant de légèreté qu'à la sortie du cours. Fanny a imité Stillman et son accent so british et je n'ai pas pu résister. J'ai quand même jeté un œil alentour avant de me laisser aller à rire. Il n'était pas question de me griller dès le premier jour.

Ensuite, nous avions sport. Le prof nous a présenté le programme de l'année. Je n'ai retenu qu'une seule chose. Au second trimestre, nous allions à la piscine. L'horreur absolue pour moi. Impossible de me mettre en maillot de bain devant tout le monde. Je n'avais pas encore d'idée sur la manière d'y échapper, mais j'allais en trouver une.

Comme nous n'avions pas nos affaires, le prof nous a laissés partir plus tôt. Fanny a essayé de me traîner pour une deuxième tournée au bar, mais je n'avais plus qu'une hâte, c'était de rentrer chez moi. Cette histoire de piscine m'avait miné le moral. Elle n'a pas insisté. Le beau Karim terminait ses cours une demi-heure plus tard et me remplacerait haut la main. Elle m'a accompagnée à l'arrêt de bus et n'a pas arrêté de parler jusqu'à ce qu'il arrive. Ce flot ininterrompu de paroles était à la fois fatigant et reposant. Je n'avais pas à fournir d'effort de conversation, elle s'en chargeait très bien toute seule.

Quand je suis arrivée à la maison, ma mère m'est tombée dessus direct. Elle avait quitté le boulot plus tôt pour partager les premières impressions de sa fille en ce jour de rentrée...

« Alors ma chérie, comment ça s'est passé ?

– Ça a été.

– Il est comment ton emploi du temps ?

– Bof...

– Vas-y, montre-moi. »

J'écoutais vaguement ses commentaires en me préparant avec soin une tartine de Nutella. Elle en était à me conseiller d'optimiser le temps que j'avais entre mes heures de cours pour travailler au lycée. Super idée maman ! Je me voyais bien dire à Fanny que je préférais bosser en bibli qu'aller papoter avec elle au café…

« Et les gens de ta classe, ils sont comment ?

– J'ai pas parlé à grand monde… j'ai passé la journée avec une fille, Fanny, elle a l'air sympa. »

Je me suis abstenue de préciser que Fanny triplait sa seconde, qu'elle semblait être l'ennemie jurée de tous les profs et que c'était une habituée du bar à côté du lycée. J'ai aussi caché qu'elle fumait et qu'elle avait des piercings. Ma mère découvrirait tout ça bien assez tôt.

*

Le placard de Fanny débordait de fringues. Noires pour la plupart. De grandes jupes de gitane, des pantalons évasés, des hauts à bretelles avec des slogans comme « Trop bonne pour toi ! », « Même pas dans tes rêves ! » ou « Bouge de là ! ». Ses sous-vêtements ressemblaient davantage à ceux de ma mère qu'aux miens. Des strings, de la dentelle, des soutifs rembourrés. Pas de culottes, pas de coton, pas de bonnets D.

Tailles : 36, Small, 85B.

J'étais déprimée.

« Qu'est-ce que tu fous ?

– Rien, je regarde tes fringues. J'aime bien comment tu t'habilles.

– Je croyais que t'en avais rien à foutre des fringues toi.

– J'ai jamais dit ça...

– Ben nan mais...

– Mais vu comment je suis sapée c'est ça ?

– Ouais... enfin nan, c'est pas ce que je voulais dire mais t'es toujours fringuée pareil alors je pensais que tu t'en foutais. »

J'avais envie de chialer. Je me suis retenue. Puis je me suis laissée aller.

« Merde, qu'est-ce qui t'arrive ma loute ?

– ...

– Je t'ai vexée c'est ça ? Je suis trop conne moi.

– C'est pas toi le problème, c'est moi. Regarde, je ressemble à rien. Je suis grosse, moche, mal sapée.

– Arrête tes conneries, t'es mignonne comme tout. Il faudrait juste que tu te mettes un peu plus en valeur, un changement de coupe de cheveux, une séance de shopping et hop ! T'as du fric pour t'acheter des fringues ?

– J'peux en demander à ma mère. Elle est chiante mais pas radine.

– Super ! Le week-end prochain, on va à Créteil Soleil. Et pour ce soir, je te coupe les cheveux et je te maquille, tu vas voir, tu vas être canon !

– Tu sais couper les cheveux toi ?

– Ben ouais, je coupe les cheveux de tout le monde dans ma famille. »

Je n'étais pas rassurée mais une pointe d'excitation commençait à m'envahir à l'idée d'un peu de changement. Fanny a réussi à vaincre mes dernières réticences.

J'avais beaucoup de chance d'avoir rencontré Fanny. Ma vie était devenue beaucoup plus marrante depuis que nous étions ensemble.

Elle était pleine d'énergie et débordait d'idées pour ne pas s'ennuyer. Nous allions un peu partout sur son scooter. Elle connaissait plein de monde et nous étions sans arrêt invitées à des soirées. Malgré sa popularité, pour une raison qui m'échappait, c'était moi qu'elle avait choisie comme meilleure amie. Nous étions devenues inséparables. Pas une soirée où elle allait sans moi. Pas un événement qu'elle ne partageait avec moi. Elle accordait de l'importance à mon avis et moi au sien. Nous passions des heures pendues au téléphone, ce qui avait le don d'exaspérer ma mère qui, comme prévu, n'aimait pas beaucoup Fanny.

Nous nous sommes installées dans la cuisine. Il n'y avait pas de miroir pour me permettre de suivre les changements. J'avais dit à Fanny de suivre son inspiration, et je voyais maintenant de longues mèches tapisser le carrelage. Fanny ne parlait pas beaucoup, elle était concentrée. Elle semblait sûre d'elle, et quand mon regard croisait le sien, son grand sourire me disait de ne pas m'inquiéter.

Je portais les cheveux longs depuis des années. Je ne me rappelais pas vraiment les avoir eus plus courts. J'avais vu des photos, mais c'étaient des photos de moi petite fille. Moi avant. Pas vraiment moi. Je n'étais pas certaine de l'enthousiasme de ma mère quand j'allais rentrer.

« Qu'est-ce qui te fait sourire ?

– Je pensais à la tête de mes parents quand ils me verront comme ça.

– Ils ne pourront rien dire parce que ta nouvelle coupe t'ira trop bien.

– T'as bientôt fini ?

– Presque…

– J'ai hâte de voir.

– Tu veux que je te maquille après ?

– …

– T'inquiète, je vais pas t'en mettre des tonnes mais tu vas voir, ça change tout. Ce soir, tu vas faire des ravages ! »

J'arrivais presque à la croire. Quand je secouais la tête, j'avais une impression nouvelle de légèreté. Je tentais de me rendre compte du résultat en touchant mes cheveux, mais Fanny faisait mine de se mettre en colère et me répétait d'arrêter de bouger. J'étais branchée sur du cent mille volts. Surexcitée.

« Je peux voir mes cheveux avant le maquillage ?

– Nan, je veux que tu voies tout d'un coup.

– Allez…

– Non.

– Allez…

– Je vais chercher le maquillage, tu ne bouges pas de cette chaise. »

À peine avait-elle tourné le dos que j'étais sur pied, essayant de trouver quelque chose dans lequel me regarder.

« Mais tu vas t'asseoir ! C'est pas possible ça ! »

Je me suis assise en prenant un air de petite fille boudeuse que j'ai tenu à peine dix secondes. Je me suis mise à me dandiner sur mon tabouret au rythme de la musique.

« J'adore cette chanson !

– Ouais, ben t'as intérêt à te calmer sinon je vais te crever un œil. »

Je me suis calmée et me suis mise à penser à Sébastien. C'était chez lui que nous allions ce soir. J'étais amoureuse de lui depuis des semaines. Je n'en avais jamais parlé à qui que ce soit. Même pas à Fanny. Surtout pas à Fanny. Si elle avait été au courant, Sébastien n'aurait pas tardé à l'être. Je ne voulais pas prendre ce risque. Je préférais que les choses restent comme ça. Mais peut-être que ce soir, avec ce nouveau look, quelque chose allait arriver. Je m'imaginais des scènes romantiques tout en obéissant aux ordres de Fanny : fermer les yeux, les ouvrir, la regarder bien en face, entrouvrir la bouche, sourire, me tourner vers la lumière. Et enfin, embrasser Sébastien.

Fanny m'a autorisée à la suivre dans la salle de bains pour voir le résultat. Elle m'a laissée entrer la première, lumière éteinte.

« T'es prête ?

– Ouais. »

Elle a allumé et j'ai découvert en face de moi une nouvelle Mélanie. C'était moi, bien sûr, je me reconnaissais. Mais moi en beaucoup plus jolie. Elle m'avait coupé les cheveux assez courts. Ma frange était toujours là, mais plus aérée. Mes yeux semblaient plus ouverts, plus pétillants. L'eye-liner et le mascara me donnaient un regard plus profond. Mes lèvres crayonnées et coloriées me donnaient une bouche un peu boudeuse que je trouvais très sexy. Je n'en revenais pas.

« C'est génial ! »

Je me suis tournée vers Fanny qui me regardait avec un sourire éclatant.

« J'adore ! C'est trop classe ! Merci, merci, merci ! »

En descendant du scooter, j'ai enlevé mon casque avec mille et une précautions. Je me suis penchée pour observer mon reflet dans le rétroviseur. Pas de casse. Fanny me regardait avec un sourire en coin.

« Ben quoi ?

– Nan rien. Ça me fait marrer. Toi qui fuis ton image d'habitude… »

J'ai haussé les épaules en souriant. Nous avons sonné et sommes entrées. La soirée démarrait à peine. Il n'y avait que six personnes qui discutaient tranquillement, affalées dans les canapés des parents de Sébastien.

« Ouah ! Super ta nouvelle coupe !

– Merci Séb. C'est Fanny qui m'a coupé les cheveux avant de venir.

– Ça te va vachement mieux comme ça, c'est hallucinant comme ça te change ! »

J'étais sur un nuage.

« Fanny, tu t'occupes aussi des hommes ?

– Pourquoi, ça t'intéresse ?

– Ouais ! Surtout si y a une option massage de cuir chevelu !

– Faut voir… »

Fanny avait son regard de charmeuse. Je n'aimais pas ça. Sébastien, il était pour moi. J'ai tenté de revenir dans la course.

« Alors Séb, va y avoir qui ce soir ?

– Un peu les mêmes que d'habitude. Qu'est-ce que vous voulez boire les filles ? Fanny, bière ?

– Ouais s'il te plaît.

– Mélanie ?

– Pareil. »

Je n'aimais pas trop la bière mais je m'y habituais petit à petit au cours des soirées. J'ai accompagné Sébastien à la cuisine pour l'aider. J'espérais une scène ultraromantique où il me coincerait entre le frigo et la table pour m'embrasser fougueusement. Il m'a juste mis un pack de bières dans les bras en me chargeant de le rapporter au salon.

J'ai distribué les bouteilles pendant que Fanny racontait son week-end précédent. Elle était allée dans une branche de sa famille où la beauf attitude était un art de vivre. Tout le monde était hilare dès qu'elle imitait un certain Francis, particulièrement gratiné.

« Bon, en tout cas, à cause de ton week-end à Beaufland, t'as raté une fête bien sympa chez Sylvain.

– Ah ouais ? C'était quoi cette fête ?

– Un truc de dernière minute. Ses vieux ont dû partir chez ses grands-parents. Du coup, il a invité tout le monde chez lui… c'était cool. On était dans un état…

– C'est sympa de m'avoir appelée… », ai-je dit en aparté à Sylvain qui se trouvait juste à côté de moi.

« Merde, c'est vrai. Je suis désolé Mélanie. Comme Fanny n'était pas là… »

J'ai encaissé sans rien répondre. Mon moral venait de plonger à une vitesse vertigineuse. J'ai attrapé une bière et suis sortie dans le jardin. J'avais envie d'être seule, mais Fanny n'a pas tardé à me rejoindre.

« Ça va ma cocotte ?

– Bof.

– Qu'est-ce qui se passe ? Quand on est arrivées, t'étais en superforme.

– …

– Hé ho, y a quelqu'un ?

– J'ai les boules.

– Ben pourquoi ?

– …

– Allez dis.

– Nan rien, laisse tomber. »

Je me suis levée et suis rentrée. Il valait mieux que je ne laisse pas libre cours à ma mauvaise humeur. Je lui en voulais de prendre toute la place, d'être celle qu'on appelait pour les soirées. Je n'étais que son ombre. On m'accueillait sans problème mais au fond, on se moquait de savoir si j'étais là ou non. Fanny avait besoin d'être le centre du monde et elle œuvrait sans relâche pour ça. Moi j'étais discrète, je lui laissais la vedette. Elle pouvait briller et moi j'applaudissais. C'était sans doute ce qui lui plaisait chez moi.

J'ai attrapé une autre bière et me suis installée dans un coin de la pièce. Les gens se sont mis à danser. Moi, je ne dansais jamais. J'ai observé les autres se déhancher et s'amuser pendant un moment, puis j'ai ouvert un magazine qui traînait pour me donner une contenance. J'espérais que Sébastien vienne me parler, inquiet de me voir seule, mais il avait l'air de beaucoup s'amuser et ne se souciait pas de moi.

Je me suis levée pour aller aux toilettes. J'y ai ruminé ma colère contre le monde entier. Quand j'en suis sortie, je me suis dirigée vers la cuisine pour me laver les mains. Je suis restée bloquée sur le pas de la porte. Fanny rinçait un verre dans l'évier et Sébastien était derrière elle, collé à elle, il lui parlait à l'oreille et l'embrassait dans le cou. Je ne voulais pas en voir plus mais je n'arrivais pas à bouger. Fanny rigolait. Elle a coupé l'eau, s'est essuyé les mains, puis lui a fait face. Il a caressé son visage et a posé ses lèvres contre les siennes, avec beaucoup de douceur.

Je me suis enfin éloignée. J'étais assommée. Fanny et Sébastien. Jamais elle ne m'avait parlé de lui. Jamais. Il fallait qu'elle les séduise tous, c'était plus fort qu'elle. Et moi, là-dedans ?

Il était onze heures et demie, mes parents ne devaient pas encore être couchés. J'ai décidé de les appeler pour qu'ils viennent me chercher. Après avoir eu ma mère, j'ai pris mes affaires et suis sortie l'attendre sur le trottoir. Je ne voulais pas croiser Fanny ou qui que ce soit d'autre. J'espérais qu'elle s'inquiéterait en se rendant compte que je n'étais plus là. Peut-être même culpabiliserait-elle de m'avoir abandonnée, je pouvais toujours rêver. J'ai pris un chewing-gum pour masquer l'odeur de la bière.

Quand je suis montée dans la voiture, j'avais oublié les cheveux, le maquillage et tout ça. C'est quand j'ai vu la tête de ma mère que ça m'est revenu.

« C'est joli, non ?

– Oui, oui…

– C'est Fanny qui m'a coupé les cheveux.

– Si t'avais envie de te faire couper les cheveux, t'avais qu'à me le dire, je t'aurais emmenée chez le coiffeur.

– Qu'est-ce que ça change ? T'as fait des économies.

– C'est pas le problème… ton père va être contrarié, il aimait bien tes cheveux longs. »

Elle m'énervait à parler comme ça à la place de tout le monde, et puis je n'étais pas d'humeur.

« Il s'y fera. Allez démarre. »

Elle continuait de me regarder sans bouger.

« Mais démarre, on va pas passer la nuit ici. »

Elle s'est enfin décidée. J'aurais aimé que le trajet soit silencieux mais c'était sans espoir avec ma mère.

« Alors, qu'est-ce qui s'est passé à cette soirée ? Ça ne te ressemble pas de m'appeler pour que je vienne te chercher.

– …

– Je te parle Mélanie.

– Je t'ai entendue. C'était… chiant.

– Surveille ton langage. Et Fanny, elle y est toujours ?

– Oui, en train de bécoter dans tous les coins. »

Ça m'avait échappé.

« Elle a un nouvel amoureux ?

– Si on veut.

– Et du coup, tu t'es retrouvée toute seule, c'est ça ?

– …

– Je vois. »

Je ne savais pas ce qu'elle voyait et je n'avais pas envie de le savoir. Pour éviter qu'elle ne développe, j'ai changé de sujet.

« Maman, je voudrais aller faire du shopping avec Fanny la semaine prochaine.

– Super, on ira à Créteil Soleil.

– Comment ça "on" ? C'est bon, j'ai plus huit ans maman. On peut y aller sans toi.

– Ce n'est pas le problème. Soit je viens avec vous, soit tu oublies cette idée de shopping.

– …

– Quand il s'agit de venir te chercher à une soirée, t'es bien contente que je sois là. »

Elle marquait un point.

« Laisse tomber, puisque c'est comme ça…

– Mais non, c'est une très bonne idée ! Parce que franchement…

– J'ai l'air d'un sac, je sais. »

Ma mère a souri, contente d'elle. Je lui

aurais bien donné quelques coups de couteau si j'en avais eu un sur moi à ce moment-là.

Nous sommes arrivées à la maison, et après un rapide baiser, je me suis réfugiée dans ma chambre. J'ai attendu que ma mère soit couchée pour redescendre à la cuisine. J'ai ouvert les placards, sans bruit, et je me suis préparé un plateau réconfort : pain, fromage, chips et cookies au chocolat. Je me suis installée devant la télé, sans le son, pour ne pas risquer d'alerter ma mère.

Je les détestais tous. Y compris Sébastien qui m'avait laissée croire que je lui plaisais, au moins un peu, toujours gentil et attentionné avec moi, tu parles, tout ça pour se taper Fanny. Et moi, je n'avais rien vu venir. J'en avais marre que tout le monde me prenne pour une conne.

« Qu'est-ce que tu fais à manger ces cochonneries au milieu de la nuit, non mais ça va pas hein ! »

J'étais si perdue dans mes pensées que je n'avais pas entendu ma mère arriver.

« Je... on n'a pas pris le temps de manger avant d'aller à la soirée et...

– C'est ça, toutes les excuses sont bonnes. Tu vas me ranger ça tout de suite et tu montes te coucher. »

Je me suis mise à pleurer. En silence d'abord. Puis à gros sanglots. Je ne me contrôlais plus. J'en avais marre. Marre d'être comme ça. Marre d'être moi. Je ne demandais pas grand-chose, juste d'avoir ma part. Comme tout le monde. Mais apparemment, c'était déjà trop.

Ma mère s'est radoucie.

« Qu'est-ce qui se passe ma chérie ? C'est juste, tu sais, je n'aime pas que tu manges en dehors des repas. »

Je ne pouvais pas lui parler. Je hoquetais dès que j'essayais de lui dire quoi que ce soit.

« Calme-toi, calme-toi. Ça va aller. Qu'est-ce qui ne va pas mon bébé ? Tu peux me parler.

– Je… j'en ai marre… personne ne m'aime. »

C'était tout ce que j'étais capable de dire. Elle est restée silencieuse un court instant avant de me répondre.

« Bien sûr que si, il y a des gens qui t'aiment. Ton père et moi, on t'aime.

– Vous, c'est pas pareil.

– Fanny aussi t'aime.

– …

– Allez, va au lit, je suis sûre que ça ira mieux demain. »

*

J'avais tout essayé pour annuler ce maudit shopping mais ma mère était trop enthousiaste pour lâcher l'affaire. Quant à Fanny, je pense qu'elle s'en serait bien passée vu le climat qui régnait entre nous depuis la soirée chez Sébastien (je lui faisais plus ou moins la gueule, mais pas complètement, tout en disant que je ne la faisais pas), mais quand j'avais compris que je subirais Créteil Soleil avec ma mère, que Fanny vienne ou non, j'avais jugé préférable qu'elle soit là. Si moi je n'étais pas capable d'imposer mes goûts à ma mère sans que nous frôlions la crise de nerfs, Fanny, elle, arriverait peut-être à m'y aider.

Nous étions donc en route toutes les trois pour le centre commercial. Fanny était assise près de ma mère qui affichait une insupportable bonne humeur. Elle discutait et plaisantait avec Fanny, oubliant pour l'occasion tout le mal qu'elle en pensait. Cette hypocrisie me mettait hors de moi. Quant à Fanny, elle rentrait dans son jeu, elle jouait les grandes et rigolait bêtement. Elle était ridicule. J'observais la scène, du siège arrière, en bougonnant en silence.

Nous sommes entrées dans une première boutique et Fanny m'a demandé ma taille. Je lui ai répondu du bout des lèvres qu'il me fallait du L ou du 40-42. J'ai cru voir ma mère faire un signe à Fanny, genre « C'est pas gagné ! ». J'ai pris sur moi pour ne rien dire. Fanny est partie en chasseuse solitaire et, confiante, m'a donné rendez-vous dix minutes plus tard aux cabines d'essayage.

J'allais partir moi aussi de mon côté, mais ma mère m'a mis le grappin dessus en me demandant mon avis sur un haut qui semblait taillé soit pour une gamine de dix ans, soit pour une anorexique. Je me demandais si elle plaisantait tant il était évident que je ne pouvais pas rentrer dedans.

Je l'ai laissée en plan sans lui répondre, me contentant de hausser les épaules. Je me suis baladée dans la boutique, en me forçant à regarder les hauts suspendus un peu partout, mais le cœur n'y était pas. Je n'avais qu'une envie, rentrer à la maison et me prendre un bon goûter devant la télé.

Je me suis dirigée vers les cabines. J'étais bredouille. Ma mère et Fanny, elles, se réjouissaient de leurs diverses trouvailles, se congratulant pour leur bon goût et leur capacité à dénicher des trésors cachés. Elles m'ont poussée dans la cabine sans ménagement.

J'ai refermé le rideau, goûtant cette brève solitude. J'ai attrapé le premier haut. C'était une tunique avec un grand décolleté. J'ai retiré mon tee-shirt. J'ai jeté un œil dans le miroir. Une baleine. Je ressemblais à une baleine. Je ne me suis pas attardée. J'ai enfilé la tunique. Un élastique la resserrait sous la poitrine et donnait un effet vaporeux au niveau du ventre. On voyait la naissance de mes seins. Beurk. Je suis sortie à contrecœur. Fanny a émis un sifflement.

« Ça te va trop bien !

– Je suis d'accord avec Fanny, c'est très bien ça. »

Bien sûr, elles étaient d'accord. Moi, j'avais l'impression qu'on ne voyait que mes seins et ça n'était pas du tout à mon goût.

« Je trouve ça trop décolleté…

– Pas plus que le haut que je porte, a répondu Fanny.

– Oui, enfin, sur toi, ça ne fait pas vraiment le même effet…

– Nan, t'as raison, c'est beaucoup plus joli sur toi. »

J'ai essayé de me regarder dans la glace d'un œil objectif. Ça me changeait pas mal. C'était même assez joli. Avec ma nouvelle coupe de cheveux, tout ça, je ressemblais davantage aux autres filles, mais au niveau des seins… non, ça n'était pas possible.

« On voit trop mes seins.

– Arrête…

– Mais putain, maman, me dis pas d'arrêter ! Déjà qu'en temps normal, les gens ne matent que mes seins. C'est bon, je vais pas en rajouter. »

Je suis retournée bien vite dans la cabine. Je me suis regardée encore une fois dans la glace. Elles ne pouvaient me comprendre ni l'une ni l'autre avec leurs petits seins presque invisibles. J'entendais ma mère chuchoter à l'extérieur. Elle disait à Fanny qu'elle ne comprenait pas pourquoi j'étais aussi obnubilée par mes kilos et ma poitrine. Elle a ensuite ajouté quelque chose, à voix plus basse, que je n'ai pas compris, et Fanny a éclaté de rire.

Ma mère et Fanny riaient de moi.

« Alors Mélanie, on peut voir la suite ? »

Je n'ai rien répondu.

Je regardais mon corps dans la glace. Mes larmes m'empêchaient de bien le voir, mais je percevais ses contours mous.

« Mélanie, qu'est-ce que tu fous ? »

Elles riaient de moi et il y avait de quoi.

« Le second ne m'allait pas du tout, je passe direct au troisième. »

Ma voix tremblotait mais elles n'y ont pas prêté attention. Je les ai entendues reprendre leur conversation.

Je n'étais pas capable de les affronter.

J'ai attrapé un haut noir avec un décolleté rond pas trop plongeant et des manches longues. Je l'ai enfilé en priant pour qu'il m'aille bien. J'ai respiré à fond et suis sortie.

Fanny a levé son pouce en l'air. J'ai évité son regard et me suis concentrée sur mon reflet dans le miroir. Je trouvais le haut joli, mais un peu court. Quand je l'ai dit, ma mère a levé les yeux au ciel et s'est tournée vers Fanny.

« Mélanie est persuadée qu'un tee-shirt doit arriver à mi-cuisse ! »

Je n'ai rien dit.

« Mélanie, ce n'est pas une robe ! », a ajouté ma mère avec une pointe d'énervement.

Je me contorsionnais devant la glace pour me rendre compte de l'effet de dos. Un peu gros cul quand même.

« Alors Mélanie, tu te décides ? a embrayé ma mère.

– Non, il est trop court. Tant pis. »

Ma mère a poussé un long soupir et ce soupir m'a libérée de la paralysie dans laquelle leurs rires m'avaient plongée. La colère a repris le dessus.

« Ben quoi, ce n'est pas de ma faute si ces fringues me vont pas !

– Mais non, ma chérie, bien sûr que non. »

L'ironie dans sa voix, sa manière de m'appeler « ma chérie », c'était insupportable.

« On va rien trouver, ça me saoule.

– Mais non, prends ton temps.

– Nan, c'est bon. Ça va être pareil avec tout.

– Mélanie, ta crise d'enfant gâtée, ça va bien. Fanny et moi, on essaie de t'aider et toi, tu ne fais aucun effort.

– C'est ça, vous, vous êtes formidables et moi je ne fais aucun effort. Allez, on remballe. »

Je me suis réfugiée dans la cabine. J'ai enfilé mon tee-shirt et j'ai remis les affaires sur les cintres, histoire de laisser le temps à mon menton et à mes mains de s'arrêter de trembler. Je suis passée sans un regard pour ma mère et j'ai filé tout droit vers la sortie du magasin. Elles m'ont rattrapée et Fanny a tenté de détendre l'atmosphère.

« Allez, on va boire quelque chose. Et puis après, on verra si on a envie de refaire une tentative…

– …

– …

– On va pas abandonner comme ça ?

– …

– …

– Bon, on rentre alors… »

Ma mère n'avait plus envie de copiner avec Fanny. Elle marchait d'un pas rapide devant nous. Fanny en a profité pour me donner son avis éclairé.

« C'est con…

– Ben c'est comme ça.

– On peut encore y retourner.

– …

– Mais si, allez, remballe ta fierté. Ça arrive à tout le monde de s'énerver.

– Surtout quand ta mère et ta soi-disant meilleure amie se foutent de ta gueule…

– Qu'est-ce que tu racontes ?

– Laisse tomber.

– Je laisse rien tomber du tout, t'es en train de te monter le ciboulot ! Tu vas venir à la maison, on va discuter. »

Ma mère nous a déposées chez Fanny, pas mécontente de se débarrasser de nous, je crois. Je n'étais pas très à l'aise. Fanny est restée silencieuse jusqu'à ce que nous soyons installées dans sa chambre. Elle a sorti un paquet de Carambar du tiroir de son bureau et me l'a tendu.

« Allez, sers-toi et explique-moi ce qui se passe dans ta petite tête.

– …

– Allez, on va pas rester comme ça ! »

J'ai pris un Carambar pour gagner un peu de temps et réfléchir à ce que j'allais dire.

« Je t'ai entendue te marrer avec ma mère quand j'étais dans la cabine…

– Et t'as cru qu'on se foutait de toi ?

– …

– On rigolait d'une nana qu'essayait un futal trois tailles trop petit pour elle ! »

Fanny disait la vérité, j'en étais sûre. Je me suis sentie ridicule.

« C'est… c'est que… c'est tellement pénible pour moi les séances de shopping, j'espère toujours trouver des trucs et puis, y a jamais rien qui me va, j'ai trop de bide, trop de seins, trop de cul et ça me rend… je sais pas… »

Pour ne pas pleurer, j'ai attrapé un autre Carambar. Fanny me regardait avec son air le plus sérieux.

« Qu'est-ce que tu changerais à ton corps, là, maintenant, si t'avais une baguette magique ?

– Tout. J'en demanderais un neuf. Avec de

longues jambes, un cul rebondi, un ventre plat et des seins plus petits.

– Oui mais en priorité, si tu pouvais demander un seul truc.

– Les seins.

– C'est marrant. Moi, j'ai longtemps été complexée de ne pas en avoir. J'ai une cousine qu'était comme toi, elle détestait ses seins et elle s'est fait opérer l'année dernière.

– Ah ouais ?

– Je te jure, comment c'est bien ce qu'ils lui ont fait. Y a pas de cicatrice, rien. Des seins tout ronds qui regardent droit devant.

– Elle a quel âge ?

– Seize ans.

– Si je pouvais, je ferais comme elle.

– Et pourquoi tu pourrais pas ?

– Ma mère ne veut pas que je fasse de régime, alors la chirurgie esthétique, c'est même pas la peine.

– T'as qu'à dire que t'as mal au dos.

– Comment ça ?

– Ben les gros seins, ça donne mal au dos. À cause du poids. T'as pas mal au dos, toi ?

– Si, ça arrive...

– Tu vois !

– Ça marcherait jamais un truc pareil avec ma mère. Elle me dirait de faire du sport pour me muscler et la discussion serait close.

– Tu devrais quand même essayer... »

*

Le médecin regardait avec attention les radios que j'avais passées la veille. J'avais lu cent fois le rapport : début de scoliose pouvant être à l'origine des maux de dos dont se plaint la patiente. Moi.

Il a reposé les clichés sur le bureau, a enlevé ses lunettes et les a nettoyées. Il était clair qu'il essayait de gagner du temps. Il connaissait ma mère et savait que ça allait être délicat.

« Alors docteur ?

– Eh bien, Mélanie a un début de scoliose, ce qui ne m'étonne guère.

– Et ?

– Et voilà ce que je pense. Cette scoliose peut avoir deux causes. »

Il a cessé de regarder ma mère pour me parler à moi.

« Mélanie, ne prends pas mal ce que je vais te dire… »

J'ai senti mon sang me descendre dans les orteils. Il allait me dire que j'exagérais et que je devais arrêter mon cinéma.

« Il y a d'abord tes kilos en trop, on y reviendra. Il y a aussi ta poitrine, assez volumineuse. Les femmes, et plus particulièrement les jeunes femmes comme toi, ont tendance, quand elles sont gênées par la taille de leurs seins, à se tenir voûtées, pour qu'on les remarque moins. C'est très mauvais pour leur dos. »

J'étais aux anges. J'avais envie d'embrasser le médecin. Ma mère semblait moins ravie que moi.

« Et qu'est-ce que vous préconisez ?

– Tout d'abord, qu'elle suive un régime pour perdre quelques kilos.

– À son âge ?

– Écoutez, il ne s'agit pas de faire n'importe quoi. Si vous êtes d'accord, je vous donnerai l'adresse de l'un de mes confrères nutritionniste qui pourra la suivre et lui prescrire un régime sur mesure.»

Ma mère n'a pas moufté.

«J'aimerais maintenant parler à Mélanie en privé si cela ne vous dérange pas.

– Pourquoi?

– Ne le prenez pas mal madame Lagrange, mais à partir d'un certain âge, il est parfois préférable de ne plus voir les enfants accompagnés de leurs parents.

– Je ne vois pas ce qu'elle peut avoir à me cacher.

– Ce n'est pas la question.»

Ma mère était furieuse. Moi, je ne savais pas trop à quoi m'attendre. Elle a ramassé ses affaires sans me jeter un regard.

«Mélanie, ta scoliose n'est pas en soi très inquiétante, mais suffisante pour te causer tes douleurs. En revanche, si elle venait à s'aggraver, cela pourrait devenir préoccupant. Il est important de bien suivre ce régime. Est-ce que tu te sens prête à faire des efforts dans ce sens?

– Oui, bien sûr. Moi ça fait longtemps que je veux faire un régime mais ma mère n'a jamais été d'accord.

– Je vois. Avec, disons dix kilos de moins, tu penses que tu te sentirais mieux ?

– C'est clair !

– Il n'y a rien d'autre dont tu veuilles me parler ? »

C'était le moment de jouer le tout pour le tout.

« En fait, si...

– Je t'écoute.

– Je... je sais pas comment vous dire ça...

– Je suis là pour t'aider Mélanie.

– Je... je déteste ma poitrine. Je la trouve moche... encombrante... je... enfin, vous devez trouver ça un peu ridicule mais...

– Pas du tout Mélanie. Dès lors que ça te pose un problème, ce n'est pas ridicule.

– J'ai l'impression qu'on ne voit que ça quand on me regarde. Quand je dois courir ou quoi, j'ai l'impression qu'elle bouge dans tous les sens et c'est douloureux. Je camoufle comme je peux mais...

– Tu sais qu'en perdant des kilos, ta poitrine va diminuer...

– Oui... oui... sans doute un peu... »

Je devais aller jusqu'au bout, c'était l'occasion ou jamais. J'ai inspiré et j'ai marmonné sans oser le regarder :

«Je... enfin... j'ai entendu dire qu'on pouvait se faire opérer pour diminuer la taille des seins... enfin... je ne sais pas si dans mon cas... c'est juste que... ça m'aiderait... enfin... je crois...»

Je ne quittais plus des yeux le bout de mes chaussures. J'avais très chaud aux joues.

«Écoute Mélanie, c'est une option possible mais ce n'est pas une décision à prendre à la légère. C'est une opération qui, comme toute opération, présente des risques. En plus, tu es un peu jeune pour ce genre d'intervention... mais bon, ce serait envisageable.»

J'ai enfin relevé la tête.

«Vous croyez? ai-je demandé d'une toute petite voix.

– Il ne faut pas se précipiter. Dans un premier temps, tu dois te débarrasser de tes kilos en trop. Et si après, tu ne te sens pas mieux avec ton corps, nous pourrons en reparler.

– D'accord. Est-ce que... est-ce que ma mère...

– Tu es mineure, rien ne pourrait être envisagé sans l'accord de tes parents.

– Ils ne voudront jamais. Surtout ma mère. Elle ne voulait même pas que je suive un régime.

– Écoute Mélanie, ils ont raison d'être prudents. Tu es jeune et il ne faut pas faire n'importe quoi. Je te propose de nous revoir dans quatre mois, je compte sur toi pour respecter les consignes du nutritionniste. Nous reparlerons de tout ça à ce moment-là. Ça marche ? »

J'étais un peu déçue mais il me fallait être patiente. Au moins, les choses commençaient à bouger. Il est parti chercher ma mère. Elle faisait toujours la gueule. Elle lui a presque coupé la parole alors qu'il lui expliquait comme il était important qu'elle me soutienne dans mon régime.

« Je crois que j'ai compris. Combien je vous dois ?

– Quatre-vingt-cinq francs. »

Je redoutais le tête-à-tête qui allait suivre. Mauvaise humeur et interrogatoire garantis. Ça n'a pas raté.

« Alors qu'est-ce que vous vous êtes dit que je ne pouvais pas entendre ?

– Rien de spécial. Il voulait savoir comment je me sentais, si j'étais prête pour ce régime, des trucs comme ça...

– Je ne vois pas en quoi ma présence dérangeait.

– Ce n'est pas moi qui t'ai demandé de sortir... tu téléphones au nutritionniste en rentrant?

– Oui, oui, je vais appeler. T'es contente de suivre ce régime on dirait.

– J'en ai marre d'être grosse.

– J'attends de voir ta volonté... »

Elle n'a plus ouvert la bouche de tout le trajet, ce qui en disait long sur son niveau de contrariété. De mon côté, je préparais dans ma tête le compte-rendu que j'allais faire à Fanny. Tout ça, c'était grâce à elle. Toute seule, je n'aurais jamais pu, ne serait-ce qu'imaginer, aller contre la volonté de ma mère.

*

Jour J, quatre mois plus tard.

J'ai demandé à ma mère de rester dans la

salle d'attente mais elle n'a rien voulu savoir, plaidant qu'elle voulait entendre ce que le médecin avait à dire, et qu'il le lui demanderait s'il désirait qu'elle sorte. Il l'avait fait une fois, il saurait bien le refaire. Son raisonnement tenait la route.

Le médecin m'a adressé un grand sourire quand je suis entrée dans le cabinet.

« Eh bien Mélanie, je vois que tes efforts ont payé. Nous allons te peser pour mesurer ça. »

Je me suis déshabillée et suis montée sur la balance.

« Cinquante-cinq kilos. Et au départ... voyons, qu'est-ce que j'avais noté ? Soixante-deux. Sept kilos de moins, c'est très bien. Alors, comment tu te sens ?

– Ça va.

– Qu'est-ce que vous vous étiez fixés comme objectif avec le nutritionniste ?

– Une dizaine de kilos sur six mois.

– Tout se passe comme vous voulez alors ?

– Oui... enfin, c'est devenu plus dur ces derniers temps. Je n'arrive plus trop à perdre.

– C'est normal. Les premiers kilos sont toujours les plus faciles à éliminer. Allonge-toi, je vais te prendre ta tension. 10-7, c'est un peu faible. Tu te sens fatiguée ?

– Un peu, sans plus.

– Bon, de toute manière, c'est bientôt les grandes vacances, tu vas pouvoir te reposer. Et ce dos alors, est-ce qu'il te fait toujours souffrir ? »

Mon dos. Je l'avais un peu oublié celui-là.

« Elle ne se plaint plus.

– Bonne nouvelle ! Plus de douleurs, Mélanie ? Plus de gêne ? »

Je ne pouvais pas dire que je souffrais le martyre alors que je ne m'étais pas plainte depuis des semaines.

« Ça va mieux. Enfin, c'est pas impeccable... je veux dire... ça m'arrive toujours d'avoir mal... mais... je suppose que je m'y habitue. »

Le médecin me scrutait attentivement.

« Tu t'y habitues ?

– Oui... enfin nan mais... »

Le médecin a tourné la tête en direction de ma mère.

« Je dois sortir, c'est ça ?

– J'allais vous le demander, effectivement. »

Dès qu'elle a quitté la pièce, je me suis mise

à pleurer. Le médecin m'a tendu une boîte de Kleenex.

« Qu'est-ce qui se passe Mélanie ?

– J'ai beau avoir maigri, tout ça, je ne me sens pas mieux.

– Mélanie, par rapport à l'option que nous avions mentionnée ensemble la dernière fois, tu vas devoir être encore patiente. J'ai appelé ton nutritionniste avant que tu ne viennes. Il m'a dit qu'il ne te pensait pas stabilisée dans ton régime alimentaire, qu'il t'arrivait d'avoir des comportements compulsifs, et que la phase de stabilisation pouvait s'avérer difficile. Tu dois bien comprendre, Mélanie. Il ne s'agit pas de maigrir, de te refaire la poitrine et de jouer ensuite au yo-yo avec ton poids. Il doit absolument être stable pour envisager l'opération et cela va encore prendre un peu de temps.

– Combien de temps ?

– Le temps nécessaire pour que tu atteignes ton objectif de poids et que tu t'y stabilises sans que cela ne te pose plus de problèmes.

– …

– Tu vas y arriver Mélanie, j'ai confiance en toi. »

Je me suis remise à pleurer. Moi, je n'étais pas certaine d'y arriver. Pas certaine du tout. Il a attendu que je sois calmée pour appeler ma mère. J'avais les yeux trop rouges pour qu'elle ne devine pas que j'avais pleuré, mais elle n'a émis aucun commentaire. Jusqu'à la voiture.

« Qu'est-ce qui s'est passé ?

– Rien.

– Ne me prends pas pour une idiote Mélanie, tu as pleuré, tu as les yeux tout rouges.

– C'est juste que... ça devient dur le régime. »

Et je me suis remise à pleurer. Ma mère n'a rien dit. J'avais voulu à tout prix suivre ce régime, contre son avis, je ne méritais ni compassion, ni réconfort.

*

Quand septembre est arrivé, avec sa fichue rentrée des classes, j'avais déjà repris deux kilos. Fanny avait enfin réussi à convaincre sa mère pour son BEP d'esthéticienne, et n'était plus au lycée. Je me sentais plus mal que jamais.

Après, les kilos sont revenus un à un. Il n'a plus jamais été question ni d'être mince, ni de me faire opérer des seins.

Vingt-cinq ans

Je parcourais mon désert sentimental de long en large depuis pas mal d'années, presque résignée, quand Fanny, toujours elle, m'a fait découvrir qu'il y avait sur cette terre des hommes sains d'esprit a priori, qui avaient une préférence définitive pour les femmes bien en chair.

Oui, je sais, tous les goûts sont dans la nature, mais il faut admettre que la nature présente des normes assez marquées, à savoir que les pies sont attirées par ce qui brille, les requins par ce qui saigne, les marins par les sirènes, les sirènes par les rochers, les riches par Monaco, les pauvres par les riches et les hommes par les femmes aux mensurations de rêve, à savoir le triptyque magique 90-60-90.

Donc, quand Fanny m'a parlé de ce site Internet dédié aux hommes aimant les femmes aux formes généreuses, je m'attendais à ce que ce soit plus un site pour pervers qu'autre chose. Et puis, passer par des petites annonces pour tenter de me caser voulait dire renier les dernières miettes d'amour-propre qu'il me restait.

Mais quand Fanny pensait tenir une bonne idée, elle ne la lâchait pas comme ça. Elle me répétait sans cesse que les rencontres sur Internet allaient devenir super tendance et qu'il fallait tordre le cou aux vieux a priori. Elle était emballée à l'idée que j'aille pavaner au milieu de ce cybermarché de l'obésité. Moi, beaucoup moins. Même si je devais bien reconnaître que c'était peut-être là ma meilleure chance de ne pas finir vieille fille.

Comme toujours avec Fanny, j'ai fini par céder. Un dimanche après-midi, après un brunch fastueux que je digérais en me lamentant une fois de plus sur mon sort, elle m'a vaincue.

« Allez, on essaie, ça va être marrant. Et puis, ça n'engage à rien. On te crée un profil, on met une photo et…

– T'es dingue, je ne mets pas de photo !

– Si tu mets pas de photo, ça marchera pas…

– …

– Allez, bouge tes fesses, on se lance. »

Le site s'appelait rondeDesRencontres.fr. Gratuit pour les filles, payant pour les garçons. Motivés les gars !

Nous avons commencé par jeter un œil à quelques fiches. Personne ne pesait moins de quatre-vingts kilos. Bienvenue dans la quatrième dimension. Les filles arboraient des sourires éclatants au milieu de visages aux joues rondes, des décolletés aux reliefs vertigineux et des mensurations à faire vomir une anorexique. Leurs fiches étaient rigolotes et coquines. Il y avait là de quoi mettre une sacrée claque à tous mes complexes. C'est donc avec un regain de confiance que je me suis lancée avec Fanny dans la rédaction de ma fiche.

Pseudo : …
Âge : 25 ans
Mensurations : 1,58 m – 85 kg – 100E
Recherche : homme entre 20 et 30 ans (Paris)
Aime : …
Déteste : …

J'étais bloquée.

Qu'est-ce que j'aimais ? Qu'est-ce que je détestais ?

Fanny débitait vingt conneries à la seconde. Je riais beaucoup mais ne trouvais rien pour remplir les cases. Je n'avais pas de passions si dingues qu'elles méritent d'être citées. Il y avait la peinture, mais cette activité solitaire ne me semblait pas être un très bon argument de drague. Fanny n'était pas d'accord avec moi. Elle était certaine qu'une touche bohème intriguerait et attirerait plein de beaux mâles. Elle en était même à me suggérer de mettre que j'étais spécialiste du nu, et que je recherchais de beaux spécimens du sexe masculin pour me servir de modèles. Bien sûr…

Qu'est-ce que j'aimais? Qu'est-ce que je détestais?

Rien ne me venait. J'ai relu quelques fiches... il y en avait des vraiment bien, la concurrence était rude! Qu'est-ce que je pouvais bien mettre? J'aime... j'aime... ça me bloquait d'avoir Fanny qui lisait par-dessus mon épaule. Je lui ai demandé de me laisser un quart d'heure, promettant de trouver quelque chose dans ce laps de temps. Elle s'est éloignée en chantonnant des conneries comme quoi j'aimais les jolies fesses et les gros zizis.

Pseudo : Mél25
Âge : 25 ans
Mensurations : 1,58 m – 85 kg – 100E
Recherche : homme entre 20 et 30 ans (Paris)
Aime : les Chamallow grillés au feu de bois si c'est un beau brun ténébreux qui les lui a préparés en fredonnant une chanson de Radiohead
Déteste : les Chamallow grillés au feu de bois si elle doit les partager avec un

pauvre type qui ne comprend rien à la magnifique tristesse de Radiohead.

Je n'étais pas mécontente. Ce n'était pas transcendant mais ça sonnait bien. J'ai appelé Fanny pour qu'elle valide.

« Ouais, c'est cool et ça te ressemble bien.

– On envoie ?

– Attends, attends, on n'a pas mis la photo ! »

La sélection de la photo nous a donné du mal. Je trouvais toujours quelque chose à redire. Au final, nous en avons choisi une où j'étais bronzée et souriante, plutôt jolie, même de mon point de vue, pourtant sévère.

À peine cinq minutes après m'être enregistrée, je recevais mon premier message : « Salut Mél25 ! Quel sourire… »

Quelle originalité !

Et voilà comment a débuté une longue série de soirées passées devant mon ordinateur.

*

Le premier type que j'ai accepté de rencontrer s'appelait Paul. Je flirtais avec assiduité sur le site depuis quelques semaines déjà, sans jamais me décider à franchir le cap de la rencontre en chair et en os (surtout en chair en ce qui me concernait). J'étais du clan des allumeuses. Toujours là pour tchater jusqu'à pas d'heure, mais systématiquement aux abonnés absents dès qu'on cherchait à me rencontrer. Je pratiquais les smileys, les LOL et autres acronymes avec la dextérité des habitués, mais pour ce qui était de me rendre à un tête-à-tête, il n'y avait plus personne.

Difficile d'expliquer l'intérêt que je trouvais à draguer sans jamais chercher à concrétiser, mais je crois que je me moquais pas mal d'avoir une autre langue que la mienne dans ma bouche ou de m'encastrer avec qui que ce soit. En revanche, j'éprouvais un grand plaisir à attirer les prétendants, à les sentir suspendus à mes messages, mes réponses, mes blagues, à jouer un rôle qui n'était pas le mien, celui de la fille à l'aise, drôle, presque mondaine au milieu de tout ce réseau d'habitués, de drogués du clavier.

Et puis, il y a eu Paul. Paul était un beau métis antillais. Il a su se montrer plus malin que les autres, et surtout, plus malin que moi. Paul m'a laissée faire la belle. En tout cas au début. Et puis très vite, il a décelé la supercherie et il m'a balancé mes quatre vérités.

« C'est facile de faire la maligne planquée derrière ton ordi...

– ???

– Je suis sûr que t'es du genre coincée dans la vraie vie.

– T'es psy ? Médium ? ;-))) »

Je pensais encore m'en sortir à ce moment-là.

« À quoi tu joues ?

– ???

– À QUOI TU JOUES ? »

Là, j'ai commencé à flipper.

« Comment ça ?

– Ça fait un mois qu'on tchate.

– Et ?

– Arrête de jouer la nana cool.

– Ça existe les nanas cool...

– Ouais, dans les soirées, les bars... toi tu te

planques en faisant semblant de pas te planquer.

– J'me planque pas.

– Tu te planques et t'es coincée.

– Pourquoi ? Parce que j'ai pas couché avec toi ? ;-)))

– Ni avec personne d'autre je parie. Ça me saoule les nanas comme toi.

– Je te retiens pas !

– À quand remonte ton dernier rancard ? »

Au secours ! Je ne pouvais pas avouer que je ne m'étais jamais rendue à aucun rancard.

« Ça te regarde pas.

– Je vois…

– T'as jamais demandé à ce qu'on se rencontre !

– Peine perdue… »

Il m'insupportait ce monsieur je-sais-tout.

« Ben t'avais tort ! »

Un mensonge n'avait jamais tué personne.

« Ah ouais… tu fais quoi demain soir ? »

Là, j'étais un peu coincée. Si je me défilais, je lui donnais raison.

« Je suppose que t'es prise…

– Nan.

– Demain soir, 20 h, devant l'opéra Bastille ?

– OK. »

C'est comme ça que je suis allée à mon premier rendez-vous. Tétanisée. Pas du tout excitée par la rencontre.

J'avais bu un verre avant. Pour me détendre. En espérant être plus bavarde avec un peu d'alcool dans le sang. Je m'étais faite jolie mais pas trop, je ne voulais pas avoir l'air de m'être préparée. Je voulais avoir l'air cool. L'air de m'en moquer. L'air d'être blasée de ces rendez-vous auxquels je ne pouvais me rendre comme à une banale soirée entre potes.

Je suis arrivée un peu en retard, en espérant qu'il ne serait plus là. Qu'il n'aurait pas eu la patience d'attendre. Il était là. Il était beau. Beau à calmer un troupeau complet d'hystériques. N'étant pas hystérique, ça m'a carrément paralysée. J'ai marmonné un timide bonjour alors que j'étais encore à deux mètres de lui. Il n'a pas entendu. Alors je me suis approchée davantage. Un pas de plus et je lui marchais sur les pieds, mais il ne m'avait toujours pas vue. Il a enfin tourné la tête dans ma direction.

« Ah salut !

– Salut. »

Qu'est-ce qu'on est censé faire dans ce genre de situations, on se serre la main ou on se roule direct une pelle ? Je n'en savais rien. Je me suis contentée d'un sourire et d'un hochement de tête.

« Je n'étais pas certain que tu viendrais...

– Ben si, si... »

Quelle réplique fulgurante !

« On va boire un verre ?

– Ben si, si... enfin je veux dire... oui.

– T'as un endroit de prédilection ?

– Je te laisse choisir... »

Nous avons marché en silence. J'espérais qu'il mette ça sur le compte de la foule compacte qui envahissait Bastille et qui rendait la conversation difficile alors que nous nous faufilions pour nous rendre dans le bar de son choix.

À peine installés, il a pris l'avantage en étant le premier à poser cette question, cette question stupide qui m'a fait me sentir débile. Il m'a demandé :

« Alors, qui es-tu Mélanie ? »

Je me suis embarquée dans un autoportrait aussi drôle que possible. Je ramais. Et lui me regardait ramer. Ce type était un sadique ! Mais un sadique au sourire si envoûtant qu'à aucun moment je n'ai envisagé de l'envoyer balader. J'étais convaincue d'avoir l'entière responsabilité de cette rencontre. J'étais obnubilée par ma peur du silence, par la nécessité de le combler et par son jugement.

Au bout d'une heure, la sentence est tombée. Il a regardé sa montre et m'a dit qu'il avait rancard avec des potes. Il a ajouté, avec un sourire ironique, que ça avait été très agréable de me rencontrer.

Je n'ai plus fait d'effort. Je n'ai plus essayé de maintenir un semblant de conversation, ni pendant que nous attendions le serveur pour payer, ni pendant que nous marchions en direction du métro. J'acceptais le verdict. La réalité venait de me rattraper, cette réalité que j'avais oubliée pendant les longues heures passées devant mon ordinateur. J'étais une handicapée sociale. Une nullité. Je n'avais plus qu'à retourner à ma peinture et à me faire oublier.

Il a fallu toute la force de persuasion de Fanny pour me remettre en selle après ce malheureux épisode. Je ne voulais plus tchater, je ne voulais même plus approcher mon ordinateur. Je voulais retourner à ma vie d'avant, celle où je restais dans mon coin et où on me laissait en paix.

Mais Fanny l'a emporté. Elle a réussi à me convaincre que je devais m'entraîner en acceptant davantage de rendez-vous. D'après elle, seul le manque d'expérience était à l'origine de ce fiasco. Le manque d'expérience et le fait que ce Paul était un pauvre con, mais ça, comme disait Fanny, nous n'y pouvions rien.

J'ai suivi ses conseils. Quand les types me proposaient de les rencontrer, je les rencontrais. Toujours à reculons. Toujours avec une boule d'angoisse au fond du ventre, mais j'y allais. Je le faisais comme on se débarrasse d'une corvée utile, sans rechigner, mais pressée que ce soit terminé.

Je suis tombée sur des mecs sympas que j'ai revus plusieurs fois. J'ai couché avec certains d'entre eux. J'ai rencontré des tordus qui aimaient les grosses pour des raisons suspectes, d'autres juste parce qu'ils aimaient les gros seins ou les gros culs. J'ai raconté maintes fois ma vie, mes goûts musicaux, les derniers films que j'avais vus, les derniers livres que j'avais lus. Des fois je parlais de ma peinture, des fois non.

La stratégie de Fanny s'avérait efficace, j'étais de plus en plus à l'aise dans ces confrontations.

*

Sans que je m'en rende compte tant l'approche était discrète, Pascal, un gars plus timide encore que moi, est entré dans ma vie.

Au début, je ne lui ai pas prêté une grande attention. Il n'appartenait pas à la catégorie des spécimens top glamour sur lesquels je me polarisais à tort. Pascal était un peu enrobé, chose rare sur ce site, comme si c'était réservé aux filles et que les garçons se devaient d'être filiformes pour compenser.

Je recevais de ses nouvelles régulièrement, et petit à petit, je me suis mise à guetter ses messages. Je les trouvais drôles et intelligents. Quand j'étais repue de blagues lourdingues et de drague façon bulldozer, j'aimais discuter avec lui.

Nous avons passé de plus en plus de temps à tchater ensemble sans que jamais il ne demande à me rencontrer. C'est moi qui ai fini par le lui proposer. Comme ça, sur un coup de tête. Je devais aller à une soirée le samedi suivant, une soirée avec beaucoup de monde et je l'ai invité à y passer.

Quand il est arrivé, j'avais bu quelques verres de rhum et j'étais très détendue. On ne pouvait pas en dire autant de lui. J'observais son malaise comme on se regarde dans le miroir, tout en essayant de me comporter comme si de rien n'était. Je parlais pour deux en attendant que ça s'arrange, et je lui servais verres sur verres.

Ma technique a bien fonctionné. Il a commencé à se détendre et à blaguer. Nous avons parlé, parlé, parlé. De tout, de rien. Nous avons ri aussi. Je ne saurais dire comment se passait la soirée pour les autres. Nous étions dans notre bulle. Je ne me souciais plus de paraître intelligente ou drôle. À ses yeux je l'étais et ça me suffisait.

Attention, je ne suis pas en train de dire que Cupidon m'avait mitraillée de fléchettes et que j'étais sous le charme, prête à me marier le lendemain ou quoi... non... mais les choses étaient faciles, évidentes. C'était si rare pour moi... je savourais. J'aurais aimé qu'il soit plus beau, plus sociable, plus sexy mais je savais aussi que s'il avait été parfait, ça m'aurait bloquée.

Ce soir-là, il ne s'est rien passé de plus. Chacun est rentré chez soi. Je m'en suis un peu voulue, mais pas trop non plus. Je savais que ça n'était que partie remise.

Dès le lendemain, Pascal m'appelait pour m'inviter à dîner chez lui le samedi suivant. Il voulait que je goûte sa tartiflette qui était, de l'avis de ses amis, la meilleure au monde. J'étais moi-même une spécialiste et chacun de nous revendiquait le titre de champion. Il fallait bien que nous en ayons le cœur net. Et rapidement de préférence. J'étais ravie.

Je suis arrivée chez lui avec deux bouteilles de vin blanc sous le bras, une pour faciliter la digestion du fromage fondu, et l'autre pour combattre la timidité. J'avais beau me sentir à l'aise avec Pascal, je ne voulais prendre aucun risque.

Son appartement se trouvait au sixième étage sans ascenseur. J'ai eu le temps de les compter en gravissant péniblement les marches. Je suis arrivée en haut à bout de souffle et en sueur. J'ai marqué une pause pour ne pas avoir l'air d'être sur le point de rendre l'âme à peine franchi le pas de sa porte. Il m'a fallu cinq bonnes minutes pour récupérer.

J'ai sonné.

« Salut ! C'est ici qu'on peut soi-disant manger la meilleure tartiflette de Paris ?

– Attends de la goûter, tu n'oseras plus parler de la tienne !

– C'est ça oui, je préfère entendre ça que d'être sourde !

– Ça a été les escaliers ?

– J'ai cru que j'allais claquer mais à part ça, rien à signaler.

– On s'y habitue, tu verras. »

Il a rougi dans la seconde qui a suivi la fin de sa phrase et a tout de suite enchaîné :

« Enfin moi, je m'y suis habitué. Mets-toi à l'aise, donne-moi ton manteau, je vais le mettre dans la chambre.

– Je peux visiter ? J'adore visiter les appartements.

– Bien sûr, suis-moi.

– C'est toujours aussi propre et bien rangé chez toi ? Je ne vais jamais oser t'inviter chez moi !

– J'avoue que c'est un peu de la publicité mensongère... c'est un peu moins clean d'habitude.

– Ça me rassure ! »

Je l'ai imaginé passant son après-midi à transformer son repaire de célibataire en endroit accueillant. Je trouvais ça charmant.

« J'ouvre une bouteille de vin blanc pour l'apéro ?

– Ouais.

– Installe-toi au salon, j'arrive. »

Il a débarqué avec un plateau recouvert de cochonneries à grignoter. Mais attention, ce n'étaient pas n'importe quelles cochonneries !

Pas des chips et des cacahuètes, non non ! Il y avait des toasts de tarama, de tapenade et de guacamole, des feuilletés à la saucisse tout droit sortis du four et d'appétissants rouleaux de saumon fumé. Un tableau idyllique !

« Ouah ! Trop classe ! »

Nous avons trinqué et je me suis jetée sur un premier toast. Il me regardait avec ravissement.

« Ça fait plaisir à voir !

– Je suis gourmande, c'est plus fort que moi !

– Moi, je trouve ça très bien.

– Malgré les rondeurs qui vont de pair ? »

Il était toujours agréable de s'entendre répéter que les maigrichonnes des magazines n'avaient pas toujours la cote.

« Moi, je n'ai rien contre les rondeurs. Je préfère quelqu'un de bien vivant, qui profite d'un bon repas et d'une bonne bouteille de vin à une nana toute mince qui calcule le nombre de calories qu'elle avale à chaque bouchée, alors que je me suis cassé le cul à préparer à manger. »

Nous nous sommes regardés en souriant. Il était un peu tôt pour nous laisser aller à nous embrasser, l'alcool ne nous en avait pas encore donné le courage, mais il était clair que ça allait arriver, que nous le savions tous les deux, clair que j'avais apporté mon kit de découchage, qu'il avait dû acheter des préservatifs, clair que nous nous plaisions, que nous partagions le péché de gourmandise et que cette soirée ne serait pas la dernière, clair que ses feuilletés à la saucisse étaient une tuerie.

« Tes feuilletés à la saucisse, c'est une tuerie !

– Alors t'es toujours aussi sûre de toi pour le challenge tartiflette ?

– Après des préliminaires pareils, évidemment, le doute s'immisce... »

Nous avons traîné à l'apéritif.

Une gorgée de vin, un toast de tarama, une gorgée de vin, un feuilleté... la conversation s'est installée... encore une gorgée de vin, un rouleau de saumon, une gorgée de vin, un peu de guacamole... j'ai eu un fou rire quand il m'a imité ses collègues instits... gorgée de vin, feuilleté, gorgée de vin, tapenade... et à mon tour, je me suis lancée dans une galerie de portraits de mes collègues informaticiens, rien à envier aux enseignants… encore un dernier rouleau de saumon… ah ! J'étais comblée.

À ce stade, nous avions les joues rouges et les yeux qui pétillaient déjà pas mal.

Je suis allée me repoudrer le nez comme on dit, pendant qu'il mettait le couvert sur la table basse. Je souriais toute seule pendant que j'entendais Pascal siffloter tout en s'activant entre la cuisine et le salon. J'étais un peu paf. Je suis passée à la salle de bains me laver les mains avant de revenir au salon où la tartiflette répandait son délicieux fumet. J'en avais les papilles toutes retournées. Une salade verte trônait à côté du plat, caution morale de la ligue des nutritionnistes.

« Miam, ça sent bon !

– Assieds-toi et goûte ça. »

Il m'a servi une part généreuse. J'ai ajouté trois feuilles de salade dans un coin de l'assiette et je me suis obligée à l'attendre. Il avait l'air fier de lui. Il a lancé les festivités :

« À vos marques… »

J'ai levé ma fourchette pour signifier que j'étais prête.

« Partez ! »

J'ai attrapé un mélange de pomme de terre, de reblochon, de lardons et d'oignon, j'ai soufflé un peu parce que ça avait l'air très chaud et j'ai mis en bouche...

« Hummmmm... presque aussi bonne que la mienne !

– Meilleure, tu veux dire.

– N'exagérons rien, mais je dois reconnaître que tu ne t'en sors pas trop mal. »

Après trois assiettes, nous avons repris une conversation plus tranquille en écoutant de la musique. Mise en confiance par l'ambiance feutrée, j'ai osé poser ma tête sur son épaule. Nous ne parlions plus. Il me caressait les cheveux en fredonnant. J'ai fermé les yeux. Il en a profité pour venir poser ses lèvres sur les miennes, comme si seul mon regard l'en avait jusque-là empêché. C'était un baiser très doux, très tendre. J'ai gardé les yeux fermés. Il a quitté ma bouche pour m'embrasser dans le cou, tout en laissant ses mains se promener sur mon corps, d'abord timidement, le long de mon dos, puis avec plus d'audace, sa main s'est aventurée sur mes fesses.

Il a suspendu ses baisers pour me glisser à l'oreille qu'il adorait mes formes. C'était le moment que je préférais. Celui où le désir de l'autre me rendait belle. Il fallait en profiter. Je savais qu'après, mes formes perdaient très vite leur pouvoir magique. J'ai chassé ces idées et me suis assise à califourchon sur ses genoux, face à lui, et me suis mise à l'embrasser dans le cou, tout près de l'oreille. Je voulais me sentir plus belle encore. J'entendais sa respiration devenir courte. Ses mains, posées sur mes fesses, m'ont attirée contre son sexe que je sentais tendu malgré l'épaisseur des jeans. Je me suis frottée à lui, doucement, tout en continuant à l'embrasser. Il a passé ses mains sous mon haut et j'ai pris l'initiative de l'enlever, pour lui dévoiler cette poitrine qui les faisait tant fantasmer. Il a plongé dans mon décolleté, embrassant gloutonnement tout ce qu'il y rencontrait. Je l'ai laissé faire un instant puis je me suis écartée de lui. Je l'ai regardé, il était hagard. Je me suis levée et lui ai tendu la main pour l'entraîner dans la chambre.

Nous avons retiré nos jeans sans rien dire. Je me suis assise au bord du lit. Il s'est agenouillé devant moi et m'a enlevé ma culotte avec fébrilité alors que je lui baissais calmement son caleçon. Il a attrapé un préservatif dans sa table de nuit que je lui ai pris des mains pour le lui enfiler. Son sexe semblait prêt à exploser. Il était trop excité pour perdre une seconde. Il est entré en moi et a démarré un lent va-et-vient. Très lent. Je me rappelle m'être dit qu'il devait avoir peur de jouir trop vite. Et puis, j'ai stoppé là mes réflexions. Des sensations nouvelles envahissaient mon ventre. Il a effleuré mes seins, sans rien changer à son rythme langoureux, et les sensations se sont amplifiées, propagées. Je ne voulais plus que ça s'arrête, tout en craignant cette montée presque vertigineuse, et puis tout à coup, une rafale de secousses libératrices s'est emparée de mon corps, et j'ai entendu Pascal pousser un cri à l'unisson du mien.

Nous sommes restés sans rien dire, essoufflés, calmés, comme repus une seconde fois. Il a ramené la couette sur moi pour que je ne prenne pas froid, geste tendre qui est venu parfaire le moment. Je me suis blottie dans ses bras.

J'avais souvent joué à faire l'amour, pris la pose et poussé des cris, toujours un peu surprise de constater l'importance de ce pouvoir qui était en ma possession. Même si le lendemain les types me jetaient sans plus de précaution, c'était l'heure de ma toute-puissance. Mais je n'en avais jamais tiré de plaisir. Je n'avais jamais joui et je n'avais jamais espéré que ça puisse être différent.

Là, je venais d'être clouée sur place. J'en étais la première surprise.

*

Après…

Après, les choses sont allées si vite que j'ai eu l'impression de n'avoir aucune prise sur leur déroulement.

Fanny adorait Pascal.

Ma mère adorait Pascal.

Pascal adorait tout le monde.

Nous enchaînions les soirées et les nuits.

Chez l'un, chez l'autre.

Nous avons fêté nos six mois.

Nous avons emménagé ensemble.

Nous sommes allés chez Ikea.

Nous avons fêté nos un an.

Nous avons organisé des soirées. Des dîners.

Nous sommes partis en week-end. En vacances.

À la mer. À la campagne. Avec des amis. En famille.

Nous avons fêté nos deux ans.

J'ai fini par oublier que j'étais timide, que les gens m'effrayaient. Ils étaient moins impressionnants depuis que nous étions deux pour les affronter. Au pire, je pouvais toujours me réfugier dans notre appartement douillet, oublier le monde dans les bras de mon amoureux qui était toujours là pour me rassurer. Non, je n'étais pas pire qu'une autre, pas plus débile, pas plus handicapée que la moyenne puisque j'avais réussi à entrer dans le moule : un boulot, un appartement, un chéri, des amis… tout était en ordre.

Et puis un soir, Pascal m'a invitée au restaurant. Il a commandé une bouteille de champagne, et au moment de trinquer, il a pris un air grave, a rougi, et s'est lancé dans une jolie demande en mariage.

Que dire ? C'était ultraclassique, ultraconventionnel. Nous baignions en plein cliché avec la larme à l'œil et la bague sortie de nulle part. Il n'empêche que ça m'a émue bien plus que je n'aurais pu l'imaginer. Le garçon que j'avais en face de moi envisageait, souhaitait, espérait passer le restant de ses jours avec moi. C'était quand même quelque chose. Mon ego ne pouvait pas rester indifférent à ça. J'ai été prise d'une énorme bouffée d'amour. J'ai répondu oui sans hésiter. Je pleurais, je riais, j'étais heureuse.

Trente-cinq ans

« Qu'est-ce qu'il y a ?

– Rien, rien…

– Bon ben si y a rien, arrête de me regarder comme ça. »

Pascal a soupiré et a préféré sortir de la cuisine. Cette énième tentative de régime était un échec. Un de plus. Je regardais les croûtes de fromage dans mon assiette. C'était tout ce qu'il restait du plateau qui était dans le frigo à peine une demi-heure plus tôt. J'avais lutté aussi longtemps que possible, mais l'idée d'une tartine, juste une, avait germé dans mon esprit en rentrant du travail. Je n'avais pas réussi à m'en débarrasser. Une tartine en avait entraîné une autre et je n'avais pas su m'arrêter.

Pascal était déçu, je le savais. Il n'avait rien dit mais je savais interpréter chacun de ses regards, et celui qu'il m'avait lancé en entrant dans la cuisine m'accusait de saboter une fois de plus nos chances d'avoir un bébé.

J'étais d'accord avec lui. C'était de ma faute. Nous ne pouvions pas avoir d'enfant parce que je ne pouvais pas avoir d'enfant. Mon corps avait décrété qu'il en avait marre de mon grand n'importe quoi, qu'il avait fait son maximum, et il s'était mis en grève. Plus de règles, plus d'ovulation, plus rien. Le médecin que j'avais consulté m'avait expliqué que c'était courant chez les personnes obèses, tout comme chez les personnes trop maigres. J'avais été contente d'apprendre que je partageais quelque chose avec cette catégorie de la population.

J'avais franchi le cap de l'obésité sans m'en rendre vraiment compte. Il n'y avait pas eu un jour précis où j'étais devenue obèse, un jour anniversaire que j'aurais pu fêter chaque année. Non, c'était arrivé de manière plus insidieuse. J'étais longtemps restée avec l'idée que j'étais ronde. Ronde, c'était acceptable. Ronde, c'était presque un style. Ronde, ça plaisait à Pascal, alors il n'y avait pas lieu de s'inquiéter. J'avais traversé une période de paix avec mon corps. Je ne lui avais plus prêté attention. Je l'avais laissé vivre. Il en avait profité pour s'épanouir et s'étaler. À mon insu.

Mais une fois, dans le métro, le nez rivé à la fenêtre derrière laquelle défilaient les murs du tunnel, j'avais entendu une voix murmurer qu'elle préférait ne pas s'asseoir là, que la dame était trop grosse et qu'elle sentait sûrement mauvais. Comme tous les gros. Cette déclaration avait failli être entassée avec les centaines de phrases que j'entendais pendant chaque trajet, ces bribes de conversation qui ne me concernaient pas, mais elle avait émergé in extremis du côté de ma conscience, me sortant de ma rêverie et m'interpellant sans ménagement.

Cette fille parlait peut-être de moi.

J'avais décollé le nez de la vitre. Il y avait une

place libre près de moi et une adolescente, juste à côté, debout, qui discutait. C'était sa voix. J'étais la grosse dame dont elle parlait.

Cet épisode avait marqué un tournant. J'avais renoué avec la balance chaque matin et repris mes inspections devant la glace. Mon corps, ce traître qui avait profité de mon inattention, s'était transformé en une masse informe. Moi qui croyais posséder les rondeurs et le charme d'une mamma italienne, je me rendais compte que j'avais dépassé depuis longtemps ce stade des courbes rassurantes.

Ma vie s'était transformée en un perpétuel cauchemar de culpabilité. J'avais accumulé les tentatives de régimes ratées, les alternances de privations et d'excès, les engueulades avec Pascal qui ne me soutenait pas assez ou pas comme il fallait, et les crises de paranoïa face au regard des autres. Je m'en voulais quand je manquais de volonté et j'en manquais sans arrêt. Je continuais de grossir. Inexorablement.

L'arrêt de mes règles avait été pire que tout. J'avais gardé du mythe de la mamma italienne l'envie d'avoir une nombreuse marmaille autour de moi, des bouts de chou à aimer, à dorloter, à couver. Alors, même s'il y avait longtemps que nos parties de jambes en l'air étaient devenues à mes yeux un truc grotesque et fatigant, avec nos ventres qui débordaient de toutes parts et nos sexes qui ne pouvaient se rencontrer qu'au prix de contorsions insensées, je m'étais toujours donnée à fond, imaginant à chaque fois que la vie allait peut-être germer, là, maintenant, dans mon ventre. Ce rêve s'était envolé.

Plus rien n'avait de sens.

À quoi rimait ce ventre qui ne pouvait abriter un enfant ?

À quoi rimait ce couple qui ne se transformerait jamais en famille ?

À quoi rimait cette sexualité ridicule ?

À quoi je rimais, moi ?

Voilà les idées qui tournaient dans ma tête pendant que je gardais les yeux rivés à mes croûtes de fromage bien que les larmes m'empêchent de vraiment les voir.

*

C'était un soir comme beaucoup d'autres. Pascal préparait ses fameuses activités pédagogiques dans son bureau, comme trois soirs par semaine au moins, et je ruminais sur mon sort en grignotant les restes de notre dîner-pizza. Je zappais machinalement sans trouver aucun programme qui retienne mon attention.

Je suis tombée sur *Relooking Extrême*, une émission de télé-réalité. Ça avait l'air débile, mais fatiguée comme j'étais, je n'étais pas en mesure de regarder quoi que ce soit qui demande à mes neurones de s'agiter. Par flemme donc, j'ai décidé de voir ce qui se cachait comme nouveau concept derrière ce titre aguicheur.

L'émission a commencé par un portrait de Jessica.

Jessica avait vingt-six ans (elle en paraissait quarante), elle était plutôt grosse (les images de Jessica en sous-vêtements nous permettaient de le constater), elle portait des lunettes (le genre culs de bouteille) et elle avait une vilaine cicatrice au milieu de la joue gauche (un peu comme Albator d'après mes souvenirs). Autant dire qu'elle n'avait pas été gâtée par Dame Nature. Elle était institutrice mais rêvait de devenir comédienne, et pour ça, elle prenait des cours de théâtre mais nous expliquait qu'à cause de son physique, il lui était impossible d'envisager d'en faire plus qu'un hobby.

Lors de l'un de ses cours, celui auquel nous assistions, comme par hasard, son prof lui a annoncé, d'un ton désolé, qu'elle ne pourrait pas participer au spectacle de fin d'année.

Zoom sur la tronche déconfite de Jessica.

Le prof l'a laissée mariner dans son jus, puis lui a annoncé sur un ton d'animateur de supermarché, qu'elle ne pourrait pas participer parce qu'elle serait… tatata… à *Relooking Extrême* !

Seconde d'incompréhension chez Jessica qui a mis les mains devant sa bouche genre « Je ne peux pas y croire, ce n'est pas possible ! », avant que sa famille et ses amis ne la rejoignent sur la scène pour partager ce grand bonheur.

Ça démarrait très fort. J'ai profité de la coupure de pub pour faire une incursion du côté du frigo. Une glace accompagnerait à la perfection cette mauvaise émission.

Nous avons retrouvé Jessica alors qu'elle arrivait en limousine dans une résidence luxueuse. Elle était tout excitée. Elle n'arrêtait pas de pleurer et de remercier. Ils lui ont posé des tas de questions débiles avant de la laisser rencontrer le spécialiste mondial de la chirurgie esthétique.

Le chirurgien ressemblait à Superman, avec la peau si tendue que j'avais mal pour lui à chaque fois qu'il souriait. Il allait transformer Jessica, lui donner un corps et un visage parfaits. Il a pris un air de confident pour recueillir ses desiderata. Elle voulait qu'il la débarrasse de son ventre, qu'il lui retende les seins et qu'il fasse disparaître sa cicatrice. En bonus, il lui a proposé de lui refaire le nez, de lui relever les paupières, de lui gonfler les pommettes et de lui raboter le menton. Jessica a dit oui à tout. Quand on a affaire à un spécialiste d'une telle éminence, on ne discute pas, on dit oui et on remercie. Surtout quand c'est gratuit.

Jessica a ensuite passé une batterie d'examens pour vérifier qu'elle était en bonne santé, pendant que défilaient en bas de l'écran quelques rappels sur les risques présentés par toute chirurgie, y compris esthétique. La tension est montée d'un cran, Jessica était potentiellement en danger ! En attendant, comme nous pouvions nous y attendre, elle était apte à continuer l'aventure.

Nous nous sommes retrouvés dans la salle d'opération. Jessica commençait à paniquer, mais une infirmière super lui tenait la main et tentait de la rassurer. Tout le monde était très gentil, très compétent et tout allait bien se passer.

Sur ce, ils l'ont endormie, et c'est devenu très gore. Le chirurgien maniait le scalpel avec dextérité, tout comme le technicien sa caméra, ce qui nous a permis d'admirer jets de sang et organes internes en mouvement. Des explications accompagnaient chaque étape, que ce soit les coups de burin sur l'arête du nez, le vigoureux va-et-vient du tuyau de liposuccion dans les chairs ou le décollage de la peau pour poser les prothèses mammaires.

Tout ce chantier a duré cinq heures. Le chirurgien est ressorti de là fatigué mais satisfait de son travail, et nous, complètement écœurés.

Jessica, quant à elle, a eu un réveil difficile. Elle a commencé par vomir, puis s'est inquiétée de ne pas pouvoir bouger. Sans prendre la peine de la rassurer, ils lui ont demandé si elle était contente, et elle a répondu péniblement que oui, elle était très contente. Elle avait surtout l'air de souffrir le martyre.

Ils ne se sont pas appesantis sur les jours qui ont suivi, ils étaient là pour vendre du rêve, pas de la gueule de bois post-opératoire.

Nous avons donc retrouvé Jessica alors qu'ils allaient lui retirer les pansements qui lui couvraient la tête. Elle avait hâte de voir, et nous aussi ! Loin d'être devenue toute jolie, elle était tuméfiée et enflée de partout. Pourtant, en voyant le résultat dans le miroir, elle s'est exclamé que c'était super, qu'elle n'avait jamais espéré un tel résultat ! Je me suis demandé s'ils ne l'avaient pas rendue aveugle en lui retendant les paupières.

Le médecin a ensuite écarté les pans de son peignoir. Le ventre de Jessica était plat. Plus aucun bourrelet. Elle en avait les larmes aux yeux.

Comme je la comprenais ! Comme je pouvais imaginer les heures qu'elle allait passer devant sa glace, enfin satisfaite de ce qu'elle y verrait. Pas comme moi. J'ai jeté un œil sur mon propre ventre qui s'étalait, libéré de l'entrave de mon jean que j'avais déboutonné pour regarder la télé à mon aise. Indécent. J'ai tiré sur ma tunique pour le cacher. J'enviais Jessica. J'aurais donné cher pour être à sa place et voir soudain ma vie transformée.

J'ai reporté mon attention sur Jessica qui apparaissait, resplendissante dans sa robe de soirée, devant les regards médusés de ses amis et de sa famille lors de la soirée de retrouvailles.

Je me suis décollée du canapé pour aller raconter à Pascal ce que je venais de voir. Il a levé les yeux au ciel en grommelant qu'il n'y avait plus de limites à ce qu'on pouvait imaginer pour faire de l'audience. Je me suis un peu énervée. Il n'avait pas vu la métamorphose de cette fille. Elle allait démarrer une nouvelle vie, elle ! Il ne m'écoutait déjà plus.

Tout en allumant l'ordinateur au salon, je me demandais quelle impression ça me ferait de subir une telle transformation. Sûr que ça me remettrait sur les rails. Fini la dépression, les cachetons, les crises de larmes et de dégoût. Je suis allée sur Google et j'ai tapé « chirurgie esthétique ventre ». Je voulais plus de renseignements sur ce type d'opérations. Je n'avais jamais envisagé ce genre de solutions, mais pourquoi pas ?

J'ai vite déchanté. C'était cher, trop cher ! Une plastie abdominale coûtait environ quatre mille cinq cents euros et une liposuccion importante, trois mille. En plus, tous les articles disaient que ces opérations n'étaient pas destinées à amaigrir mais à corriger la silhouette après que le patient eut déjà perdu ses kilos.

J'étais déçue.

Jessica n'était pas mince. Pas grosse comme moi non plus, c'est vrai, mais quand même… et ils l'avaient opérée sans préalable. J'ai continué à fouiller mais tous les sites disaient la même chose. Ça paraissait logique en y réfléchissant. Connerie d'émission qui m'avait donné l'illusion qu'il pouvait y avoir des solutions miracles. J'avais accumulé trop de kilos maintenant. J'étais au stade où je devais passer par le régime, chose dont je me savais incapable, ou me satisfaire de mon état. Et m'habituer à l'idée de ne jamais avoir d'enfants.

J'étais d'une humeur de chien au moment de me coucher. Pascal, lui, était au contraire très satisfait de sa soirée, très content de ce qu'il avait mijoté pour sa classe. Il m'a expliqué les grandes lignes de sa nouvelle approche de la multiplication, nouvelle approche révolutionnaire à l'écouter, qui permettrait à une génération complète de devenir de grands mathématiciens. Je me demandais comment il arrivait encore à s'enthousiasmer comme ça, depuis dix ans qu'il répétait chaque année les mêmes programmes à quelques variantes près.

Pascal était de si bonne humeur qu'il s'est mis en tête de faire l'amour. Je n'ai jamais compris le rapport qu'il pouvait y avoir entre la libido et la recherche pédagogique, mais à chaque fois que Pascal avait l'impression d'avoir eu une idée géniale pour enseigner quelque chose, il avait envie de baiser. C'était automatique. Sauf que là, il tombait mal. J'avais plus que jamais conscience de mon image, et son désir aveugle m'était insupportable.

J'ai aussitôt refroidi ses ardeurs. Avec un peu de culpabilité quand même. Comme toujours dans ces cas-là. Mais je ne pouvais pas. Je lui ai donné un rapide baiser de bonne nuit et me suis réfugiée dans mon coin du lit pour trouver le sommeil.

Deux heures plus tard, j'étais toujours éveillée. Souvent, pour m'endormir, je me racontais des histoires. Ce soir-là, je m'étais concocté un scénario inspiré de ma soirée télé, dans lequel je m'inscrivais pour participer à *Relooking Extrême*. Je retenais tout de suite l'attention du type qui sélectionnait les candidatures car, comme il me le disait lors de notre première rencontre, j'avais un potentiel formidable, de très jolis traits derrière mon embonpoint, une histoire touchante avec cette grossesse impossible et une personnalité intéressante qui plairait beaucoup aux téléspectateurs. Je partais donc dans la limousine et je rencontrais le chirurgien qui me rassurait tout de suite en me disant qu'il n'était pas nécessaire que je perde du poids avant de subir les interventions.

D'habitude, ces scénarios me duraient des semaines entières car je m'endormais en cinq minutes, et rien que pour peaufiner le démarrage de l'histoire, il me fallait plusieurs soirs. Mais il arrivait parfois, comme ce soir-là, que le sommeil n'arrive pas et que j'aie le temps de retourner le scénario dans tous les sens, arrangeant les détails, reprenant la même scène jusqu'à ce qu'elle soit parfaite. Jusqu'à en être saturée.

Je me suis relevée pour aller boire. En revenant de la cuisine, j'ai fait un crochet par la salle de bains. Je me suis déshabillée et me suis regardée dans la glace. Sans complaisance. Mon corps était un amas de graisse qui dégoulinait de partout. Mon cou se noyait dans mon double menton et mes bras ressemblaient aux ailes d'une chauve-souris. Mes seins, plus que jamais attirés par le sol, reposaient sur mon ventre qui s'était dédoublé pour former un abominable tablier abdominal. Mes hanches servaient de socle à des monticules absurdes qui annonçaient les rondeurs disproportionnées et molles de mes fesses. Quant à mes cuisses, elles étaient envahies par la cellulite, toujours la cellulite, à l'infini la cellulite.

J'ai attrapé un rouge à lèvres et j'ai marqué sur mon corps tout ce qui devait être corrigé, comme le chirurgien avec son feutre avant l'opération de Jessica. J'imaginais le dégoût et le mépris que je lui inspirerais et j'entendais ses mots résonner dans ma tête : « Attrapez un grand couteau, que dis-je, une hache, et taillez-moi ce ventre dégueulasse, pelez ce cul comme une orange jusqu'à ce qu'il ait une taille normale, et ces seins, enlevez tout, ça vaudra encore mieux que ça, donnez-moi un couteau, arrêtez de pleurer madame, c'est pour votre bien, frappez ces chairs molles pour les tonifier, frappez plus fort je vous dis, elle n'avait qu'à pas tant bouffer cette salope ! »

Combien de temps s'était-il passé ? Je n'en avais aucune idée. J'ai repris peu à peu mes esprits. J'étais en position fœtale dans la baignoire. J'ai regardé mon corps barbouillé de rouge à lèvres. Un bel hématome commençait à se dessiner sur ma cuisse gauche. Qu'est-ce que j'avais fait ? J'ai mis l'eau à couler pour me nettoyer. Je laissais mon esprit vagabonder. Le bain me faisait du bien. Je me sentais plus calme. Je repensais à Jessica. Pourquoi elle et pas moi ? Cette phrase rebondissait dans ma tête. Je cherchais à la chasser mais elle revenait, entêtante. Pourquoi elle et pas moi ? Pourquoi elle et pas moi ?

Tout à coup, ça m'a paru évident. Je suis sortie de la baignoire en toute hâte et j'ai enfilé mon peignoir. Je suis allée dans le salon sans prendre le temps de me sécher. Je devais participer à cette émission, c'était aussi simple que ça. J'ai allumé l'ordinateur. Il devait bien y avoir moyen de savoir comment postuler. Je suis allée sur le site de la chaîne. Il y avait une page dédiée à toutes les émissions pour lesquelles ils cherchaient des candidats, et parmi elles, *Relooking Extrême*. Le processus était ultrasimple. Je pouvais m'inscrire en ligne, il suffisait de remplir un questionnaire et de leur envoyer deux photos, un portrait et une en maillot de bain. Je devais avoir ça en stock.

Une heure plus tard, le questionnaire était rempli et les photos sélectionnées. Au moment d'envoyer le tout, j'avais les mains moites et le cœur qui battait la chamade. C'était peut-être une énorme connerie, mais ça ne m'a pas empêchée d'appuyer sur le bouton de confirmation avec un grand sourire aux lèvres.

Le lendemain matin, je me suis réveillée avec difficulté, accusant le coup pour cette nuit mouvementée. J'ai marmonné de vagues réponses à Pascal qui s'étonnait de mon bain nocturne (j'avais oublié de vider la baignoire) et de ma mine défaite.

J'ai évité de lui raconter mon inscription impulsive à *Relooking Extrême*. Si jamais je n'étais pas sélectionnée, ça ne valait pas la peine d'affronter ses sarcasmes et sa désapprobation. À vrai dire, assise devant mon petit déjeuner, tout ça ne me semblait plus très réel. Je me rappelais l'avoir fait mais c'était un peu comme dans un rêve.

Dans les jours qui ont suivi, j'ai essayé de ne pas trop y penser. En vain. Je ne pouvais m'empêcher d'espérer. J'avais reçu un accusé de réception de ma candidature dans lequel ils me remerciaient de l'intérêt porté à leur chaîne et à leur émission, et blablabla ils étudieraient mon cas avec beaucoup d'attention, et blablabla ils me répondraient au plus vite.

Leur notion du « au plus vite » était toute relative ! Je n'ai pas entendu parler d'eux pendant les six mois qui ont suivi. Au début, je me jetais sur ma boîte mail cent fois par jour avec excitation, espoir, mais petit à petit, j'ai perdu la foi… je n'étais pas assez moche pour eux… ou peut-être trop…

*

Ce matin, j'ai reçu ce mail. Ce mail que je n'attendais plus. Ce mail où Mylène, chargée de casting pour *Relooking Extrême*, me disait qu'elle souhaitait me rencontrer. Il y avait le numéro de téléphone de Mylène. Elle attendait mon appel. J'étais au boulot, je devais partir en réunion. Je ne pouvais pas la rappeler. Pas tout de suite.

J'allais peut-être participer à *Relooking Extrême*. Je n'en revenais pas. Tout à coup, tout me semblait possible. Ouvert. Il suffisait parfois de donner des coups de pouce au destin. Arrêter de subir la vie. Oser. La voix de ma mère a résonné dans ma tête : « Ne t'emballe pas, ils veulent juste te rencontrer. Ils doivent convoquer plein de candidats pour n'en retenir qu'un. » Bien sûr, je le savais mais il y avait une possibilité.

Je n'arrivais pas à me concentrer sur ce qui se passait dans cette réunion. Dommage parce que tous les regards étaient maintenant posés sur moi. J'en ai déduit qu'ils attendaient que je dise quelque chose, mais je n'avais aucune idée de ce dont ils parlaient.

« Je... est-ce que vous pouvez... heu... préciser votre question ?

– Oui, bien sûr. »

Je me suis efforcée d'être plus attentive pendant le reste de la réunion.

À peine sortie, je me suis isolée avec mon portable. J'ai composé le numéro d'une main tremblotante.

« Allô...

– Bonjour, je suis Mélanie Bertier... »

Je m'attendais à ce que ce début suffise pour qu'elle s'exclame qu'elle était ravie que je rappelle aussi vite, mais visiblement, mon nom ne lui rappelait pas grand-chose.

« Je... vous... enfin... j'avais postulé pour participer à *Relooking Extrême* et vous m'avez envoyé un mail me demandant de vous rappeler...

– Quel nom vous m'avez dit ?

– Mélanie Bertier... »

Je l'entendais farfouiller dans ses papiers.

« Ah voilà. Mélanie Bertier, c'est ça. Bonjour, je m'appelle Mylène et je suis chargée de sélectionner les meilleures candidatures pour participer à *Rex*.

– Heu... à quoi ?

– Ah oui... excusez-moi... l'habitude... *Rex*, c'est le diminutif pour *Relooking Extrême*. Votre dossier a tout de suite retenu mon attention ! »

Je n'ai pas jugé nécessaire de rappeler que ça faisait presque six mois que j'avais postulé, et que loin de lui avoir sauté aux yeux, ma candidature avait plutôt dû être repêchée au fond d'un tiroir.

« Ah ?

– Oui, j'aime beaucoup vos photos, vous avez le potentiel pour être jolie ! D'ailleurs vous avez dû être jolie à une époque, quand vous étiez moins grosse, hein ?

– Je ne sais pas, je...

– En plus, vous avez fait des études, c'est très bon ça ! Je ne vais rien vous cacher, on nous accuse de ne faire venir que des ploucs dans l'émission et ce n'est pas bon pour notre image. On nous a demandé de trouver des profils comme le vôtre pour montrer que la chirurgie s'adresse à tout le monde. Comme notre émission d'ailleurs. Vous voyez ?

– Je vois.

– Alors Mélanie, quand peut-on se rencontrer ? Demain à quinze heures, c'est possible ?

– C'est que… je travaille… je ne sais pas si je vais pouvoir me libérer si vite…

– Vous devez être rapide Mélanie, très rapide… ne laissez pas passer cette opportunité !

– Oui bon, je vais m'arranger…

– Parfait ! »

J'ai à peine eu le temps de noter l'adresse qu'elle me donnait. Elle avait déjà raccroché. Je suis restée le téléphone à la main, hébétée, à remettre de l'ordre dans mes idées. Cette Mylène était à vomir et je ne mourais pas d'envie de la rencontrer, mais je ne devais pas perdre de vue ce qui allait suivre si j'étais sélectionnée. Le jeu en valait la chandelle.

J'étais nerveuse en me rendant dans les bureaux de la chaîne. J'avais soigné la manière dont j'étais habillée et maquillée. J'avais cru comprendre que plus elle aurait l'impression que j'étais jolie sous mes kilos, plus j'aurais mes chances.

À peine les portes de l'ascenseur s'étaient-elles entrouvertes que la fameuse Mylène me sautait dessus.

« Mélanie, je suis ra-vie de vous rencontrer !

– Moi aussi, enchantée.

– Suivez-moi... »

Malgré la hauteur de ses talons aiguilles, elle avançait très vite, m'obligeant à trottiner derrière pour ne pas être larguée.

Nous sommes arrivées dans son bureau, une pièce exiguë encombrée de dossiers dans des pochettes de toutes les couleurs. Elle m'a montré une chaise en me disant de m'asseoir, tout en contournant son bureau et en s'installant dans son large fauteuil en cuir.

Elle m'a répété en guise d'introduction ce qu'elle m'avait déjà dit, en gros, au téléphone. Puis, l'interrogatoire a démarré. Elle voulait tout savoir. Depuis quand j'étais grosse, si j'étais dépressive, si j'avais des amis, depuis quand j'étais avec Pascal, quel était mon idéal de beauté féminine, si j'avais déjà eu recours à la chirurgie esthétique... les questions fusaient sans jamais me laisser le temps de reprendre mon souffle. J'ai eu du mal au début, m'emmêlant dans mes réponses, hésitant à dévoiler ce qui ne me semblait pas la regarder, mais le tempo frénétique des questions m'a vite fait oublier où j'étais, pourquoi j'étais là et à qui je parlais (une inconnue). Je répondais mécaniquement à tout ce qu'elle me demandait.

Tout à coup, ça s'est arrêté. Mylène me regardait en souriant.

« Je crois que nous allons faire quelque chose ensemble.

– C'est vrai ? Je...

– Oui, je crois que ça va être bien, très bien même.

– Je...

– Notre entrevue va être visionnée par d'autres personnes pour avoir leurs avis et je vous rappelle sous huit jours. Ça vous va ? »

Je n'avais pas remarqué que j'étais filmée. Heureusement.

« Oui, bien sûr, très bien.

– Je vous raccompagne ! »

J'aurais aimé en savoir plus sur ce qui se passerait si ma candidature était retenue, mais je n'ai rien osé demander. Elle m'a remise dans l'ascenseur en deux temps trois mouvements, en me répétant qu'elle me rappellerait très vite.

En sortant, j'étais sonnée. J'ai marché un moment avant de réaliser ce qui venait de se passer et ce que ça allait entraîner. C'était dingue. Complètement dingue. Je devais en parler à quelqu'un pour arriver à y croire. J'ai appelé Fanny.

« Il faut absolument que je te voie. Tu fais quoi là ?

– Je suis au boulot mais ma prochaine cliente est dans une heure. T'es où toi, t'es pas au boulot ?

– Naaaan…

– Qu'est-ce que tu mijotes ?

– Je te rejoins dans un quart d'heure, ça te va ?

– Magne-toi, tu m'as mis l'eau à la bouche maintenant. »

Le trajet m'a semblé long, je bouillais d'impatience. J'ai parcouru les derniers mètres qui séparaient le métro de l'institut de beauté où travaillait Fanny au pas de course. Elle m'avait à peine dit bonjour qu'elle attaquait.

«Alors, qu'est-ce qui se passe?

– Je ne sais pas par où commencer... tu connais l'émission *Relooking Extrême*?

– Ouais.

– Je vais peut-être y participer...

– ...

– Je te jure! Je sors d'un entretien avec la nana qui s'occupe du casting et elle avait l'air super enthousiaste! Ce n'est pas encore sûr hein, elle doit me rappeler dans la semaine, mais ça a l'air bien parti...

– ...

– Tu ne dis rien?

– C'est ouf. C'est complètement ouf. Surtout venant de toi.

– Je sais!

– Raconte-moi les détails, je veux tout savoir!»

Je lui ai raconté mon inscription au milieu de la nuit sur le site Internet, le coup de fil de la veille et l'entretien avec Mylène dans les détails. Elle n'en revenait pas. Moi non plus. Mais elle n'a pas tardé à trouver ça génial et à s'enflammer en imaginant la suite des événements.

Trois jours plus tard, Mylène me rappelait et m'annonçait que j'avais beaucoup plu aux autres membres du comité de sélection. C'était donc décidé, je serais une des heureuses participantes de *Rex*.

Il ne me restait plus qu'à le dire à Pascal, qui risquait de ne pas être aussi enthousiaste que Fanny et moi. Le soir, à table, je lui ai annoncé que j'avais été retenue pour participer à une émission de télé.

« Ah ouais, quel genre d'émission ?

– Le genre que tu détestes…

– …

– …

– Ben vas-y, dis-moi !

– Télé-réalité…

– *Koh-Lanta* ?

– Très drôle…

– *Le Loft*, ça n'existe plus, hein ?

– Je vais participer à *Relooking Extrême*…

– …

– …

– Ce truc où ils charcutent les candidats à coups de bistouri ?

– Oui…

– C'est une blague ?

– Non.

– Mais…

– Y a pas de mais, Pascal. C'est pour moi une opportunité de…

– De quoi ? De ressembler à Pamela Anderson ? Mais putain Mélanie, c'est quoi ces conneries ? Oui, tu es bien en chair… et alors ? Moi, je t'aime comme tu es !

– Toi, peut-être… mais pas moi.

– D'accord, d'accord, admettons… on peut s'attaquer au problème sans pour autant s'exhiber sur un plateau télé où ils n'auront qu'une idée en tête, faire de l'Audimat sans se soucier le moins du monde de toi Mélanie !

– Au moins, je serai prise en charge…

– Écoute, si c'est juste d'une structure que tu as besoin, il existe des cliniques spécialisées, ce genre de trucs…

– Ah ouais et on s'endette sur cinquante ans pour payer ?

– Écoute, je ne sais pas mais on pourrait y réfléchir avant que tu ne t'embringues dans ce…

– C'est tout réfléchi. Je suis prête à m'asseoir sur ma pudeur. La seule chose qui m'importe, c'est le résultat.

– …

– J'aimerais que tu essaies de considérer les choses de mon point de vue, Pascal…

– Moi aussi, j'aimerais que tu essaies de considérer les choses de mon point de vue…

– Je ne vois pas ce qui te dérange tant.

– …

– …

– Ce qui me dérange, c'est que tu aies l'air de croire qu'en trois coups de bistouri, tous tes problèmes vont s'évanouir…

– Je n'ai pas dit ça, mais je suis sûre que je me sentirais beaucoup mieux…

– Ah oui ? Et quand tu étais plus jeune, que tu étais un peu ronde mais sans plus, tu avais l'impression que tout allait bien dans ta vie ? Il me semble que les choses n'étaient déjà pas très simples pour toi… je me trompe ?

– J'ai toujours été grosse.

– C'est faux Mélanie et tu le sais très bien. Quand tu vas sortir de cette émission, tu seras peut-être à peu près comme quand je t'ai connue… et après ?

– Tu n'es qu'un rabat-joie !

– J'essaie juste de t'ouvrir les yeux. J'ai peur que tu ne sois très déçue, c'est tout…

– Tu peux dire ce que tu veux, ma décision est prise. »

Relooking Extrême

Je me suis levée ce matin vers six heures, chose exceptionnelle pour moi. Je ne pouvais plus rester allongée dans mon lit, j'étais si excitée que les jambes m'en démangeaient. C'était le 23 septembre, jour du tournage de l'annonce « surprise » de ma sélection à *Relooking Extrême.*

La scène devait se dérouler au cours d'abdos-fessiers où je m'efforçais d'aller une fois par semaine. Cette idée ne m'emballait pas plus que ça, car j'imaginais comme j'allais être à mon avantage, boudinée dans mon survêtement, mais c'était exactement pour ça qu'ils avaient fait ce choix.

Pascal avait refusé de venir participer à

cette mascarade, mais Fanny et ma mère étaient, elles, ravies de prendre part de façon active à mon aventure. Elles devaient venir me chercher à neuf heures. Je me suis demandé comment j'allais pouvoir m'occuper jusque-là.

Je me suis offert un petit déjeuner solide, Dieu seul savait quand nous allions bien pouvoir manger avec tout ça. Je n'avais pas beaucoup d'informations sur la manière dont les choses allaient s'organiser. Je devais me rendre au club de gym à neuf heures et demie pour avoir le temps de me préparer avant que ne commence la séance, à onze heures, pour laquelle les participants habituels avaient accepté d'être figurants.

Ma mère est arrivée à huit heures et demie. Elle était encore plus excitée que moi. Elle s'était pomponnée pour l'occasion, ne voulant surtout pas rater son instant de gloire télévisuelle. Elle était belle. Si belle que cela ne manquerait pas d'interroger les téléspectateurs sur les mystères de la génétique, en nous voyant côte à côte, ma mère, fine, élégante et jolie, et moi, hippopotame aux joues rouges et au front transpirant dans un survêt hors d'âge. Je n'étais pas loin de la soupçonner de vouloir justement créer ce contraste mais c'était sans doute de la parano de ma part. Pour ne pas démarrer cette journée avec mes chakras en vrac, j'ai évacué cette vilaine pensée.

Fanny est arrivée. Elle non plus ne tenait pas en place, elle parlait encore plus vite et plus fort que d'habitude. Mais contrairement à ma mère, elle ne semblait pas vouloir me voler la vedette. Elle était la même que tous les jours, sans chichis, sans tralala.

Pascal ne s'est pas montré avant notre départ. J'étais sûre qu'il ne dormait pas. C'était impossible avec le niveau sonore de notre conversation. Il avait accepté l'idée que je participe à cette émission, mais il ne fallait pas non plus lui demander de partager l'enthousiasme de mon fan-club. Il devait attendre notre départ, terré sous la couette, et agacé par nos babillages qui n'en finissaient pas.

Quand nous sommes arrivées au club, il y régnait déjà une ambiance survoltée. Des éclairages d'un blanc aveuglant avaient été disposés un peu partout dans la pièce, des kilomètres de câbles traînaient par terre et des techniciens s'agitaient dans tous les sens. Je ne savais pas à qui m'adresser au milieu de toute cette effervescence.

Ma mère me stressait. Elle me bombardait de questions et je sentais croître son agacement à chacun de mes «je ne sais pas». Elle ne comprenait pas que je ne me sois pas un peu mieux renseignée. Elle ne s'énervait pas mais elle avait un ton de plus en plus pincé. Je savais qu'elle me trouvait empotée, mais je n'osais plus aborder personne depuis qu'un technicien m'avait plus ou moins rembarrée quand je lui avais demandé s'il pouvait me renseigner.

Lætitia a mis fin à cette situation inconfortable. Je ne l'avais jamais rencontrée mais elle s'est adressée à moi comme si nous nous connaissions depuis toujours.

«Ah Mélanie bonjour. Je m'appelle Lætitia. Comment tu te sens, ça va? Pas trop stressée?

– Je...

– Ne t'inquiète pas ma chérie, tout va très bien se passer!

– Est-ce que je...

– Excuse-moi, je reviens dans une seconde... »

Et elle a disparu.

Mais pas ma mère.

« Alors qu'est-ce qu'elle t'a dit, comment ça va se passer ?

– Je n'en sais rien.

– Comment ça, tu n'en sais rien ? Elle t'a bien dit quelque chose.

– Si on veut... elle revient dans une seconde. »

Ma prof est arrivée. Elle m'a serrée dans ses bras en me disant qu'elle était très contente pour moi. Elle me l'a répété en me regardant bien en face, comme pour insister sur la sincérité de ses sentiments. J'ai répondu « merci » en baissant les yeux tandis que j'essayais de chasser les souvenirs qui affluaient, souvenirs dans lesquels ce petit bout de bonne femme tout en nerfs me bousculait sans ménagement quand je ralentissais tout le monde pendant les exercices. Ça ne l'empêchait pas forcément de ne pas être sincère aujourd'hui. Parmi les autres élèves, certains me saluaient de loin sans oser venir me parler, d'autres, comme la prof, se sentaient soudain très proches de moi...

Lætitia est enfin revenue. Sa seconde avait duré vingt minutes. Elle a demandé un peu de silence et nous a donné les instructions. Ça semblait simple. Je me suis dit qu'en une demi-heure ce serait bouclé, mais c'était mal connaître les aléas d'un tournage.

Nous avons démarré notre séance comme à notre habitude, histoire de transpirer et rougir un peu. Avec les éclairages qui surchauffaient la pièce, ça n'a pas demandé longtemps. Lætitia a fait un signe à la prof qui a interrompu l'exercice pour me dire, désolée, que je devais suivre des cours plus adaptés à mon niveau. J'ai pris l'air le plus contrarié possible.

Lætitia a demandé aux techniciens de couper et s'est précipitée vers moi.

« Ça ne va pas du tout Mélanie, ma chérie ! Ce qu'elle te dit est très vexant, tu dois avoir l'air au bord du gouffre ! Allez, c'est pas grave, on reprend. Exercice, interruption, vexation, je compte sur toi. »

Il a fallu je ne sais combien de prises avant que Lætitia ne me trouve assez désespérée. Elle m'avait tellement poussée à bout que ça n'était pas loin de correspondre à mon véritable état. Difficile ensuite d'être « ivre de bonheur » quand la prof m'annonçait que j'allais bénéficier d'une remise en forme personnalisée grâce à *Relooking Extrême* ! Mais Lætitia gardait une exigence « high level » et nous avons recommencé jusqu'à ce que ça lui convienne. Même ma mère et Fanny ont fini par se lasser de répéter la scène finale où elles partageaient mon grand bonheur face à la caméra.

L'équipe de tournage a applaudi et remercié tout le monde, marquant ainsi la fin de cette pénible séance. Les techniciens ont commencé à ranger leur matériel et Lætitia est venue me prendre dans ses bras, en me disant que c'était super. Je ne voyais pas en quoi ça avait été super mais je la laissais me pétrir les bras en guettant un créneau où je pourrais enfin poser mes questions.

« Bon Mélanie, nous avons planifié les tournages de la semaine prochaine. Je t'ai tout noté là. On se voit lundi matin chez toi, mardi matin chez Fanny, mercredi toute la journée chez tes parents et jeudi matin en extérieur au jardin du Luxembourg. Est-ce que tu as pu convaincre ton mari de nous donner une interview ?

– Non, il ne veut pas.

– Tant pis, on fera sans, allez je file. Je te dis à lundi, je t'embrasse, je suis à la bourre. »

Et dans la seconde suivante, elle a lâché mon bras, dégainé son téléphone et s'est éloignée en faisant de grands gestes d'au revoir à tout le monde. J'étais sonnée. Je me suis tournée vers Fanny qui m'a glissé à l'oreille « Allez ma chérie, c'est supeeeeeer ! », en imitant à la perfection le ton snobinard de Lætitia.

*

Les tournages suivants ont été à l'image du premier. Personne ne s'occupait de moi hors caméra, j'étais invisible, et quand nous tournions, je vivais un enfer, subissant les remarques en rafales de Lætitia qui restait égale à elle-même, détestable. Je n'essayais plus de lui parler. J'en avais pris mon parti.

Pourtant, ça me manquait de ne pas avoir quelqu'un de sympa qui soit là pour me tenir la main tout au long de cette aventure, pour me rassurer, m'expliquer les choses et pour combler l'absence de soutien de Pascal.

À la résidence, les visites étaient interdites, Lætitia serait ma seule compagnie et je savais que ça serait difficile, mais j'essayais de faire preuve d'humour et de détachement. La seule chose qui comptait, c'était de ressortir de là avec un corps et un visage qui me donneraient un nouveau départ. Je pouvais m'arranger avec le reste.

*

Le check-up médical devait avoir lieu à l'hôpital de la Pitié-Salpêtrière. Tout était prévu pour que je ne m'inquiète de rien : un taxi est venu me prendre à mon domicile et Lætitia était à l'hôpital pour me soutenir. Tu parles d'un soutien, elle passait son temps au téléphone.

Je n'en menais pas large mais j'essayais de ne pas le montrer. Si je reculais devant ce genre d'examen, qu'est-ce que ce serait lorsqu'il s'agirait de me charcuter dans tous les sens ? Je me suis donc laissé radiographier, piquer, intuber et j'en passe, sans rechigner, avec le sourire même quand j'y arrivais.

Au bout de deux jours, j'étais contente de rentrer chez moi et de retrouver Pascal, mais quand j'ai entamé le récit de mon séjour à l'hôpital, une boule d'amertume est venue se loger au creux de mon ventre. Il était si ironique ! Je n'attendais pas de lui qu'il me plaigne, juste qu'il m'écoute. Mais dès ses premières remarques, j'ai compris que ça n'était pas la peine. J'ai pris le parti de saupoudrer d'une bonne dose d'humour et de supprimer toute trace de plainte ou de regret, en attendant de me rattraper avec Fanny.

*

Les deux semaines pendant lesquelles l'équipe médicale de *Relooking Extrême* a étudié mon dossier m'ont semblé interminables.

J'y pensais dès le saut du lit et jusqu'au soir avant de m'endormir.

Je n'avais envie de parler que de ça.

Je me retenais avec Pascal.

Je me lâchais avec Fanny et ma mère.

*

La limousine est venue me chercher. C'était absurde mais j'étais fière en la voyant m'attendre en bas de mon immeuble. Pendant le trajet, outre Lætitia qui m'accompagnait, il y avait une équipe de tournage qui m'a poussée à dire comme j'étais heureuse et impatiente de démarrer cette aventure.

Je devais rester deux jours à la résidence. J'ai installé mes affaires dans ma chambre et je me suis rafraîchie avant de me rendre à l'interview. Ils voulaient connaître mon état d'esprit à quelques minutes de ma rencontre avec le médecin. Je n'avais pas à jouer la comédie pour avoir l'air nerveuse. J'étais très stressée. J'avais essayé de tester Lætitia pour voir si elle savait ce que le médecin allait m'annoncer, mais elle m'avait juré ses grands dieux qu'elle n'en savait rien. J'ai donc confié mes craintes au type qui m'interrogeait. Il semblait très satisfait de me voir aussi anxieuse.

*

Lætitia m'a conduite au cabinet de consultation où je me suis retrouvée en blouse et culotte devant pas moins de huit techniciens. Je me sentais très vulnérable à moitié nue au milieu de tous ces gens habillés. J'ai resserré la ceinture de ma blouse autour de mes hanches.

On a demandé le silence dans la salle pour démarrer le tournage et un médecin est entré dans la pièce. Ce n'était pas le chirurgien plastique, le fameux clone de Superman.

« Bonjour Mélanie, je suis ravi de vous rencontrer. Je suis le docteur Fitoussi, je suis gastro-entérologue. »

Je ne comprenais pas la présence ici de ce gastro-entérologue. J'avais regardé des dizaines d'épisodes et c'était toujours le chirurgien plastique qui menait ce premier entretien. Mauvais signe…

« Alors, comment vous sentez-vous Mélanie ?

– Je suis un peu nerveuse…

– Il ne faut pas, détendez-vous. »

Il en avait de bonnes. Ce n'est pas lui qui était à moitié à poil devant tout le monde et à qui on allait annoncer ce qui allait advenir de sa personne.

« Mélanie, je ne vais pas y aller par quatre chemins. J'ai reçu l'ensemble des résultats de vos examens médicaux et nous nous sommes longuement concertés avec mes collègues. »

J'ai senti un grand vide m'envahir et les larmes me monter aux yeux. Son entrée en matière annonçait forcément une catastrophe.

« Nous ne voulons vous faire courir aucun risque Mélanie. C'est pourquoi nous aimerions que vous perdiez du poids avant de subir quelque opération que ce soit. »

J'étais projetée vingt ans en arrière. La même scène. La même déception. Le mot régime emplissait ma tête, associé au mot échec.

« Mélanie ?

– …

– Je comprends votre déception Mélanie, mais c'est pour votre bien. Ne vous inquiétez pas, il ne s'agit pas de vous renvoyer chez vous en vous disant de vous débrouiller pour perdre vos kilos. Nous allons vous y aider. Ce que nous vous proposons, c'est de vous implanter un ballon intragastrique. Est-ce que vous connaissez cette technique ?

– C'est comme l'anneau gastrique ?

– Non, pas tout à fait. Le principe du ballon intragastrique, c'est d'introduire un ballon dans l'estomac, puis de le remplir d'air en vue d'occuper une partie de la surface interne de l'estomac, pour duper les récepteurs de la satiété. En bref, le patient qui a ce ballon a l'impression d'être repu après avoir mangé de très petites quantités de nourriture. Le ballon reste en place pendant six mois, puis on le retire.

– Et combien on perd en six mois ?

– En moyenne, entre quinze et vingt-cinq kilos.

– Pas mal…

– Pas mal, oui. En ce qui vous concerne, nous

pensons qu'il serait bien que vous perdiez au moins vingt kilos, et idéalement trente, ce qui vous ferait passer de quatre-vingt-dix à soixante. Qu'est-ce que vous en pensez?

– Ce serait inespéré... »

Soixante kilos... Je n'avais jamais pesé si peu. Enfin si, forcément, mais c'était il y a si longtemps que je ne me souvenais plus à quoi je pouvais ressembler à ce poids.

« Nous vous expliquerons cet après-midi tous les avantages et inconvénients de cette méthode. Nous verrons comment cela pourra s'organiser pendant les six mois d'amaigrissement. Nous n'allons, bien sûr, pas vous bloquer ici pendant toute cette période. Vous rentrerez chez vous et reprendrez votre vie normalement, mais nous assurerons un suivi très rapproché avec un nutritionniste, un psychologue et aussi un coach sportif qui vous fera travailler pour améliorer les résultats du ballon gastrique.

– De toute façon, je ne pense pas pouvoir y arriver toute seule...

– Nous allons voir tout ça ensemble. Vous seriez a priori partante?

– Oui…

– Ça manque d'enthousiasme…

– C'est que… je pensais que les choses seraient rapides et…

– Avec le ballon gastrique, vous commencerez à perdre très vite vous savez. Les résultats sont spectaculaires ! »

*

Après de longues discussions avec le gastro-entérologue, le nutritionniste et la psychologue, j'ai décidé d'essayer. En réalité, ils ne me proposaient aucune alternative. C'était ça ou la fin de l'aventure.

Nous avons fixé le rendez-vous pour l'implantation du ballon à la semaine suivante. Après l'opération, je devais rester un mois à la résidence avec visite quotidienne du nutritionniste et de la psy. Le travail avec le coach sportif commencerait dès que je serais remise de l'opération. De retour chez moi, les visites deviendraient hebdomadaires chez le nutritionniste et la psy, bihebdomadaires avec le coach sportif. Au bout de six mois, je devais revenir à la résidence pour attaquer la chirurgie plastique. Voilà pour le programme.

*

J'ai ouvert un œil. Je me sentais mal. J'avais un goût désagréable dans la bouche. J'ai essayé de changer de position, je n'étais pas bien sur le dos. J'avais des tubes fichés dans le bras gauche mais rien côté droit. J'ai donné l'ordre à mon corps d'exécuter un quart de tour à tribord, mais à peine le mouvement entamé, j'ai ressenti un douloureux élancement au ventre. J'ai abandonné. Une violente crampe me broyait l'estomac, bientôt accompagnée d'une irrépressible envie de vomir. Des litres de salive m'ont envahi la bouche pendant que je me concentrais pour bien respirer. Je devais me retenir, j'étais sur le dos, incapable de me tourner et je ne voulais pas mourir étouffée dans ma propre gerbe.

J'en étais là de mes réflexions, sur le point de paniquer, quand une infirmière est apparue dans mon champ de vision. Elle a tout de suite compris ce qui se passait et m'a aidée à basculer sur le côté, juste à temps pour que je vomisse sur mon oreiller. Je n'avais rien mangé depuis la veille au soir et ce que je rendais était liquide, acide et me tirait sur l'estomac sans ménagement.

« Ne vous inquiétez pas, c'est courant au réveil d'une anesthésie générale.

– Je ne me sens pas bien, j'ai froid.

– Je vais vous apporter une couverture supplémentaire. Vous allez rester en salle de réveil encore un peu puis nous vous remonterons dans votre chambre. D'accord ? »

Je ne sais pas pourquoi elle me demandait mon avis, je n'étais pas en mesure de me rebeller, j'étais en train de mourir.

*

« Alors, comment vous sentez-vous aujourd'hui ?

– Un peu faible mais ça va. Ce matin, j'ai réussi à boire un bouillon de légumes sans vomir. C'est la première fois depuis l'opération. D'habitude, c'est impossible de garder quoi que ce soit.

– C'est très bien ça ! Et côté douleurs, où est-ce que ça en est ?

– J'ai encore des crampes d'estomac assez douloureuses.

– Bon, c'est normal, il n'y a que cinq jours que vous avez été opérée. On va faire une radio pour voir si tout est bien en place. »

*

« Bonjour Mélanie. On va commencer par vous peser si vous voulez bien. Je vous laisse vous déshabiller. »

C'était le rituel du matin. Je me levais à dix heures, je prenais mon petit déjeuner, enfin ce que je pouvais avaler au lever, c'est-à-dire pas grand-chose en général, je prenais ma douche, puis je me rendais à ma consultation chez le nutritionniste à onze heures.

Une fois par semaine, il me pesait.

Le reste du temps, je n'avais pas de balance à ma disposition. Le nutritionniste m'avait expliqué que c'était pour m'éviter de m'affoler pour d'insignifiantes variations de poids. J'avais donc hâte de savoir à combien j'étais.

« Alors, vous êtes aujourd'hui à quatre-vingt-six kilos, soit quatre kilos perdus en dix jours. C'est très bien ! Je pense qu'on peut miser sur une perte de huit kilos sur le premier mois.

– Vous croyez vraiment ? »

Il faut dire que mon comportement alimentaire était mis à rude épreuve par l'intrus qui habitait dans mon estomac. Il ne tolérait pas grand-chose et renvoyait tout ce qui ne lui plaisait pas. La cuisinière de la résidence me préparait des bouillons et des purées qui étaient à peu près tout ce que je pouvais avaler, et encore, dans des proportions de nouveau-né.

J'étais bichonnée ici. Ce qui m'inquiétait, c'était l'idée de devoir continuer à avoir cette alimentation quand je serais de retour chez moi. Nous passions beaucoup de temps avec le nutritionniste à travailler sur ce sujet, à me préparer des fiches menu conciliables avec mon mode de vie et mon ballon gastrique.

*

« Alors Mélanie, on m'a dit que tu étais assez rétablie pour démarrer les séances de sport. Je m'appelle Michaël, je suis le tortionnaire avec qui tu vas travailler chaque après-midi. »

Ça faisait maintenant plus de deux semaines que j'avais été opérée. La dernière pesée avait annoncé quatre-vingt-quatre kilos et je commençais en effet à me sentir mieux. Je n'avais plus de douleurs, sauf après les repas et de manière très supportable, et si je m'appliquais à manger lentement, je ne vomissais plus.

Je n'étais pas mécontente de démarrer mon programme avec Michaël car je commençais à m'ennuyer un peu à la résidence.

L'équipe de tournage était au grand complet. Michaël souriait beaucoup à la caméra, semblant oublier que j'étais là et que c'était à moi qu'il parlait et non aux futurs téléspectateurs. Mais ça n'entamait pas ma bonne humeur, je m'étais habituée aux différents effets que les caméras pouvaient avoir sur les gens.

« Mélanie, on va obliger ton corps à puiser dans ses réserves en lui demandant des efforts supplémentaires.

– Ça me paraît bien !

– Est-ce que tu fais du sport en temps normal Mélanie ?

– Pas vraiment, non.

– Je suis sûre que tu vas y prendre goût pendant toutes ces semaines que nous allons passer ensemble !

– J'en doute mais bon…

– Mais si, tu verras ! On va démarrer en douceur. Notre programme initial sera surtout composé de marche et de natation. Pas de grimace Mélanie, tu vas voir, ça va être super ! »

Je me suis retrouvée à passer chaque jour deux heures avec Michaël, Mike pour les intimes, et j'ai fini par trouver ça… non pas super, ce serait exagéré… mais plutôt agréable.

*

Je suis sortie du bureau en claquant la porte. Je commençais à en avoir ras le cul de cette psy et de ses théories fumeuses.

Tout se passait pour le mieux, j'en étais à sept kilos perdus en trois semaines, je me sentais en forme et je commençais à être rassurée sur ma capacité à continuer à suivre le régime en rentrant chez moi.

Mais cette connasse de psy ne voulait rien entendre. Elle voulait à tout prix que j'aie de graves problèmes relationnels avec mon père, cause de tous mes désordres alimentaires. Mon père ! Franchement ! Avec la mère que j'avais, aller chercher des poux dans la tête de mon père, c'était tordu. Mais elle n'en démordait pas. D'après elle, il ne m'avait pas assez regardée, alors je m'étais mise à grossir pour qu'il me voie, comblant du même coup le manque d'attention par la bouffe. Complexe d'Œdipe, version contrariée. Bien plus grave apparemment que les vexations que je subissais de la part de ma mère depuis la nuit des temps.

Et quand j'osais exprimer l'hypothèse que, peut-être, j'étais plus gourmande que névrosée, elle secouait la tête avec un air agacé. Pour elle, la gourmandise pure et simple n'existait pas. Tu m'étonnes ! Elle était toute maigre ! Elle n'avait jamais dû se faire plaisir avec la bouffe, elle. Ni avec grand-chose d'autre d'ailleurs.

Je suis partie à la recherche de Lætitia. Je ne pouvais pas continuer les séances avec cette bonne femme.

*

Lætitia est entrée dans ma chambre sans frapper, comme à son habitude, avec un grand sourire aux lèvres.

« Mélanie ma chérie, aujourd'hui pas de sport, on part faire du shopping !

– C'est vrai ? C'est super, regarde. »

Je me suis levée pour montrer à Lætitia les poches que faisait mon jean sous mes fesses.

« À ton avis, combien j'ai perdu de tailles ?

– Au moins deux, voire trois…

– Yes ! Et où on va ?

– On a des arrangements avec quelques enseignes dans Paris qui font les grandes tailles. Tu vas voir, ce sont de très chouettes boutiques, je suis sûre que tu vas trouver ton bonheur.

– J'espère ! À quelle heure on y va ?

– On part à treize heures avec la limou, les caméras et tout le bordel…

– Budget ?

– Ce n'est pas ton problème !

– J'adoooooore *Relooking Extrême* !

– Dommage qu'il n'y ait pas les caméras, la production aurait adoré ça !

– Je la referai cet après-midi ! J'adoooooore *Relooking Extrême* !

– Économise-toi ! Allez, je te laisse, on se retrouve à midi et demi dans le hall d'entrée. »

*

Je préparais mes valises, empilant avec le sourire tous mes nouveaux habits. C'était bizarre de partir d'ici. Je m'étais habituée au rythme, aux gens.

J'avais hâte de revoir Pascal. Je lui avais parlé presque tous les jours au téléphone. Il me soutenait maintenant dans ma démarche. L'approche régime lui plaisait plus que celle du bistouri, un vieux réflexe judéo-chrétien qui accordait à l'effort et la privation une valeur supérieure à la facilité. J'avais envie de me retrouver dans ses bras, de voir ses yeux briller, de l'embrasser et de lui tourner la tête avec mes nouvelles formes, moins généreuses mais plus gracieuses…

J'ai rangé avec précaution le dossier constitué avec le nutritionniste, toute ma ligne de conduite pour les semaines à venir. Je me sentais une volonté de fer. J'étais boostée par les résultats de ce premier mois (huit kilos et six cents grammes). J'étais maintenant convaincue de pouvoir redevenir une jeune femme normale.

*

« Nous retrouvons Mélanie après ses six mois de régime. Comme vous allez le constater, la transformation est spectaculaire. Nous rappelons que nous avions implanté, il y a six mois, un ballon intragastrique dans l'estomac de Mélanie. Pendant sa convalescence à la résidence de *Relooking Extrême*, Mélanie avait déjà perdu huit kilos et six cents grammes. Elle pesait au début de l'aventure quatre-vingt-dix kilos et espérait perdre trente kilos au total. Aura-t-elle réussi à les perdre ? Vous le saurez tout de suite après la page de publicité ! »

« Mélanie, tu es prête ?
– Oui, c'est bon.
– On reprend dans trente secondes… »

« Mélanie, bonjour !
– Bonjour !
– Vous avez littéralement fon-du ! Je vous reconnais à peine. Combien avez-vous perdu Mélanie ?
– Trente-trois kilos…
– Trente-trois kilos ! C'est extraordinaire ! Pouvez-vous vous lever pour que nous puissions constater le résultat ? C'est fabuleux ! Comment se sont passés ces six mois Mélanie, est-ce que ça a été difficile ?
– Ça va peut-être vous paraître bizarre mais ça a été plutôt facile… ce ballon gastrique, c'est magique ! Il a complètement modifié mes habitudes alimentaires. Moi qui m'empiffrais à chaque repas, j'ai pris l'habitude de manger des quantités raisonnables. Je suis

aussi devenue accro au sport ! Et ça, ça en a étonné plus d'un, moi la première !

– À aucun moment, vous n'avez flanché pour des sucreries ou du MacDo dont vous raffoliez il me semble, ou n'importe quoi de ce genre ? Vous pouvez nous le dire, nous ne le répéterons pas à votre nutritionniste…

– C'est étrange mais je ne l'ai même pas envisagé. J'étais dans un état d'esprit où il n'y avait pas de négociation possible… un truc presque excessif… j'étais capable de me fâcher si mon mari me proposait quelque chose à manger auquel je n'avais pas le droit par exemple…

– Demain, le docteur Fitoussi va vous retirer votre ballon gastrique, est-ce que vous redoutez qu'à la suite de ça, l'appétit ne revienne ?

– J'en ai beaucoup parlé avec le nutritionniste et la psy, et en six mois, j'ai modifié en profondeur mon rapport à la nourriture. J'espère donc que tout ira bien.

– Êtes-vous aujourd'hui satisfaite de votre corps ?

– À vrai dire, j'ai la peau très distendue mais

je compte sur *Relooking Extrême* pour remédier à tout ça !

– Et vous avez bien raison ! Vous avez l'air en pleine forme Mélanie !

– Je le suis, je ne m'étais pas sentie aussi bien depuis longtemps.

– Je vous remercie Mélanie, je vais vous laisser rejoindre Lætitia qui va vous accompagner jusqu'à la résidence. »

C'était un bien joli portrait que je leur avais dressé là, conforme à ce que voulait la production. La vérité était un peu moins rose. Le nutritionniste n'était pas content parce qu'il pensait que mon comportement tirait vers l'anorexie. La psy, cette connasse que je n'avais jamais pu saquer, lui donnait raison alors que je respectais toutes leurs instructions à la lettre. J'arrangeais un peu les quantités, il est vrai, jamais en plus, toujours en moins, mais enfin, ils chipotaient.

Moi, je considérais que j'avais une alimentation normale. Mais, d'après eux, ce que j'appelais « alimentation normale » ne l'était pas du tout. Pour autant que je sache, aucune des analyses de sang des derniers mois n'avait mis en évidence quoi que ce soit d'inquiétant, alors c'était quoi leur problème ? J'avais l'impression que dans leur esprit, quelqu'un qui avait été gros ne pouvait se mettre à avoir une alimentation raisonnable sans que ça soit suspect ! Je voulais maigrir et je m'en donnais les moyens, je ne vois pas pourquoi ils stressaient avec ça. J'étais loin d'être maigre, il n'y avait pas lieu de s'inquiéter. Le nutritionniste m'avait fait tout un sketch, l'autre semaine, quand un mannequin était mort d'anorexie. Je lui avais ri au nez. Il me parlait d'une nana qui pesait trente-six kilos pour un mètre soixante-quinze, alors que je pesais soixante kilos pour un mètre cinquante-huit. Nous ne jouions pas dans la même cour !

Pour le sport, ils trouvaient aussi que j'étais excessive, que je passais trop de temps à la salle et sur mon vélo d'appartement, à mesurer le nombre de calories brûlées. Mon vélo, c'était mon antidote aux envies de bouffe, chacun son truc. Dès que je sentais un tiraillement dans l'estomac, je grimpais dessus et je n'en redescendais que quand j'avais pédalé au moins trente minutes. J'accompagnais ça d'un litre d'eau, et dans la plupart des cas, la fringale disparaissait. Pas de quoi non plus en faire tout un plat !

J'avais décidé d'uniformiser mes repas. Ça aussi, ça les chiffonnait, alors que c'était juste plus simple à gérer comme ça pour moi. Tous les midis, je mangeais une salade composée sans assaisonnement (l'huile de la vinaigrette me semblait annuler tout le bénéfice de la salade), une tranche de pain complet avec un fromage maigre et un fruit. Je n'allais plus jamais à la cantine avec mes collègues, au début pour ne pas être tentée, et ensuite parce que je n'en avais plus eu envie. Leurs frites brillantes de gras et leurs pizzas dégoulinantes de fromage fondu me dégoûtaient. Le soir, j'avalais un bouillon de légumes, une tranche de jambon blanc avec une tranche de pain complet et un yaourt.

Je ne partageais plus mes dîners avec Pascal. Je ne supportais plus ses remarques concernant la composition de mes repas. Et vice versa. Au début, il avait fait des efforts, il s'était mis au régime pour m'encourager, mais très vite, il avait tout laissé tomber. Je ne pouvais pas lui en vouloir, j'avais de nombreuses fois essuyé cet échec. Manque de motivation et de volonté. Je crois qu'il était envieux de ce que moi, je ne flanchais pas. Il reprenait à son compte les arguments du nutritionniste et de la psy, martelait que j'étais obnubilée par les calories et que ça n'était pas sain, mais au fond, je pense qu'il était juste jaloux.

Seul Mike était content de mon évolution sans aucune réserve. Je n'étais censée le voir que deux ou trois fois par semaine, mais j'allais à la salle de sport tous les soirs après le travail, au moins une heure, voire deux, ainsi que le samedi. Il prenait toujours le temps de me faire travailler et de me donner de nouveaux conseils. J'étais un peu son œuvre. Il était très fier de la manière dont il avait transformé mon corps. Il était comme moi impatient que je passe sur le billard pour retirer les poches de peau sur lesquelles nous ne pouvions plus rien.

Le dimanche, la salle était fermée. J'en profitais pour aller à la piscine, en général avec Fanny, qui n'en revenait pas, elle non plus, de ma transformation. Elle aussi manifestait parfois une vague inquiétude à propos de mon excessive motivation, mais sa nature enthousiaste l'emportait toujours. Elle disait en rigolant que j'allais bientôt être plus mince qu'elle. Cette idée n'était pas pour me déplaire.

*

J'ai enfilé la blouse réglementaire comme six mois auparavant. On nous a demandé le silence. J'allais enfin rencontrer l'imminent chirurgien plastique de *Rex*.

« Bonjour, Mélanie ! Je suis le docteur Cohen et je suis ravi de vous rencontrer...

– Bonjour... moi aussi ! J'aime bien le docteur Fitoussi, il est super, mais j'avoue avoir été déçue, il y a six mois, de devoir passer entre ses mains avant de passer entre les vôtres !

– Ça en valait la peine d'après ce que je vois !

– Oui, ça en valait la peine ! Le problème maintenant, c'est ça... »

J'ai ouvert ma blouse pour lui montrer la poche de peau qui pendait de mon ventre.

« C'est classique dans des cas comme le vôtre Mélanie, mais ne vous inquiétez pas, nous allons y remédier. J'imagine qu'il y a d'autres zones présentant le même problème ? »

J'ai retiré la blouse, plus consciente que jamais du regard des techniciens. Je n'étais pas du tout sexy en sous-vêtements… avec toute cette peau en trop… je ne pouvais donner le change qu'habillée.

« Très bien, je pense que nous arriverons à rattraper tout ça. Nous retirerons des fuseaux de peau et de graisse sur chacune des zones qui pose problème. Êtes-vous satisfaite de vos seins ?

– À vrai dire, j'en ai beaucoup perdu pendant le régime et ils sont encore plus mous qu'avant…

– Je vais mettre en place des prothèses, pas trop volumineuses, mais qui donneront une plus jolie forme à votre poitrine. Au niveau du visage ?

– J'ai un horrible double menton…

– Je peux effectuer un dégraissage de cette zone sans aucun problème… j'aimerais aussi retoucher vos paupières. Vous aurez un plus joli regard si je retends un peu tout ça… ça vous va ?

– Je suis un peu inquiète mais je vous fais confiance…

– Vous verrez, tout se passera très bien !

– Je n'arrive pas à y croire… c'est comme si on m'offrait une seconde naissance… »

Le docteur Cohen m'a posé la main sur l'épaule en un geste ridicule qui se voulait chargé de sens. Pas plus ridicule que ma tirade sur la seconde naissance, d'accord, mais c'était pour contenter la production qui ne me trouvait pas assez expressive. Ils m'avaient demandé, via Lætitia, de faire un effort. Je voulais bien faire tous les efforts du monde. J'étais même prête à me ridiculiser ou à passer pour une imbécile si c'était le prix à payer pour bénéficier de toutes ces opérations.

*

« Je suis restée sept heures sur la table d'opération ! Sept heures, tu te rends compte ? étais-je en train de raconter à Fanny.

– Putain, c'est pas de la rigolade. Et t'étais dans quel état en te réveillant ?

– Horrible... je te passe la gerbe post-anesthésie ?

– Ouais, classique.

– J'avais l'impression qu'on m'avait passé tout le corps sous un rouleau compresseur, c'était horrible ! Je ne pouvais bouger ni les bras, ni les jambes, ni la tête...

– Alouette...

– Je ressemble à une momie avec mes pansements de contention dans tous les sens... je te jure, j'ai morflé pendant trois jours ! Là, ça commence tout juste à aller mieux.

– Tu vas bientôt pouvoir te lever ?

– Non. À cause des coutures que j'ai au niveau des fesses, je dois rester allongée le plus possible pendant quinze jours...

– Quinze jours, c'est long ! Je sais pas comment tu supportes tout ça...

– Ce n'est qu'un mauvais moment à passer...

– Ouais, en tout cas, j'ai hâte que tout ça soit fini, que tu nous reviennes toute jolie et bien dans tes baskets.

– …

– Hé ho, y a quelqu'un ?

– …

– Ben tu pleures ? Eh cocotte, qu'est-ce qui se passe ?

– Je ne sais pas, j'ai un coup de blues… je suis contente mais… tout à coup… ça me semble absurde… toute cette souffrance que j'inflige à mon corps…

– Arrête, tu vas être superbe, ça va changer ta vie ! Fini les complexes ma belle, tu vas conquérir le monde !

– Je me sens seule, j'aimerais bien que tu sois là avec moi…

– Eh ! J'ai pas que ça à foutre moi de garder les momies !

– T'es conne toi ! Bon, allez, je te laisse, ça me fait mal au bras de tenir le téléphone.

– OK, je te rappelle demain, je t'embrasse bien fort, hein ! »

*

Mon moral est remonté en flèche quand ils ont retiré mes divers pansements.

Mon nouveau menton était parfait.

Pour mon nouveau regard, je ne savais pas encore. Ils ne m'avaient pas retiré les fils des paupières, ce qui me faisait ressembler à Frankenstein. Heureusement que j'avais déjà vu ça sur d'autres candidats, sinon j'aurais eu quelques angoisses.

Mes seins étaient très volumineux. Trop volumineux. Enfin, c'est ce que je me suis dit en les découvrant la première fois. Le chirurgien a tenté de me rassurer en me disant que c'était encore un peu enflé… mais quand même ! Et puis, de fil en aiguille, à force de me redécouvrir dans le miroir, j'ai commencé à les aimer ces seins très ronds, très fermes. J'ai essayé des hauts décolletés et je les ai carrément adorés ! J'étais super sexy ! La naissance de mes seins me semblait captivante, voire envoûtante. Un jour, j'ai testé leur effet sur Mike qui passait me voir. J'avais choisi un haut noir qui mettait mon décolleté bien en évidence, et j'observais les regards de Mike. Eh bien, comme je le pensais, mon nouveau décolleté exerçait un fort magnétisme. Ses yeux étaient attirés sans qu'il puisse lutter. Je le voyais se débattre, le pauvre diable, essayer de raccrocher ses yeux aux miens, mais ils finissaient toujours par déraper de nouveau jusqu'à la naissance de mes seins.

Mes bras et mes cuisses avaient maintenant la peau bien tendue. Le chirurgien y était allé franco dans son découpage. Plus aucun surplus. Je pouvais agiter les bras, applaudir, sans que ça ne tremblote comme une horrible gelée telle que seuls nos amis anglais peuvent l'apprécier.

J'avais du mal à bien regarder mes fesses, mais ça semblait être la partie la moins réussie. Tant pis. Je pouvais accepter l'idée de ne pas devenir une diva du string. Planquées dans une culotte, elles avaient une allure correcte.

Enfin, j'ai gardé le meilleur pour la fin... mon ventre... mon ennemi juré... celui qui me donnait l'air d'une maman kangourou depuis que j'avais maigri... il avait disparu. J'avais le ventre plat. Je voyais mes poils pubiens juste comme ça, en baissant la tête. Plus aucun obstacle entre mon sexe et moi. La peau n'avait pas l'aspect lisse, souple et tendre d'une peau de bébé, on voyait que c'était une vieille routière qui avait déjà pas mal souffert, mais j'allais la soigner, la chouchouter, lui offrir toutes les crèmes de l'univers de la cosmétique pour lui redonner une deuxième jeunesse.

*

Un mois après les opérations, j'avais dégonflé de partout et le chirurgien m'avait retiré tous mes fils. J'étais autorisée à reprendre le sport avec Mike, à condition d'y aller en douceur.

Ça me fascinait de voir mes abdominaux travailler. Ils étaient là, à fleur de peau, je les regardais se contracter à chaque effort. Avant, je ne pouvais qu'imaginer qu'ils existaient, en coulisse, qu'ils travaillaient planqués derrière les amas de graisse et de peau. Maintenant qu'ils étaient visibles, je ne quittais plus des yeux le miroir pendant les exercices.

Il n'y avait pas que mon regard sur mon corps qui avait changé, celui de Mike aussi. Il perdait en professionnalisme. Ses mains s'attardaient sur mon corps un peu plus que nécessaire lorsqu'il me montrait un nouvel exercice ou qu'il me corrigeait une posture. Je laissais faire. Je ne nourrissais pas de désir particulier pour Mike, mais j'éprouvais la même curiosité vis-à-vis de cette nouveauté que vis-à-vis de toutes les autres.

Un après-midi, je suis arrivée à mon cours de gym en avance et de très bonne humeur car j'étrennais une nouvelle tenue dans laquelle je me sentais très à mon avantage. C'était un short noir rikiki et un top à bretelle décolleté, en matière si moulante qu'on les aurait crus cousus à même ma peau. Mon corps était devenu une fierté que j'avais envie d'exhiber.

Pour ne pas perdre de temps, j'ai mis en route le tapis de marche. J'avais déjà parcouru trois kilomètres et je commençais à avoir chaud quand Mike est arrivé. Il m'a à peine dit bonjour. Sans arrêter ma balade sur place, je lui ai demandé :

« T'en as une tête ! Qu'est-ce qui se passe ce matin, un souci ?

– Non, non…

– Panne de réveil ?
– Mélanie, je...
– Oui ? »

Il n'a pas été plus loin. Il s'est approché de moi et a arrêté le tapis.

« Qu'est-ce que tu fais ? Je n'avais pas fini !
– Descends de là, il faut que je te parle. »

Nous nous sommes assis sur le banc.

« Alors, qu'est-ce qu'il y a ? »

Il ne semblait pas dans son assiette. Je lui ai donné des pichenettes sur le bras pour détendre l'atmosphère. Il a stoppé mes taquineries en attrapant mes mains. Il ne les a pas relâchées. Il me regardait maintenant droit dans les yeux. Une vague de chaleur a envahi mon ventre.

Qu'est-ce qui m'arrivait ?

Je devais retirer mes mains, me lever.

Je n'ai pas bougé.

Mike a approché son visage du mien. Il était encore temps de tout arrêter mais je l'ai laissé m'embrasser. Je ne contrôlais plus rien. Mike a retiré mon haut et a enfoui son visage entre mes seins. La scène m'a électrisée. J'avais l'impression d'être l'héroïne d'un film porno, et bizarrement, ça me plaisait. Il m'a prise sur la planche sur laquelle je travaillais d'habitude mes abdos, avec brutalité, et j'ai aimé cette brutalité.

De ce jour, les séances de sport ont pris un tour différent. Nous ne commencions à travailler qu'après avoir soulagé le désir qui nous taraudait. La culpabilité avait beau grignoter mes moments de solitude, c'était plus fort que moi. J'attendais de voir Mike avec l'impatience d'une adolescente. Je n'étais pas amoureuse de lui, mais il y avait une telle intensité dans nos rapports que j'étouffais mes bouffées de mauvaise conscience. Cette histoire prendrait fin avec *Relooking Extrême* et personne n'en saurait jamais rien.

*

La maquilleuse procédait aux dernières retouches avant mon entrée en scène. Je me regardais dans la glace en essayant de retrouver mon visage. Je me reconnaissais dans certaines expressions mais c'était à peu près tout.

« Voilà, j'ai fini, vous êtes ravissante !

– Je… merci ! Est-ce que vous avez vu des photos de moi avant ?

– Oui, oui…

– C'est étrange de changer à ce point, vous ne trouvez pas ?

– Sans doute…

– …

– Mais vous allez très vite vous y habituer je pense !

– Oui, je vais m'y habituer. »

Lætitia a débarqué dans la loge, plus gesticulante que jamais.

« Mélanie, ma chérie, tu es magnifique ! Qui pourrait croire qu'il y a de ça quelques mois, tu étais… enfin bref ! Tu entres en scène dans trente minutes ! Tiens-toi prête ! »

Je n'ai comme d'habitude pas eu le temps de répondre qu'elle était déjà repartie. Je me suis levée pour me regarder dans le miroir. Je portais une longue robe de soirée, noire, avec un décolleté qui mettait en valeur ma nouvelle poitrine. Je me suis tournée pour me voir de profil. J'avais ce ventre plat dont j'avais toujours rêvé, plus aucun double menton, des fesses enfin normales…

Alors pourquoi cette tristesse ? C'était comme ça depuis la veille au soir. Une sorte de baby blues ? Depuis un mois et demi que j'étais à la résidence, mes journées étaient organisées autour de mon bien-être et de mon apparence, je passais des moments intenses avec Mike, et dès demain, tout ça serait terminé. J'allais reprendre le rythme métro-boulot-dodo. Il y avait de quoi ne pas sauter de joie.

Bien sûr, j'allais retrouver Pascal… mais justement, j'appréhendais. La veille, j'avais dit à Mike que nous ne nous reverrions pas. Ma culpabilité avait grandi au fur et à mesure que la date de mon départ s'était rapprochée. Au fond de moi, je me sentais moche. Pas du tout en phase avec ma nouvelle beauté extérieure… Comment regarder Pascal dans les yeux après toutes mes parties de jambes en l'air avec Mike ? Rien que lui parler au téléphone m'était devenu difficile. J'avais d'ailleurs espacé mes appels. Il ne semblait pas l'avoir remarqué et continuait de me dire à chaque fois que je lui manquais (je répondais

« moi aussi » du bout des lèvres), qu'il ne restait plus que tant de jours, et que, et que, et que... j'en sortais à chaque fois déprimée.

« Mélanie, tu viens !

– J'arrive !

– Tu te souviens de tout ? On lance la musique, tu commences à monter les marches, lentement, la pression doit s'installer, OK ?

– Je ne risque pas de marcher très vite avec cette robe, tu sais !

– Tu marques une pause derrière le rideau et tu attends la fin de mon speech. Ensuite le rideau s'ouvre et tu avances sur le podium, OK ?

– OK.

– Après, place à l'émotion, hein, je compte sur toi ma chérie ! »

J'ai avancé de quelques pas sur le podium et les lumières se sont allumées, permettant à tous mes proches (et plus tard aux téléspectateurs) de me découvrir dans ma nouvelle version. J'attendais leur réaction avant d'oser me montrer davantage. J'ai entendu un sifflement. J'étais sûre qu'il provenait de Fanny et ça m'a fait sourire. Puis les applaudissements ont fusé et j'ai tourné sur moi-même pour qu'ils puissent admirer ma silhouette dans son intégralité. Les larmes me sont montées aux yeux en voyant Pascal me regarder avec de grands yeux ronds. J'ai lu sur ses lèvres plus que je n'ai entendu qu'il me disait que j'étais belle.

Lætitia m'a autorisée à descendre du podium et rejoindre mes proches. Je me suis exécutée en me demandant vers qui j'étais censée me diriger en premier. Question inutile. Pascal m'a accueillie en bas des marches et m'a serrée dans ses grands bras costauds et rassurants. Il pleurait, me disait qu'il était si content que je revienne, qu'il m'aimait déjà avant mais que là, j'étais si jolie… si jolie ! Fanny m'a libérée de cette étreinte, elle me tenait les épaules à bout de bras et rigolait de me voir si belle sans trouver les mots. Derrière elle, j'ai vu ma mère qui trépignait en attendant son tour. Tout le monde se bousculait, riait et parlait fort.

Les coupes de champagne ont circulé et j'ai

porté un toast à la santé de *Relooking Extrême* grâce à qui patati patata.

Quand Mike est venu trinquer avec moi, j'avais déjà bu pas mal de champagne. Il m'a embrassée tout près de l'oreille pour me féliciter, et je crois lui avoir susurré quelque chose comme quoi je voulais le revoir. Il ne m'a pas répondu, a juste levé à nouveau son verre en souriant.

Et après…

« À quelle heure ils arrivent ?

– Je leur ai dit de venir vers sept heures et demie, ça nous laissera le temps de manger tranquille avant que l'émission ne commence. »

C'était le grand soir ! Mon heure de gloire ! Celle où le monde me verrait grosse et moche pour la dernière fois. Je n'avais pas vu l'émission avant la diffusion officielle, et j'étais curieuse de voir ce que ça donnait.

« Qu'est-ce que tu fous, là ?

– Mon heure de vélo quotidienne.

– Tes invités arrivent dans trois quarts d'heure, y a rien qu'est prêt, et toi, t'es en train de pédaler sur cette connerie de vélo d'appartement !

– Ben oui.

– Tu comptes sur moi pour tout préparer ?

– Mais non ! Je n'en ai plus que pour sept minutes.

– Et tu ne vas pas te doucher après ?

– Si... »

Pascal est sorti de la pièce avec de la fumée qui lui sortait des oreilles. Il ne comprenait pas que c'était important pour moi de ne m'autoriser aucune exception. Si je passais une journée sans aucun exercice physique, je sentais aussitôt les bourrelets repousser.

De toute façon, je savais que ma mère arriverait en avance, comme d'habitude, et qu'elle serait ravie de prendre les choses en main. Ça m'éviterait en plus ses réflexions sur ma manière de faire ceci ou cela qui n'était jamais la bonne.

On a sonné à la porte. Qu'est-ce que je disais ? Mes parents. Quarante minutes d'avance.

« Bonjour ma chérie ! Toujours perchée sur ce foutu vélo... si on m'avait un jour dit que tu deviendrais une accro du sport ! Enfin, c'est bien, c'est très bien ! Tu as une mine superbe ! Bonjour Pascal ! Comment ça va ? Ouh là là, tu as l'air fatigué toi en revanche… tes petits monstres te font la vie dure à l'école ? Je t'admire tu sais ! Qu'est-ce que je peux faire pour vous aider ? »

Je suis descendue de mon vélo juste à temps pour éloigner ma mère de Pascal et de ses éventuels sarcasmes.

« Je n'ai pas eu le temps de préparer, je suis rentrée tard du boulot… je pensais faire une salade en entrée, j'ai acheté des crevettes, des tomates, de l'avocat, du pamplemousse. Et puis j'ai préparé de la sauce bolognaise hier soir, y a plus qu'à faire cuire les pâtes.

– Allez oust ! va vite te doucher, je m'occupe de la salade.

– T'es sûre ?

– Va, je te dis ! »

J'ai regardé Pascal avec un sourire triomphant.

Quand je suis sortie de la salle de bains, Pascal et mon père étaient installés au salon. Ils buvaient une bière en descendant un bol de cacahuètes… une vision cauchemardesque ! J'ai rejoint ma mère à la cuisine.

« Tu n'as pas assaisonné la salade hein ?

– Mais non, j'ai préparé la sauce à côté dans ce bol que tu vois là, afin que ma petite fille chérie puisse manger sa salade toute sèche !

– Et rester mince !

– Et rester mince. Tu n'as pas encore maigri ? J'ai l'impression… non ?

– Non non.

– T'es sûre ?

– Mais oui, je suis sûre ! Tu n'es pas encore habituée à ma nouvelle silhouette, c'est tout ! »

J'avais perdu deux kilos depuis la fin de l'émission et j'espérais en perdre encore autant pour atteindre le chiffre symbolique de cinquante. Je préférais le cacher. Personne ne semblait plus approuver mes pertes de poids. La même réprobation planait que lorsque j'étais grosse et que je m'empiffrais. Comme disait ma mère, il faut être raisonnable en tout, et visiblement, pour beaucoup, j'avais dépassé ce seuil.

« Ça va avec Pascal ? J'ai l'impression que c'est tendu entre vous…

– Ça va.

– C'est ça, prends-moi pour une idiote.

– Tous ces changements nous ont pas mal bousculés…

– Ça ne m'étonne pas. T'es devenue trop jolie pour lui.

– C'est délicat ça maman, vraiment…

– Écoute, il ne faut pas se voiler la face. Tant que vous étiez gros tous les deux, c'était parfait, mais maintenant…

– Maintenant quoi ?

– Ne me dis pas que le regard des hommes sur toi n'a pas changé !

– …

– Et que ça ne te fait pas plaisir…

– …

– Et que tu ne compares pas Pascal aux autres hommes…

– Tu dis n'importe quoi maman !

– Je ne suis pas née de la dernière pluie Mélanie. »

Pour clore la conversation, j'ai emporté la pile d'assiettes pour mettre la table au salon. Elle avait raison et c'était exaspérant.

Quand Fanny est arrivée, en retard comme l'a souligné ma mère, nous sommes passés à table.

«Je sers Mélanie la première. On pourra ajouter la sauce dans le saladier après, c'est plus pratique que de devoir mélanger dans son assiette. Ça va comme ça ma chérie?

– Parfait.»

Ça m'agaçait qu'elle fasse remarquer que je mangeais ma salade sans sauce. Fanny a lu dans mes pensées et m'a souri avant de lancer la conversation.

«Alors, t'as hâte de voir l'émission?

– Oui, ça va être marrant…

– T'as prévenu les gens à ton boulot? a lancé Pascal d'un ton un peu mauvais. Attention mesdames et messieurs, si vous voulez entrer dans l'intimité de votre collègue de bureau, la voir exhiber son corps aux caméras, ne ratez surtout pas ce soir *Relooking Extrême* avec Mélanie Bertier!

– Ha! Ha! Ha! Très drôle. Elle t'emmerde Mélanie Bertier.

– Du calme, du calme, les enfants. Tu n'es pas content, Pascal, d'avoir une femme plus jolie?

– Moi, je l'ai dit mille fois, je la trouvais jolie avant, et je préférais quand on faisait de bonnes bouffes, qu'on buvait de bonnes bouteilles de vin, qu'on parlait d'autre chose que de régime et… »

Et qu'on baisait, ai-je complété dans ma tête.

« Non mais regardez, elle trie ses morceaux d'avocat, je ne peux pas vivre comme ça moi !

– Tout va revenir à la normale, a lancé ma mère conciliante, elle est en phase de stabilisation, c'est normal, ça ne durera pas. Mélanie, tu ne manges pas tes morceaux d'avocat ?

– Non, c'est trop gras.

– T'exagères un peu quand même.

– Vous voyez ! Deux mois qu'elle est en soi-disant stabilisation et c'est pire que si elle était au régime !

– C'est bon, Pascal. On ne va pas laver notre linge sale en public ! »

Il m'a lancé un regard assassin mais n'a rien répondu. Je me suis levée pour débarrasser.

Je suis restée dans la cuisine à regarder les pâtes cuire, en espérant que ça allait me calmer. Fanny m'a rejointe pour fumer une clope.

« C'est pas la joie hein ?

– C'est le moins qu'on puisse dire. Tu te souviens comme c'était avant, jamais on ne s'engueulait avec Pascal, mais depuis que je suis rentrée… c'est comme ça sans arrêt. »

J'ai poussé la porte et j'ai repris à voix basse.

« Il est super en colère mais ce n'est pas vraiment à cause de mon comportement alimentaire…

– C'est à cause de quoi alors ?

– Je t'ai dit que j'avais à nouveau mes règles ?

– Ouais, tu m'as dit ça.

– Pascal voudrait qu'on essaie d'avoir un enfant et… le truc, c'est que je n'en ai plus du tout envie… en tout cas, pas pour l'instant.

– Ah ouais ? Mais avant…

– Avant oui, mais maintenant… je veux profiter un peu, rester mince, tu vois… et Pascal, il ne comprend pas ça…

– Je vois.

– Et puis, y a autre chose, c'est que… de toute façon… je n'ai plus envie de faire l'amour avec lui… je… quand je le vois nu, c'est dégueulasse de dire ça mais… je ne peux plus.

– Je comprends mieux…

– Ouais…

– Je sais pas quoi te dire, il faut peut-être que vous vous laissiez du temps…

– C'est ce que je me dis. Mais tu vois l'ambiance…

– Ouais. »

J'ai hésité à aller jusqu'au bout de mes confidences et raconter à Fanny mon histoire avec Mike, histoire qui durait même si elle battait de l'aile.

Ma mère en a décidé autrement.

« Alors les filles, elles viennent ces pâtes ? a-t-elle lancé depuis le salon.

– Ça vient, ça vient. Plus que deux minutes. »

J'ai levé les yeux au ciel en mimant ma mère pour faire marrer Fanny.

J'ai servi tout le monde en pâtes. Pour ne pas déchaîner les passions, j'ai mis quelques spaghettis dans mon assiette, recouverts d'un peu de sauce. Personne n'a remarqué les portions riquiqui que je me servais. Tant mieux. La discussion a suivi son bonhomme de chemin, et j'ai enfourné deux fourchettes, histoire d'avoir autour de la bouche le minimum syndical de sauce tomate qui permettrait d'attester que j'avais mangé. J'ai tassé le peu qui restait dans un coin de mon assiette pour que ça ait juste un air de je-n'ai-pas-fini et non de je-n'ai-rien-mangé. Quand tout le monde a déclaré avoir terminé, je me suis empressée de débarrasser en empilant l'assiette de Fanny sur la mienne. Je m'en étais bien sortie.

Le générique de *Relooking Extrême* a retenti. Nous avons emporté en vitesse nos desserts devant la télé (j'en ai profité pour oublier le mien sur la table). Je suis apparue en gros plan à l'écran.

« Malheur, comme je suis !

– Comme t'étais, a corrigé Fanny avec un grand sourire.

– Oui, comme j'étais… »

Pascal a secoué la tête en poussant un soupir exaspéré.

« Ben quoi ? Tu ne vas pas me dire que j'étais mieux comme ça !

– Ho ! vous n'allez pas recommencer tous les deux, c'est pas vrai, est intervenue ma mère. Tiens, ouvre donc la bouteille de champagne Pascal au lieu de t'énerver.

– Oh là là ! Lætitia avait raison de s'arracher les cheveux, je suis nulle ! On dirait une demeurée qui ne comprend rien de ce qui se passe !

– Moi, je te trouve très bien. Hé, Fanny, regarde, c'est à notre tour d'être interviewées. On n'est pas mal hein ?

– Vous êtes très bien, ai-je répondu bonne joueuse.

– Vous faites super jeune, a ajouté Fanny en me pinçant discrètement le mollet.

– C'est gentil ça Fanny. Tu trouves toi ? a-t-elle demandé à mon père.

– T'es magnifique, comme toujours ! »

Et le pire, c'est qu'il était sincère. Au bout de quarante ans de mariage, il continuait de la regarder avec ce mélange d'admiration et de soumission qui me mettait hors de moi.

« La tronche que tu fais Mélanie !

– Tu parles, je m'attends à rencontrer le chirurgien plastique et à ce qu'il m'annonce qu'en deux coups de bistouri ça va être réglé, et je rencontre un gastro-entérologue qui m'annonce six mois de régime… »

Ils montraient ensuite ma transformation en morphing avec les séquences qu'ils avaient filmées à intervalles réguliers pendant mes six mois de régime.

« C'est quand même hallucinant comme t'as réussi à maigrir, a lancé Fanny.

– Oui, félicitations Mélanie. Ça a dû te demander pas mal d'efforts. Je suis très fier de toi.

– Merci papa. »

J'étais aux anges. Mon père n'était démonstratif qu'avec ma mère d'habitude. Ce jour était à marquer d'une pierre blanche.

Je me suis crispée quand a démarré la séquence avec Mike. C'était bizarre de nous voir là, dans cette salle de sport pleine de souvenirs adultères et de regarder ça avec Pascal. J'aurais aimé passer à la suite sans plus de commentaires, mais ma mère étant ma mère…

« Dis donc, t'as de la chance, il était pas mal ton prof de sport ! Quand je pense à la vieille bique qui me donne mes cours…

– Ouais. »

J'ai piqué un fard mais tout le monde avait les yeux rivés sur la télé. Personne ne l'a remarqué.

« C'est trop bizarre la matière de ta peau. Regarde, là, quand ils montrent au niveau de tes bras, on dirait du vieux parchemin.

– Merci pour la comparaison Fanny. »

J'apparaissais ensuite en momie. Puis, telle une strip-teaseuse de cabaret, je me défaisais progressivement de tous mes bandages.

J'étais très émue de revivre ces instants-là.

La cérémonie des retrouvailles venait clôturer l'aventure en apothéose. J'espérais que nous n'avions pas été filmés avec Mike. J'ai croisé les doigts. Ouf rien, c'était terminé. L'émission passait au candidat suivant.

*

Je suis rentrée sur la pointe des pieds. La soirée s'était prolongée plus tard que prévu et il était deux heures du matin. Si je réveillais Pascal, j'étais sûre de passer un mauvais quart d'heure, et je n'avais aucune envie de gâcher cette bonne soirée avec une énième scène de ménage.

Et t'étais où ? Avec qui ? Et vous avez fait quoi ? Et pourquoi tu rentres si tard ?

Vous avez demandé la police, veuillez patienter. Mon mari s'était transformé en grand inquisiteur. Il ne supportait plus que je sorte sans lui, particulièrement lorsqu'il s'agissait de soirées avec mes collègues de travail. Les soirées filles avec Fanny lui posaient moins de problèmes. Comme par hasard. S'il avait su que c'était de mes séances de sport qu'il aurait dû le plus se méfier… enfin ça, c'était du passé. Mike avait trouvé moins confortable notre relation une fois revenus à Paris. Il disait que je demandais trop. Il avait flippé, pourri la situation et j'avais fini par y mettre un terme parce qu'il en était incapable.

Pascal me fatiguait maintenant avec sa mine triste et ses perpétuels ronchonnements. J'en avais ras le bol de regarder la télé pendant que Monsieur préparait ses cours. Je m'emmerdais.

L'ancienne Mélanie le supportait, la nouvelle avait décidé que ça devait changer.

Comme au travail.

J'avais demandé et obtenu d'être mutée au siège social pour me débarrasser de mon étiquette d'ancienne grosse qui s'était métamorphosée grâce à une émission de télé-réalité. La nouvelle équipe dans laquelle j'étais fourmillait de jeunes qui avaient l'habitude d'organiser des soirées. Ils m'avaient adoptée dès mon arrivée. Je m'amusais bien plus avec eux que chez moi.

J'aurais pu proposer à Pascal de se joindre à nous, mais personne d'autre ne le faisait. De toute façon, il se serait ennuyé. Et puis Pascal était un pantouflard qui se levait tôt le matin (l'Éducation nationale n'attend pas!) et il m'aurait envoyé des signaux dès onze heures pour rentrer, alors que la soirée venait de commencer.

Pour être honnête, ce qui m'aurait le plus dérangé si Pascal était venu, c'est que je n'aurais pas pu tester mon tout nouveau pouvoir de séduction. Ce n'est pas que je voulais tromper Pascal (j'avais eu ma dose avec Mike) ou que je m'intéressais à untel ou untel, mais je papillonnais et ça me faisait beaucoup de bien. S'il avait été là, je n'aurais pas pu me permettre de minauder comme ça, et les soirées auraient perdu beaucoup de leur intérêt.

« Putain, mais t'as vu l'heure ? »

Et merde, il était réveillé.

« Ouais, c'est l'heure de dormir. Bonne nuit.

– C'est ça, fais la maligne. J'en ai marre de tes conneries.

– …

– Tu pourrais me répondre au moins.

– Je ne vois pas ce qu'il y a à dire.

– Putain, tu me rends dingue Mélanie !

– …

– Mais dis quelque chose !

– Je ne sais pas quoi te dire.

– Tu es déjà sortie deux fois cette semaine avec tes collègues…

– Et ?

– Ça te semble normal ?

– …

– Ça t'arrive de te demander ce que je ressens ?

– …

– Je ne compte plus pour toi ?

– Mais si, bien sûr. Mais... Oh et puis merde, traite-moi d'égoïste si tu veux mais je ne peux plus vivre comme avant Pascal. Je me sens à l'étroit, j'étouffe. J'ai l'impression de passer à côté de plein d'autres choses.

– Ah oui, comme quoi ? Te taper d'autres mecs ? T'as déjà choisi parmi tes collègues ? Ils m'appellent comment à ton boulot ? Monsieur Cocu ? À moins qu'ils ne sachent même pas que j'existe !

– Arrête...

– Mais non, pourquoi... crevons l'abcès !

– Écoute, si on n'arrive pas à se parler, il vaut mieux qu'on dorme.

– Parce que tu crois que je vais pouvoir dormir, là ?

– Je crois que cette discussion ne nous mène à rien. De toute façon...

– De toute façon quoi ?

– Je ne sais pas, on devrait peut-être faire un break...

– ...

– Ça nous permettrait de faire le point. Calmement.

– Tu veux me quitter, c'est ça ?
– J'en sais rien…
– …
– Je suis désolée Pascal. »
J'ai posé ma main sur son épaule pour le réconforter. Il s'est dégagé.
« Je vais dormir dans mon bureau.
– Mais arrête Pascal, tu peux rester dormir ici !
– Non. »

*

Je suis rentrée du boulot avec une enclume au creux de l'estomac. Ma décision était prise.

Depuis que nous faisions chambre à part, Pascal ne m'adressait quasiment plus la parole. Il avait transformé son bureau en une forteresse dans laquelle il travaillait, mangeait, regardait la télé, dormait. Sa porte était toujours fermée.

Quand il sortait de son antre pour aller dans la salle de bains ou la cuisine, il se comportait comme si je n'existais plus. Si j'essayais de profiter de ses apparitions pour lui parler, je n'obtenais que des réponses minimalistes, cassantes. Je ne me décourageais pas. Je voulais comprendre. Je voulais faire la paix. Même si nous devions nous quitter.

Il avait fini par me demander de ne plus lui adresser la parole, en me regardant droit dans les yeux, comme pour me défier de risquer la moindre remarque. Je n'avais pas osé. J'avais eu peur qu'il n'explose. Je savais qu'il trouverait les mots pour me blesser.

Je devais lui laisser du temps. C'était l'idée à laquelle je m'étais raccrochée. Je ne devais plus rien faire qui alimente sa colère. Je ne sortais plus beaucoup, mais j'évitais de traîner dans le salon, pour ne pas me trouver sur sa route. Comme lui, je m'étais mise à passer beaucoup de temps dans ma chambre.

Fanny s'inquiétait pour moi. Son caractère impulsif supportait mal cette étrange attente. Elle me poussait à transgresser les règles que Pascal avait imposées, à demander des comptes, à m'insurger. Elle martelait que je ne méritais pas ça, que c'était injuste.

Moi, je me sentais coupable. Coupable de

nous avoir reniés. De nous avoir bazardés pour quelques kilos en moins et quelques regards flatteurs en plus. Alors j'attendais. Mais rien ne se passait.

Pascal semblait s'accommoder de cette situation alors que pour moi, elle devenait insupportable. Au bout de quelques semaines, j'étais de nouveau sortie. Beaucoup. Je prenais la fuite. Je dormais parfois chez Fanny, parfois chez des hommes que je connaissais à peine, parfois chez moi, quand je n'avais pas d'autres choix.

Fanny m'exhortait à partir. Pour de bon. Je savais qu'elle avait raison mais j'avais eu besoin de beaucoup de temps pour m'y résoudre.

Pascal était dans son bureau, ce bureau où je n'avais pas mis les pieds depuis trois mois. J'ai enlevé mon blouson et j'ai respiré à fond. J'avais le cœur qui battait à tout rompre. J'ai frappé à sa porte. Je n'ai pas obtenu de réponse. J'ai frappé un peu plus fort et il m'a dit d'entrer.

« Salut. »

Il corrigeait des cahiers et n'a pas daigné lever le nez.

«Je m'en vais Pascal. Je pars vivre chez Fanny. Je ne supporte plus tout ça.»

Il a daigné lever le nez.

«J'imagine que ça devait finir comme ça...

– C'est tout ce que ça t'inspire?

– Tu voudrais quoi? Que je te supplie de rester?

– Non... bon... je vais préparer mes affaires.»

Il a replongé le nez dans ses cahiers.

*

J'avais invité pas mal de mes collègues, quelques vieux amis avec qui nous étions restés en contact depuis le lycée, et bien sûr, Fanny, l'indéboulonnable, l'irremplaçable. Il n'y avait aucun de nos amis communs à Pascal et moi. Pourtant, certains se montraient compréhensifs, mais j'avais envie d'une coupure complète. C'était ma crémaillère, le symbole de mon nouveau départ dans la vie, et je voulais que rien ne me ramène en arrière.

J'avais préparé deux marmites d'un punch

qui attaquait en traître la bonne éducation des uns et des autres. L'ambiance, doucement bourdonnante, s'est vite transformée en un joyeux brouhaha d'où fusaient des rires tonitruants et des éclats de voix.

Moi qui étais restée presque huit mois sans toucher une goutte d'alcool, régime oblige, je m'y étais remise depuis peu. Toujours obnubilée par mon poids et mon nombre de calories quotidien, je m'obligeais à ne rien manger quand je buvais. Pour compenser. Résultat, j'étais toujours très vite saoule et je m'étais fondée en un rien de temps une image de pilier de bar, de joyeuse luronne, de fêtarde sur qui on pouvait toujours compter en soirée.

Avec mon nouveau physique et les miracles de l'alcool, que j'avais eu le tort de ne jamais consommer de façon aussi déraisonnable, je me sentais pousser des ailes. Je devenais mondaine, excentrique et tapageuse. Je me remémorais avec émotion la femme invisible que j'avais longtemps été. En particulier lorsque j'étais au centre de l'attention. Comme ce soir. J'ai augmenté le volume de la musique et je me suis mise à danser en chantant à tue-tête : « Mais c'est la mort qui t'a assassinée, Marcia, c'est la mort qui t'a consumée, Marcia, c'est le cancer que tu as pris sous ton bras, maintenant, tu es en cen-en-endres. »

Richard s'est joint à moi. Un beau spécimen ce Richard ! Il était grand et athlétique, les cheveux bruns, en bataille, faussement mal coiffés, et un sourire à renier sa mère. Il avait une manière de me regarder et de me parler tout bas à l'oreille, pendant que nous dansions, qui me donnait l'impression d'être la personne la plus importante au monde.

J'avais pas mal œuvré ces derniers temps pour me rapprocher de lui. Je l'avais bombardé de mails drôles et aguicheurs. L'approche avait eu l'air de lui plaire. Il m'avait répondu sur le même ton. Je le sentais mûr maintenant, prêt à être cueilli.

Alors qu'il récupérait d'une danse frénétique, je me suis dirigée droit sur lui, et lui ai dit que j'avais envie de l'embrasser. Il s'est marré. Il m'a tendu la main et m'a attirée vers lui pour un baiser comme n'importe quelle fille normalement constituée en a toujours rêvé. Je suis retournée danser pour me remettre de mes émotions. Il m'a rejointe et s'est collé à moi pour m'embarquer dans une danse très très sexy…

J'ai passé le reste de la soirée sur un nuage. Je dansais, je buvais, je riais avec les uns, les autres, je parlais beaucoup et sans doute très fort. Je trouvais que la vie était belle.

Les gens sont partis vers trois heures du matin, sauf Richard, bien sûr, qui tenait à être là le lendemain pour m'aider à tout ranger… Malgré notre niveau d'ébriété, nous avons fait l'amour avant de nous réfugier, sourire aux lèvres, dans les bras de Morphée.

Au bout de trois semaines, Richard a mis fin à notre idylle. Il était en proie à ses propres démons. Rien à voir avec moi. Il me l'a bien répété. Il était traumatisé par son histoire précédente. La femme de sa vie. Au bout de trois ans, elle avait rencontré un type avec qui elle était partie du jour au lendemain. Moche.

J'ai fait bonne figure, je me suis montrée sympa et compréhensive, la bonne copine quoi… qui morfle mais ne te le balance pas en pleine gueule. Par fierté. Par stratégie aussi. Avec des idées de reconquête plein la tête. Il croyait pouvoir me quitter comme ça ! Tut tut tut... à chaque soirée, c'était la rechute, il finissait dans mes bras, dans mon lit. Jusqu'au lendemain, où il prenait à nouveau la fuite.

Je n'écoutais pas ce qu'il me disait. Pas vraiment. Je me voilais la face, ne voyant pas beaucoup plus loin que ma prochaine opération séduction. Tant que j'arrivais à le mettre dans mon lit, je me sentais exister. Quelle misère ! Un jour, il a rencontré une nana avec qui il a sans doute trouvé à partager plus que ça.

J'ai préféré ne pas trop creuser l'analyse de cette histoire, alors j'ai ouvert un nouveau dossier, comme nous aimions dire avec Fanny. Ma nouvelle proie s'appelait Luc. Il travaillait au service marketing de ma boîte. Une mine d'or ce job. Je ne sais pas qui s'occupait du recrutement mais elle avait beaucoup de goût. Luc et moi, nous ne nous connaissions pas, mais après le conseil de guerre tenu avec Fanny, la stratégie était au point.

Étape 1 : migrer les pauses café au deuxième étage où se trouvait son service.

Étape 2 : instaurer un semblant de relation genre « Salut », « Salut », « Ça va ? ».

Étape 3 : démarrer une campagne de mails.

Étape 4 : l'inviter à une soirée entre collègues.

Étape 5 : conclure.

Fanny avait toujours été une sacrée coquine, une dévoreuse d'hommes, et elle ne manquait jamais d'imagination pour mettre au point une nouvelle stratégie de séduction. Nous passions des heures à préparer des pièges à beaux gosses. Les pauvres passaient de sales quarts d'heure entre nos griffes. Nous les examinions au microscope, les dépecions. Chaque épisode marquant s'accompagnait d'un débriefing complet, commentaires et ricanements inclus.

Nous étions des pestes, en apparence solidaires. Mais il m'arrivait parfois de percevoir chez Fanny, au détour d'une remarque, un agacement devant mon succès grandissant. Je n'en étais pas certaine, mais quelque chose planait, une compétition cachée. D'ailleurs, elle avait interdit le principe de chasse gardée. J'avais accepté. Prête à me venger du vieil épisode Sébastien si l'occasion s'en présentait. Juste une fois. Juste pour rétablir l'équilibre. Elle l'avait quand même bien mérité.

Ainsi soit-il

En un an, j'avais ouvert pas mal de dossiers qui s'étaient tous déroulés de manière identique : succès en phase de séduction, échec en phase de relation. Avec plus ou moins d'élégance, ils avaient tous pris la fuite au bout d'un nombre de nuits qui allait de une (quel con !) à quelques-unes (juste le temps de commencer à y croire). Après, il y avait toujours eu une fausse bonne raison pour expliquer leur départ.

J'ai décidé d'arrêter. Je m'y perdais. Je rigolais beaucoup en période de « chasse » mais je morflais trop après. Les histoires sans lendemain ne m'intéressaient pas. Je n'étais pas aussi frivole que je l'affichais. Au contraire. Je voulais être aimée.

Je devais me recentrer, ne plus attendre après qui que ce soit. Je n'avais pas réussi à exister pour ce que j'étais vraiment auprès de ces garçons. D'ailleurs, je ne savais plus qui j'étais vraiment.

J'ai « fêté » cette nouvelle résolution en m'autorisant une orgie de bouffe. Ça ne m'était pas arrivé depuis des lustres. Je bravais l'interdit suprême. Je suis allée au supermarché pour préparer ma soirée, car il n'y avait rien chez moi pour me livrer à ce genre de festivités. J'ai empilé dans mon Caddie des cacahuètes et des bières, une pizza, deux cheeseburgers, une bouteille de rosé et un litre de glace à la vanille. En passant devant la boulangerie, j'ai repéré une tarte aux framboises, très tentante, mais pour six personnes. Qu'à cela ne tienne, je l'ai achetée.

C'était ma manière de dire merde au monde entier. Merde à tous ces pauvres cons qui ne m'aimaient pas assez, merde aux nutritionnistes qui me brimaient sans cesse, aux psys qui me faisaient chialer sans pour autant me soulager, merde à Pascal qui venait d'emménager avec une autre nana, à Fanny qui était séduisante sans tricher, merde à ma mère qui ne pensait qu'à elle en laissant croire le contraire et à mon père qui ne lui disait jamais de se taire, merde, merde et merde.

Je suis rentrée chez moi.

J'ai ouvert une première bière. Puis une deuxième. J'alternais sans interruption poignées de cacahuètes et gorgées de bière.

J'ai mis la pizza au four. Quinze minutes. C'était ce qui était marqué sur l'emballage. Je suis restée à regarder le fromage fondre et la pâte dorer à travers la vitre. Je ne pensais à rien. J'attendais.

Je suis retournée au salon. J'ai débouché la bouteille de rosé et j'ai bu quelques gorgées au goulot. Il n'était pas terrible. Aucune importance.

Bouchée après bouchée, je suis venue à bout de la pizza.

Je me suis accordé une pause. J'ai zappé un peu pour voir ce qu'il y avait à la télé. Coïncidence ? Je suis tombée sur *Relooking Extrême*.

Pendant la coupure publicitaire, je suis allée mettre mes cheeseburgers au micro-ondes.

Quel plaisir de me goinfrer en regardant le nutritionniste et la psy faire leurs speeches aux nouveaux candidats !

J'ai avalé la dernière gorgée de rosé.

J'ai couru aux toilettes. Mon estomac n'en pouvait plus. J'ai tout vomi jusqu'à la dernière olive.

Je lui ai laissé un répit avant d'attaquer la tarte et la glace à la vanille.

Et une cuillère pour maman, une cuillère pour papa, une pour le nutritionniste, une pour la psy. J'ai maintenu la cadence jusqu'à ce qu'il ne reste plus une miette de quoi que ce soit.

J'avais le bide explosé.

J'ai hésité un peu et puis je me suis dit que quitte à organiser une boulimie-partie, autant aller jusqu'au bout du concept.

Je suis retournée aux toilettes et me suis mis deux doigts au fond de la gorge.

Je suis revenue au salon, hébétée.

J'ai passé la nuit recroquevillée sur le canapé.

Je me suis réveillée vaseuse et écœurée. La vue des reliefs de la veille ne m'a pas aidée à me sentir mieux. Qu'est-ce qui m'avait pris? Je n'avais plus qu'à tout nettoyer et pédaler une bonne heure sur mon vélo d'appartement pour éliminer les effets désastreux de cette crise.

J'allais me reprendre en main, arrêter toutes ces sorties vides de sens où le jeu consistait à se bourrer la gueule le plus vite possible pour devenir Super-Mél, l'intrépide dragueuse à gros nichons. Il était temps que je me mette à la recherche de Mélanie, la vraie, celle qui se planquait sans arrêt. J'allais aussi perdre les trois kilos pris à force de faire la fête. J'allais me remettre au régime et au sport. Il était temps de reprendre le contrôle.

Pleine de ces bonnes résolutions prises en pédalant comme une dératée, je me suis attaquée à un grand ménage. Ça m'a pris cinq heures. J'ai traqué la poussière dans les moindres recoins, j'ai mené une chasse au calcaire et à la bactérie sans ménagement et j'ai manié l'éponge avec hargne et détermination, jusqu'à ce que mon appartement reprenne une apparence propre. Nette.

J'ai vidé mon frigo de tout ce qui, de près ou de loin, pouvait représenter une infraction au règlement. Les bières ont fini dans l'évier, et tout aliment trop éloigné de la calorie zéro à la poubelle.

À la fin de la journée, j'étais fourbue mais contente. J'étais plus calme, plus détendue. J'y voyais plus clair sur ma ligne de conduite des prochaines semaines. J'allais m'astreindre à un mode de vie moins chaotique, plus structuré. C'était ce dont j'avais besoin.

J'ai encore trouvé l'énergie pour aller au supermarché acheter de quoi manger pour les jours à venir : salades, tomates, concombres, champignons, quelques fruits et des yaourts maigres. J'ai aussi pris du thé brûle-graisses et de la tisane diurétique. J'étais armée.

*

Pendant le mois qui a suivi, j'ai décliné toutes les invitations. Pour mes collègues, j'avais des soucis familiaux. Pour Fanny, je m'étais remise à peindre et je ne voulais pas me couper dans mon élan. Pour ma mère, j'avais un nouvel amoureux avec qui je passais tout mon temps.

J'ai pris plaisir à mettre en place mon nouveau rituel. Chaque jour, après le travail, je passais à la salle de gym pour une heure de cours où je transpirais à grosses gouttes. Ensuite, je rentrais chez moi et j'enchaînais avec une heure de vélo devant la télé. Au début, mon ventre avait tendance à gargouiller. Il faut reconnaître, à sa décharge, que c'était un peu long entre le petit déjeuner et le repas du soir car j'avais supprimé celui du midi. Mais à force de volonté, il s'y est habitué. Je me préparais ensuite une salade avec juste un peu de vinaigre balsamique en assaisonnement, que je mangeais devant la télé, en prenant bien mon temps. Avec un yaourt et un ou deux fruits en plus, j'étais calée. Je me couchais tôt pour être en forme et me lever de bonne heure le matin, ce qui me permettait d'aller à la piscine avant le travail.

Je voyais avec plaisir mes efforts payer. De cinquante-trois kilos, j'étais passée à cinquante en deux semaines. C'était un bon début mais je ne voulais pas m'arrêter là. Quand je me regardais dans la glace, je voyais encore du gras et de la cellulite. Je m'étais fixé de perdre quatre ou cinq kilos supplémentaires.

Je n'ai pas pu tenir Fanny éloignée plus longtemps. Elle avait beau avoir des paillettes dans les yeux en parlant de son Laurent, le nouveau chéri dont elle semblait très éprise, elle n'en restait pas moins Fanny, la meilleure copine avec qui je partageais tout et le reste. Alors, plutôt que de prendre le risque de la voir débarquer chez moi à l'improviste et d'avoir à lui expliquer pourquoi il n'y avait aucune toile dans mon salon, pas la moindre odeur de peinture et pas un pinceau à tremper, j'ai pris les devants en lui proposant de passer chez elle. Elle était ravie et moi aussi. J'étais sûre que sa nouvelle histoire allait prendre un maximum de place. Aucun risque d'interrogatoire, donc, sur ma peinture.

Elle a à peine ouvert la porte qu'elle s'est exclamée que j'avais maigri. J'étais à la fois contente que ça se voie et tracassée de ce qu'elle allait en dire. Mais je m'inquiétais à tort. Ce jour-là, Fanny avait l'insouciance et la légèreté des amoureux. Elle m'a regardée un peu mieux, et dans un même élan, m'a embrassée et dit que j'étais plus jolie de jour en jour. J'aimais cette fille pour toujours.

Elle m'a proposé un thé, que j'ai accepté, mais sans les gâteaux secs qui allaient avec. Fanny grignotait toujours beaucoup de cochonneries, et pourtant, je l'avais toujours connue mince, voire maigre. Elle semblait partie pour le rester jusqu'à la fin de sa vie. J'en étais un peu jalouse.

Elle m'a raconté dans les moindres détails sa rencontre avec Laurent dans un bar à Belleville. Il lui avait tout de suite tapé dans l'œil, et elle, la grande gueule, s'était retrouvée tout intimidée, ce qu'elle me racontait d'une voix émerveillée.

Pendant qu'elle me déballait les détails de son histoire, sans laisser la moindre zone d'ombre, je me suis demandé pourquoi je lui avais menti pendant tout ce mois, pourquoi je ne lui avais pas juste expliqué mon envie de souffler, de me reposer, et de prendre le temps de réfléchir au sens de ma vie. C'était absurde.

Qu'y avait-il de mal à ça ?

Rien.

Qu'est-ce que j'avais à cacher ?

Rien.

Il n'était pas trop tard pour lui dire tout ça mais je n'y suis pas arrivée.

Je me suis alors dit que j'allais me remettre à la peinture. Pour de vrai. Comme ça, il n'y aurait plus de mensonge. Ça ne m'avait pas effleuré jusque-là, mais tout à coup, ça m'a semblé évident. Indispensable même. Dès le lendemain, j'allais m'acheter du matériel au lieu de transpirer à la salle de sport.

*

Je suis rentrée chez moi, contente de pouvoir enfin me délester de mes paquets. J'avais les doigts sciés par les sacs en plastique. Je n'avais pu prendre que des toiles sur châssis de petite taille et j'avais dû me limiter sur les tubes de couleur pour tout ramener en métro, mais ça n'avait aucune importance, j'avais de quoi peindre, c'était l'essentiel. J'avais envie de m'y mettre tout de suite et c'est ce que j'ai fait après avoir accordé un regard coupable à mon vélo d'appartement. Cette journée sans sport était acceptable si je sautais le repas du soir. Marché conclu.

J'ai mis de l'eau à chauffer pour un thé et je me suis changée, troquant ma tenue de jeune cadre dynamique contre un jean et un tee-shirt que j'avais hésité à jeter peu de temps auparavant. J'ai installé un châssis sur mon vieux chevalet. Je n'avais pas encore une idée précise de ce que je voulais peindre, juste des envies de couleur. Les premiers coups de pinceau m'ont paru malhabiles, incertains. Et puis les sensations sont revenues. Je n'essayais pas de représenter quoi que ce soit, je me laissais aller à juxtaposer les couleurs selon mon humeur. J'ai peint, sans interruption, sans voir le temps passer. Quand je me suis accordé une pause, il était déjà minuit. Je me sentais presque heureuse. J'ai mis mes pinceaux à tremper et je suis allée prendre ma douche.

J'ai modifié le programme de mes soirées. J'allais toujours à la salle de gym et je faisais toujours une heure de vélo d'appartement, mais après, je me lançais dans la peinture sans plus tarder. Je ne passais plus ma soirée devant la télé en mangeant ma salade et mes yaourts. Il n'y avait plus de repas à proprement parler. Je n'avais plus le temps. Je croquais une pomme. J'avalais un yaourt. C'était selon.

Ce fonctionnement m'a permis de perdre trois kilos supplémentaires, sans presque y penser. Les os de mon bassin étaient de plus en plus visibles, et je trouvais que j'avais une allure folle quand je portais un jean taille basse. Je devenais aussi longiligne que j'en avais toujours rêvé. J'aimais porter de grands décolletés qui permettaient de voir la naissance de mes seins mais aussi mes clavicules saillantes. Je trouvais le contraste élégant. Mes pommettes ressortaient davantage aussi, donnant un caractère plus slave à mon visage.

Ma peinture tournait autour de cette thématique de la silhouette. La première toile sur laquelle j'avais travaillé représentait des femmes éléphantesques bavardant avec des femmes girafes, très fines, très élégantes, avec le port altier que leur conférait leur long cou cerclé de colliers. Je m'étais ensuite acharnée sur une série d'autoportraits d'après photos, cinq au total, me montrant aux différents stades de ma transformation. Et enfin, celle que je venais de terminer, ma préférée, représentait des femmes dont la peau translucide dévoilait le squelette.

J'étais contente de mon travail mais je ne l'avais encore montré à personne. Fanny a été la première à les découvrir. Elle est restée un long moment à les regarder sans rien dire. Je ne voulais pas la brusquer même si je mourais d'impatience d'entendre ce qu'elle en pensait.

« C'est... dérangeant...

– ...

– J'ai un pote à qui tu devrais montrer ton travail. Il a de bonnes connexions et... je suis sûre que ça tiendrait la route pour une expo. C'est si... je sais pas...

– Tu penses vraiment ?

– Mais oui ! Regarde mes bras, j'ai la chair de poule ! »

J'étais contente. Il me semblait bien avoir

réussi à atteindre quelque chose, mais je n'en étais pas sûre jusque-là. Fanny venait de me le confirmer.

« Ça va toi ? Je veux dire... je trouve ça cool que tu peignes et je trouve le résultat très réussi, mais aussi... très torturé...

– Ça va, ne t'inquiète pas. J'exorcise un peu tout ce que j'ai vécu depuis deux ans. Ça me fait du bien au contraire. J'ai l'impression que quand j'en aurai fini avec cette série, toutes ces idées fixes autour du poids et de la silhouette seront derrière moi.

– T'as encore maigri, non ?

– Peut-être un peu, je ne sais pas.

– ...

– OK, j'ai maigri. Je suis si obnubilée par ma peinture que je ne prends pas toujours le temps de manger, mais ne t'inquiète pas, je vais me reprendre.

– Tu me le promets ? »

*

J'ai commencé à transpirer et à avoir les tempes bourdonnantes. Mes jambes sont devenues molles, j'avais besoin de m'asseoir. Il n'y avait pas un siège à l'horizon près de cette machine à café. Je devais vite retourner à mon bureau. À ma chaise. Je suis partie sans un mot à mes collègues. Je n'avais pas le temps. Je devais arriver avant que mes jambes ne cessent de me soutenir.

D'après ce qu'on m'a ensuite raconté, je me suis écroulée sur le pas de la porte de mon bureau.

Quand j'ai repris conscience, on me conduisait à l'infirmerie. J'entendais les voix des deux personnes qui me soutenaient à travers un épais brouillard. J'essayais de commander mes jambes mais elles restaient molles, incapables de me porter.

Je suis de nouveau tombée dans les pommes.

Je me suis réveillée et j'ai aperçu le médecin qui s'agitait près du lit sur lequel j'étais allongée.

« Ah ! Vous revoilà parmi nous. Comment vous vous appelez ?

– Mélanie. »

Il me prenait pour une gourde ou quoi ?

« Savez-vous où vous êtes Mélanie ?

– Au travail… j'ai eu un malaise.

– Bon, ça va. Est-ce que vous êtes souvent sujette à ce genre de malaise ?

– Non, c'est la première fois.

– Tendez votre bras Mélanie, je vais prendre votre tension.

– …

– 8-6… ce n'est pas très bon ça. Est-ce que vous vous sentez fatiguée en ce moment ?

– Un peu, mais ça va.

– Est-ce que vous dormez bien ?

– Oui.

– Est-ce que vous vous alimentez correctement ?

– Je… oui oui.

– Combien pesez-vous Mélanie ?

– Je ne sais pas.

– Est-ce que vous pouvez vous lever ? J'aimerais vous peser. Allez-y doucement, voilà, comme ça. »

À peine sur mes jambes, j'ai senti de nouveau ma tête tourner.

« Quarante et un kilos. Mélanie, vous mesurez combien ?

– Un mètre cinquante-huit. »

Je me suis évanouie une troisième fois et on a dû me remettre au lit. Dans un demi-sommeil, j'entendais le médecin parler à je ne sais qui. Il disait que j'étais trop maigre et le mot anorexie revenait en boucle.

À mon réveil, le médecin m'a longuement parlé. Il se sentait investi d'une mission très importante : arriver à me sauver de moi-même. Pathétique… J'en connaissais plus que lui en matière de nutrition et de psychologie alimentaire. Il était inquiet de mon poids qu'il jugeait beaucoup trop bas. Il n'a pas employé une seule fois le terme d'anorexie devant moi. Il m'a fait une ordonnance pour des analyses de sang. Il craignait que j'aie des carences. Il m'a donné les coordonnées de confrères, nutritionniste et psychologue, spécialistes dans les troubles alimentaires. Je me suis retenue pour ne pas lui rire au nez. Je n'avais pas largué les miens pour remettre maintenant le couvert. La seule chose qui m'intéressait dans tout ça, c'était l'arrêt de travail de deux mois. J'allais avoir du temps pour peindre. Il voulait me revoir d'ici une semaine avec les résultats des analyses. Je le soupçonnais de vouloir s'assurer que j'avais bien contacté ses confrères. Qu'à cela ne tienne...

Fanny est venue me tirer de ce bourbier et m'a ramenée chez moi. Je voyais qu'elle était inquiète. En arrivant à la maison, elle a inspecté mon frigo et mes placards. Face au vide absolu qu'elle y a trouvé, elle s'est mise à m'engueuler. Et qu'est-ce que je foutais? À quoi je jouais? Et blablabla. Puisque c'était comme ça, elle passerait chaque soir avec de quoi manger et resterait dîner avec moi. Je n'avais pas la force de lutter, là, maintenant, tout de suite, alors je l'ai laissée parler. Il serait toujours temps de trouver une solution plus tard. Pour le moment, je voulais juste dormir.

*

J'avais oublié comme Fanny pouvait être tenace. Comme convenu avec elle-même, elle s'est pointée chez moi tous les soirs.

Quand je me suis retrouvée assise en face d'elle, avec devant moi une assiette, je me suis sentie prise au piège. Je n'avais aucune envie de manger. Mais si je ne mangeais pas, son inquiétude augmenterait et elle me pisterait d'encore plus près. Elle irait même peut-être jusqu'à en parler à ma mère, alors que j'avais réussi pour l'instant à négocier son silence.

Je ne m'étais pas retrouvée à table devant une assiette depuis si longtemps que c'était tout juste si je savais encore m'y prendre. Je regardais le riz cantonnais et les crevettes qui m'attendaient, et j'essayais de calculer le nombre d'heures de vélo supplémentaires que ça représentait. Ce n'était pas si terrible. Je ne travaillais pas, j'en aurais tout le temps.

J'ai avalé la première fourchette sous les applaudissements de Fanny, qui, à son habitude, en faisait des tonnes. Puis une seconde. Une troisième. Plus j'avançais et plus apparaissaient d'énormes traces de gras au fond de l'assiette.

Il me devenait difficile de continuer.

À mi-chemin, j'ai demandé à Fanny de m'arrêter.

Elle a négocié deux fourchettes supplémentaires.

Je me sentais mal. Souillée.

Je n'avais plus qu'une idée en tête, voir partir Fanny pour vomir. Plus elle traînait, plus la digestion était entamée. Mais malgré mes bâillements, Fanny n'a pas levé le camp avant une heure avancée. Je suis quand même allée vomir, mais c'était beaucoup trop tard.

Les journées se suivaient et se ressemblaient.

Je ne sortais plus de chez moi. Fanny se chargeait de mes courses. Quand je me levais, je préparais un litre de thé et je pédalais trois heures sur mon vélo devant la télé en le sirotant. C'était alors le moment sacro-saint de la journée où je me pesais. Je continuais de maigrir avec régularité mais pas assez vite à mon goût. Avec les bons soins quotidiens de Fanny, c'était difficile de faire mieux. L'après-midi, je peignais en mangeant ma portion quotidienne de pommes (deux) et en vidant mon litre de tisane diurétique. Je préparais ensuite l'arrivée de Fanny en jetant dans le vide-ordures ce que j'étais censée avoir ingurgité dans la journée. Quand elle arrivait, elle préparait le repas et nous restions à table jusqu'à ce qu'elle considère que j'avais assez mangé. Nous papotions ensuite au salon ou regardions ensemble la télévision. Dès qu'elle partait, je vomissais.

Au fil des jours, son enthousiasme s'est effrité. Elle avait pensé me remplumer en quelques semaines, mais elle voyait bien que malgré ses efforts, rien ne se passait. Un soir, elle a explosé.

« Est-ce que tu peux m'expliquer, Mél, pourquoi tu ne reprends pas de poids malgré tout ce que je te fais manger ?

– Je ne sais pas...

– Moi, je vais te dire comment ça se fait. Je suis certaine que dès que je passe le pas de cette porte, tu te fais vomir ! Voilà comment ça se fait !

– Mais non, n'importe quoi !

– Oui, c'est ça. Tu me prends pour une conne ?

– Non, bien sûr que non.

– Qu'est-ce que tu veux ? Te suicider ?

– Qu'est-ce que tu racontes ?

– Tu crois que ton corps va supporter ça

jusqu'à quand ? Tu n'as jamais entendu parler d'anorexiques qui crèvent à force de ne rien bouffer ?

– Si mais…

– Mais quoi ?

– Je ne suis pas anorexique…

– Regarde-toi, Mél, bordel ! Tu es aussi squelettique que les femmes de tes tableaux ! Tu fais peur à voir ! Tu as vu les résultats de tes analyses, tu as des carences dans tous les sens ! Jusqu'où tu vas aller ? Je peux plus me taire. Je vais en parler à tes parents. J'ai essayé de t'aider mais ça n'a pas marché. Peut-être qu'eux pourront t'obliger à te faire hospitaliser ou je sais pas…

– Non !

– Quoi non ?

– N'en parle pas à mes parents, je t'en supplie, je vais faire des efforts. »

Mes larmes m'ont empêchée d'aller plus loin. Je venais de me prendre la vérité en pleine gueule. Je ne m'étais jamais considérée comme anorexique. Je savais que j'étais un peu excessive dans ma manière d'être au régime, mais…

« Je vais faire un effort Fanny, je te le promets.

– …

– Promis juré…

– OK, mais si cette fois ça ne s'arrange pas…

– Ça va s'arranger. »

*

J'avais la trouille. Je pesais trente-huit kilos et j'avais beau ne pas me trouver assez mince quand je me regardais dans la glace, je savais que j'avais atteint un poids dangereusement bas.

Je n'avais pas de chance. J'étais ainsi faite que même en étant très légère, je restais grosse. C'était un problème de morphologie. On voyait mes côtes mais j'avais toujours de la cellulite. Ça me désespérait. Fanny me disait que je fabulais, que je n'avais plus un gramme de graisse, mais moi, je la voyais. C'était insupportable. J'avais envie de perdre encore deux ou trois kilos pour voir si ce serait mieux, mais je savais que c'était un jeu dangereux.

Et puis, je savais que Fanny était à deux doigts de flancher et d'appeler ma mère à la rescousse. C'était pour moi inenvisageable. Je l'imaginais déjà débarquer chez moi et s'y installer sept jours sur sept, vingt-quatre heures sur vingt-quatre.

Je préférais mourir. Non. Je ne voulais pas mourir.

Je devais manger. Mais malgré ma bonne volonté, je n'y arrivais pas. Mon corps n'acceptait plus rien. Le matin, je m'obligeais à manger des céréales. Quand au bout d'une heure j'arrivais au fond du bol, des crampes insupportables m'étreignaient l'estomac. En général, je me couchais et j'essayais de dormir pour ne pas flancher. Ne pas vomir. Parfois ça marchait. Souvent pas.

Je ne faisais plus de vélo, j'avais la tête qui tournait au moindre effort. Ça m'angoissait. Mes muscles allaient se transformer en graisse.

Dans l'après-midi, je peignais. J'atteignais des états de transe où je ne savais plus très bien ce que je dessinais. J'en sortais épuisée.

L'arrivée de Fanny annonçait la grande épreuve du soir. Je la redoutais mais je la souhaitais aussi. C'était mon ultime rempart pour ne pas sombrer. Je ne trichais plus avec Fanny. Je lui demandais souvent de rester dormir avec moi pour être sûre de ne pas me faire vomir. Et elle disait oui. Toujours. Elle était formidable. Mais elle ne riait plus beaucoup. Elle avait la trouille, elle aussi.

*

Un soir, quand Fanny est arrivée chez moi, elle m'a trouvée évanouie dans le salon. Elle a appelé le SAMU qui m'a amenée à l'hôpital.

Quand je me suis réveillée et que j'ai compris où j'étais, j'en ai ressenti une espèce de soulagement. Je n'étais plus capable de m'occuper de moi. Fanny me tenait la main en retenant ses larmes.

« Je n'ai pas eu le choix cette fois.

– C'est bien, tu as eu raison.

– Ils vont prendre bien soin de toi ici.

– Ma mère est là ?

– Ouais.

– Comment elle est ?

– Hystérique comme d'hab'.

– Et… et mon père ?

– Retenu à son boulot, il vient dès qu'il peut.

– Je vois. »

*

Mélanie Bertier est décédée à l'hôpital, dix jours plus tard. Elle venait d'avoir quarante ans.

Ce 238e titre du Dilettante
a été achevé d'imprimer
à 2 222 exemplaires
le 7 décembre 2007
par l'imprimerie
Floch, à
Mayenne
(Mayenne).
Il a
été tiré,
en outre,
13 exemplaires
sur vélin marais,
numérotés à la main.
L'ensemble de ces exemplaires
constitue l'édition originale
de « Le Strip-tease de la femme
invisible », de Murielle Renault.

Dépôt légal : 4e trimestre 2007
(69795)
Imprimé en France